Social Theory in the Twentieth Century and Beyond

Second Edition

Social Theory in the Twentieth Century and Beyond

Second Edition

PATRICK BAERT AND FILIPE CARREIRA DA SILVA

polity

First edition published in 1998 by Polity Press.
This edition published in 2010 by Polity Press.

Polity Press
65 Bridge Street
Cambridge CB2 1UR, UK

Polity Press
350 Main Street
Malden, MA 02148, USA

ISBN-13: 978-0-7456-3980-2
ISBN-13: 978-0-7456-3981-9(pb)

A catalogue record for this book is available from the British Library.

Typeset in 11.25 on 13 pt Monotype Dante
by Toppan Best-set Premedia Limited
Printed and bound in Great Britain by MPG Books Limited, Bodmin, Cornwall.

The publisher has used its best endeavours to ensure that the URLs for external websites referred to in this book are correct and active at the time of going to press. However, the publisher has no responsibility for the websites and can make no guarantee that a site will remain live or that the content is or will remain appropriate.

Every effort has been made to trace all copyright holders, but if any have been inadvertently overlooked the publisher will be pleased to include any necessary credits in any subsequent reprint or edition.

For further information on Polity, visit our website: www.politybooks.com

Contents

Preface to the Second Edition

The first edition of this book appeared more than a decade ago. Ten years is a substantial amount of time in a rapidly moving field like social theory, hence the need to revise this book. One obvious difference between the first and the second editions is that what was initially a single-authored volume is now the work of two authors, and this cooperation has largely shaped the changes and additions that have been made. Our aim has been to update the first edition in the face of the changes that have occurred in social theory over the past decade. In particular, our concern has been to expand its scope so as to include the new generation of social theorists, as well as the emergent themes at the dawn of this millennium. As it currently stands, this book aims to be a critical overview of the main contributions to social theory in the twentieth and early twenty-first century.

Three major changes are worth mentioning. First, all chapters have been updated and expanded. Our intention has been to provide an overview of the cutting-edge lines of research currently being pursued in the various strands of social theory. For instance, the work of Luc Boltanski is now included in our discussion of contemporary French social theory (chapter 1); Randall Collins and Russell Hardin are discussed in the chapter on micro-sociology (chapter 3); and Claus Offe and Axel Honneth have been added to our analysis of critical social theory (chapter 7). The order of the chapters is roughly the same, the exception being the chapter on rational choice theory (chapter 7 in the first edition), which is now chapter 4 (including a new section on neo-institutionalism). Second, this edition includes a whole new chapter (chapter 8) on current trends in social theory. Third, this edition includes a long section on historical sociology, in particular Charles Tilly, Theda Skocpol, Michael Mann and Shmuel Eisenstadt. Major contemporary social thinkers, such as Manuel Castells, Zygmunt Bauman, Ulrich Beck, Richard Sennett and Saskia Sassen, are discussed in this chapter. Finally, we felt that the concluding chapter of the previous edition did not do justice to the challenges of social theory today, so chapter 9 has been completely rewritten. The increasing influence of pragmatism on the social sciences (see also chapter 1) as well as on our own thought is now given due attention. Chapter 9 is based on sections from previously published articles: P. Baert, 'Social Theory and the Social Sciences', in G. Delanty (ed.), *Handbook of Contemporary European Social Theory*, London: Routledge (2006), pp. 14–24; P. Baert, 'Why Study the Social', in P. Baert and B.S. Turner (eds), *Pragmatism and European Social Theory*, Oxford: Bardwell Press (2007), pp. 45–68; and P. Baert, 'A Neo-pragmatist Agenda for Social Research; Integrating Levinas, Gadamer and Mead', in H. Bauer and E. Brighi (eds), *Pragmatism in International Relations*, London: Routledge (2009), pp. 44–62. We thank both Routledge and Bardwell Press for granting us permission to publish this material here.

As we are well into the twenty-first century, the old title (*Social Theory in the Twentieth Century*) is now out of date. The new title, *Social Theory in the Twentieth Century and Beyond*, captures both the distinctiveness and the continuity of this new edition vis-à-vis its predecessor.

We want to thank the whole Polity team, and in particular Emma Longstaff, John Thompson and Jonathan Skerrett, for suggesting that we write this second edition in the first place and also for their encouragement and patience throughout the project.

Patrick Baert
Filipe Carreira da Silva

Introduction

What this book is about

We take social theory to be a relatively systematic, abstract and general reflection on the workings of the social world. However elementary this definition might be, a number of consequences follow from it. First, we will only discuss theories which reach a high level of *abstraction*. This is certainly not to say that social theories are necessarily independent of the empirical study of society. Of course, some theories have hardly any bearing on empirical research, while others very much rely upon or inform empirical sociology. But whether they are empirically grounded or not, the main purpose of social theorists is obviously to theorize, and there is thus a clear distinction between the abstract nature of social theory and the practical orientations of empirical sociology. Second (and relatedly), we will explore theories which reach a high level of *generality*. That is, they aim to cover various aspects of the social realm, across different periods and across different societies. Third, there is the *systematic* nature of social theories. Compared to mere opinions and beliefs, they exhibit a high level of internal consistency and coherence. Even recent attempts to move away from grand theory-building are systematic endeavours; they are not mere amalgams of opinions.

Our starting point is the early twentieth century, but this is not to suggest that social theory was created in this period. The tradition of social theory goes a long way back. From the classic Greek thinkers to the eighteenth-century *philosophes*, the social realm has long been a motif for theoretical reflection. Furthermore, social theory was central to the emergence of sociology as a separate discipline in the course of the nineteenth century. Auguste Comte, Émile Durkheim, Max Weber and Karl Marx (to name only a few) developed extremely elaborate views about the mechanisms of the social world. Nevertheless, contemporary social theory is, at least in some respects, quite distinct from its nineteenth-century predecessor. Three main differences can be pointed out.

First, although Comte, Durkheim and others made great efforts to establish sociology as a separate discipline, theory-building and empirical research were far from being institutionalized specialisms. By contrast, in many countries, social theory has increasingly become a separate academic field – clearly distinct from empirical sociology. Second, social theory has become professionalized. In the nineteenth century it was practised by people who were educated in aligned fields (namely philosophy). Few occupied academic positions which would have allowed them to train others. Most classic social theorists (Tocqueville, Comte, Marx, Spencer and Simmel, for example), never occupied permanent posts in universities at all. Nowadays, formal training in social theory has become a massive industry enrolling tens of thousands each year in graduate schools around the world. Third, social theories are now less clearly tied to political action and social reform than they used to be. Sociology, one should not forget, emerged as the scientific answer to the so-called 'social question' afflicting nineteenth-century European societies – i.e., the social and political upheavals created by the Industrial Revolution. Social theories were then tools for dealing with social and political problems. For example, Comte (and to some extent Durkheim) wondered how social order could be reinstated following the political and economic turmoil of the time. Tocqueville tried to ascertain how equality of opportunity and freedom could be reconciled, and Marx aimed to develop a more equal and less alienating type of society. For all of them, social theory was not an aim in itself; it was considered to be a necessary medium for dealing with current social and political issues. Today there is a much more pronounced consciousness that social reform and political activism are not internally linked to social theory. When contemporary thinkers like Jürgen Habermas intervene in the public sphere, they do so as public intellectuals, i.e., as citizens concerned with the public good. Habermas's social theory, however, is not at stake. Its validity comes from its intellectual depth and internal consistency, characteristics to be established through academic procedures like anonymous peer review or empirical verification, not from its ability to 'solve' political problems. Today, social theory and political life are highly differentiated professional domains, with separate organizational principles and goals.

Social theory has undergone profound changes in the past four decades. In the 1960s, events like the student revolts of May 1968 in Paris and the civil rights movement in the US contributed decisively to a sea change in the intellectual landscape. As a result, the intellectual edifice that Talcott Parsons had been carefully building since the 1930s was spectacularly ruined. In less than a decade, Parsonian structural-functionalism passed from being the dominant paradigm in sociology to being the consensual target of an entire generation of social theorists. The 1970s were devoted to the working out of feasible alternatives to structural-functionalism: symbolic interactionism, ethnomethodology, conflict theory and exchange theory were among the paradigms presented as the solution for the crisis generated by the demise of Parsons's project. In the early 1980s, the tradition of grand social theorizing returned. In a few years, sociology bookshelves were invaded by multivolume attempts at grand theoretical synthesis. Jeffrey Alexander's neo-functionalism, Pierre Bourdieu's genetic structuralism, Anthony Giddens's structuration theory and Habermas's critical theory came to the forefront in this period.

These theories have two features in common. First, they all attempt to integrate opposing philosophical and theoretical traditions. For example, they aim to integrate structuralist notions and insights from interpretative sociology, and they seek to transcend the opposition between determinism and voluntarism. Second, they all wish to overcome previously held dualisms. For example, they try to move beyond the opposition between the individual and society. Besides these two features, genetic structuralism and structuration theory have other characteristics in common. Both reject mechanistic views of the social world in which structures are seen as imposed upon people. Instead, people are portrayed as active agents – their behaviour being constrained, but not determined. Both Bourdieu and Giddens argue that people's daily routines are rooted in a taken-for-granted world. In general, people know how to act in accordance with the implicit, shared rules which make up that world. They draw upon these rules and, in so doing, they unintentionally reproduce them.

Fin-de-siècle social theory differs from the recent past in three important respects. First, there is what we call the 'empirical turn' in contemporary social theory. We refer to the trend of contemporary theorists to abandon universal ambitions and instead to reflect on the transition towards modernity and towards society today. This intellectual enterprise is 'empirical' in that it provides a diagnosis of the empirical nature of modernity and contemporary society. Those who follow the empirical turn do not abandon theory as such. Rather, they develop a theoretical frame of reference that facilitates the understanding of the distinctiveness and problems of modern contemporary society. The epochal sociologies of authors like Richard Sennett, Ulrich Beck or Zygmunt Bauman exemplify this empirical turn (see chapter 8).

Second, there is a 'normative turn'. Until recently, issues of justice, equality and democracy were considered off-limits to objective social theorizing. From the 1990s onwards, however, social theorists have enthusiastically included these moral and political topics in their agendas. From Habermas's discourse ethics to Bauman's postmodern ethics and Judith Butler's writings on the performative nature of gender identity, normative social theorizing has firmly established itself as a legitimate mode of social thinking. Third, globalization has become a major topic of interest to social theorists. If modernization was the central preoccupation for the post-war generation and the new social movements were the chief interest for social theorists in the 1970s and early 1980s, today there is hardly any major social theorist who does not address globalization. There are, however, noticeable differences in the treatment of this topic. There are those who try to develop a general new social theory about global networks, such as Manuel Castells; there are those who, like Habermas or Axel Honneth, try to explore the democratic and emancipatory potential of this process of growing cosmopolitanism; and there are those who try to develop global, intercivilizational comparisons in order to advance non-ethnocentric modes of social theorizing (Shmuel Eisenstadt is one such example).

The structure of this book can be described as follows. Most contemporary perspectives are influenced by some nineteenth-century precursors. Both structuralism (see chapter 1) and functionalism (see chapter 2) have a lot in common in that they adopt Durkheim's holistic picture of society. According to the doctrine of holism, society is to be studied as a whole, and this whole cannot be reduced to a mere sum of its components. Like Comte, Durkheim emphasized that society is an entity *sui generis*; that is, an entity with its own complexity. Society can therefore not be seen merely as an aggregation of people pursuing their individual interests. Likewise, both structuralism and functionalism are interested in the extent to which different parts of a social system are interrelated, and how they contribute to that system. Structuralists search for those underlying social structures which constrain and determine people's action and thought. The individuals themselves are not necessarily aware of the existence of the structures, and they are a fortiori rarely conscious of the constraining effects of the very same structures. In addition, structuralist social theorists often employ analogies with language in order to make sense of non-linguistic, social phenomena. They do so, often, by relying upon the work of Ferdinand de Saussure, a Swiss linguist and founding father of structural linguistics.

Functionalists, instead, believe in the existence of so-called universal functional prerequisites. That is, they hold that for any social system to survive, a number of functions or needs must be fulfilled. For example, for a system not to disintegrate, a minimum level of solidarity is needed amongst its members. Functionalists thus pay attention to how various social practices fulfil (or might fulfil) the central needs of the wider system in which these practices are embedded. Just as structuralism pays attention to the underlying structures of which people are rarely aware, so functionalism focuses on functions of which the individuals involved tend not to be conscious. Like structuralism, functionalism became especially dominant in the 1950s and 1960s. Many theorists then adhered to both perspectives, and tried to integrate the two in a 'structural-functionalist' framework. Parsons was the main exponent of this view. Functionalism became highly unfashionable in the 1970s, but there has been a revival of functionalist reasoning in the 1990s. Compared to its forerunner, 'neo-functionalism' is a broad church in that it attempts to integrate functionalist notions with insights from rival theories.

For a long time, so-called 'interpretative sociologies' (see chapter 3) were the main alternatives to the hegemony of structural-functionalism. These include symbolic interactionism, the dramaturgical approach and ethnomethodology. Both symbolic interactionism and the dramaturgical approach draw upon the work of the American philosopher G. H. Mead. Like Mead's theories (but unlike structuralism and functionalism), they emphasize the social relevance of the human self; that is, society is possible only because individuals have the ability to reflect upon their (imaginary or real) actions and upon the actions of others. In opposition to structuralism and functionalism, people's actions are not seen as merely the product of social structures imposed upon them. Instead, these 'interpretative schools' stress that people actively interpret their surrounding reality, and act accordingly. The same emphasis on human agency and reflectivity is present in Harold Garfinkel's ethnomethodology and related theories. Also, we discuss the use of micro-sociology in general social theory, for instance, in the work of Randall Collins.

Other micro-sociological proposals are non-interpretative, however. The most obvious example is rational choice theory (see chapter 4). Rational choice theorists hold that it is possible to explain and predict social and political phenomena by drawing upon the notion of a rational, self-interested agent. So, like Weber and Tocqueville, they account for social life by referring to the fact that people act intentionally, and produce numerous effects some of which are intended, some unintended. However, they also assume a constant rationality. There is a vast amount of literature on what rationality consists of. It means, inter alia, that people have a clear ordering of preferences, that they gather information about the costs involved in obtaining the preferences and that they act accordingly. The model suggested is basically derived from economics; hence some rational choice theorists refer to their view as the 'economic approach'. They attempt to show the usefulness of their theory to areas which are traditionally not associated with economics. Take, for example, marriage patterns, rates of fertility or criminal behaviour. Rational choice theorists feel that the more a practice is prima facie irrational, the greater their accomplishment in showing that the practice is rational after all. Rational choice theory became more popular in the 1980s and 1990s, a fact partly related to the re-emergence of an interest in the role of institutions.

Both ethnomethodology and structuration theory are heavily influenced by Alfred Schutz's social phenomenology and the later Wittgenstein. Garfinkel and other ethnomethodologists investigate the extent to which people actively (though unintentionally) reconstitute social order in their daily routine activities. Anthony Giddens's structuration theory (see chapter 5) relies upon both Erving Goffman and Garfinkel to demonstrate that order is indeed a practical accomplishment by knowledgeable individuals who know a great deal about social life. That knowledge tends to be tacit (where the understanding is unspoken), rather than discursive (where the understanding can be put into words). These interpretative schools came to the surface especially in the 1960s; structuration theory emerged in the late 1970s and early 1980s. The analysis of modernity offered by Giddens will be contrasted to other historical sociological accounts. Charles Tilly, Theda Skocpol, Michael Mann and Eisenstadt are the authors of the theoretical proposals we discuss in this regard.

French structuralism eventually led to post-structuralism in the course of the 1970s and 1980s. Structuralism and post-structuralism have quite a lot in common. For example, the modern concept of the individual is not prior to society. It emerges out of time- and space-specific structures or discourses. But post-structuralists differ from their predecessors in that, for example, they abandon the scientistic pretensions of structuralism. Post-structuralists flirt with Friedrich Nietzsche's perspectivism, according to which there is no absolute standpoint from which to make statements regarding what is or what ought to be. They are often inclined to adopt some kind of relativism: different epistemological frameworks bring about new meanings, and each framework is accompanied by novel standards of rationality and truth. The best-known post-structuralists are Jacques Derrida, Gilles Deleuze and Michel Foucault. Derrida had an enormous influence on literary theory and literary criticism, Deleuze on philosophy. For our purposes, Foucault's work (see chapter 6) is especially relevant. Although a historian by training, his writings have had an enormous impact on social theory. We will focus on his historical methodology, since doing so sheds light on the highly original nature of his project. Some of Foucault's ideas have been pursued by a number of contemporary social theorists. We discuss two such cases: David Garland's sociology of punishment and Nikolas Rose's analysis of biopolitics.

Bourdieu and Giddens acknowledge that sociology and social theory have a critical potential. Social theory especially can help us to reflect critically upon society. Nevertheless, the task of developing the foundations of a critical theory is very much that taken on by the Frankfurt School, and particularly by Habermas (see chapter 7). We will focus on Habermas, since his version of critical theory is highly sophisticated. It is extremely elaborate, and it integrates a wide variety of philosophical and sociological traditions. Like other liberal rationalists, Habermas promotes the implementation of procedures of an open, unrestrained debate amongst equals. His notions of 'communicative rationality' and 'ideal speech situation' are situated around this vision. Habermas's utopia looks suspiciously like an academic seminar: society is to be organized so that people are able to criticize openly what others say. Likewise, everybody should be able to defend their viewpoint against the criticisms of others. For Habermas, this vision of an open, unrestrained debate underlies Enlightenment philosophy. If Habermas is the most important representative of the second generation of the Frankfurt School, Honneth is certainly the most influential of the third. We will discuss his theory of recognition, a sophisticated attempt to update Hegel's model of recognition with the help of Mead's theory of the self.

In chapter 8, we discuss current trends in social theory that focus on the empirical nature of our 'late modern', globalized epoch. We begin by analysing Sennett's suggestive depictions of the hidden consequences for personal life of economic globalization. Both Zygmunt Bauman and Ulrich Beck are prime examples of this empirical turn, and this chapter also discusses their work. In particular, we will assess the validity of Bauman's argument that the shift towards a modern society (and towards modern techniques of organization) entails various dangers. In *Modernity and the Holocaust*, Bauman points out that the shift towards modernity goes hand in hand with the vision of a homogeneous nation-state, with the conviction that people and society can be perfected, and with a decline of individual responsibility in its bureaucratic institutions. For Bauman, this means that there might be a link between modernity and atrocities like the Holocaust. We will also evaluate Beck's view that society today is a risk society and therefore radically different from previous stages of modernity. According to Beck, the difference is so enormous that it necessitates a new sociological vocabulary. Castells's social theory of the 'network society' and Saskia Sassen's political economic analysis of the urban hierarchy of global cities are two other proposals discussed in this chapter.

In the conclusion, we reconsider the precise status of social theory today and reassess what it can achieve and what it is for. We begin by discussing the roles of social theory. Our argument is that it not only performs the function of an intellectual facilitator between different disciplines, but it also helps in setting the agenda for sociologists, anthropologists and many other social scientists. We then present our case for the study of social theory. Instead of trying to capture a previously hidden reality, as suggested by traditional models of social research, we argue that innovative readings of the social should be the aim of social theorizing. Our 'hermeneutics-inspired pragmatism' entails four distinct components – conceptualization, critique, edification and imagination – and urges contemporary social practitioners to take a broader perspective and reflect on the world we have hitherto taken for granted. Rather than conceiving of social research as, primarily, an explanatory or predictive endeavour, our neo-pragmatist perspective promotes social research in terms of an ongoing engagement with otherness, a process which ultimately contributes to the pursuit of richer forms of collective redescription.

Our agenda

Underlying this book is a particular view of what is a fruitful way of thinking about social theory. This view also has consequences for how social theory should be taught. We can contrast it with the way in which numerous (introductory or advanced) books on the subject tend to proceed. First, several commentators commit the 'fallacy of explanatory reductionism': they presuppose that theories necessarily aim to *explain* (and possibly predict) empirical social phenomena. Indeed, when sociologists talk about '*sociological* theory' (rather than *social* theory), they often adopt this more restrictive notion of theory as an exclusively explanatory endeavour. Underlying this book is the pragmatist assumption that knowledge can be connected to a variety of objectives, explanation being only one such objective. This means that any student of social theory ought to reflect on what the theory under consideration is supposed to achieve. For instance, some theories are designed to provide understanding rather than explanation; other theories aim at critique and self-emancipation (see chapter 6). Yet other theories, as we will try to show, enable us to develop self-understanding: they allow us to reconsider some of our presuppositions and to re-describe and reassess our present societal constellation (see chapters 5 and 8). In sum, while assessing any theory, it is important to take into account precisely what it is trying to achieve.

Second, some commentators commit what we call the 'fallacy of perspectivism'. By 'perspectivism', we mean here the (often implicit) view that no independent yardstick exists which would enable one to judge and compare between rival theories. Very few explicitly adhere to this, but many more actually practise it. One recognizes perspectivists by the way in which they describe differences between theories. They seem to believe that what distinguishes various theories is merely that they shed light on different aspects of social life. For example, one theory focuses on power, another one on daily interaction and yet another on values and norms. None of them is regarded as superior to any other; they highlight different features of the social realm. Underlying this book is the strongly held conviction that differences between social theories cannot be reduced to mere differences in emphasis or subject-matter. There are indeed a number of yardsticks by which social theories can be judged and compared, the main ones of which are intellectual depth, originality, analytical clarity, explanatory power and internal consistency. Without explicitly referring to these criteria, we employ them throughout what follows.

Third, some commentators on social theory commit the 'fallacy of externalism', in that they present *external* criticisms of the authors discussed. That is, social theories are often criticized for failing to accomplish something which the theorists did not set out to pursue in the first place. For example, many have criticized Garfinkel for not sufficiently taking into account broader social structures. This, in isolation, is obviously an external criticism because the issue of wider structures falls outside Garfinkel's project. We consider external criticisms (at least in isolation) generally to be less desirable, and we try to avoid them in what follows. Nobody can accomplish everything. To criticize a theory for ignoring something is unlikely to be particularly informative. In general, it is more appropriate to evaluate theories from within – to evaluate their internal consistency. This is not to say that all projects have the same value. Some theoretical assumptions or aims are, indeed, more plausible or interesting than others. Neither is it to say that external criticisms are always inadequate. As a matter of fact, there are at least two ways in which they might be useful: they can be a stepping-stone towards an internal critique – for example, it might be shown that taking broader structural issues into account undermines some of Garfinkel's propositions; and they can be used as a medium for developing one's own social theory – for example, Giddens's structuration theory rests upon a series of external criticisms.

Fourth (and related to the previous point), some commentators commit what we call the 'political fallacy'. They criticize theories for their potential or actual *effects* on socio-political matters. For example, a common criticism of functionalist social theory has been that it maintains or reinforces the political status quo. Now, we do not doubt that some publications in social theory *might* affect society. Neither do we wish to argue that it is impossible to ascertain or predict the likely effects of a given theory. For example, it is probably true that, compared with some other theories, functionalist theory can be used more effectively as a justification for the (or any) existing socio-political order. But the identification of possible or actual consequences of a theory should *not* normally interfere with the intellectual appreciation of that theory. We can see only a few exceptions to this rule, one of which refers to the phenomenon of the so-called self-denying prophecy. That is, in some cases, once a theory becomes public knowledge, people start to act in ways which lead to the erosion of that theory. Here, the identification of effects of the theory are crucial to one's judgment regarding its validity. Generally, however, this is not the case. In what follows, we will be concerned with the intellectual validity of social theories, not with their intended or unintended effects on society.

With all this in mind, we wish now to make two points regarding the structure of the book. First, apart from chapters 3, 8 and 9, all chapters deal with a particular school or viewpoint in social theory, namely: structuralism (chapter 1), functionalism and neo-functionalism (chapter 2), rational choice theory (chapter 4), Giddens's structuration theory (chapter 5), Foucault's post-structuralist view (chapter 6), Habermas's and Honneth's critical theory (chapter 7). Chapter 3 discusses several theories which deal with more micro-sociological issues: symbolic interactionism, ethnomethodology, the dramaturgical approach and the rational choice analysis of trust. Chapter 8 deals with current social theoretical attempts at making sense of globalization and late or reflexive modernity. Second, every chapter follows a clear temporal sequence. For example, chapter 1 starts with the predecessors of structuralism (Durkheim and Ferdinand de Saussure), then moves on to Claude Lévi-Strauss's structuralist anthropology, and finally discusses recent attempts to link structuralism with some insights from Heidegger and the later Wittgenstein. A less strict temporal logic applies to the sequence of the chapters.

This book should normally be accessible to undergraduates and postgraduates in the arts and humanities. Each chapter can be read independently of the others.

One Hundred Years of French Social Theory
From Structuralism to Pragmatism

St Augustine argued that he knew what time was until he was asked. One interpretation of this enigmatic statement is that time is so essential to being human that knowledge of it cannot be put discursively. In a sense, structuralism has occupied a similar role in twentieth-century intellectual life. It is indeed virtually impossible to conceive of social theory without taking on board structuralist notions. Yet it is equally difficult to provide an accurate definition of structuralism precisely because it is so much intertwined with current ways of theorizing about the social. The task of defining structuralism is even more complicated because of the wide range of subject-matter that it covers. Its area of application is not restricted to social theory, and it is at least equally prominent in a wide variety of other disciplines. Structuralism incorporates Ferdinand de Saussure and Roman Jakobson's linguistics, Claude Lévi-Strauss's anthropology, Jean Piaget's contributions to the psychology of development, François Jabob's biology and Louis Althusser's reading of Marx.

Being aware of the above reservations and focusing solely upon the social sciences, we think that, nevertheless, four features can be distinguished. First, the most obvious characteristic of structuralism is that it advocates a 'holistic view'. Holism suggests that the various parts of a system should not be investigated independently of each other. The parts can only be understood in terms of their interrelations, and, eventually, in terms of their connections to the whole. Holism is often accompanied by a holistic theory of meaning. According to the latter, the meaning of signs, concepts or practices depends on the broader structure or context in which they are embedded. For example, the meaning of an utterance depends on which language is spoken; the meaning of any scientific term is dependent on the scientific theory in which it is employed; and the meaning of gestures or practices depends on the broader culture in which they take place. It follows that the same utterance might mean something different if spoken in another language; that the meaning of a scientific term might change with a new theory; and that the same gestures or practices could mean something else in a different culture.

The second feature of structuralism is that it tends to prioritize the invariant over the transient. Structuralism downgrades the flux of actions and events, and looks instead for social structures that are more stable across time. Structuralism assumes that these relatively unchanging social structures are either the 'real' causal powers behind actions and events, or that they are crucial in attributing meaning to these observed phenomena. Owing partly to its search for invariant structures, structuralism has a distinctive and controversial method of enquiry. Structuralism has affinities with 'synchronic analysis'. Synchronic analyses merely take a snapshot of society, as opposed to diachronic analyses which look at developments over time. Structuralists tend to downgrade the flow of time; some of them go as far as holding that a snapshot will do. Yet even if they embark upon diachronic analysis, they do so in a distinctive manner. Structuralist historians, for instance, are not particularly interested in the minutiae of historical events. Instead, they search for those factors which, although not immediately visible to the people involved, play a central role in the shaping of their destiny: climate, geography, cultural frameworks, to name a few.

The third characteristic of structuralism is that it opposes positivism. Positivist philosophy will be discussed in detail at a later stage (see chapter 8). It will suffice to say here that positivists prefer to explain things only in terms of entities that are immediately observable. For positivists, to explain is to invoke causes, and causes are to be derived merely from observed regularities. In contrast, structuralists acknowledge the existence of a deeper stratum of reality far below the surface level of observed phenomena. The underlying structures are not immediately visible to the people subjected to them, or to an observer. It is the task of the social scientist to uncover these latent structures in order to explain the surface level. Structuralists also distance themselves from a positivist notion of causality. First, they often refuse to commit themselves to statements regarding causality; they prefer to talk about 'laws of transformation'. Second, even if structuralists do employ causality, their notion is radically different from a positivist one. For structuralists, causality cannot be derived simply from observed regularities. Causes are not immediately available to sensory observation; social structures are latent, but nevertheless exercise causal power.

The fourth characteristic, which most structuralists have in common, is that they acknowledge the *constraining* nature of social structures. That is, structuralists tend to hold that people's actions and thoughts are heavily constrained and determined by underlying structures. It is possible to distinguish both a weak and a strong version of this structuralist position. The weak version is basically a methodological dictum. It suggests that the social researcher needs to search for those parameters which set limits to people's choices. This methodological position leaves open whether or not, in spite of the existence of structures, people really have choice and freedom. The strong version is a philosophical statement with far-reaching consequences. It does not simply say that structures are constraining, but that they are constraining to the extent that they preclude the possibility of the individual's agency. That is, although people might be under the impression that they are in control of their own destiny, they never really are. In its strong version, structuralism should be seen as a reaction against some philosophical currents of the 1940s and 1950s. The assumption that the individual cannot help but be free was indeed a central starting point of existentialist philosophy; structuralism set out to show otherwise.

Most self-declared structuralists would subscribe to the above four features. But in spite of these similarities, it would be a mistake to conceive of structuralism as simply a unified doctrine. There are at least two strands in structuralist thought: one goes back to Émile Durkheim's sociology, the other to Saussure's structuralist linguistics. The first strand emphasizes the extent to which social structures impose themselves and exercise power upon agency. Social structures are regarded as constraining in that they mould people's actions or thoughts, and in that it is difficult, if not impossible, for one person to transform these structures. The second strand draws upon semiology, a general science of signs. Authors within this tradition borrow insights from and analogies with the study of linguistic activities for understanding non-linguistic, rule-governed behaviour. Culture is then conceived of as a 'system of signs'. Fernand Braudel was a clear example of the Durkheimian version of structuralism, Roland Barthes of the Saussurean strand. Lévi-Strauss incorporated both Saussure and Durkheim.

In this chapter we will first deal with the founding fathers of both versions of structuralism: Durkheim and Saussure. We will then elaborate upon Lévi-Strauss's structuralist anthropology, which will allow us to explain some of the deficiencies of structuralist thinking. This will subsequently lead us to Pierre Bourdieu's work, which is one of the major attempts to overcome these inadequacies.

Durkheim's contribution

Émile Durkheim (1858–1917) studied at the École Normale, a selective institution in France for the training of teachers and academics, where he developed a keen interest in social and political philosophy, and an equally keen dislike of what he saw as the humanistic, non-methodical and literary nature of the Parisian intellectual scene. He subsequently spent some time in Germany, where the cultural climate was somewhat more to his liking. On his return to his homeland, he was soon to receive a post at the University of Bordeaux, and 15 years later he returned to Paris. The irony is that this man, who devoted his whole life to the foundation of the discipline of sociology, never officially held a post in his favourite subject until late in his life. Sociology was still associated with Auguste Comte (1798–1857), whose ideas, it was thought, matched his disreputable personality. Durkheim was supposed to teach educational science, but this was hardly a deterrent for a man with such a zealous devotion. He took every opportunity to smuggle sociology into the bastions of the French academic establishment.[1]

A useful way of introducing Durkheim's sociology is by showing how he relates to two other icons of nineteenth-century thought: Comte and Herbert Spencer (1820–1903). This is not to suggest that either Comte or Spencer's influence on Durkheim exceeds the impact of any other author. As a matter of fact, the effect of neither should be overrated; Charles Renouvier, Émile Boutroux and Wilhelm Wundt, for example, were at least as influential. But the advantage of focusing upon Comte and Spencer is that they enable one to locate Durkheim within the broader intellectual spectrum of the nineteenth century.

Through his teacher Boutroux, Durkheim came across Comte's hierarchical division of various domains of reality, where the higher levels are irreducible to the lower ones. Hence the social domain cannot be seen as an aggregate of its psychological components. As society has *sui generis* features, a holistic view is called for. From Comte, Durkheim borrowed the notion that, as in other realms of reality, society can be studied according to rigorous scientific methods. Like Comte, he called this study sociology, and believed it to be not only possible, but also desirable; it would enable one to steer society rationally and to eradicate 'pathological' forms. Also like Comte, Durkheim thought that, given the current crisis of society, steering was not just desirable, but necessary. But like J. S. Mill, Durkheim thought that Comte's sociology was still too speculative and dogmatic. Consequently, Durkheim's theories have a more solid empirical foundation, and he tried to use methods that were as rigorous as possible. Hence he expressed more admiration for the detailed, methodological research conducted by Alfred Espinas and Albert Schaeffle. On the same theme, whereas Comte made sweeping generalizations about 'humanity' in general, Durkheim was more sensitive to differences between societies (Durkheim 1982: 63ff.; see also Lukes 1973: 67ff.).

Evolutionary theory, and especially Spencer's version of it, was another source of inspiration. Durkheim was attracted to Spencer's sophisticated use of social analogies with biological evolution. Like Spencer and many other theorists at the time, Durkheim introduced a dichotomy to portray the evolution of society. Spencer wrote about a transition from military to industrial societies, Ferdinand Tönnies saw a shift from *Gemeinschaft* to *Gesellschaft* and H. S. Maine was struck by the demise of a society based on status and the emergence of a society based on contract. Durkheim preferred to talk about the replacement of mechanical by organic solidarity. Whereas the former is a type of solidarity based on similarities, the latter is based on division of labour and mutual dependency (Durkheim 1984: 31–87). As with Comte, Durkheim did not find Spencer's writings empirical or detailed enough (Durkheim 1982: 64ff.). He also disagreed with Spencer (and with Maine and Tönnies) that modernization goes together with the weakening of social bonds. One of the main propositions in his *Division of Labour* is that, with the advent of industrial society, a new type of solidarity is formed. He distanced himself from Spencer's (and Maine's) view that in modern society people engage in free contractual relations devoid of any moral basis. Contracts presuppose, rather than create, a social order (Durkheim 1984: 149–75).

Partly because of the wide variety of influences on Durkheim's thought, his work does not always present a unifying picture. Equally compelling arguments can be presented for reading him in radically different ways; indeed, authors with different theoretical outlooks have found inspiration in his writings. For instance, it is possible to see Durkheim as the founding father of modern positivist sociology, as can be inferred from a glance at his methodological pamphlet, *Rules of Sociological Method*, and its application in *Suicide*. It is equally plausible to regard some aspects of his work (notably the underpinning theoretical framework of his doctoral dissertation in *Division of Labour*, and sections of his *Rules of Sociological Method* (1982: especially pp. 119–46)) as foreshadowing modern functionalism (see also chapter 2).

Finally, there are undoubtedly structuralist tenets in Durkheim's work. Some argue that these features only appear in his later work on religion, but this is to ignore the more subtle, though equally strong, structuralist claims in his *Rules of Sociological Method*. Be that as it may, it is true that his commitment to structuralism is nowhere as clearly stated as in his *Elementary Forms of Religious Life*.

We will now select those aspects of Durkheim's work which are relevant to the history of structuralism. The Durkheimian concept which deserves our attention is the notion of a 'social fact', of which Durkheim insisted that the subject-matter of sociology consists. He defined the latter as 'any way of acting, whether fixed or not, capable of exerting over the individual an external constraint . . . [and] which is general over the whole of a given society whilst having an existence of its own, independent of its individual manifestations' (1982: 59). One of Durkheim's methodological dictums is that social facts have to be treated as 'things'. By this he meant that they have to be studied like natural objects. That is, social facts exist independent of one's framework or one's perception, and can only be found through empirical research (ibid.: 60ff.). An example of a social fact is a 'collective representation'. Being a state of the collective consciousness of a group, collective representations show how that group envisions itself and its surroundings (ibid.: 40ff.). Collective representations are social in two ways. They have social origins (they emerge out of social associations) and they deal with social phenomena (Lukes 1973: 6–7).

Durkheim's definition of social facts, as outlined, is not exactly what one would call an elegant formulation, but it does reveal three of their most important characteristics: they are external, constraining and general. By the externality of social facts, Durkheim meant that they are prior to the individual, and, more controversially, that their functioning is independent of the individual's use of them. For instance, the individual does not define the duties which he or she has to perform; these obligations are prescribed in law and custom which are external to the individual (Durkheim 1982: 50–1). By the constraining nature of social facts, Durkheim meant that they have 'compelling and coercive power' through which they exercise control over the individual. People tend not to recognize this as coercion because they generally comply with the social facts out of free choice. Durkheim demonstrated this coercive power by imagining what would happen if the individual were to decide not to acquiesce – it would lead to punishments and result in failure (ibid.: 51–2). Finally, generality indicates that social facts are beliefs and practices which are neither individual nor universal attributes, but which refer to those feelings, thoughts and practices that would have been different if people had lived in other groups. Social facts take public-collective forms, as opposed to their individual applications (ibid.: 52ff.).

Like Boutroux and Comte, Durkheim argued that every scientific domain needs to be understood according to 'its own principles'. Just as the biological realm cannot be reduced to physico-chemical forces, society is not an aggregate of psychological phenomena. Through social associations, emergent properties occur which transcend and transform the individuals involved, similar to the numerous 'creative syntheses' in the biochemical realm. Advocating a strict methodological holism, society is considered to be an entity *sui generis* and therefore subject to its own laws. More precisely and polemically, social facts are only to be explained by other social facts (ibid.: 119–46).

Durkheim's later work dealt particularly with the sociology of knowledge and the sociology of religion (see especially 1915; 1963). Whereas his earlier work aimed at demonstrating that it is erroneous to conceive of moral codes in a social vacuum, he continued his sociological crusade by attempting to show the social nature of the Kantian elementary categories of thought. Even the concepts of number, space and time do not escape Durkheim's vigorous campaign. The exact nature of his 'sociological Kantianism' is not entirely clear. It has been shown convincingly that he conflated four separate claims.[2] First, he argued that basic categories are shared by members of the same society. Second, he claimed that these Kantian categories are caused by the underlying social conditions. Third, he argued that the very same categories demonstrate a structural homology with the social conditions out of which they emerge. Fourth, he maintained that the categories fulfil essential functions for the social conditions out of which they evolved. Durkheim's attempt to use sociology in order to rectify Kant's apriorism inspired structuralist anthropology. Like Durkheim, Lévi-Strauss too searched for the latent structures by which people categorize the external world.

It should be obvious from this brief survey that Durkheim's work adumbrated the development of structuralist thought in a number of ways. Let us recapitulate why he was a structuralist *avant la lettre*. First, he drew attention to those features of social life which cannot be reduced to a mere aggregate of its component parts. In structuralism one finds a similar commitment to holistic types of explanation. Second, the notion of constraint was essential to Durkheim's concept of social facts. He was trying to demonstrate the extent to which society moulds and penetrates the individual. Likewise, structuralism allocates coercive power to social structure. Third, Durkheim often relied upon a structuralist two-level world-view, opposing a superficial level of self-mastery to a deeper, more real level of unconscious structures. Fourth, he attempted to eradicate those explanations which refer to subjective states of individuals (intentions, motives, purposes). This shows striking affinities with the 'objectivist' ambitions of structuralist sociology and anthropology in the course of the twentieth century. Fifth, Durkheim's rejection of Kantian apriorism culminated in an attempt to demonstrate the social nature of the basic categories by which people order and classify the surrounding world.

Saussure's approach to linguistics

Having studied at Leipzig and Berlin, Ferdinand de Saussure (1857–1911) taught Sanskrit, Gothic and Old High German, first at the University of Paris and subsequently in Geneva. An obviously gifted man, at the age of 21 Saussure wrote a splendid dissertation ('Mémoire sur le système primitif des voyelles dans les langues indo-européennes'), which already anticipated pivotal features of his mature thought. But with age, Saussure wrote less, and by the time he died he had published not more than 600 pages. His ideas only became widespread through the posthumous publication of his *Course in General Linguistics*, which was based on his lectures at the University of Geneva. For almost half a century the readership of this work was limited to linguists, but once the structuralist bandwagon was well on its way, other social scientists became fascinated with it.

It is, first, important to compare Saussure's structuralism with that of Durkheim. Three differences are worth mentioning here. First, whereas Durkheim's *oeuvre* is Janus-faced, Saussure's is not. We have already referred to the fact that various theoretical research programmes can be attributed to Durkheim; structuralism is only one of them. This is not the case for Saussure, whose theoretical contribution forms much more of a unity. Second, whereas Durkheim's structuralism was meant to be a contribution to sociology, Saussure's was not. Saussure was concerned with linguistic matters and only occasionally explored the possibilities of extending his ideas beyond the boundaries of the study of language. It was the accomplishment of others to demonstrate the wider sociological significance of his insights into linguistics. It also follows that, whereas Durkheim's propositions for sociology are clear-cut, the implications of Saussure for the social sciences remain open to discussion. Third, one of Durkheim's main concerns throughout his life was to explain social facts as *caused* by other social facts, similar to the way in which physico-chemical forces operate. Drawing upon analogies with thermo-dynamics and electricity, structuralist notions are subordinated to a causal analysis. As will be shown shortly, the purpose of a Saussurean approach to language was to reveal the underlying 'syntagmatic' and 'paradigmatic' relations. In this structuralist theory of semiotics, there is hardly any place for a fully developed notion of causality.

Linguists today argue that the importance of Saussure's *Course* lies in the fact that the author distanced himself from two established opinions on language. First, there was the view, initially introduced by Claude Lancelot and Antoine Arnauld as early as the seventeenth century, that language is a mirror of thoughts and intrinsically rational. Second, there were the *Junggram-matiker* (the 'neogrammarians') such as Franz Bopp and Karl Brugmann, and Saussure's teachers Hermann Osthoff and August Leskien. According to their view, very much in vogue in the nineteenth century, the history of a language informs one about its current form. Sanskrit was believed to be the oldest language, and knowledge of it made it possible to trace back the history of other languages and to reveal their mutual roots. These two views had two features in common. First, both assumed that it could be established why, within any language, a particular name or pattern of sound is used to express a certain idea or concept. The further back one goes in history, the less arbitrary is the relationship between naming and concepts. Second, both conceived of language as a nomenclature. That is, both took it to be a set of names attached to universal concepts which are unchangeable and which exist independent of language.

With the appearance of Saussure's *Course* this picture was changed altogether. First, contrary to the atomistic nature of these earlier beliefs, Saussure introduced a holistic view of language. Whereas his predecessors conceived of language as nothing but the sum of its component parts, Saussure insisted that it needs to be seen as a structure in which the meaning of individual concepts is dependent on their relationship within a larger whole. Second, in contrast with, for instance, Bopp's bias in favour of diachronic analysis, Saussure's view of language attributes more importance to the synchronic investigation of language (1960: 71–100). Third, Saussure demonstrated successfully that language is not a nomenclature. If it were, translation would be an easy task, but it is not, and this can be explained by the fact that different languages structure the world differently. Likewise, the boundaries and semantics of concepts continuously change through time, and this again shows that languages organize the world differently.

Central to Saussure's theory is his distinction between 'langue' and 'parole'. Saussure introduced this distinction in his attempt to identify the object of linguistic investigation (ibid.: 7–23). What Saussure called *parole* or the 'executive side of language' alludes to actual utterances. *Langue* refers to the shared set of structural properties underlying language usage. Saussure insisted that the major concern of linguistics should be with *langue*, not *parole*. Similar to Durkheim's notion of the externality of social facts, Saussure argued that the simultaneous system of *langue* precedes *parole*, and that the former is the *sine qua non* for the latter. What people say or write makes sense because of the pre-existent structural properties of language. Language is a shared, social experience: people can speak and write because of the intersubjective nature of language usage.

Equally important is his distinction between 'sign', 'signifier' and 'signified'. The sign refers to both the signifier and the signified (ibid.: 65–7). Whereas the signifier is the utterance or trace, the signified is the concept attached to it. If we say 'horse', the utterance or trace 'horse' is the signifier, the concept 'horse' is the signified and the sign refers to both. These distinctions are relevant for understanding his notion of the 'arbitrary nature of the sign' (ibid.: 67–70). The arbitrariness refers to the bond between the signifier and the signified. Saussure's use of 'arbitrary' calls for further explanation here. What he meant is that a different signified could have been attached to a particular signifier, were it not for the relationship between the sign that links them and other signs within that language. Now, we mentioned earlier that, in Saussure's view, language is not a nomenclature and that there are thus no unchangeable universal signifiers. Hence, his notion of the 'arbitrary nature of the sign' not only designated the 'unmotivated' bond between sound-image and concept, but also the arbitrary nature of both the signified and the signifier in themselves (Culler 1986: 28–33).

Still regarding Saussure's concept of the arbitrary nature of the sign, there is a potential misunderstanding, which we briefly wish to point out. The notion of an arbitrary nature of the sign could well be understood to mean that the individual speaker can decide which signifier to use. But Saussure insisted that he did not mean this at all (1960: 68–9). As a matter of fact, he very much denied individuals that power. Reminiscent of Durkheim's reflections upon the constraining features of social facts, Saussure went to great lengths to show that, because of its public-collective features, language is 'necessary' in that no individual is able to choose different signifiers from the ones in use. This particular view of language, as both arbitrary and necessary, is sometimes referred to as 'conventional' (see, e.g., Harland 1988: 13).

Closely related to the notion of the arbitrary nature of the sign is the principle of difference. Saussure's famous analogy between language and a chess game is useful here (1960: 88ff., 110–11). The meaning of a piece is not derived from its material form in itself, but depends on how that piece can be distinguished from the other pieces. Likewise, in language, identity is a function of differences within a system. This applies to both signifier and signified. The meaning of the utterance 'man' is dependent on its difference from the utterances 'can', 'gen', 'mean', 'mess', etc. Likewise, the meaning of any colour, say green, is dependent on its differences from the other colours currently in use: blue, yellow, red, etc. Another way of expressing this insight is by saying that identity depends on difference from an 'absent totality'. For instance, when we refer to the colour green, the meaning of green is derived from its difference within a *system* of colours which is currently in use and which, although not uttered, is nevertheless *implied*. Notice that the principle of difference operates at several linguistic levels, say from phonemes to grammatical facts. The phoneme (for instance, *c* in the word 'cat') is defined by its opposition to other phonemes which can potentially replace it and still make sense (in this case: 'bat', 'mat', 'sat', etc.). Grammatical facts comply with the very same notion of the relational nature of the sign: for instance, the future tense of a verb is dependent on its opposition to its present tense (ibid.: 120–2).

Saussure's distinction between synchronic and diachronic analyses of language is well known. Initially, he used the terms 'static' and 'evolutionary' linguistics, but then opted for synchronic and diachronic analysis (ibid.: 79–81). Whereas the former takes a snapshot of language, the latter follows its evolution through time. Although critics of Saussurean linguistics tend to portray it as simply 'ahistorical', Saussure's own position was more subtle. Contrary to what the textbooks say of him, he recognized the historicity of language. The arbitrary nature of the sign implies that there are no essential, universal features to meaning, and meaning is thus constantly in flux. Now comes the interesting twist in his argument. Whereas most scholars would conclude from this the priority of diachronic over synchronic analysis, for Saussure it meant exactly the opposite. The arbitrary nature of the sign not only makes for the historicity of language, but also for the necessity of analysing language synchronically. From a Saussurean perspective, the explanation for this paradox is rather straightforward. The arbitrary nature of the sign means that the sign does not possess any essential features of its own. In structuralist parlance, there are no positive, self-defined signs in language. Every sign is entirely defined by its relationship with other signs which are currently in use, and it must therefore be taken to be a relational entity. Now, if the meaning of a sign is dependent on its relationship with other signs at a given time, it follows that a synchronic analysis is called for (ibid.: 79–100; see also Culler 1986: 46–57).

We finish the exposition of Saussure's thought with a brief note regarding the distinction between paradigmatic and syntagmatic relations. Whereas the former refer to oppositional relations between replaceable items, the latter refer to combinatory relations between signs. Hitherto, we have only dealt with relations of paradigmatic contrast. Regarding syntagmatic relations, 'I love', for instance, can be followed by 'you', 'flying', 'them', 'Bruges', 'that film', etc. It cannot be followed by 'underwent', 'she', etc. There is thus a group of words which, according to the rules of syntagmatic relations, can follow 'I love'. Each two members of that group are in paradigmatic opposition to one another. Saussure's bold conjecture is that, at any level (i.e. whether one is dealing with phonemes, morphemes or 'grammatical facts'), language can be reduced to a combination of paradigmatic and syntagmatic relations (1960: 122–7).

Saussure's impact on the development of social theory has been considerable. First, his distinction between *langue* and *parole* (and his prioritizing of the former over the latter) struck a chord with those who were disenchanted with the positivist pursuit of regularity conjunctions (see also chapter 8). The relevance of the distinction between *langue* and *parole* indeed extends beyond the realm of language. It can be seen as derived from a more general opposition between underlying structures on the one hand, and their particular instantiations on the other. From that general dualism follows, for instance, the hierarchical opposition between social structure and behavioural patterns. With this model in mind, the positivist preoccupation with statistical regularities was in vain: it was a mere search at the superficial non-structural level. Second, various social scientists became aware that, like language, other systems of discourse could be studied semiotically. Whether scientific theories, hairstyles, restaurant menus or ancient myths, they can all be studied as systems of signs (see, e.g., Barthes 1972; 1983). For example, there are clear rules regarding appropriate combinations of meal courses and vis-à-vis potential substitute courses. The meaning of each course depends on its difference from alternative choices. Compared with a light course, heavy and filling courses might suggest (in some social circles) a lack of delicacy or sophistication.

Durkheim and Saussure set the stage for a structuralist movement in the social sciences. Three Frenchmen were essential to the further development of structuralist thinking. First, Fernand Braudel introduced Durkheimian notions in history (Braudel 1972: preface; 1980). As opposed to a mere history of events or 'small-scale science of contingency', Braudel searched for what he coined the *longue durée*. This refers to underlying structures which are relatively stable and which stretch over long periods of time. These geophysical, climatological or demographic structures constrain people's action and thought. Braudel was one of the founders of the highly influential Annales School; most of its members carried out historical research in a similar vein.[3] Second, Louis Althusser argued that there is an epistemological break between the early and the later Marx (Althusser 1972; Althusser and Balibar 1970). Whereas the former was still indebted to German idealism and classical political economy, the latter went further and developed a structuralist 'science of history'. Against existentialist readings of Marx, Althusser argued that the later Marx rejected any a priori conceptions of human needs. Individuals are not the real subjects of history any longer; the hidden relations of production are. Others soon followed Althusser in the pursuit of structuralist Marxism; Étienne Balibar and Nicos Poulantzas were probably the best known amongst them (Althusser and Balibar 1970; Poulantzas 1968). Third, by drawing upon Roman Jakobson, Sigmund Freud and Durkheim, Lévi-Strauss developed a structuralist anthropology. With the help of the structuralist method, he analysed diverse social phenomena, ranging from myths to kinship systems. Compared with Braudel and Althusser, Lévi-Strauss has been the most influential. His structuralist method was emulated by Edmund Leach and many other anthropologists. Given the abstract nature of his work, his influence went far beyond anthropology. We will therefore pay special attention to his work.

Lévi-Strauss's anthropology

The name of Claude Lévi-Strauss (1908–) is closely associated with the structuralist tradition. Born in Belgium, Lévi-Strauss moved to France as a child, and studied philosophy at the Sorbonne. During his studies in Paris he became acquainted with French sociology, notably the works of Comte, Durkheim and Marcel Mauss. His interest soon shifted to cultural anthropology when he moved to Brazil, first in a teaching capacity at the University of São Paulo, then on a research expedition funded by the French government. During the Second World War he fled to the United States, and taught at the New School of Social Research in New York. It was there that he met the linguist Jakobson – an encounter which would lastingly shape Lévi-Strauss's intellectual development. In his later life he moved back to France – first to the École Pratique des Hautes Études, subsequently as Professor of Anthropology at the Collège de France – where he established himself as one of the leading figures of the structuralist movement.

It has occasionally been asserted that Lévi-Strauss's structuralist analysis of culture is very much indebted to Durkheim. Although there is some truth in this claim, it certainly requires further qualification. As a matter of fact, a brief comparison of the intellectual projects of Durkheim and Lévi-Strauss will help in elucidating the latter's. Insofar as there has been an appropriation of Durkheim's thought by Lévi-Strauss, it has been a highly selective one. Lévi-Strauss distanced himself from the functionalist or positivist readings of Durkheim which were prominent at the time (see also chapters 2 and 8). Not that these readings were necessarily false depictions of Durkheim's thought at certain points in his life. Yet for Lévi-Strauss these aspects of Durkheim's work were less attractive, probably erroneous and largely to be ignored. More worthy of attention, but seriously in need of a contemporary reassessment, were Durkheim's earlier propositions regarding social facts and collective representations. Finally, the most important contribution to Lévi-Strauss's intellectual development are Durkheim's later writings on religion.

Lévi-Strauss's selective appropriation of Durkheim is symptomatic of the significant differences between the two men. First, whereas especially the earlier work of Durkheim is still very much embedded in the *Weltanschauung* of the nineteenth century, Lévi-Strauss's work is, in many respects, a reaction to this intellectual tradition. In *Division of Labour* Durkheim drew upon analogies with biological evolution to explain the transition from 'mechanical' to 'organic' types of solidarity. In contrast, Lévi-Strauss has always been hostile to evolutionist types of explanation. The early Durkheim was concerned mainly with those theoretical principles that only reveal themselves across longer temporal spans. *Ex adverso*, Lévi-Strauss focused upon those mechanisms that reveal themselves across cultures. Durkheim was aware of the problems which accompanied industrialization and modernization, but he nevertheless defended the cultural and structural transformations which the West was undergoing. Certain adjustments needed to be made, but the overall trend was one of progress. By contrast, Lévi-Strauss's *oeuvre* can be read as a fierce critique of the Western project of modernity.

Second, in some respects the aims of Durkheim and Lévi-Strauss are diametrically opposed. To clarify this, it is useful to consider the not uncommon view that anthropologists belong to either of two categories. On the one hand, there are those who are struck by and sensitive to the enormous cultural differences between societies. Underlying their work is an inclination to focus on the more malleable features of people's personality or practices, or, more strongly, a tendency towards an outright *tabula rasa* conception of the individual. On the other hand, there are those who find these differences superficial, and who are overwhelmed by that which all human beings have in common. They dedicate their life to a search for the universal features of humankind. However crude this distinction, it is a very useful one within the context of our discussion, for whereas Durkheim is very much representative of the former, Lévi-Strauss is an almost archetypal example of the latter. Durkheim was sensitive to the differences between various cultures. The existence of these differences (which can be ascertained empirically) was, for instance, central to his refutation of any a priori moral theory. Lévi-Strauss's project could not be more different. Normally, one would expect a collection of ethnographic details about numerous foreign cultures to back the insight that cultures radically differ from each other, but Lévi-Strauss used that information to convince the reader about the similarities between human beings. For him, people cannot help but structure the world in the same way.

Third, some of the ideas of Durkheim reached Lévi-Strauss through his reading of the work of Durkheim's nephew, Mauss. This is not to suggest that Durkheim did not exercise any direct influence on Lévi-Strauss. But Mauss's influence is at least as important, and whenever he deviated from his uncle's path (a rare occurrence indeed), Lévi-Strauss was likely to follow the nephew. In particular, Lévi-Strauss seemed very much taken by Mauss's notion of a 'total social fact'. Through that notion, both Mauss and Lévi-Strauss purported to transcend the opposition between atomism and holism. They followed Durkheim in his critique of individualist forms of explanation, but deplored the reifying tendencies in his notions of a collective mind or collective consciousness. In an attempt to avoid the deterministic pitfalls of Durkheim's idea of a collective consciousness, Mauss outlined the concept of a total social fact as embedded within actual patterns of social interactions. This seemed attractive to Lévi-Strauss, who also attributed to Mauss the uncovering of unconscious structures under-lying the surface level of ethnographic results. For Lévi-Strauss, this was remarkably similar to the way in which linguistics reveal structures under-neath the immediately accessible level of speech patterns (1994: 5ff.).

Fourth, Durkheim and Lévi-Strauss were different personalities, involved in different kinds of practice. To put it bluntly: Durkheim was a scientist at heart, and Lévi-Strauss was not. Although Durkheim con-templated following in the religious footsteps of his father (who was a chief rabbi) and although there are some obvious traces of a religious upbringing in his work, his outlook on the world was, from an early age onwards, a rational-scientific one. We have already briefly sketched Durkheim's antagonistic attitude to the literary 'brilliance' of his Parisian contemporaries, and how his life was devoted to the development of a scientific approach to society. Durkheim aimed at applying as much sci-entific rigour as was employed in the natural sciences, and he tried to achieve this by rigidly adhering to the rules of logic, and by putting his theories through severe empirical tests.[4] Lévi-Strauss is very different indeed. Although he (and structuralism in general for that matter) aimed at a science of society, he regularly broke the most elementary rules of scientific investigation. We are dealing here with a very different mind: a man with great sensitivity, but surely not a scientist. For anybody who is acquainted with Lévi-Strauss's writings, it will come as no surprise that his home background was artistic, and that he himself was an accom-plished musician. Leach was not far from the truth when he referred to Lévi-Strauss as a 'visionary'. We are dealing with a highly imaginative, artistic mind, which *expresses* intuitions about the world, rather than *exam-ining* their validity.

If Durkheim's influence on Lévi-Strauss is ambiguous, the impact of structuralist linguistics is less so. While lecturing in New York during the war, Lévi-Strauss developed a friendship with the Russian linguist and folklorist Jakobson. Jakobson introduced Lévi-Strauss to Saussure's work, the linguistics of the Prague School and, obviously, his own contributions. Jakobson was very much influenced by Saussure's notion that the meaning of a linguistic item depends on its *difference* from other items currently in use. With this Saussurean framework as his starting point, Jakobson con-ceived of language in terms of binary oppositions. That is, people are able to distinguish a consonant from a vowel, an acute sound from a grave one, and a voiced sound from an unvoiced sound. By extending Jakob-son's theory to non-linguistic domains, Lévi-Strauss became one of the first to investigate social life by systematically employing analogies with linguistic systems. He analysed kinship and myths in terms of binary oppositions, correlation, inversion and permutation, similar to Jakobson's treatment of the phoneme on the phonological level. What is important, however, is Lévi-Strauss's systematic attempt to go beyond the conscious level, looking for those universal, unconscious features of the mind which uniformly force a particular structure onto the world. As we suggested earlier, from Lévi-Strauss's perspective, this search for the universal, unconscious level is loyal to both Mauss and structural linguistics.

Lévi-Strauss deplored the fact that Freud and Marx had been excluded from the syllabus when he was a student. He did become acquainted with the writings of both later in his life. Here again, his readings of these authors deviated from the prevailing interpretations of his time. During the 1940s and 1950s, an attempt was made to merge existentialist philosophy with Marxism, and to interpret the latter in terms of the former. Lévi-Strauss's understanding of Marx could not be more different. He saw in Marx a structuralist *avant la lettre* who constantly searched beyond the surface level for economic structures. The same applies to his reading of Freud. Freud was initially introduced into the social sciences by members of the Frankfurt School (e.g., Theodor Adorno and Max Horkheimer) and theoreticians with close affinities to critical theory (e.g., Wilhelm Reich and Erich Fromm). Most of them attempted to integrate Freud (and Marx) with a humanist tradition, and they interpreted the work of Freud along these lines. Lévi-Strauss's reading was different indeed. What was appealing for him was Freud's attempt to develop a scientific explanation of psychological phenomena by moving beyond the conscious level and searching for the underlying structure and power of the unconscious. The merging of structuralism and psychoanalysis became prominent in Lévi-Strauss's analysis of myths, to which we will turn shortly.

First, we need to outline Lévi-Strauss's overall scheme. His starting point is that human beings have certain features in common, one of these being the way they construct and divide up the external world. The surrounding world is potentially open to many categorizations, but human beings employ particular ones. They interpret their surroundings by reducing them to discontinuous units. Lévi-Strauss came to this conclusion through generalizing from Jakobson's structuralist treatment of language. According to this theory, people have an in-built ability to discriminate vowels from consonants. The former have high noise energy, while the latter are less loud. People are also able to distinguish compact sounds (*a* or *k*) from diffuse sounds (*u*, *p*, *i* or *t*), and acute sounds (sounds with a high frequency pitch, such as *i* or *t*) from grave sounds (sounds with a low frequency pitch, such as *u* or *p*). So one arrives at Jakobson's primary vowel (and consonant) triangle (see figure 1.1).

According to Jakobson's triangle, people unwittingly process linguistic information through binary oppositions. Lévi-Strauss used this simple idea to analyse non-linguistic cultural phenomena. Take, for example, food and culinary activities. Simple binary oppositions ('nature versus culture' and 'altered versus unaltered') are at work here. It is obvious that ordinary raw food has not undergone any transformation, whereas cooked or rotten food has. But there is a difference between cooked food and rotten food. The former has been altered through cultural means, whereas the latter has been transformed through nature. So Lévi-Strauss arrived at a primary culinary triangle (see figure 1.2), which allows him to distinguish and analyse the main types of culinary activity. Boiling, for instance, is similar to rotting, because it also leads to the decomposition of food.

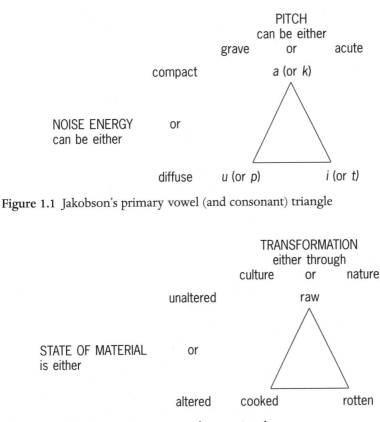

Figure 1.1 Jakobson's primary vowel (and consonant) triangle

Figure 1.2 Lévi-Strauss's primary culinary triangle

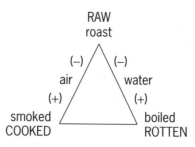

Figure 1.3 Lévi-Strauss's developed culinary triangle
Source: Lévi-Strauss 1978: 490

But it is different from rotting in that it can only take place through the medium of water plus cultural means (one needs a container). Smoking leads to complete cooking, with the medium of air, but without any cultural means. Roasting leads to only a partial transformation, and it is accomplished without the medium of air, water or any cultural means. Lévi-Strauss thus arrived at his *developed* culinary triangle (see figure 1.3). This example gives some indication of how, through simple binary oppositions, Lévi-Strauss tried to tackle elaborate cultural procedures.

Let us now move to Lévi-Strauss's treatment of myths, which, amongst other things, will give some indication of the extent to which both structuralism and psychoanalysis have influenced his work. He started off by pointing out a particular ambiguity in the study of myths. That is, on the one hand, a myth is one amongst many linguistic manifestations, and, on the other hand, it belongs to a more complex order than other linguistic expressions (1993: 206–11). Indicative of the fact that myths are both 'part of and above language' is that, contrary to other linguistic phenomena, they employ a dual time referent. On the one hand, they allude to reversible time in that they refer to events which have taken place a long time ago. On the other hand, they operate outside time in that they inform us not only about the meaning of the past, but also about the present and the future. Now, this means that in order to understand myths, they need to be analysed at both temporal levels. Lévi-Strauss invoked the example of an orchestra score to support his method of analysis. In order to find harmony, one needs to read the orchestra score both 'diachronically' and 'synchronically'. The former means that it is read as if it were a book: from left to right and top to bottom, starting with page one, then page two, etc. The latter means that one tries to conceive of the notes along

Cadmos seeks
his sister Europa,
ravished by Zeus

Cadmos kills the
dragon

The Spartoi kill
one another

Labdacos, Laios'
father = lame

Oedipus kills his
father, Laios

Laios, Oedipus'
father = left-sided

Oedipus kills the
Sphinx

Oedipus = swollen
foot

Oedipus marries
his mother,
Jocasta

Eteocles kills his
brother, Polynices

Antigone buries
her brother,
Polynices despite
prohibition

Figure 1.4 Lévi-Strauss's treatment of the Oedipus myth
Source: Based on Lévi-Strauss 1993: 214

each axis as one bundle of relations. Now, Lévi-Strauss invited us to 'read' myths in a similar fashion (ibid.: 211ff.).

Take, for example, the Oedipus myth, which Lévi-Strauss transformed as a chart (see figure 1.4). If one wanted to tell the story, one would read from left to right, and from top to bottom. But if one wants to understand the myth, Lévi-Strauss argued, one would read column by column (ibid.: 214ff.). The columns are constructed such that each one involves events which have something substantial in common. For instance, the events included in the first column indicate blood relationships which are too intimate or too close, whereas events in the second column imply the underrating of blood relationships. The third column refers to the killings of those monsters who are a threat to the coming to life, or the living of, human beings. The fourth column concerns the names of Oedipus and his ancestors, and all indicate problems with walking or standing up (ibid.: 213–15).

Now, whereas the first and the second columns are rather straightforward, the third and the fourth are obviously not self-explanatory and necessitate further interpretation. Here, the interpretative abilities of the structuralist researcher become important. Partly drawing upon psychoanalytic accounts of symbols and partly inferring from his general knowledge of other myths, Lévi-Strauss suggested that the events in column three symbolize the denial of the autochthonous origin of human beings, whereas column four symbolizes the continuance of that very same autochthonous origin. It follows that column four is to three as column two is to one. That is, 'the overrating of blood relations is to the underrating of blood relations as the attempt to escape autochthony is to the impossibility to succeed in it' (ibid.: 216). So, the myth deals with the contradiction between the belief that human beings are authochthonous and the knowledge that they are born from the union of man and woman (ibid.: 215ff.).

This example is indicative of Lévi-Strauss's structuralist analysis of myths, and it allows us to summarize the main features of that analysis. First, there is no intrinsic or invariable meaning to any 'mytheme' or 'gross constituent unit'. Their meaning depends on their opposition to other symbolic units within that myth. Second, myths should not be conceived of in isolation from each other. A closer look shows the extent to which, through necessary transformations like symmetrical inversion, one myth is related to another. Whether we study Oedipus, Antigone or Phaedra, myths express the basic polarities such as 'nature versus culture', 'gods versus man' or 'life versus death'. Third, myths enable people to articulate and come to terms with the basic contradictions of human existence. The contradictions at stake are those between people's unconscious wishes or anxieties on the one hand, and their conscious experience on the other. Myths have an existential value in that they enable people to transcend these contradictions, somehow to reduce these in-built tensions.

Lévi-Strauss's analysis of myths shows most effectively that his work meant a radical break with nineteenth-century ways of theorizing about the social. Against nineteenth-century unilinear evolutionism and its attendant notion of progress, Lévi-Strauss argued for the importance of synchronic analysis through which foreign cultures, prima facie very different, end up remarkably similar to ours. Through an in-depth comparative analysis of different cultures, he attempted to demonstrate the universal, innate properties of the human mind which bring the old and the new together, and which show distant societies to be much closer to us than was once believed. There is, no doubt, a political or ideological message to Lévi-Strauss's anthropology. Whereas, for decades, armchair anthropologists had somehow assumed the West to be the ultimate outcome of a necessary, linear process, Lévi-Strauss's notion of a universal mind looks for that which necessarily links us all together (1993: 1–27; 1994: 312–62).

Attempting to capture the innate properties of the human mind, Lévi-Strauss's work is one of the most ambitious and challenging attempts to develop a grand theory about culture. But it is evidently not devoid of problems, and two arguments, which have been held against him, are especially worth mentioning. First, it has been pointed out correctly that, contrary to what Lévi-Strauss believed, not all cultural forms are reducible to the logic of binary oppositions. Second, it has been argued (again convincingly) that, rather than attempting to put his theory to the test, Lévi-Strauss seemed to *select* empirical evidence in order to support his argument. Both are valid points, but it seems to us that there are more severe problems with his project. First, his work exhibits a remarkably closed, circular form of argument. He always seems to have a set of tools at hand (inversions and permutations) which turn those myths that do not prima facie fit his scheme into transformations of ones that do. There is an uncertainty regarding which potential or real myths would, within the parameters of his structuralist theory, be potential falsifiers of that very same theory. Second, an aura of mystery surrounds his choice of the basic dichotomies, and the reader is expected to accept uncritically the 'superior' intuition of the *maître-penseur* in these matters. It is perfectly possible, without deviating from the structuralist cause, to account for the same phenomena by invoking a different set of universal dichotomies from the ones used by Lévi-Strauss. It is not clear which criteria should be employed to judge and compare between these distinct structuralist readings. Third, from the perspective of evolutionary biology, there might be grounds to support Lévi-Strauss's assumption that there are innate, universal structures of the human mind. More contentious, however, is his belief that he can have access to these innate structures as they are. If innate universal structures of the human mind did exist, any attempt, including Lévi-Strauss's, to get access to them would only be possible by drawing upon the very same innate structures. These universal structures are both the object of research and the medium through which that research becomes possible. It is obvious that the dual nature of this type of knowledge formation (as both medium and object) is not unproblematic, and calls for more epistemological foundation than provided in Lévi-Strauss's work.

By the end of the 1960s, structuralism had developed into two different schools. Both criticized central features of the structuralist project, but both also shared a lot in common with structuralism. First, there is post-structuralism, associated with the work of Jacques Lacan (1989), Jacques Derrida (1973; 1976; 1978) and Michel Foucault.[5] Post-structuralists build further upon the work of Friedrich Nietzsche, Martin Heidegger and Ludwig Wittgenstein. The theory shares with structuralism an anti-humanist and anti-Cartesian stance. But whereas structuralists aimed at a science of signs (and a science of society), post-structuralism purports to undermine notions of truth and scientific objectivity. Post-structuralists tend to commit themselves to conceptual or epistemological relativism. A more radical version of the post-structuralist position is taken up by some feminist authors, such as Hélène Cixous (1981), Luce Irigaray (1985) and Julia Kristeva (1982; see also Marks and de Courtivron 1981). We will deal with Foucault and post-structuralism in chapter 5. Second, there is Pierre Bourdieu's genetic structuralism and Anthony Giddens's structuration theory. Both feel uneasy with the reifying tendencies of structuralist reasoning and its neglect of social praxis. Both also feel uncomfortable with the structuralists' exclusive emphasis on the constraining nature of structure. This explains why structuralism fails to account sufficiently for how structures are reproduced through time. While accepting some structuralist notions, both Bourdieu and Giddens attempt to link these with insights from social phenomenology and hermeneutics. The reproduction of structure is then seen as a continuous practical accomplishment by competent individuals. Bourdieu is clearly embedded in the French structuralist tradition, whereas Giddens is more eclectic. This explains why we leave Giddens for a separate chapter (see chapter 5), and why we will turn to Bourdieu now.

Bourdieu's genetic structuralism

Pierre Bourdieu (1930–2002) initially studied philosophy at the École Normale Supérieure, but subsequently moved in the direction of social anthropology and sociology. He first became well known in anthropological circles because of his critique of Lévi-Strauss and because of his meticulous anthropological analyses of Algeria. His work on the sociology of education in the 1960s introduced him to a wider audience. Meanwhile, he had worked out a sophisticated theoretical frame of reference which enabled him to develop a perspicacious analysis of his collected data. By the late 1960s, Bourdieu had introduced many of the key notions of his framework: *habitus*, *doxa*, field, capital, etc. His empirical analyses already adumbrated his subsequent conceptual endeavours to connect structuralist notions with social phenomenology. These theoretical attempts were summarized in his highly influential *Outline of a Theory of Practice* and later in his lucid *Logic of Practice*. The very same theoretical considerations also underlie his more recent empirical writings, which range from studies of culture and symbolic power to the intricacies of higher educational establishments and similar elite formations.

This résumé allows us to introduce a number of features of Bourdieu's work. First, there is his relationship to theory. It is obvious from the above that Bourdieu is not merely a theorist, in that he has carried out numerous empirical researches. But there is a more fundamental way in which he distances himself from what he sees as the Anglo-Saxon notion of social theory; that is, a coherent, abstract project independent of any empirical basis. For him theory should grow out of research, and it should be directed towards that research. In this view, theory is a set of tools or directives, which suggest to the reader the questions that ought to be asked. Without an empirical base, social theory becomes a pointless and empty enterprise (see Bourdieu 1993: 29–30; Bourdieu et al. 1991; Bourdieu and Wacquant 1992b: 158–62; see also Wacquant, 1992: 26–35).

Second, there is Bourdieu's relationship to other French intellectual traditions. During his formative years at the École Normale Supérieure, he came across three philosophical strands: French Marxism, Jean-Paul Sartre's existentialism and Lévi-Strauss's structuralist anthropology. Of these three, Bourdieu seems to be most sympathetic towards Lévi-Strauss. He strongly distances himself from the economic determinism of French Marxism. Although he agrees with Marxist sociologists that power struggles are central to social life, he insists that they are not exclusively economic; they often operate on a symbolic level. Bourdieu is equally critical of Sartre's philosophy. Sartre's writings were still embedded in a Cartesian philosophy of consciousness, whereas Bourdieu draws upon social phenomenology, Heidegger and the later Wittgenstein, learning from them the importance of shared, practical knowledge. Existentialist views are justified in emphasizing the pivotal role of agency, but they fail to acknowledge the objective constraints of the social world. Bourdieu saw Lévi-Strauss's anthropology as a systematic attempt to reveal these structural constraints, and this accounts for why he was initially favourably disposed to Lévi-Strauss. However, Bourdieu soon became dissatisfied with the structuralist neglect of social praxis. Rather than opting for either structuralist or agency-orientated views, Bourdieu's conceptual frame of reference aims at transcending that opposition (1977: 1–30; 1990: 25–51).

This brings us to one of the *idées maîtresses* of Bourdieu's viewpoint: to transcend the antinomy between what he coins 'subjectivism' and 'objectivism' (1977: 3–10; 1990: 30–51). By objectivism, Bourdieu means a search for underlying structures independent of people's knowledge, concepts or purposes. Subjectivism tries to capture how people experience or conceptualize the world, and then how they act in accordance with it. By ignoring one vital aspect of social reality, each viewpoint inevitably distorts its complexity. Subjectivism tends to conceive of the social world as created *de novo*, failing to take into account the extent to which people's mental framework and their practices are adjusted to social constraints. Contrary to the premises of subjectivism, social life is not created from nothing. People's hopes, expectations and goals are in tune with the social environment in which they have been brought up. However problematic subjectivism may be, one cannot find rescue in objectivist accounts either. By abandoning insights from hermeneutics altogether, objectivism erroneously adopts a mechanistic view of human conduct, ignoring the extent to which social life is a practical achievement by skilful actors (1977: 10–16, 22–30). Objectivism reduces the complexity of social life to, for example, a mere role-playing or a following of rules. It fails to take seriously the ability of people to cope with novel situations and their capacity to improvise whenever necessary.

Bourdieu's attempt to transcend the opposition between the objective and the subjective culminates in two methodological notions. First, his research aims at what he calls 'participant objectivation'. That is, the researcher first objectifies the object of research, then scrutinizes the validity and presuppositions of that objectification, and finally takes into account people's improvisations and skilful achievements. Second, Bourdieu attempts to break with the traditional positivist distinction between the researcher and object of research. That is, given that the social sciences are embedded in structural conditions and power struggles themselves, the researcher needs also to take up a critical attitude to his or her own practices. Hence his appeal for 'reflexive sociology', which aims at just such a critical distance.

From social phenomenology, and from Heidegger, Wittgenstein and Goffman, Bourdieu learns the importance of people's *practical mastery* of the complex logic of everyday life. He insists that this practical mastery should not be reduced to conscious intervention or theoretical knowledge. Nor should people's practical sense be conflated with the unconscious realm, because this would imply some notion of repression. People know how to go on with their daily activities, without needing to put that knowledge discursively. People's practical mastery draws upon *doxa*, or 'doxic experience', referring to a taken-for-granted world beyond reflection (see, e.g., ibid.: 164–71). Bourdieu's notion of practical sense and *doxa* culminates in his highly acclaimed and widely misused concept of *habitus*. *Habitus* is a generative scheme of dispositions, tacitly acquired through early childhood and therefore durable. The dispositions generate people's practices, improvisations, attitudes or bodily movements. The *habitus* provides a 'feeling for the game' or 'practical sense', allowing people to develop an infinite number of strategies to cope with an infinite number of situations.[6] As the dispositions are adjusted to the constraints of the social surroundings in which they emerge, the *habitus* differs according to background. Manners of speaking or bodily gestures, concepts of beauty or self-identity – all these indeed differ according to class background. Notice that these differences in *habitus* often imply inequality in resources. For instance, compared with members of the working class, the middle class feels more confident with public speaking or with formal occasions, and this might be an important asset in the economic sphere. It is thus not surprising that Bourdieu's concept of *habitus* is central in his analysis of various forms of reproduction of social inequality.

Bourdieu uses the concept of 'field' to refer to those areas of social life in which, through strategies, struggles take place with respect to valuable goods or resources.[7] In the context of fields, Bourdieu relies rather heavily upon economic metaphors, and this has occasionally led to confusion amongst commentators. For example, he coins the term 'capital' to refer to the goods and resources which are at stake, but it would be mistaken to restrict fields only to struggles over economic capital. Fields might also deal with social capital (where the main issue is who you know, and how you are related to that person), cultural capital (dealing with education, culture and aligned skills) or symbolic capital (dealing with social prestige and distinction).[8] Neither does Bourdieu's use of 'strategy' mean that, as assumed in mainstream economics, people necessarily adopt a conscious calculative orientation towards the interests at stake. On the contrary, people's strategies should be seen as skilful achievements operating against the background of the pre-reflective *doxa*.[9]

Some of these ideas might appear less striking and innovative now than they used to be. We would say two things in favour of Bourdieu. First, he introduced most of these ideas in the 1960s and he brought them together as early as 1972 in his *Outline of a Theory of Practice*. By the time that *le tout Paris* celebrated the achievements of structuralism, Bourdieu had already become aware of its limitations and had tried to supersede these. He anticipated some important developments of social theory in the Anglo-Saxon world, especially key aspects of Giddens's structuration theory (see chapter 5) and Roy Bhaskar's transformational model of social action (see chapter 9). Amongst the similarities with Giddens and Bhaskar is, for example, Bourdieu's attempt to transcend the opposition between the individual and society (or, if you like, between subjectivism and objectivism), and his attempt to link structural notions to Wittgensteinian and phenomenological insights vis-à-vis shared, practical knowledge. Like Giddens and Bhaskar, Bourdieu notes that structures should not merely be seen as constraining; they are also enabling in that they allow for agency to be exercised (cf. Bourdieu 1977 and 1990 with Giddens 1984 and Bhaskar 1989).

The second point in favour of Bourdieu is that his strength lies in the way in which his theory is interwoven with empirical research. Let us remind the reader that, for Bourdieu, theorizing should not be an isolated practice; it ought to emerge out of contact with empirical reality. Bourdieu's framework has shown itself to be very successful in elucidating empirical findings. First, consider the sociology of education and related fields, in which he has pointed out the subtle mechanisms through which 'symbolic power' or 'symbolic violence' operates. That is, with the help of various forms of 'pedagogic action', dominant groups of society are able to impose their culture onto others – to make it, in spite of the arbitrary nature of any culture, appear as legitimate or superior. Whether formal (for example, school) or informal (for example, the family or the peer group), pedagogic action may lead to cultural reproduction and eventually to the reproduction of underlying power relationships (see, e.g., Bourdieu and Passeron 1977). Second, in *Distinction* and related writings, Bourdieu takes up again the issue of reproduction. Once members of the less privileged classes enter the struggle for status, the differences in *habitus* make for an unequal fight and hence for the reproduction of inequality. That inequality is both the medium and the outcome of their practices. For example, for some people 'high culture' is intrinsic to their way of life, and dealing with culture appears 'natural'. For others, culture can only be *achieved*, hence the slightly laboured, artificial manner in which this is done, or the lack of subtlety involved. In the battlefield over cultural or educational matters, members of the lower classes are bound to lose, entering an unfair game in which they are often forced to deny their own *habitus*. Every encounter implies that they can be 'found out', either because they inadvertently display a lack of knowledge, or because they display too much anxiety and lack of grace. More importantly, by attempting to emulate the higher strata and so uplift their status, the *petits bourgeois* implicitly acknowledge the legitimacy or superiority of the dominant culture.

Bourdieu's writings have sometimes been subject to pedantic criticisms. Some have argued that his conceptual scheme lacks analytical rigour; others that he reads too much into his empirical material. There is certainly some truth in these points, but they hardly hit the core of Bourdieu's writings. We would argue that his strengths reveal his weaknesses. His incisiveness lies in his account of stability, as becomes apparent in his notion of a skilful, unquestioned reproduction of structures or in the presupposition that the *habitus* tends to be adjusted to social constraints. One of the consequences of this is that Bourdieu pays less attention to the ability of individuals to distance themselves from the facticity of daily existence – the ability to turn tacit knowledge into theoretical knowledge. Bourdieu tends to focus on this only insofar as it is a result of social scientific intervention. He thereby fails to acknowledge fully that people may also exhibit the ability to distance themselves in the *absence* of scientific interference. If people's theoretical knowledge enters the public-collective realm, it might become an important source of change or deliberate maintenance of structures. Given Bourdieu's interest in reproduction of inequality, he could have been more sensitive to the extent to which people's theoretical, discursive knowledge about underlying structures is often constitutive of the maintenance of the very same structures. In *Learning to Labour* (1993), for instance, Paul Willis shows how working-class children have clearly articulated conceptions about their limited opportunities. Ironically, the very same conceptions are central to the fact that such adolescents drop out of school, and these conceptions therefore contribute to the reproduction of inequality. It is important, however, that this reproduction does not take place in the unquestioned world of Bourdieu's *doxa*.

On a related theme, Bourdieu has shown convincingly and repeatedly how the 'practical sense' of individuals makes for the unintended reproduction of social inequalities. He has shown the empirical validity of maintaining, for instance, that the *habitus* is relatively durable, that it takes different forms in different classes, and that it is adjusted to objective external constraints. Meanwhile, these assertions beg for explanation, rather than providing one. How is one to account for, say, the inflexibility of dispositions across the individual lifespan, or for the adjustment of the *habitus* to objective structural conditions? Given Bourdieu's hostility to tight theoretical system-building, he would probably dismiss these questions as chimerical constructions to haunt solely the abstract theorist. But for those who expect theories to answer adequately 'why?' or 'how?' questions, that response would be found to be unsatisfactory.

One major theme runs through Bourdieu's latter years, a theme that has actually accompanied him ever since his early works on Algeria in the 1950s. It is the attempt to provide an alternative to the ahistoricism of individualistic economic theories (see chapter 4). Such an alternative points to a sociological analysis of economic action that incorporates history and culture. Contrary to what cultural sociologists claim (see chapter 3), Bourdieu insists that the object of sociology is *not* culture but the practices of the 'agents and institutions of economic, cultural and social production and reproduction' (2005: 13), i.e., the study of economy and society. In *The Social Structures of the Economy*, he provides us with an example of how this approach can be applied to the study of economic phenomena such as the housing market. In this detailed empirical study of the field of housing in France since the 1980s, Bourdieu shows that the direct exchange between buyer and seller in the market, the sole interest of economic research, is actually of little relevance in comparison with the finance and planning policies that established mortgage and housing markets, the structure of the building industry, the marketing sales strategies, the class basis of home ownership, and the individual reasons behind the purchases as well as the subsequent reflections on those decisions.

This theme has been pursued in two other ways, one philosophical and another political and polemicist. In the *Pascalian Meditations*, Bourdieu's hostility to abstract theorizing is given a new and elaborate expression. Although this is a philosophical text, aimed at a philosophical audience, it is nonetheless an anti-philosophical text, as the reference to Pascal's *Pensées* should make clear. Bourdieu, of course, is not criticizing philosophy as a discipline, but a specific modality of philosophical thinking. This he calls, following Plato, the 'scholastic condition' or *skholè*. For Bourdieu, the *skholè*, the idea that intellectual life is beyond social determination, is an illusion responsible for serious epistemological distortions (2000: 49ff.). One such distortion is the projection of the *skholè*'s own conventions on human behaviour in general. When this occurs, scholastic thinking is unable to understand any modality of thought other than its own. This is particularly true insofar as practical knowledge is concerned, incidentally the kind of thinking characteristic of social life. Hence Bourdieu's concern with the *skholè* – it is closely related to abstract, ahistorical social theorizing. The alternative to this intellectual form of ethnocentrism is a historically sensitive sociology that shows the limits of philosophical reason. Only in this way can the original emancipatory project of philosophy be salvaged. Furthermore, Bourdieu argues that *skholè's* nefarious influence extends well beyond philosophical academic circles and encompasses democratic politics. Contending that a similar unmasking process must also take place in this field, Bourdieu introduces the notion of a '*Realpolitik* of the universal' (ibid.: 80). By this he means a specific form of political struggle aimed at unmasking truth and rendering it universally available, putting an end to the scholastic thinker's monopoly of reason.

This radical democratic agenda is developed in several of Bourdieu's other works of this period, from the massive ethnography on the social consequences of neo-liberal politics in France, *The Weight of the World*, to the shorter volumes *Acts of Resistance* and *Firing Back*. Indeed, deeply disillusioned with the socialist governments of François Mitterrand and Alain Juppé, Bourdieu devotes his last years to mobilizing the 'left of the left' against neo-liberal globalization. At this time, Bourdieu is France's most prominent public intellectual. Fully aware of the responsibility associated with that status, he strives to mobilize progressive intellectuals in a new internationalism. In 1999, he engages in a fascinating dialogue with Günter Grass, who had been given the Nobel prize for literature earlier that year (Grass and Bourdieu 2002). By taking the side of the losers, by exposing the tragic consequences of neo-liberal policies in Europe and by questioning the role of television and opinion-makers, Grass and Bourdieu engage in a Franco-German dialogue in the old European tradition of the 'republic of letters'. Like Zola and Sartre before him, Bourdieu had become the critical consciousness of his age. By the time of his death, in 2002, his influence on French sociology was unrivalled and his followers dominated the discipline. There were already those, however, who were attempting to move beyond Bourdieu's sociology.

The work of Bernard Lahire, a former student and colleague of Bourdieu, provides a good example of this attempt. Take his work on the self. Though sympathetic with his old mentor's conception of *habitus*, Lahire has been nonetheless developing a more nuanced and flexible alternative. His conception of 'the plural man' is worth mentioning for two reasons. First, he criticizes the one-dimensional conception of self presupposed by most current social analyses. When one studies, say, 'the student', 'the worker' or 'the voter', the inherently plural nature of the self subsides. Lahire's alternative is to make the human self's plural nature the starting point of sociological analysis. To question how multiple, sometimes contradictory, experiences are incorporated by individuals, and to study human action in different scenes, should thus replace the current bias for one-dimensional social scientific analyses. Second, Lahire suggests that the idea of an absolute subjectivity and the related myths of an 'inner world' and totally unconstrained free choice should be discarded in favour of a conception of action that emerges out of the tensions between forces and counter-forces, some internal (dispositions), others external (contexts of action). Lahire has been applying these social theoretical insights in his empirical studies of culture, literacy and the school system with a remarkable degree of success.

French pragmatism

Other contemporary French social theorists, however, are often less sympathetic to Bourdieu's critical sociology programme than Lahire. One could even go as far as suggesting that there are two main contemporary French conceptions of sociology. On the one hand, there is Bourdieu's critical sociology, whose systematic denunciation of social inequalities comes close to Paul Ricoeur's celebrated phrase 'the hermeneutic of suspicion'.[10] On the other, there is a smaller yet growing movement in the direction of a pragmatic sociology. In this latter case, one of the most representative figures is Bruno Latour, especially his more recent work. Taking inspiration in part from the philosophical tradition of American pragmatism, French pragmatic sociology aims at describing the plurality of regimes of human action. In the case of Latour's work on sociology of science (1987), this pragmatic approach assumes the character of a sociological inquiry of the actions performed by scientists while doing their work and the actions of science itself on the social world. An important implication of this line of work is the suggestion that the subject–object relationship needs to be reconsidered. The relations between material objects and human interpretations are given centre stage by pragmatic sociologists: while Latour focuses on how objects as spokespersons are able to extend the space of interpretation beyond the concrete situation, others focus on the set of forms of justification available to human agents. The collaborative work of Luc Boltanski and Laurent Thévenot, another example of the so-called 'new French social sciences', exemplifies this second strategy. Let us now elaborate on their work.

Boltanski and Thévenot's research programme aims at reconnecting normative political philosophy with empirical social science. They try to achieve this general goal by focusing on a specific aspect of social life, namely on how people's repertoire of justifications in concrete controversies mirrors the formalized figures of justification in treatises of political philosophy. Assuming that disputes are a characteristic feature of our modern complex societies, they look at how individuals negotiate their way in such problematic situations – i.e. how social relationships today are fundamentally structured by the requirement of providing moral justifications. The most complete expression of this 'sociology of disputes' (Boltanski 1990: 25) is their joint volume, *On Justification*. Originally published in 1991, but only translated into English in 2006, this book is generally considered to be the single most important sociological treatise of post-Bourdieu French sociology. It can also be seen as an alternative to Bourdieu's critical sociology towards a more pragmatic sociology: instead of a single discourse of social denunciation, whose own status is never made explicit, Boltanski and Thévenot suggest that there are several such orders of discourse in which individuals are free to enter and leave as they wish (2006: 342). Its starting point is a well-known pragmatist theme. The authors focus on those particular moments in time in which the ordinary course of action is interrupted. In these 'critical moments,' social agents realize 'that something is going wrong; that they cannot get along any more; that something has to change' (1999: 359). In order to reach an agreement, the parties in dispute have to refer to something that transcends that concrete controversy, to resources that they share and reach beyond the situation. There are two kinds of resources: material objects and orders of justification or worth (*grandeur*). The description of these orders of justification (or *cités*) is the main contribution of *On Justification* to contemporary social theory.

Siding with Michael Walzer's communitarian philosophy, which sees different conceptions of justice operating in different settings (or 'spheres of justice'), against John Rawls's neo-Kantian attempt to ground a theory of justice in rationally derived principles, Boltanski and Thévenot identify six such orders of justification. Each order is governed by one dominant principle. These are the orders of the market, inspiration, the public sphere, the domestic order, the civic order and industry. Aiming at connecting political philosophy with empirical social science, Boltanski and Thévenot conceive of each of these six *cités* as being governed by a specific grammar. This grammar – including subjects, objects, qualifiers, verbs, etc. – gives each economy of worth a more structured nature than a mere discourse: social relationships involve not only words but 'objects' as well, which vary according to the world in question (e.g., good manners in the domestic world or laws in the civic order). In each *cité*, individuals are naturally aware of what counts, the value of each thing, and of the relative positioning of that thing within that specific order of worth. In a real-life dispute, the first task of social agents is to determine to which order of justification it belongs. This task is all the more difficult as all six orders of justification can be found in any specific context of action, from a multinational company to the local flower shop. This delineation of the mechanisms of value construction and dispute management through multiple practices (ranging from compromise to denunciation or critique), without ignoring the world of 'objects' within which these disputes occur, is the book's main achievement. One of its main contributions is the nuanced view it offers of the social process of institution building, as well as of the related theme of trust (see chapter 4).

Luc Boltanski has meanwhile published a second important social treatise, this time co-authored with Eve Chiapello, *The New Spirit of Capitalism* (first published in 1999 and translated into English in 2005). As hinted by the book's title, Boltanski and Chiapello propose a follow-up study of Max Weber's *The Protestant Ethic and the Spirit of Capitalism*. Focused on the social and normative structure of capitalism since the 1960s, this monumental study (more than 600 pages) is an application of Boltanski's theoretical model as laid down in his previous *On Justification*. Primarily based on the French case, the book's main thesis is that late twentieth-century capitalism has incorporated, transformed and ultimately benefited from the social and artistic critiques created in the streets of Paris in May 1968. This recovery of the well-known Marxist theme that capitalism feeds on its own critique is undertaken by focusing on how the available set of forms of justification in the areas of work and management has evolved during this period. Three major stages in the spirit of modern capitalism are identified. In the first stage, the spirit of capitalism focused on the individual figure of the capitalist and its justification was associated with the domestic order. In the second stage, the capitalist gives way to the manager and the domestic order of justification is substituted by the industrial, organizational one. Finally, the new spirit of capitalism finds its home in the 'network city', the distinctive order of justification of contemporary political communities. *The New Spirit of Capitalism* focuses on the transition from the second to the third spirit of capitalism, i.e. the transition from the hierarchical and centralized spirit of Fordism to the flexible and highly mobile post-Fordist spirit.

Boltanski and Chiapello's neo-Marxist account identifies four central motifs that have been the target of the critique of capitalism in the past 200 years. These 'sources of indignation' (2005: 37) have been developed by two different sorts of critique. The artistic critique has focused on inauthenticity and oppression, whereas inequality and egoism have been the topics of the social critique. Boltanski and Chiapello intend to bring these two types of critique together. They propose to do so by analysing the justifications provided for managers in proscriptive books ('Why be a manager?,' 'How to become a successful manager'). The comparison of the management literature from the 1960s and the 1990s grants them, they believe, a privileged vantage point from which to assess the development of the normative fabric of the capitalist system in this period. Their findings suggest that the events of May 1968 provoked a crisis of justification of capitalism in the ensuing years that eventually led to the latter's incorporation of the critiques that had been levelled at it. Especially since the 1990s, a new order of justification has been emerging, an order that emphasizes global, flexible and cooperatively organized networks of people working on multiple projects. In other words, neo-liberal capitalism has incorporated the artistic critique that flowered in 1968 and used it to reframe the terms of the social critique. As social exclusion replaced social class as the principle of social differentiation, inequality and poverty are now seen as resulting from the personal lack of attributes, not from one's relative position in the economic and social structure.

This ambitiously conceived analysis of modern capitalism can be criticized from three different angles. First, the combination of a neo-Marxist agenda and an almost exclusive focus on the French case prevents the authors from seriously engaging in debates that are taking place either in other regions of the world (namely, the Anglophone world), or outside their ideological terrain, or both. As a consequence, this otherwise empirically detailed book has remarkably little to say about globalization or anything else besides the French experience. Even though Boltanski and Chiapello purport to analyse the 'spirit of capitalism' as a global category, they become subject to the old methodological error of *pars pro toto*, i.e. taking a part for the whole: they study one single manifestation of this 'spirit' assuming it represents the whole phenomenon. In an epoch when capitalism has expanded to include China, Southeast Asia, and the Indian subcontinent's 3 billion inhabitants, this sort of French-centred, Parisian-style of grand social theorizing lacks much of the appeal it once had. More concretely, one wonders whether Boltanski and Chiapello are not over-playing the importance of the students' revolts of May 1968 in the development of contemporary capitalism. After all, it is far from clear how this social revolt against the paternalism of the French post-war welfare state actually defined the character of such a regionally diversified global phenomenon as today's capitalism. To understand and explain the current stage of development of this mode of production, a comparative, global and context-sensitive approach is needed. As we will see (chapter 7), Peter A. Hall's 'variants of capitalism' approach seems to be in a better position to meet these requirements.

Second, as noted above, Boltanski and Chiapello choose to paraphrase Weber's celebrated study *The Protestant Ethic and the Spirit of Capitalism.* Is the absence of a substantive analysis of ethnic and religious disputes to be understood as if the new spirit of capitalism is, contrary to previous ones, unrelated to the religious dimension of social life? That would be not only empirically unsustainable, but, in an epoch when religion is making a spectacular return to the centre of the political and scientific agenda (see, e.g., Taylor 2007), such an argument would seem utterly out of tune with the spirit of our times.

A third and more general critical remark concerns the very theoretical and methodological strategy employed by Boltanski and his colleagues. Consider the strategy employed to reconstruct the several *cités* to which people turn in the course of a dispute. In order to reconstruct each order of justification, Boltanski and Thévenot use three bodies of data: empirical data from their fieldwork on the process of disputation, a set of classical texts from political philosophy and contemporary handbooks of behaviour directed at laypersons. In the case of the market world, for instance, they supplement their fieldwork data with the first chapters of Adam Smith's *Wealth of Nations* and an American popular guide to the art of business, *What They Don't Teach You at Harvard Business School* (2006: 43ff., 193–201). Not surprisingly, the image of the market world that Boltanski and Thévenot offer is inadequate to guide empirical analyses: 'In a market world, important persons are buyers and sellers. They are worthy when they are rich' (1999: 372). Similar criticisms can be levelled at Boltanski and Chiapello's usage of management textbooks in *The New Spirit of Capitalism.* Directed at managers, their influence upon other types of workers is far from clear, let alone upon the population in general. It is understandable that Weber resorted to management texts to gain an understanding of the spirit of capitalism in the early twentieth century – there was hardly any other data available. But with sound cross-national survey data on values and practices since the 1950s for most developed countries readily available, it is hard to see why Boltanski and Chiapello are still focusing on management texts to gain an understanding of the new spirit of capitalism. Not to mention, of course, richly textured ethnographic methodologies. A case in point is Richard Lloyd's 2006 *Neo-Bohemia*, a study of Chicago's Wicker Park neighbourhood in the 1990s. Boltanski and Chiapello's 600-page volume is intended to show how the neo-liberal economy incorporated the artistic critique of the 1960s and subverted it. What Lloyd's fine-grained work demonstrates is that such incorporation does not necessarily lead to a loss of authenticity or freedom. Wicker Park's highly creative 'neo-bohemian scene' possesses a productive character that sets it apart from its nineteenth-century predecessor, but it is no less authentic. The neo-bohemians of Wicker Park, producing arts and culture, are the entrepreneurs of the new economy – creative, mobile, tolerant *and* authentic.

The divide separating Bourdieu's critical sociology and the more recent pragmatic sociology of Boltanski and Thévenot and many others should be clear by now. The social determinism of Bourdieu's genetic structuralism is gradually being replaced by a social theory much more concerned with agency. There still are, however, some residues of structuralism in Boltanski's sociology of disputes. For instance, the aim of producing a 'grammar of morality', despite all the efforts to liberate social agents from the constraints of macro-level structures, is a form of structuralism nonetheless. One further instance is terminological. Whereas Bourdieu's conceptual apparatus included such notions as 'field', '*habitus*' or 'capitals', pragmatic sociologists prefer instead to use concepts such as 'black boxes', 'inscriptions', 'lactic ferments' (Latour) or 'orders' and 'worth' (Boltanski and Thévenot). These differences in terminology reflect deeper divergences in the theoretical strategy of these two strands of French social theory. Whereas Bourdieu's genetic structuralism shows great awareness of power struggles and the reproduction of inequality, pragmatic sociology is chiefly concerned with describing the plurality of repertoires of action. This is true of Boltanski's earlier book *On Justification* and less so in the case of *The New Spirit of Capitalism*, which rivals Bourdieu's *The Weight of the World* in its denunciation of the free market economy. In both cases, however, the rejection of utilitarian, ahistorical modes of social theorizing remains a key point. The favoured alternative by contemporary French sociologists (with the notable exception of Raymond Boudon), continuing the tradition inaugurated by Durkheim over a century ago, is a social and historically sensitive conception of human action and rationality. This fundamental disagreement on the anthropological foundations of social theory remains up to this day the single most important source of disagreement between the Anglo-Saxon mode of social theorizing and French sociology.

Further reading

For an accessible introduction to structuralism and post-structuralism, Sturrock's *Structuralism and Since* or Harland's *Superstructuralism* can be recommended. Culler's *Ferdinand de Saussure* is an excellent introduction to the life and work of the Swiss linguist. The core of Saussure's ideas can be found in parts 1 and 2 of his *Course in General Linguistics*. Lukes's *Emile Durkheim; His Life and Work* remains by far the most comprehensive account of Durkheim's work. But this biography is long, and as a shorter introduction, Giddens's lucid *Durkheim* will do. For an overview of Lévi-Strauss's intellectual development, it is worth reading his own autobiographical *Tristes Tropiques* or Pace's *Claude Lévi-Strauss: The Bearer of Ashes*. For a first approach to genetic structuralism, we suggest the excellent introduction to Bourdieu's work by Wacquant in Bourdieu and Wacquant's *An Invitation to Reflexive Sociology*. Both Bourdieu's *Outline of a Theory of Practice* and *The Logic of Practice* summarize the key notions of his theoretical viewpoint; the latter is more accessible. The size of *The Weight of the World* should not put off readers: its chapters can be read autonomously, and chapters like the introductory 'Jonquil Street' are among Bourdieu's finest mature writings. A useful collection of articles assessing the continuing relevance of Bourdieu's ideas is Swartz and Zolberg's *After Bourdieu*. Latour's *Science in Action* is an accessible introduction to science studies. On Boltanski's work, *The New Spirit of Capitalism* provides an easier reading than the previous *On Justification*.

References

Althusser, L. 1972. *For Marx.* New York: Pantheon (originally in French, 1965).

Althusser, L. and Balibar, E. 1970. *Reading Capital.* London: New Left Books (originally in French, 1968).

Barthes, R. 1972. *Mythologies.* London: Cape (originally in French, 1957).

Barthes, R. 1983. *The Fashion System.* New York: Hill and Wang (originally in French, 1967).

Bhaskar, R. 1989. *The Possibility of Naturalism.* Brighton: Harvester (2nd edn).

Boltanski, L. 1990. *L'Amour et la justice comme compétences. Trois essais de sociologie de l'action.* Paris: Métailié.

Boltanski, L. and Chiapello, E. 2005. *The New Spirit of Capitalism*. London: Verso (originally in French, 1999).

Boltanski, L. and Thévenot, L. 1999. The sociology of critical capacity. *European Journal of Social Theory* 2(3): 359–77.

Boltanski, L. and Thévenot, L. 2006. *On Justification. Economies of Worth*. Princeton, NJ: Princeton University Press (originally in French, 1999).

Bourdieu, P. 1969. Intellectual field and creative project. *Social Science Information* 8: 89–119 (originally in French, 1966).

Bourdieu, P. 1971. Champ du pouvoir, champ intellectuel et habitus de classe. *Scolies* 1: 7–26.

Bourdieu, P. 1973. Le marché des biens symboliques. *L'Année sociologique* 22: 49–126.

Bourdieu, P. 1977. *Outline of a Theory of Practice*. Cambridge: Cambridge University Press (originally in French, 1972).

Bourdieu, P. 1984. *Distinction: A Social Critique of the Judgement of Taste*. London: Routledge & Kegan Paul (originally in French, 1979).

Bourdieu, P. 1990. *The Logic of Practice*. Cambridge: Polity (originally in French, 1980).

Bourdieu, P. 1993. *Sociology in Question*. London: Sage (originally in French, 1984).

Bourdieu, P. 1998. *Acts of Resistance: Against the New Myths of Our Time*. Cambridge: Polity (originally in French, 1998).

Bourdieu, P. et al. 1999. *The Weight of the World. Social Suffering in Contemporary Society*. Cambridge: Polity (originally in French, 1993).

Bourdieu, P. 2000. *Pascalian Meditations*. Cambridge: Polity (originally in French, 1997).

Bourdieu, P. 2003. *Firing Back. Against the Tyranny of the Market*. New York: New Press (originally in French, 2001).

Bourdieu, P. 2005. *The Social Structures of the Economy*. Cambridge: Polity (originally in French, 2000).

Bourdieu, P. and Passeron, J.-C. 1977. *Reproduction in Education, Society and Culture*. London: Sage (originally in French, 1970).

Bourdieu, P. and Wacquant, L. J. D. 1992a. *An Invitation to Reflexive Sociology*. Cambridge: Polity.

Bourdieu, P. and Wacquant, L. J. D. 1992b. The purpose of reflexive sociology. In *An Invitation to Reflexive Sociology*. Cambridge: Polity, pp. 61–216.

Bourdieu, P., Chamboredon, J.-C. and Passeron, J.-C. 1991. *The Craft of Sociology: Epistemological Preliminaries*. New York: Walter de Gruyter (originally in French, 1968).

Braudel, F. 1972. *The Mediterranean and the Mediterranean World in the Age of Phillip II*, vol. 1. Glasgow: William Collins (originally in French, 1966).

Braudel, F. 1980. *On History*. Chicago, IL: University of Chicago Press (originally in French, 1969).

Burke, P. 1990. *The French Historical Revolution: The Annales School, 1929–89.* Cambridge: Polity; Stanford, CA: Stanford University Press.

Cixous, H. 1981. The laugh of the Medusa. In E. Marks and I. de Courtivron (eds), *New French Feminisms.* New York: Schocken, pp. 245–64.

Culler, J. 1986. *Ferdinand de Saussure.* Ithaca, NY: Cornell University Press (2nd edn).

Derrida, J. 1973. *Speech and Phenomena, and Other Essays on Husserl's Theory of Signs.* Evanston, IL: Northwestern University Press (originally in French, 1967).

Derrida, J. 1976. *Of Grammatology.* Baltimore, MD: Johns Hopkins University Press (originally in French, 1967).

Derrida, J. 1978. *Writing and Differences.* London: Routledge & Kegan Paul (originally in French, 1967).

Durkheim, E. 1915. *The Elementary Forms of Religious Life.* London: Allen and Unwin (originally in French, 1912).

Durkheim, E. 1952. *Suicide; A Study in Sociology.* London: Routledge (originally in French, 1897).

Durkheim, E. 1963. *Primitive Classification.* Chicago, IL: University of Chicago Press (originally in French, 1903).

Durkheim, E. 1982. *The Rules of Sociological Method, and Selected Texts on Sociology and its Method.* London: Macmillan (originally in French, 1895).

Durkheim, E. 1984. *The Division of Labour in Society.* London: Macmillan (originally in French, 1893).

Foucault, M. 1977. *Language, Counter-memory, Practice.* Ithaca, NY: Cornell University Press.

Foucault, M. 1980. *Power/Knowledge; Selected Interviews and Other Writings 1972–1977.* Hemel Hempstead: Harvester Wheatsheaf.

Giddens, A. 1978. *Durkheim.* London: Fontana (reprinted 1990).

Giddens, A. 1984. *The Constitution of Society; Outline of the Theory of Structuration.* Cambridge: Polity.

Grass, G. and Bourdieu, P. 2002. The 'progressive' restoration. *New Left Review* 14: 62–77.

Harland, R. 1988. *Superstructuralism; The Philosophy of Structuralism and Post-structuralism.* London: Routledge.

Irigaray, L. 1985. *The Sex Which Is Not One.* Ithaca, NY: Cornell University Press.

Kristeva, J. 1982. *Desire in Language.* New York: Columbia University Press.

Lacan, J. 1989. *Écrits; A Selection.* London: Routledge (originally in French, 1966).

Lahire, B. 1998. *L'Homme pluriel: les ressorts de l'action.* Paris: Nathan.

Lane, M. (ed.) 1970. *Structuralism; A Reader.* London: Jonathan Cape.

Latour, B. 1987. *Science in Action: How to Follow Scientists and Engineers Through Society.* Cambridge, MA: Harvard University Press.

Lévi-Strauss, C. 1973. *Tristes Tropiques.* New York: Cape (originally in French, 1955).

Lévi-Strauss, C. 1978. *The Origin of Table Manners; Introduction to a Science of Mythology 3*. London: Jonathan Cape (originally in French, 1968).

Lévi-Strauss, C. 1993. *Structural Anthropology, Part 1*. London: Penguin (originally in French, 1963).

Lévi-Strauss, C. 1994. *Structural Anthropology, Part 2*. London: Penguin (originally in French, 1973).

Lloyd, R. 2006. *Neo-Bohemia: Art and Commerce in the Postindustrial City*. New York: Routledge.

Lukes, S. 1973. *Émile Durkheim; His Life and Work: A Historical and Critical Study*. London: Penguin.

Marks, E. and de Courtivron, I. (eds) 1981. *New French Feminisms*. New York: Schocken.

Pace, D. 1986. *Claude Lévi-Strauss; The Bearer of Ashes*. London: Routledge & Kegan Paul.

Poulantzas, N. 1968. *Political Power and Social Classes*. London: New Left Books (originally in French, 1968).

Ricoeur, P. 1970. *Freud and Philosophy: An Essay on Interpretation* (trans. Denis Savage). New Haven, CT: Yale University Press (originally in French, 1965).

Saussure, F. de 1960. *Course in General Linguistics*. London: Peter Owen (originally in French, 1916).

Sturrock, J. 1979. *Structuralism and Since: From Lévi-Strauss to Derrida*. Oxford: Oxford University Press (reprinted 1992).

Swartz, D. L. and Zolberg, V. L. (eds) 2005. *After Bourdieu: Influence, Critique, Elaboration*. Dordrecht: Springer.

Taylor, C. 2007. *A Secular Age*. Cambridge, MA: Belknap Press of Harvard University Press.

Wacquant, L. J. D. 1992. Toward a social praxeology: the structure and logic of Bourdieu's sociology. In P. Bourdieu and L. J. D. Wacquant, *An Invitation to Reflexive Sociology*. Cambridge: Polity, pp. 1–60.

Willis, P. 1993. *Learning to Labour: How Working Class Kids get Working Class Jobs*. Aldershot: Ashgate.

The Biological Metaphor
Functionalism and Neo-functionalism

This chapter deals with the rise and fall of functionalist theory. The functionalist label is used in many disciplines: for example, in linguistics, psychology and architecture. Although they share the same name, the frameworks which are used do not necessarily have much in common. We will in the following merely focus on functionalist theories of society.

'Functionalism' in sociology covers a wide variety of authors and schools which nevertheless tend to share a number of central tenets. First, they explain the persistence of social practices by referring to those (often unintended) effects which are beneficial for the equilibrium or integration of the social system in which these practices are embedded. Second, functionalism reconstructs the notion of rationality: it is assumed that certain practices which appear irrational can be made intelligible once their social functions are spelled out. Beneath the surface lies a deeper social rationality, which it is the task of the sociologist to uncover. Third, functionalism draws upon the notion of functional prerequisites. The argument is often that these prerequisites need to be fulfilled for a given society to survive, or alternatively that society operates such that these needs tend to be fulfilled.

During its emergence and rise in the 1940s and 1950s, functionalism fitted in well with the intellectual climate. First, it soon emerged that functionalist reasoning was not incompatible with some aspects of neo-positivist epistemology, the latter being one of the dominant strands in the philosophy of science at the time (see chapter 8). By paying attention to consequences of actions (instead of purposes or motives behind practices), functionalism fits, for instance, the positivist inclination to avoid reference to entities that are not immediately accessible to observation. Some philosophers of science attempted to merge the two doctrines by demonstrating that functionalist formats of explanation can be moulded within the straitjacket of the deductive-nomological method. Second, functionalism was even more compatible with the core features of structuralism – another important theoretical strand at the time (see chapter

1). Both support a holistic picture of society in which the interrelationship of subsystems and practices is central. Both assume that the task of the social scientist is to unravel a deeper reality behind the conscious level of purposive action – for structuralists, that hidden realm refers to unacknowledged structures, whereas functionalists search for latent functions. Both functionalism and structuralism minimize the role of agency, attributing importance to the broader social forces which transcend the individual. Finally, functionalist and structuralist frameworks strongly object to the interpretative claims of hermeneutics and phenomenology.

Although structuralism and functionalism have a different pedigree and are distinct from each other, they did coalesce on several occasions. The alliance is exemplified by both Alfred Reginald Radcliffe-Brown's and Talcott Parsons's structural-functionalism; we will pay special attention to the latter later in this chapter. Parsons's writings had a decisive impact on American sociology over several decades. Parsons was heavily influenced by German, French and Italian authors, but, on the whole, European sociology has been more resistant to the Parsonian challenge. For the American audience, however, the structuralist-functionalist paradigm was considered the ultimate successful attempt to bring together the sociological classics within one consistent theoretical frame of reference. The term 'paradigm' is not misplaced here. For a while it looked as if the new creed was so persuasive that a consensus might arise within the sociological community vis-à-vis its main assumptions. Although some expressed doubts at a remarkably early stage with respect to the validity of some of these structural-functional presuppositions, it was only in the late 1960s that a more coherent assault against structural-functionalism developed.

Early functionalism

Functionalism as a label and as a separate school only emerged in the course of the twentieth century, but functionalist reasoning in itself is much older. Many of the so-called founding fathers of sociology attempted to explain social phenomena by drawing upon analogies with the biological realm. Herbert Spencer and Émile Durkheim are especially important in this regard. First, these functionalists *avant la lettre* saw society as an organic whole, with the different subsystems or practices functionally directed towards the persistence of the larger entity in which they are embedded. This notion of society as an organic entity became central to the functionalist argument in the twentieth century (see chapter 1). Second, many sociologists in the nineteenth century were fascinated with the application of evolutionary epistemology to the social sphere. Central to their analysis was the notion that, for social systems to survive, they needed somehow to adjust to their environment. Increasing complexity and system differentiation leads to forms of superior adjustment. Likewise, twentieth-century functionalist theories reconstruct history in terms of intensifying complexity, compartmentalization and system differentiation. Third, these predecessors of the functionalist movement introduced the notion of societal needs. For social systems to be healthy, or at least to survive, certain needs have to be fulfilled. The task of the sociologist is to identify these needs, and to help steer society such that its needs are fulfilled. The modern notion of 'functional prerequisites' denotes the same idea.

Given that Durkheim has inspired numerous sociologists and anthropologists in the twentieth century, we will briefly sketch the main functionalist tenets in his work. Durkheim himself does not need introduction, and has already been mentioned in chapter 1. The functionalist features are to be found in his *Rules of Sociological Method* and *Division of Labour*. In *Rules* Durkheim insisted that any adequate explanation combines both causal and functional analysis. Causal analysis explains the succession of social phenomena, whereas functional analysis accounts for the persistence of social practices in terms of the 'general needs of the social organism' in which these practices are embedded (1982: 199–46). At several places, Durkheim insisted that one should distinguish analytically between functions and intentions. After all, the functions of practices might be different from people's purposes in carrying out these practices (1984: 11ff.). Functional analysis is central to Durkheim's distinction between normal and pathological phenomena. Certain forms are normal in a given society if they regularly occur in similar types of society and if they fulfil essential functions in society. Phenomena are pathological if they do not fulfil these conditions. The distinction between normal and pathological forms is, in its turn, essential to Durkheim's attempts to prescribe what needs to be done. Normal forms are to be promoted, pathological forms to be eradicated. Social policy thus rests upon functional analysis (1982: 85–107).

In *Division of Labour* Durkheim noted that through time societies become more complex and differentiated. There is hardly any division of labour in earlier forms of society. Society is then kept together through what Durkheim called 'mechanical solidarity' – that is, a form of cohesion based on similarity of beliefs and sentiments (1984: 31–67). Modern societies are characterized by an increasing division of labour. They can only be kept together through 'organic solidarity' – that is, cohesion based on interdependence and cooperation of its component parts (ibid.: 68–87). The increasing division of labour needs to be explained by the increase in 'dynamic or moral density', which is itself to be explained by increasing population growth. The argument is basically Darwinian. Population growth amongst animals leads to functional specialization such that they can coexist. An analogous mechanism operates in the social realm where division of labour resolves the increased competition amongst human beings (ibid.: 200–88).

But the transition towards a differentiated society has not run very smoothly. Durkheim diagnosed 'anomie' as one of the major social problems of his time. Anomie means literally 'normlessness'. In Durkheim's sociology, anomie refers to a significant lack of normative regulation in society. He believed that a healthy society is dependent on the institutionalization of central values and normative guidelines. Without these binding value patterns and norms, social and political life would be in disarray. The moral malaise of the Third Republic was indicative of the state of anomie in a differentiated society. But anomie is only a transitional phase. Sociology can contribute to the implementation of values and normative rules which fit modern society (ibid.: 291–309).

The above summary suffices as an illustration of the functionalist tenets in Durkheim's reasoning. First, it shows that his sociological outlook relied upon the notion of societal needs: societies need solidarity and shared values. Second, it reveals the organicist tenets of his thinking: social health depends on the extent to which different parts are functionally related to the whole. Third, it discloses Durkheim's preoccupation with analogies between social and biological evolution, and the central role of the notion of differentiation in his theory of evolution. It is thus not surprising that Durkheim had, and still has, an enormous impact on modern-day functionalists.

But functionalism as a separate school became dominant only after the First World War. It was first introduced by Bronislaw Malinowski (1884–1942) and Alfred Reginald Radcliffe-Brown (1881–1955). Both used the label 'functionalism' to refer to the theoretical frame of reference which they employed, although Radcliffe-Brown occasionally used 'structural functionalism' to distinguish his argument from Malinowski's.

Functionalists like Malinowski and Radcliffe-Brown rebelled against nineteenth-century anthropologists. There were basically two problems with the latter: they sometimes relied upon some kind of diffusionism and they lacked direct empirical experience. According to diffusionism, social items or practices gradually spread themselves across societies as a result of migration and trade, so similar cultural artefacts or practices are explained by a common source. The problems with diffusionism are manifold. First, diffusionists ignored the extent to which the meaning of items or practices depends on the cultural context in which they are used. Second, even assuming that it is possible to conceive of two items or practices as identical, it is difficult to substantiate empirically that they have a single source. If some nineteenth-century anthropologists did not accept diffusionism, almost all lacked systematic exposure to non-Western societies. Some had travelled abroad, but few had carried out extensive fieldwork, and of those who had, even fewer used their findings to substantiate their theories. They tended to construct theories by relying upon secondary source material.

Malinowski, Radcliffe-Brown and other early functionalists developed their views partly in opposition to diffusionism and the 'armchair' anthropology of the nineteenth century. Functionalists became hostile towards diffusionist reasoning for two reasons. First, they realized that they were dealing with societies with extremely unreliable and incomplete historical records. Hence, any attempt to comprehend these societies within an all-embracing historical narrative would lead to 'pseudo-causal' explanations. Second, they thought that it was important to conceive of societies as wholes. The meaning of a social item depends on its relationship to other items currently in use in that society, and on its contribution to the society as a whole. Cultural artefacts, which are transmitted to a new society, become reappropriated and readjusted to the requirements of the new context. To trace back the origins of social items is not only an impossible task, it is to disregard the functional rationality of the items today. The unravelling of this synchronic-cum-holistic logic can only be made possible through a thorough understanding of the whole culture as it is in operation now. And this can only be accomplished through extensive fieldwork and rigorous research methods. It is ironic that the functionalist school, which subsequently developed into the highly abstract work of Talcott Parsons, Jeffrey Alexander and Niklas Luhmann, emerged out of concerns with the necessity of detailed ethnographic research.

There is a danger of regarding functionalist anthropologists as too homogeneous a group; there is indeed significant variation within early functionalism, notably between Malinowski and Radcliffe-Brown. We will deal with Malinowski first, as his influence predated Radcliffe-Brown's. Originally from Poland, Malinowski began to study natural sciences at the universities of Cracow and Leipzig, and then anthropology at the London School of Economics. This initial training in the natural sciences might account for the strong biological bias in his work. But even before he went to England he had developed a keen interest in the social sciences. At Cracow his attention was drawn to J. G. Frazer's *Golden Bough*, and at Leipzig he became a regular attender of Karl Bücher's and Wilhelm Wundt's lectures. In Malinowski's rejection of diffusionism, for instance, one finds the resonance of Wundt's insistence that social items cannot be studied in isolation from each other. At the LSE, Malinowski became acquainted with the art of ethnography, and he subsequently carried out fieldwork in New Guinea. This research led to several articles and monographs, amongst which *Argonauts of the Western Pacific* is especially well known. Malinowski taught mainly at the LSE, where he held the first chair in anthropology. With his overpowering personality he had a decisive impact on British anthropology between the wars. He taught briefly at Yale University until his death in 1942. His posthumous *Scientific Theory of Culture* summarizes very well his views on anthropological theory.

We have already mentioned that functionalist anthropologists rebelled against some nineteenth-century frameworks. This is very much the case for Malinowski. First, he reacted strongly against Edward Burnett Tylor's and Frazer's notion that 'primitive man' does not possess the same rational faculties as 'modern man'. Malinowski tried to demonstrate that certain practices or thought processes, which are prima facie irrational, are reasonable after all, in that it can be shown that they serve certain needs, whether social or psychological (1944: 73–4). Take the phenomena of magic and religion. Previous accounts failed to capture the 'pragmatic utilitarian performance' of religious practices and rituals. Malinowski suggested taking up the view 'that magic is as magic does' (ibid.: 26). He noted that people try to know and control their environment in order to satisfy their biological needs. But the external environment is not entirely predictable, nor is it entirely controllable. This uncertainty leads to an accumulation of anxiety, which people have a need to relieve; magic and religion fulfil that function. Malinowski also stressed that people are sometimes faced with disruptions which undermine the unconscious flow of daily life. For example, when confronted with unexpected death, they resort to magic or religion to deal with these crises, as a result of which their anxiety and emotional unrest are reduced.

Second, nineteenth-century thinkers tended to believe that several contemporary cultural artefacts or practices are mere 'survivals' or 'borrowed traits' of the past. That is, current beliefs or practices might have fulfilled some purpose in the past, but as they become transmitted across generations they eventually lose their initial usefulness. They are like cultural fossils in that they are reminiscences of a distant past. Malinowski insisted that a closer look shows that many of these so-called 'survivals' are not mere 'dead-weights' at all (ibid.: 26–35). They might well have been transmitted from the past, but they are shown to fulfil vital functions in contemporary society. It is a mistake to conceive of cultural transmission as merely duplication. This would be the case only if people did not have the ability to learn from past experience and think ahead. But people do have that ability and often put it into practice. Hence, cultural items are, whenever necessary, readjusted to new contexts.

Third, many nineteenth-century social scientists attempted to establish laws or law-like generalizations which transcend the ability of individuals to interfere in the course of events. On the same theme, Comte, Durkheim and many others insisted that society is an entity *sui generis*. Of course, society consists of individuals with psychological and biological features. But it would be mistaken to attempt to explain society by attributing primal causality to either psychological or biological mechanisms. Malinowski's picture cannot be more different (see, e.g., ibid.: 69ff.). First and foremost, knowingly or unwittingly, people act in a self-interested fashion in that they ensure the satisfaction of their basic needs. These basic needs are biological. Cultural products are secondary in that they help people to satisfy the 'primary biological needs'. Furthermore, people are not mere passive recipients of external forces. Ever since the beginning of civilization, human beings have developed technologies aimed at controlling their future performance through systematic use of past experience (ibid.: 7–14).

Fourth, as already mentioned, nineteenth-century anthropological theories lacked a solid empirical basis. It should now be clear why Malinowski felt so strongly about the need for detailed ethnographic research. Only through meticulous empirical research can the anthropologist learn about the rationale behind foreign practices, about the current functions of these practices, and about how the people involved constantly manipulate their environment. Many previous anthropological works conflated customs, actions and accounts. They assumed that people's reports about their customs provided reliable information about their actions. During his fieldwork, Malinowski became very much aware of the extent to which the natives said one thing and did another, and of the extent to which they were willing to break rules or conventions whenever it was in their interest to do so. And this finding in its turn suggested the necessity of extensive fieldwork.

Malinowski's theory of needs is essential to his functionalist framework, and it is thus worth developing here. His concept of need and his notion of function are very much interrelated: social practices fulfil a function if and only if they lead to the satisfaction of needs (see, e.g., ibid.: 39, 83). Malinowski basically distinguished between three types of needs. The first level refers to the 'primary biological needs' of individuals, such as the need for food or the need for sexual satisfaction, which are essential to their survival. The second refers to social needs, like the need for cooperation and solidarity. These social needs have to be fulfilled in order for primary needs to be satisfied. The third level refers to the integrative needs of society. These comprise institutions or traditions which allow for the transmission across generations of those behavioural patterns which make for the satisfaction of the societal needs (ibid,: 75–144).

Malinowski observes some simple, but important, contrasts between humans and animals (see, e.g., ibid.: 120ff.). Animals lack culture, and they therefore cannot rely upon the satisfaction of the secondary needs in order to satisfy their primary needs. Neither do they have to do so, because their anatomical and physiological features allow them to satisfy primary needs anyway. Human beings have culture, and they can thus rely upon the fulfilment of the secondary needs in order to satisfy primary needs. But they are also dependent on culture for their survival because their anatomical and physiological characteristics do not allow them to satisfy primary needs without cultural assistance. For instance, human beings can (and must) rely upon social norms and conventions for the fulfilment of their needs for security. Given that these cultural artefacts are a *sine qua non* for the survival of the human species, it follows that humans are dependent on the continuation of culture across generations. If people had to reinvent culture with every generation, their survival capacity would indeed have been severely limited. Malinowski coined the term 'integrative imperatives' to refer to the necessity of the transmission of these norms and conventions across generations. Notice the contrast with animals again. Given that the latter are not dependent on culture, their survival is a fortiori independent of cultural transmission. But whereas animals might develop individual habit formations through instruction or trial and error, they are generally unable to transmit these skills to their offspring. In contrast, human beings have been rather ingenious in compensating for their in-built weakness: first, by invoking practices which make for the satisfaction of the secondary needs, and then, by preserving and transmitting these practices across time.

Radcliffe-Brown first studied psychology and philosophy at Cambridge, and then anthropology under W. H. R. Rivers. At Cambridge, he showed an interest in the theoretical aspects of the discipline, already developing some of his core ideas concerning anthropological theory. He had become acquainted with Durkheim's writings, which were to have a lasting influence on his thinking.

Compared to Malinowski, Radcliffe-Brown is not remembered for his fieldwork. While holding a fellowship at Trinity College, Cambridge, he did carry out some empirical research, notably on the Andamans and the Australian aborigines. But he lacked Malinowski's meticulous research methods and language skills; nor did he share Malinowski's perseverance or his genuine empathy with and passion for the people whom he studied. Instead, he became directly involved in the academic institutionalization of anthropology, contributing to the setting up of departments in various parts of the world. He held posts and established departments at the universities of Cape Town, Sydney and Alexandria. After a short spell at the University of Chicago, he took up the first Chair of Anthropology at Oxford in 1937. When he retired from Oxford in 1946, he continued teaching at various places until he was too ill to continue. His influence on anthropology was strongest in the 1940s.

Radcliffe-Brown's contribution to anthropological theory differs from Malinowski's. Remember that Malinowski's theory rests upon the causal primacy of biological drives. Culture and the transmission of culture derive from the need to satisfy these biological drives, upon which depends the survival of the species. Radcliffe-Brown's functionalism is very different. Paraphrasing Durkheim, he argued that society has its own irreducible complexity; it cannot be explained by referring to mechanisms which operate at a lower level (1958: 16ff.). Society needs to be explained by social, not psychological, mechanisms, and certainly not by biological ones. Hence, he strongly distanced himself from Malinowski's functionalism (see, e.g., Kuper 1977: 49–52). Radcliffe-Brown's anthropology is deeply sociological, although he carefully avoided that label. The reason he gave for his reluctance to refer to his work as 'sociology' was that he did not wish to be associated with what he regarded as the impressionist and shallow work often carried out in the English-speaking world under that heading (1958: 8, n.3).[1]

Like Malinowski, Radcliffe-Brown was especially suspicious of diffusionist theories. Diffusionist explanations around the turn of the century often combined psychological theory and historical guesswork. The work of Rivers, Radcliffe-Brown's teacher at Cambridge, was an example *par excellence* of the supremacy of these psychologico-historical explanations. Radcliffe-Brown's approach differed substantially. First, against Rivers's heavy reliance upon psychology, Radcliffe-Brown denied that society can be understood as an aggregate of psychological phenomena (1958: 16ff.). Second, he thought it necessary to abandon the diffusionist search for origins; any such enterprise lacks the necessary empirical support (ibid.: 52ff.). Third, instead of Rivers's attempts at making historical conjectures, Radcliffe-Brown heralded comparative sociology, which allows the anthropologist to find universal laws about synchronic relations (ibid.: 108–29). Fourth, whereas diffusionists relied upon secondary sources, Radcliffe-Brown regarded extensive fieldwork as essential to the scientific study of non-Western cultures. After all, the meaning of cultural items depends on the social context, and only systematic observation will allow the anthropologist to uncover the local meanings (ibid.: 67ff.).

Radcliffe-Brown's lifelong involvement in the academic institutionalization of anthropology was interwoven with his commitment to the subject as a scientific discipline. He thought that, hitherto, anthropology had been too often in the hands of well-meaning dilettantes, who developed highly speculative theories based on unreliable source material. Anthropology had to become a science, aimed at developing general laws of society. This meant that anthropologists needed to draw systematically upon what he called the inductive and comparative method. But Radcliffe-Brown's position also implied that anthropology was in need of professionalization. The emphasis on scientific method called for a rigorous training in fieldwork methods (ibid.: 66ff.), and this instruction was to be provided at universities. Once anthropology was established as a science, it would be able to inform and guide colonial administration, educators and policy-makers (ibid.: 90–5). Radcliffe-Brown's own prescriptions very much resemble Durkheim's. Society should aim at a state of *eunomia* as opposed to *dysnomia*. *Eunomia*, or social health, occurs when the different parts are in harmonious relation to each other. The thoroughly trained anthropologist helps colonial and local administration in the accomplishment of *eunomia* (1952: 182–3).

Radcliffe-Brown introduced a number of concepts, central to his line of argument, which include social structure, structural form and social function. Commentators have often misunderstood Radcliffe-Brown because they failed to capture the exact meaning which he attributed to these key concepts of his framework. 'Structure', especially, was used rather distinctly from its ordinary use in sociology and anthropology (see chapter 1). Radcliffe-Brown insisted that his notion of structure is not as an abstraction or model used in order to approach reality. Instead, he regarded structure (and hence *social* structure) as an observable reality. The general concept of structure refers to an arrangement of interrelated parts, and structures can be observed in different realms. For example, the structure of a piece of music refers to an arrangement of sounds, and the structure of a molecule is an arrangement of atoms. Likewise, social structure is the entire set of actually existent relations which connect certain individuals at a given time. So the ultimate components of social structure are human beings. Their relations involve well-defined rights and duties for the individuals involved. The institutionalization of incentives and sanctions ensure people's compliance with these prescriptions (Kuper 1977: 19–21, 25–42).

Some structures, such as that of a building, are relatively invariant. But many change. Like the structure of the human body, social structure is in constant flux; like the changing molecules of the human body, people come and go, or take up different positions and roles. Now, in the midst of any structural change, there is continuity. Radcliffe-Brown coined the term 'structural form' to refer to this observable structural continuity. For example, a human organism retains its structural form in spite of the changing molecules. Likewise, social structure exhibits an observable structural form: the usages or norms shared by the individuals are relatively invariant (1952: 3–4, 191ff.). The relative stability of the forms is due to what Radcliffe-Brown coined 'functions' fulfilled by the different parts of the system. By a function, he meant the sum total of all relations that a component has to the entire system in which it is embedded. The notion of function is again applicable to many realms of reality: in the same way that different parts of the human body fulfil vital functions, so too do various components of social life (Kuper 1977: 21–4, 43–8). The stability of structural form is dependent on the 'functional unity' of the whole; that is, the mutual adjustment of the different parts. Particularly central to the persistence of social forms is 'coaptation', referring to the standardization and mutual adjustment of the attitudes and behaviour of the members of that society (Radcliffe-Brown 1952: 180ff.).

Malinowski and Radcliffe-Brown had an enormous impact on social anthropology. The reception of early functionalism by social theorists was not as unequivocally positive. This ambiguous response is to be explained partly by the subsequent rise of rival functionalist theories. By the end of the 1940s, Talcott Parsons had established himself as the main exponent of functionalist theory, and very soon after that Robert Merton made his reputation. But the mild reception of early functionalist theories was also a consequence of their own shortcomings.

For illustration, two pivotal weaknesses in the argument of early functionalists can be cited. The first is their tendency to describe *all* cultural items as functional. Malinowski, for instance, postulated this 'universal functionalism' when he described culture as 'a system of objects, activities, and attitudes in which *every* part exists as a means to an end' (1944: 150; emphasis added). For him, '*every* cultural achievement that implies the use of artifacts and symbolism is an instrumental enhancement of human anatomy, and refers directly or indirectly to the satisfaction of a bodily need' (ibid.: 171; emphasis added). Now, the assumption of universal functionalism can be understood in two ways; there is a strong and a weak version. On the one hand, it can be understood to mean literally that every social item fulfils a central function. This strong version would be an untenable position to hold. Evolutionary theory might imply that highly dysfunctional items are selected out. But from this it does not follow that the items which do persist fulfil central functions. On the other, a more charitable interpretation is that universal functionalism means that only those items which fulfil central functions count as socially relevant items. For methodological purposes, every item should be treated as if it fulfils a vital function; the empirical researcher needs to be sensitive to the fact that every observed item *might* serve central needs of society. Although more plausible, this weak version of universal functionalism is not without problems either. It is unclear which criteria ought to be employed in order to decide whether or not an item *is* functional, and, if it is, which function it fulfils.

The second weakness of early functionalism is its tendency to assume that a certain amount of cohesion and cohesiveness is necessary for society to survive. Radcliffe-Brown, for instance, held to this assumption of functional unity when he wrote that 'all parts of the social system work together with a sufficient degree of harmony or internal consistency' (1952: 181). The problems with this position are twofold. One, the notion of 'survival' might have a clear meaning in the biological realm, but it does not to the same extent in the social realm. It is unclear whether the survival of a society or culture refers to continuity at a political or cultural level, or to the absence of biological extinction of its members. Also, if social survival refers to political or cultural constancy, then it remains unclear how much of that continuity constitutes survival. Two, to say that a certain degree of cohesiveness or internal consistency is necessary is a vacuous claim to make. The question is not whether or not cohesiveness is essential, but *how much* is needed. None of the early functionalists even began to answer that question. In practice, they often portrayed societies as if they were in need of high levels of standardization of sentiments and beliefs. This is not surprising given that the societies which they investigated already exhibited such high levels. But some awareness of their own culture would have taught them that although modern Western societies do not quite conform to that picture, they nevertheless manage quite well.

To avoid being too harsh on Malinowski and Radcliffe-Brown, one should not forget that they were, first and foremost, empirical anthropologists, not social theorists. Their merit lies in demonstrating that many nineteenth-century speculative theories lacked an empirical basis. They carried out detailed ethnographies, and showed their theoretical relevance. They established a tradition of rigorous empirical research. Given these achievements, it would be unfair to claim that the onus of developing a convincing and coherent functionalist framework was on them. It is ironic that this task was to be taken up by a man for whom Malinowski's lectures were one of his first exposures to the social sciences. That young American graduate student attending Malinowski's lectures in 1925 was Talcott Parsons. He was to change the face of social theory for ever.

Talcott Parsons

Talcott Parsons (1902–79) first studied philosophy and biology at Amherst College, and then social science in England and Germany. He studied under L. T. Hobhouse, Ginsberg and Malinowski at the LSE, and then embarked upon a doctoral dissertation at Heidelberg. During his stay in Europe, Parsons became heavily influenced by European social theory. His doctoral dissertation dealt with the notion of capitalism in the work of Weber, Marx and Werner Sombart. Further lasting influences on Parsons's thought include Durkheim and Vilfredo Pareto. Throughout his life, he would attempt to incorporate these various European thinkers into a unified theoretical framework. On his return to the United States, he soon took up a position at Harvard University, where he would stay until his retirement in 1973. Besides being a prolific writer, Parsons also held many offices: for instance, he was founding editor of *The American Sociological Review*, and President of the Eastern Sociological Society, the

American Sociological Association and the American Academy of Arts and Sciences. Parsons was the first ever sociologist to occupy this last position.

Parsons's abstract theorizing was initially at odds with the highly atheoretical climate of American sociology at the time. When his first book, *The Structure of Social Action*, came out in 1937, it only attracted interest amongst specialists in social theory. But his writings gradually had more impact, and by the time *The Social System* was published in 1951, he had become one of the most influential social theorists of his time. The impact was not limited to social theory; his work was now also regarded as useful for empirical purposes. However, even in Parsons's heyday in the 1950s, his work never ceased to be controversial, regarded as pure genius by some and disguised conservative ideology by others. His influence declined in the late 1960s and 1970s, and only recently has there been a revival of interest in his work; for instance, in the writings of Jeffrey Alexander and Richard Münch, as we shall see later in this chapter.

Parsons's functionalist theory differs substantially from the early functionalism of Malinowski and Radcliffe-Brown. Whereas most early functionalists were sympathetic towards a positivist conception of social science, Parsons was not. He insisted that positivist social science is erroneous because it fails to recognize the essentially purposeful nature of human action (see chapter 8). It is intrinsic to agency that it cannot be reduced to external conditions. What is needed is a theory which takes into account the fact that people are both goal-orientated and constrained. Neither the purposiveness of action nor its external constraints can be ignored; neither can be reduced to the other. This attempt to transcend both extreme forms of positivism and idealism runs throughout the whole of Parsons's *oeuvre*.

This is revealed clearly in his early work. Central to *The Structure of Social Action* is Thomas Hobbes's problem of order: how can society persist given that each of its members pursues his or her own goal? (Parsons 1937: 89–94). Idealist, positivist and utilitarian attempts to solve the problem of order are shown to be inadequate. Idealist views mistakenly ignore the extent to which human conduct is conditioned by external constraints (ibid.: 473–694). Likewise, positivist perspectives erroneously ignore the relatively independent role of the symbolic realm, and utilitarian perspectives are mistaken in reducing value patterns to a mere cost-benefit analysis (ibid.: 3–470). Instead, Parsons found inspiration for his sociological answer to Hobbes's problem of order partly in Weber's action theory, and partly in Durkheim's notions of 'collective consciousness' or 'collective representation' (see chapter 1). Parsons's solution to the problem of order is basically a Durkheimian one, referring to the internalization of shared central values and norms of society within need-dispositions of the personality structure. People tend not to adopt an instrumental attitude towards internalized values. By pursuing their own goals, socialized individuals unwittingly contribute to fulfilling the central needs of society (ibid.: 697–776).

In the course of the 1940s and 1950s, Parsons developed his 'general theory of action'. Given its central place in his work, we will pay special attention to it here. The aim of the theory was to provide a theoretical framework which united various disciplines in the social sciences: sociology, politics, psychology and economics. Parsons's attempt to develop this unifying framework fitted in with his position at that time at Harvard. After teaching in the economics and sociology departments, he became chairman of the newly founded Department of Social Relations in 1946. The new institute grouped together several disciplines. Amongst Parsons's colleagues at the department were the psychologists Gordon Allport, Henry Murray and Robert Bales, the sociologists George Homans and Samuel Stouffer, and the anthropologist Clyde Kluckhohn. Many of these collaborated with Parsons and influenced his thinking. Parsons's general theory of action was both the academic backbone and the output of his tenure in office.

Central to Parsons's general theory of action is the notion of a 'system'. System theory had become increasingly popular at the time, and Parsons was heavily influenced by it. For him, a 'system of action' refers to a durable organization of the interaction between what he called an 'actor' and a 'situation'. The actor might be an individual or a group. The situation might or might not incorporate other 'actors'. Parsons argued that there are three features to any system. First, a system is relatively structured. In the social realm, he maintained that value patterns and what he called the 'pattern variables' contribute to the structured nature of the system. Second, certain functions need to be fulfilled for a system to survive. Social systems thus have particular needs, and Parsons tried to list and classify these 'functional prerequisites'. Third, social systems change, and that change takes place in an ordered fashion. Parsons introduced the notion of cybernetic hierarchy in order to capture the phenomenon of ordered transformation in the social realm.

These three components require elaboration. Before discussing his notions of functional prerequisites and internal dynamics, we will first analyse at length Parsons's treatment of the structured nature of interaction. His starting point is that systems of action are structured by value patterns, which stipulate the ultimate objectives towards which people's action will be directed. Without those ordering principles, people would not have any guidelines regarding their conduct. But Parsons argued that the value patterns are structured as well, by what he termed 'pattern variables' (see, e.g. 1951: 46–51, 58–67). He considered these to be the ultimate principles through which systemic structure is achieved. They are universal dichotomies which represent basic choices underlying social interaction.

Parsons's pattern variables can also be seen as an attempt to reconstruct in a sophisticated manner dichotomies which were introduced by earlier authors. In particular, Tönnies's distinction between the *Gesellschaft* and the *Gemeinschaft* springs to mind. Tönnies described earlier types of society as *gemeinschaftlich*, based on personal relations and affective bonds. Modern society is more *gesellschaftlich* in that impersonal interactions are more frequent. Parsons's view was that Tönnies's typology of relationships conflates several dichotomies, and is thus too crude to have any heuristic value. Several observed relationships are indeed *gesellschaftlich* in some respects, *gemeinschaftlich* in others. Parsons set out to distinguish analytically the underlying dichotomies or pattern variables. This enabled him to redefine Tönnies's question. Rather than attempting to establish whether a given relationship is *gesellschaftlich* or *gemeinschaftlich*, Parsons's pattern variables enable him to establish *in which sense* that relationship is one or the other.

The pattern variables apply to any system of action, and refer to choices faced by an actor in relation to an object. As mentioned earlier, the actor does not have to be an individual – it can be a collectivity or a group. Likewise, the object does not have to be an inanimate object – it can be an individual or a social group. The pattern variables are universalism versus particularism, performance versus quality, specific versus diffuse relations, and affective neutrality versus affectivity. The first of each pair is characteristic of Tönnies's *Gesellschaft*, the second of each pair ties in with the *Gemeinschaft*. Underlying Parsons's scheme is the observation that our society is moving in the direction of universalism, performance, specific relations and affective neutrality. Whereas the first two pairs refer to the meaning which the actor attributes to a particular object, the remaining pairs allude to the nature of the relationship between actor and object. In Parsons's terminology again, the first two are the pattern variables of the modality of the object, and the others are the pattern variables of orientation to the object.

As to the pattern variables of the modality of the object, the actor makes use of universalistic criteria if he attributes meaning to the object according to criteria applicable to many other objects, whereas he draws upon particularistic criteria if the object is defined and judged in terms which are unique to that object. A bureaucracy, for instance, draws upon universalistic criteria, whereas relationships within the nuclear family are particularistic. Whereas the actor can judge the object in terms of its performance or achievement, the actor may also treat it in terms of its intrinsic quality. Performance is more prominent in the occupational structure, whereas quality can be exemplified in friendships. With respect to the pattern variables of orientation, the actor might adopt an attitude of affective neutrality towards the object as opposed to a relationship of affectivity. For example, the relationship between a doctor and patient demonstrates affective neutrality, whereas affectivity characterizes the interaction within the family. Finally, the actor may be involved with an object in rather specific ways, or relate to the object in multiple ways. Again, the relationship between doctor and patient is typically specific, and relationships within a family typically diffuse.

The pattern variables refer to the more voluntaristic dimensions of Parsons's theory, for they summarize and classify choices on the part of the actor. In contrast, Parsons's notion of 'functional prerequisites' points out the extent to which these attitudes or meanings are embedded within and constrained by social subsystems (see, e.g., 1951: 26–35). Parsons's functionalist theory rests upon the notion that any system of action only exists insofar as four basic needs are at least in part fulfilled by four types of function. The four needs and functional prerequisites of any system of action are, according to Parsons, adaptation (A), goal-attainment (G), integration (I) and latency or pattern-maintenance (L). Hence Parsons often refers to this aspect of his theory as the AGIL-scheme. 'Adaptation' refers to the fact that any system of action should be able to adapt to its external environment and make the environment adapt to its own needs. 'Goal-attainment' is the need of any system of action to define its goals and to mobilize resources in order to obtain them. 'Integration' refers to the need of any system of action to regulate and coordinate its parts for the sake of its stability and coherence. Finally, 'latency' or 'pattern-maintenance' means that a system must provide means for sustaining the motivational energy of its members.

Parsons noted that the four functions can be arrived at with the use of two dichotomies: external versus internal, and instrumental versus consummatory. Activities directed towards goal-attainment and integration are 'consummatory' in that they aim at the accomplishment of the ultimate goals of the system, whereas activities directed towards adaptation or latency are 'instrumental' in that they are directed towards the employment of means in order to achieve the ultimate goals. Likewise, Parsons noted that adaptation and goal-attainment refer to the interaction between the system and its external environment, whereas latency and integration refer to issues concerning the internal organization of the system. So the AGIL-scheme can be summarized by noting that any system of action needs to relate successfully to its environment and internally organize itself.

For every system of action, four subsystems can be identified, each specializing in fulfilling one of the four functions: the organism directed towards adaptation, the personality system related to goal-attainment, the social system directed towards integration, and the cultural system geared towards pattern-maintenance. The difference between the four sub-units can also be captured in terms of Parsons's 'cybernetic hierarchy'. From cybernetic theory, Parsons derives the idea that a system of action, like any other system, circulates and exchanges information and energy. The units with high information tend to control the units with high energy, whereas the latter tend to condition the former. The subsystem directed towards pattern-maintenance tends to control the other subsystems. Similarly, the subsystem geared towards adaptation conditions the other subsystems (1966: ch. 2).

Parsons's theory of action is general. For each subsystem, similar distinctions can be identified. It follows that his scheme is like a set of Russian dolls, each doll incorporating a smaller version of itself with an identical structure. For example, the social system itself can be divided up into four subsystems. There is, first, the economy, which deals with the adaptation of society towards its environment. Second, the polity of society deals primarily with goal-attainment. Third, the social community focuses upon integration and solidarity. Finally, the cultural subsystem provides values and normative regulations which make for appropriate socialization.

Parsons goes to great lengths to show the interrelationship between the AGIL-scheme and the pattern variables (1960). Systems with different functions imply different pattern variables. For instance, systems directed towards fulfilling the adaptive function are characterized by universalism, neutrality, specificity and performance, whereas systems fulfilling the integrative function emphasize particularism, affectivity, diffuseness and quality (see table 2.1).

Table 2.1 Relations between pattern variables and functional prerequisites of any system of action

	Universalism (O) Neutrality (M)	Affectivity (O) Particularism (M)	
Specificity (O) Performance (M)	ADAPTATION	GOAL-ATTAINMENT	Performance (O) Specificity (M)
Quality (O) Diffuseness (M)	PATTERN-MAINTENANCE	INTEGRATION	Diffuseness (O) Quality (M)
	Neutrality (O) Universalism (M)	Particularism (O) Affectivity (M)	

O = pattern variable of orientation to the object
M = pattern variable of object-modality
Source: Based on Parsons 1960: 470

Whereas Parsons's earlier work ignored issues related to long-term change, his later work drew upon analogies with biological evolution to develop a 'paradigm of evolutionary change' (see, e.g., 1966; 1977). Four notions are crucial here: differentiation, adaptive upgrading, inclusion and value generalization. First, with time, a process of 'differentiation' occurs in that different functions are fulfilled by subsystems within the social system. For instance, the economic and the family unit gradually become differentiated. Second, with differentiation goes the notion of 'adaptive upgrading'. This means that each differentiated subsystem has more adaptive capacity compared to the non-differentiated system out of which it emerged. Third, modern societies tend to rely upon a new system of integration. Process differentiation implies a more urgent need for special skills. This can only be accommodated by moving from a status based on 'ascription' to a status on the basis of 'achievement'. This implies the 'inclusion' of previously excluded groups. Fourth, a differentiated society needs to develop a value system that incorporates and regulates the different subsystems. This is made possible through 'value generalization': the values are pitched at a higher level in order to direct activities and functions in various subsystems.

Three basic weaknesses can be identified in Parsons's social theory. First, his general theory of action is a conceptual scheme, rather than an adequate theory. There is no doubt that, as such, the general theory is a remarkable achievement. It is, after all, analytically very tight and, because of its high level of generality, it allows us to categorize various aspects of the social realm. But equally beyond question is that the explanatory power of the theory is weak. It provides few testable propositions about social reality (for a similar argument, see Homans 1961: 10ff.; Rocher 1974: 164–5). Second, intrinsic to Parsons's theoretical frame of reference is a neglect of conflict and disequilibrium. In his earlier work he developed a theoretical argument aimed at understanding how social order is brought about. Likewise, his system analysis was primarily aimed at explaining how the stability of a system is achieved – how it manages its boundary-maintenance and its internal integration. Parsons's frame of reference not only fails to account sufficiently for widespread dissensus and major political or industrial conflicts, but also occasionally seems to exclude the very possibility of their existence (for a similar argument, see Cohen 1968: chs 2, 3, 7). Third, some of the weaknesses of early functionalism reoccur in Parsons's work. He argued that there are four functional prerequisites to any social system. Underlying his theory is thus the assumption that these pivotal functions are essential to the maintenance and survival of the system. If these pivotal functions were not fulfilled adequately, the social system would disintegrate and eventually be selected out. However, like Malinowski and Radcliffe-Brown, Parsons remains ambiguous about what exactly constitutes survival and maintenance in the social realm. And as with early functionalists, it remains unclear *how much* goal-attainment, adaptation, latency and integration are needed for a system to maintain itself.

Robert Merton

Talcott Parsons trained several promising sociologists who later turned out to be influential scholars in their own right. His long list of PhD students included, for example, Robert King Merton and Harold Garfinkel. Robert Merton (1910–2003) was one of Parsons's first doctoral students at Harvard. His dissertation dealt with science and economy in seventeenth-century England, and it already exhibited his functionalist viewpoint, albeit in an embryonic form. Other influences on Merton during his stay at Harvard included the sociologist P. A. Sorokin and the historian of science George Sarton. Amongst European scholars, Émile Durkheim and Georg Simmel had a lasting impact on his work.

Merton spent most of his teaching career at the University of Columbia, which, with him, Paul Lazarsfeld and others, became a centre of excellence for sociology. There was a remarkable compatibility between Merton's 'middle-range' functionalism and Lazarsfeld's quantitative methodology. In comparison to Parsons's abstract theorizing, Merton's middle-range theory seemed more obviously suited to empirical research, for which Lazarsfeld's sophisticated use of statistics would provide the methodological backbone. Merton had a remarkable gift for demonstrating the validity of his theoretical constructions with the help of relevant empirical applications. He dealt with several substantive topics, ranging from American politics to science. With the publication of *Social Theory and Social Structure* in 1968, he became one of the leading proselytizers of the functionalist cause.

Although once a pupil of Parsons, Merton's functionalist viewpoint differed substantially from that of his former mentor. Merton's writings were more cautious and defensive; underlying them is a constant awareness of the various criticisms levelled against previous functionalist frames of reference. A significant part of his work deals with these criticisms. Indeed, he regularly attempted to show that they were invalid, or pointed to errors which, although committed by some functionalists, were not intrinsic to the functionalist argument. Merton's proposal for a functionalist paradigm endeavoured to avoid these intellectual faults.

A similar prudence lies behind Merton's middle-range theories (ibid.: 39–72). Contrary to Parsons's grand theory, a middle-range theory does not aim to encompass the whole of society. But neither is it a sequence of unrelated empirical hypotheses. 'Theories of the middle range . . . lie between the minor but necessary working hypotheses that evolve in abundance during day-to-day research and the all-inclusive systematic efforts to develop a unified theory that will explain all the observed uniformities of social behavior, social organization and social change' (ibid.: 39). Merton believed the theory of reference groups (and relative deprivation) to be an example of a successful middle-range theory in sociology. This theory, to which Merton himself contributed, set out that individuals evaluate their own situation by comparing and contrasting it with that of a reference group. Merton thought that the theory was successful in that it counters common sense and has been validated empirically (ibid.: 40–1).

Although Merton is considered to be one of the high priests of modern functionalism, he distanced himself from a significant number of writings under that banner. He tried to demonstrate that most early functionalists drew upon untenable presuppositions. The German word *hineinlesen* summarizes well what Merton found so problematic in early functionalism. *Hineinlesen* (not a term used by Merton himself) refers to the activity of reading too much into something. And that is exactly what, according to Merton, early functionalists did. They tended *ex post facto* to read too much functional rationality into social practices.

How did early functionalists attribute too much functional rationality onto social reality? Merton argued that they did so by adhering to three erroneous principles: the postulate of functional unity of society, the postulate of universal functionalism and the postulate of indispensability (ibid.: 79–91). The first principle states that society is a functional whole, and all its parts are fully integrated and well balanced. The second principle asserts that all cultural items and social practices are functional. The third principle states that there are certain universal functional prerequisites to any society, and *only* specific cultural items or practices can fulfil these functions. Merton argued that the early functionalists were mistaken in postulating these principles in advance. They need to be shown empirically, and empirical research shows them to be incorrect. The first principle might be consistent with Malinowski's and Radcliffe-Brown's data on 'primitive' non-literate societies. But it would be a gross error to extend this principle to differentiated literate societies. The second principle fails to acknowledge the existence of social survivals: that is, items which might have fulfilled a function at some point in the past but which do so no longer. The third principle disregards the existence of 'functional alternatives' or 'functional equivalents'. The fact that a given item fulfils a particular function does not necessarily imply that the very same function cannot be fulfilled by alternative items.

Merton's proposal for a functionalist perspective was based on his criticisms of the above trinity of functional postulates. First, he abandoned the early functionalist view that we live in the best of all possible worlds. Many beliefs or practices persist in spite of the fact that they do not have notably beneficial effects for the individuals involved or for the wider society. They might have negative consequences, or they might have no socially significant effect. Merton argued that early functionalists have hitherto been biased towards exclusively focusing on the *positive* consequences of social items for the wider social system in which these items are situated. His paradigm for functional analysis, on the other hand, attributed equal status to what he coined 'functions' and 'dysfunctions'. He defined functions as those observed effects of social items which contribute to the adaptation or adjustment of a system under consideration. Dysfunctions are those observed consequences which lessen the adaptation or adjustment of a given system. Certain items might appear to be neither functional nor dysfunctional. They are 'non-functional' in that they are irrelevant for a given system. Merton believed that his attention to dysfunctions makes his functionalism well suited for analysing social transformation (ibid.: 84–6, 90, 105).

Second, early functionalists tend to focus on so-called functions for 'the society'. But the notion of society as a totality is misleading, because the same item might be functional for some individuals, group(s) or system(s), and dysfunctional for others. Merton therefore distinguished between different units for which the item might have consequences. Rather than referring to observed effects *in general*, he chose to specify the nature of the units which are affected and how these units are affected. The unit might be the society, the cultural system, a group, the psychological unit, etc. Likewise, there are societal (dys)functions, cultural (dys)functions, group functions, psychological functions, and so forth (ibid.: 79–84, 90, 106).

The phenomenon of war can be used to clarify Merton's distinction between functions and dysfunctions and his distinction between various units of analysis. Consider the following units: the society, the economic unit, the psychological level and the political realm. At the societal level, war is obviously dysfunctional in that it leads to the immediate break-up of families, and the likely injury and possible death of relatives. But war also tends to enhance the internal solidarity of a country. Confrontation with a visible external enemy tends to increase feelings of togetherness and belonging.[2] At the psychological level, some point out that the increased cohesiveness in its turn contributes to the well-being of the citizens – hence the observed decrease in suicide rates during periods of war. Notwithstanding this, going to war also has damaging psychological effects for the soldiers and their families, and for anybody who cares for peace and humanity. At the economic level, war efforts are beneficial for those sectors of the economy which are directly or indirectly involved in the production of arms. However, war also inevitably leads to the neglect of other sectors of the economy; it occasionally leads to economic sanctions from other countries; and it is almost always accompanied by decreasing trade and a decline in the standard of living. At a politico-strategic level, going to war might deflect attention from domestic problems, raise the popularity of those in power, and thus be crucial to their re-election. But strategic errors might also have the opposite effect.

Third, Merton noted that a common critique of functionalism was its conservative bias. He acknowledged that early functionalists tended to provide interpretations which legitimized the existing order, though he denied that this tendency was intrinsic to functionalism. Early functionalists came to such conservative conclusions precisely because their analysis was confined to the identification of positive effects for the society as a whole. Once functionalists include dysfunctions and once they specify various units or levels of analysis, they will be able to establish a 'net balance of an aggregate of consequences' for every item. By searching for which functional alternatives are possible in a given social structure, functionalism can help us to improve society (Merton 1968: 91–100, 106–8).

Fourth, some functionalist accounts conflated subjective states of individuals with objective consequences. Merton insisted that the function of a practice is an observable effect, and therefore to be distinguished from the motive underlying the practice. Some practices, of course, have functions which are both intended and recognized by the individuals who are involved in the practices. Merton called these 'manifest functions'. But other functions are neither intended nor recognized by the individuals involved. Merton called the latter 'latent functions'. Take the example of Christian church-going. One of its manifest functions is to commemorate Jesus and to be closer to God. One of its latent functions consists of reinforcing social integration. Functional analysis can be liberating in that it makes latent (dys)functions manifest (ibid.: 114–36).

An example of Merton's middle-range, functionalist theory can be found in his seminal articles 'Social structure and anomie' and 'Continuities in the theory of social structure and anomie' (in ibid.: 185–214, 215–48). Underlying this theory is the distinction between culture and social structure: whereas culture provides people with normative guidelines, social structure refers to the organized set of social relationships. Culture informs people about what is desirable and to be aimed at, whereas the very fact that they operate within a social structure implies various opportunities and constraints.

More specifically, Merton distinguished between the ultimate values which are central to a particular culture, on the one hand, and the availability of legitimate means to achieve these goals, on the other. Anomie is defined as a state of discrepancy between ultimate values and legitimate means. For example, whereas material and professional success are highly valued in Western society, few people have the structurally induced opportunities to achieve these goals. Merton argued that people will be driven towards reducing the discrepancy, and that deviant behaviour can be seen as an attempt to restore the equilibrium.

Merton devoted much time to the construction of a classificatory scheme about different ways in which individuals can adjust to this state of anomie (see table 2.2). 'Innovation' occurs when people accept the ultimate goals but introduce illegitimate means to achieve them. Merton cited some forms of white-collar crime as examples of this particular phenomenon. 'Ritualism' is reserved for cases in which people have lowered

Table 2.2 How people adapt to the state of anomie

Modes of adaptation	Culture goals	Institutionalized means
I. Conformity	+	+
II. Innovation	+	−
III. Ritualism	−	+
IV. Retreatism	−	−
V. Rebellion	+/−	+/−

Source: Based on Merton 1968: 194

their aims but in which they do accept the institutionalized ways of doing things. 'Retreatism' occurs when both goals and means are rejected, and when people retreat from involvement with society. Certain subcultures fall under that category. 'Rebellion' occurs when individuals seek to change the culturally prescribed goals of society and the legitimate means for achieving them. To complete the picture (although not a case of deviancy), Merton talked about 'conformity' when people accept both the ultimate goals and the institutionalized means.

Merton's accomplishment was to reflect critically upon and to elucidate pivotal concepts which were regularly in use at the time; for example, the concept of function or the notion of functional equivalent. His framework was more sophisticated than that of early functionalists, and he carefully avoided some of their errors; for instance, he distanced himself successfully from the once-widespread picture of society as an organic whole with nothing but functional and indispensable parts. But Merton's frame of reference is not without weaknesses either. First, although he developed a frame of reference, which, he hoped, would avoid the errors committed by early functionalism, he ultimately failed to provide convincing explanations for people's actions. By rejecting the simple functionalism of his predecessors in favour of a more cautious approach, he unfortunately managed to throw the baby out with the bath water. Compared to Malinowski's and Radcliffe-Brown's theories, Merton's framework has merely a descriptive and heuristic value; it might delineate and categorize social life, but that is all there is to it. Indeed, to point out existing or potential unintended effects of recurring practices, as Merton does, is, in isolation, not an explanation of those patterns.

Second, commentators have rightly indicated that some of Merton's own contributions to middle-range research can hardly be called functionalist. He does not pay much attention to the unintended outcomes of people's practices, and certainly not in the way in which functionalists normally proceed. Most of his assertions in 'Social structure and anomie', for instance, allude to a causal, non-functionalist logic. It is, of course, not surprising that, in practice, Merton deviates from his functionalist framework. Its explanatory power is so weak that he has to resort to alternative modes of explanation in order to say anything significant at all.

Third, there are a number of imprecisions in Merton's framework. These are especially problematic given that, if there is any value to the framework, it should lie in its descriptive or heuristic qualities, and therefore analytical precision is central. One example of the lack of precision concerns his definition of manifest and latent functions. In this definition, he conflated knowing something will occur and intending it to take place. Neither latent nor manifest functions cover instances where individuals wittingly, though unintentionally, bring about particular functional effects.[3]

Once a promising research programme aimed at unifying the manifold branches of the social sciences, functionalism came under severe criticism from the late 1960s onwards. At least part of the upsurge of dissident voices can be explained by the changing political climate of the time. In a period of political radicalization, students and academics became increasingly dissatisfied with the alleged ideological bias in functionalism. It is ironic that while many regarded the functionalist emphasis on equilibrium and stability as conservative, if not reactionary, quite a few of the 'radical' alternatives in vogue at the time employed functionalist types of reasoning (e.g., Althusser 1972; Althusser and Balibar 1970; Marcuse 1968). Notwithstanding this, functionalism as a school became equated with justifying the existing order and was therefore to be abandoned. Furthermore, many critics argued that, because of its focus on 'social statics', functionalism is inherently ahistorical. Functionalist research became associated with synchronic types of analysis in which a snapshot of society is regarded as sufficient for grasping the mechanisms of stability. Against this ahistorical bias, it was argued that a diachronic analysis is needed even for the purposes of explaining social order (Elias 1978; Giddens 1979: 198–233; 1981; see also chapter 4). In addition, sociologists became dissatisfied with what they saw as the functionalist neglect of agency – the ability of people to intervene in the course of events. In functionalist reasoning, people's conduct was mistakenly conceived to be the mere product of system imperatives. Relatedly, it was argued that functionalism wrongly underplayed people's knowledgeability: the fact that they know a great deal about social life and that they actually employ that knowledge in their daily interaction (Giddens 1977: 96–134; 1984; see also chapters 3 and 4).

These criticisms were often justified, but they unintentionally rein-forced a stereotyped picture of what functionalism stands for. First, the political implications of functionalism are not as clear-cut as some cri-tiques have made them out to be. It is true that functionalist reasoning *can* be used to legitimize existing patterns in society. Functionalists *have* done so in the past. However, from this does not follow that functional-ism *ipso facto* justifies the status quo. Merton's writings demonstrate that it is possible to employ functionalist notions without falling victim to a conservative bias. Second, although it is true that early forms of function-alism tended to focus only on the present, this was often due to method-ological considerations (for instance, the absence of reliable historical sources), not theoretical ones. Any type of functionalist reasoning neces-sitates some form of evolutionism, and thus a sensitivity to longer tem-poral spans. It is therefore not surprising that Parsons's later work dealt very much with long-term change, and that other functionalists were to follow him in this regard. Third, a similar argument applies to the alleged neglect of agency. Some functionalists, indeed, purposefully or unwit-tingly neglect people's active intervention in the course of events, but for others (like Parsons) agency remains a pivotal feature of their theory. But even in the case of the former, there is no need for a theory to take every-thing into account, and no theory *can* account for every feature. Neglect-ing agency is not problematic as long as the theoretical format has satisfactory explanatory power.

Neo-functionalism and Niklas Luhmann

As has been noted, from the mid-1960s onwards functionalism lost its wider appeal. Sociologists became dissatisfied with the alleged conserva-tive bias in functionalist reasoning, and they soon became attracted to a number of alternative theoretical arguments; for instance, Norbert Elias's figuration sociology, Giddens's structuration theory and Bourdieu's gen-erative structuralism (see chapters 1 and 4). But since the early 1980s there has been a revival of functionalist reasoning, at first mainly in Germany, and later in the United States. In Germany Niklas Luhmann's (1927–98) 'functionalist structuralism' has been decisive for the re-emergence of functionalist reasoning. In the United States, Jeffrey Alexander's and Paul Colomy's writings heralded the neo-functionalist movement. Both func-tionalist structuralism and neo-functionalism draw upon Parsons, but they are not uncritical inheritors of his legacy.

Niklas Luhmann has probably been the most innovative German contributor to a functionalist theory of society. His views are based on a wide variety of sources, ranging from general system theory, to Parsons's structural-functionalism, Arnold Gehlen's philosophical anthropology, and phenomenology. Luhmann also holds that there are analogies between the social world and other realms, hence his interest in the theory of autopoiesis and self-organizing systems. Although he is a theorist at heart, he has also provided many examples and applications of his viewpoint, ranging from legal and administrative matters to the issue of romantic love. Luhmann's impact on European sociology has been very important, while Anglo-Saxon sociologists seem in general to be more reluctant to adopt his ideas.

Niklas Luhmann's starting point, one could say, is the system. In his view, the workings of a system can only be fully understood if the relationship between that system and its environment is taken into account (1982: 37ff., 139ff.). Luhmann's main assertion is that systems in general reduce the complexity of the environment in which they are embedded. The complexity of an environment depends on the number of actual or possible events in that environment. Reduction of complexity refers to the process by which a system selects relevant events from the environment, and how it reduces the number of ways of dealing with that environment. The process of internal system differentiation is one of the mechanisms by which complexity becomes managed or filtered (ibid.: 213–17). In Luhmann's abstract terminology, systems can range from, say, physiological systems to social systems.

Luhmann's interest is obviously in social systems; these are defined as organized patterns of behaviour. The term 'social system' can refer to societies at large, institutions within societies or rule-governed forms of behaviour. Social systems are different from other systems in that the reduction of complexity takes place through communication of meaning (*Sinn*) (1990: 21–85). Here, Luhmann relies heavily upon Gehlen's philosophical anthropology and in particular his notion of *Entlastung*, referring to the way in which institutionalization allows human beings to compensate for their intrinsic indeterminacy and open-endedness. In contrast with animals, the innate adaptation of humans to their environment is far less developed, and this intrinsic lack of orientation leads to the necessity of regulative principles.

In Luhmann's parlance, the main regulative device is 'double contingency', referring to the process by which in interaction individuals have to take into account the orientation of others towards them. From double contingency, Luhmann argues, it follows that social systems are autopoietic systems. These are systems which, once faced with an environment which potentially endangers their autonomy, record and interpret that environment such that it contributes to their autonomy. Through double contingency, potential threats to the autonomy of the social system are processed such that they enhance that autonomy. Luhmann takes a lot of effort to explain the autopoietic nature of social systems (and hence their self-referentiality) (ibid.: 1–20). The main thrust of his argument is that there are three dimensions to self-referential systems: the 'code' of the system, its 'structure' (or programme) and its 'process'. Codes are binary procedures through which information is processed – binary oppositions such as 'true versus false', or 'significant versus insignificant'. The structure or programme involves the central values, norms and expectations held within that system, whereas the process is the ongoing interaction. For a system to reproduce itself, the code needs to remain identical, while the structure or process might be altered.

Double contingency is thus a universal ordering principle, but as modernity implies increasing contingency and complexity, more sophisticated mechanisms are needed which would allow for further reduction of complexity. Luhmann provides many examples of progressive reduction of complexity in high modernity, ranging from changes in the legal system to transformations in administration. With the advent of high modernity, 'self-reflexive' procedures and social differentiation become especially important for diminishing complexity. Self-reflexive procedures are those that can be applied not only to other phenomena but also to themselves. Teaching others how to teach, or carrying out scientific investigation of scientific activities – these are examples of self-reflexive procedures. Self-referential procedures imply the possibility of readjustment and therefore become essential for the continuous adaptation of a social system to a rapidly changing and increasingly unpredictable environment (ibid.: 123–74).

Modern social systems are not only self-reflexive; they are also differentiated. For instance, Luhmann observes that through time three levels of social system become distinct from each other: the level of situational interactions, the realm of organizations and the societal level. But Luhmann also talks about differentiation in a less trivial fashion. In a way reminiscent of Durkheim's distinction between mechanical and organic solidarity, Luhmann distinguishes between 'segmental' and 'non-segmental' differentiation: the former implies the splitting up of systems into differentiated units which perform identical functions, whereas the latter involves parts which are functionally different. The non-segmental type of differentiation can be either 'hierarchical' or 'functional': the former implies a hierarchical structure and the latter does not. With respect to the ability to lessen complexity, functional differentiation is superior to hierarchical differentiation, and the latter is superior to segmental differentiation. Given that modernity is characterized by increasing complexity in the social environment, it is not surprising to find that the evolution of society follows these different types: segmental differentiation comes first, then hierarchical differentiation and finally functional differentiation. Luhmann's evolutionary view of history relies upon three central concepts: variation, reproduction and selection. Variation refers to the fact that the emergence of social systems is accidental. Their reproduction takes place, for instance through socialization, and in the long run they are selected on the basis of their ability to adjust to the environment (1982: 232–8).

It is obvious from the above that Luhmann is highly critical of those theorists who conceive of compartmentalization and differentiation as sources of social conflict and disorder, or who see modern depersonalization in terms of alienation or 'mass culture'. For him, this is to conceive of modernity in terms of a pre-modern sociological logic: rather than a source of disorder, various forms of differentiation are central to the creation of order in modern society; rather than alienating, impersonal relations provide new forms of freedom previously unknown to mankind. Luhmann is also critical of Parsons's assertion that common values and norms are a prerequisite for social order. With the advent of modernity, social order is accomplished without central values or widespread normative integration.

There is a tension between Luhmann's philosophical anthropology, on the one hand, and his evaluation of the cultural manifestations of modernity on the other. Influenced by Gehlen and coming close to Malinowksi, Luhmann's philosophical anthropology postulates that human beings have no significant inborn traits, and that they need effective institutions to counteract the lack of an internal structure. However, this position necessitates a more critical attitude towards modernity than Luhmann is willing to adopt. He tries to get around this problem by reducing modernity mainly to differentiation and related notions. But it is obvious that modernity also implies a decrease in the power of value patterns and institutions. Taking on board Gehlen's philosophical anthropology cannot be reconciled with an uncritical appraisal of contemporary society.

Jeffrey Alexander and cultural sociology

With Luhmann's death in 2002, Richard Münch became the most significant representative of neo-functionalism in Germany. Münch's work first
gained international attention in the early 1980s, with a double set of
articles on the Kantian influence on Parsons's work. Later on, he develops
a neo-Parsonian theory of structuration trying to supplement Weber with
Durkheim. More recently, in *Ethics of Modernity* (2000) and *Nation and
Citizenship in the Global Age* (2001), Münch has been focusing on international comparative studies of late modernization processes.

A crucial element of the latter is, of course, the growing migratory
fluxes of the past few decades. Münch's neo-functionalist explanation of
how, in an increasingly globalized world economy, the social integration
of immigrants is closely related to the processes of collective identity
formation in the host societies is an important contribution to this problematic. As has been noted, at about the same time in the United States,
Jeffrey C. Alexander (1947–) was leading the American neo-functionalist
movement. The founding moment of Alexander's neo-functionalism was
the publication of *Theoretical Logic in Sociology* in the early 1980s. Written
at a time when scepticism among sociologists about the usefulness of
grand theoretical syntheses was growing, this monumental four-volume
work was not well received. It remains nonetheless one of the most
impressive sociological treatises of our time. In particular, as a conceptual
framework aiming to explain the differentiation processes that Western
modern societies went through in the past few centuries, it is certainly
unrivalled. Alexander's neo-functionalist phase reached its high tide in the
late 1980s. Much as neo-Marxists tried to draw on Marx's writings while
superseding its shortcomings, so neo-functionalists aim at producing 'significant advances relative to earlier renditions of the Parsonian tradition'
(Alexander and Colomy 1990: 55).

While following the basic outlines of a Parsonian argument, neo-functionalists aim at being less dogmatic than their predecessors, and they
address a number of criticisms. They try to merge Parsons with other
'classics' in social theory (in particular Marx and Durkheim) and with
other schools of thought (especially phenomenology, symbolic interactionism and exchange theory). Like functionalism, neo-functionalism pays
attention to the interconnections between different components of a
social system. But unlike most functionalist authors, neo-functionalists are
particularly sensitive to the potential conflicts between the different subsystems. Whereas some earlier functionalists were inclined to overesti-

mate the impact of culture onto other parts of society, neo-functionalism explicitly rejects any reductionist or mono-causal argument. Whereas some functionalists dismiss the micro-dimension of social life as irrelevant for the purposes of social theory, neo-functionalists also pay attention to the extent to which order is continually produced in our daily interactions (see chapter 3). Whereas some earlier functionalists saw social integration as given, neo-functionalism recognizes its problematic nature within modern society. Whereas former functionalist accounts of social change conceive of societal development in terms of increasing and irreversible differentiation, neo-functionalists like Colomy acknowledge the possibility of de-differentiation and uneven differentiation. The concept of de-differentiation is self-explanatory: it refers to the process by which society moves towards a less differentiated state. That is, de-differentiation occurs when several functions which were previously fulfilled by various differentiated subsystems are now fulfilled within one system. Uneven differentiation takes place when certain sectors of society are more (or less) differentiated than others. Finally, neo-functionalists like Alexander downplay one of the most distinctive features of orthodox Parsonian structural-functionalism, namely the idea that socio-cultural processes were to be studied by reference to the functions they perform within a more inclusive system. Instead of presuming that the system's functional requisites can actually explain the ongoing social processes, Alexander suggests that, at best, they establish the parameters within which individual and collective action takes place.

Alexander's interest in culture, first introduced as an illustration of a neo-functionalist research programme, soon became an exercise in paradigm formation: in the past 15 years or so, Alexander's 'cultural sociology' has been presented as nothing less than the cultural refounding of American sociology (see, e.g., Colomy 1997). Such an ambitious undertaking deserves careful attention. The movement away from neo-functionalism towards cultural sociology comprehends two steps. First, Alexander criticizes the well-known Parsonian analytical distinction between culture, society and personality. In particular, he doubts that the cultural codes and motivational patterns can actually explain human action. In order to do that, one needs to take agency into account. What does this mean? Action and agency are not to be conflated: the latter is but an analytical dimension of the former. Social actors in general should not be characterized as creative, rational, self-reflexive, etc. These are agentic qualities that actors can, in certain contexts and moments in time, exhibit (1998a: 218). Second, Alexander argues that Parsons did not study the cultural system properly. In contrast, Alexander's cultural sociology considers the cultural system as an autonomous symbolic universe that can be studied independently from other action systems (the social system and its functional requirements, for instance). In other words, this idea of 'cultural autonomy' means that culture is not to be studied as a dependent variable to be explained by external factors, but as an independent variable, 'a thread that runs through, one that can be teased out of, every conceivable social form' (2003: 7). The recognition of cultural autonomy is the single most important feature of the 'strong programme' of cultural sociology.[4]

Alexander's cultural sociology is first and foremost to be distinguished from the more traditional 'sociology of culture', especially as developed by Bourdieu (Alexander 1996; see also chapter 1). The latter is criticized for putting forth an externalist approach to the cultural realm, in which 'hard' variables of socio-economic structure shape, and are shaped by, cultural practices and belief systems. In contrast, cultural sociology begins by analytically uncoupling culture from social structure (cultural autonomy) in order to reach a textual understanding of social life. Such an impulse towards reading culture as a text should be complemented, Alexander argues, by an interest in developing 'formal models that can be applied across different comparative and historical cases' (2003: 25). Such reconciliation between the project of hermeneutic 'thick description' – Clifford Geertz's notion of a detailed and nuanced analysis of a single phenomenon that exhibits as many archetypical features as possible (Geertz 1973) – and causal analysis gives rise to Alexander's own theoretical paradigm, 'structural hermeneutics'.

However, Alexander grants possibly too much autonomy to culture. In *Cultural Trauma and Collective Identity*, for instance, his otherwise rich and detailed study of the Holocaust defines 'trauma' mainly in cultural terms (i.e., cultural memory as a social construct), thereby failing to analyse the psychological and social consequences of traumas. It is not clear what one gains from employing one single factor to explain such a complex and multilayered phenomenon. This sort of difficulty is shared by all culturalist analyses – what is left out often prevents a thorough and balanced account of the phenomenon at hand. Furthermore, Alexander's suggestion that 'structuralism and hermeneutics can be made into fine bedfellows' (2003: 26) is not without problems either. In our view, his perspective gives more analytical and empirical attention to the cultural component than to its structural counterpart. This is particularly striking in the case of Alexander's notion of 'cultural structure'. It consists of narrative frames and binary symbolic codes, such as the pure and the polluted, the sacred and the profane, the good and the evil. Such a 'soft' conception of structure is no match for political science's neo-institutionalist proposals (see chapter 4), at least as far as the 'hard' aspects of cultural structures (e.g. the economy of cultural production, power asymmetries, and the cultural elites' strategies for the maintenance of their privileged positions). Although Alexander does show some awareness concerning the control of the means of symbolic production (2003: 32), his proposal does not treat the asymmetrical distribution of power in a systematic way.

These difficulties notwithstanding, there have been two important developments in Alexander's 'strong programme' of cultural sociology. First, in 2006 he published *The Civil Sphere*, a monumental application of cultural sociology to politics. Though it is Alexander's most empirically grounded work so far, it remains as conceptually ambitious as his other more theoretically oriented writings. In the first part, Alexander reintroduces his previous thesis on real civil societies (see 1998b). Three major definitions of civil society are distinguished (2006a: 24–35). The first one (civil society I, or CSI) emerged in eighteenth-century Europe, with the struggles of the rising social classes against the absolutist monarchies. At this time, civil society was conceived as comprising all non-state institutions. The next conception of civil society, CSII, is a product of the nineteenth-century market versus state debate, and as such has two contradictory meanings: for Marxists, civil society is to be identified with bourgeois society, and therefore with capitalist exploitation, whereas for liberals it means freedom from state intervention. CSIII, Alexander's proposed definition of contemporary civil society, comprises two dialectically related dimensions. On the one hand, it refers to a universalistically oriented solidary community, which comprises a specific set of cultural codes (e.g., democratic values), institutions (e.g., free press), and integrative patterns (e.g., civic trust). On the other hand, it is patterned by a set of specific institutions (the courts and the mass media) and becomes visible in practices like civility, equality, criticism and respect. After analysing the structures and dynamics of civil societies (i.e., the binary codes of civil discourse in America and the communicative and regulative institutions), Alexander provides in-depth studies of the women's movement and the civil rights struggle. This empirical application of cultural sociology reveals how the modern institutional framework often provides the very basis for civic action: the struggle for civil rights in America, for instance, is depicted as part and parcel of a complex web of meaning that comes to life through civic engagement (2006a: 293ff.).

Second, cultural sociology is undertaking a 'performative turn' towards a 'theory of cultural pragmatics' (2006b: 29). This recent move to performance is triggered by the question, 'Why are even the most rationalized societies still enchanted and mystified in various ways?' (ibid.: 76). After all, sociological classics such as Weber and Durkheim left their mark in the discipline by predicting, over a century ago, that modernity's future was one of rationalization, bureaucratization, individualism and disenchantment. Alexander only partly agrees with this picture, pointing out that the way in which culture gets embedded in contemporary action mirrors a theatrical production. Today's social action as performance, Alexander suggests, is decisively different from old-fashioned rituals as participation in rituals nowadays is more a matter of choice than obligation. He distinguishes several elements in cultural performance. The 'collective representations' that compose culture provide the background for every performative act; 'actors' have to convince their 'audiences' of the authenticity of their cultural performances; the 'means of symbolic production' refer to the material objects and the physical space actors need to perform; the '*mise-en-scène*' is related to the temporal sequences and spatial choreographies needed for a text 'to walk and talk'; and 'social power' has to be taken into account if one wishes to understand why some performances are allowed to proceed and others are not. In short, this conceptual model is supposed to 'determine, and measure, whether and how a performance occurs, and the degree to which it succeeds or fails in its effect' (ibid.: 36).

Further reading

A concise, but critical account of functionalism can be found in Giddens's 'Functionalism: après la lutte' (in his *Studies in Social and Political Theory*). An extended, and more sympathetic, overview of functionalist theories can be found in Abrahamson's *Functionalism*. Kuper's *Anthropologists and Anthropology* includes two excellent chapters on Malinowski and Radcliffe-Brown, elucidating the intellectual background at the time. Rocher's *Talcott Parsons and American Sociology* is a remarkably lucid introduction to Parsons's writings. For those who insist on reading the master himself, *The Structure of Social Action* is probably one of Parsons's more accessible texts; *The Social System* has undoubtedly been his most influential work. Sztompka's *Robert Merton: An Intellectual Profile* remains the best introduction to Merton's functionalist framework, although it is not very critical. We very much recommend Merton's seminal article 'Manifest and Latent

Functions' (in the collection *Social Theory and Social Structure*). *The Differentiation of Society* is Luhmann's most accessible work in the English language. There are two works by Alexander that we strongly recommend: *Neo-Functionalism and After*, for the overview it provides of Alexander's neo-functionalist phase, and *The Meanings of Social Life*, an accessible entry point to his strong programme in cultural sociology.

References

Abrahamson, M. 1978. *Functionalism*. Englewood Cliffs, NJ: Prentice-Hall.

Alexander, J. C. 1982–3. *Theoretical Logic in Sociology*, vols. 1–4. Berkeley: University of California Press.

Alexander, J. C. 1996. Cultural sociology or sociology of culture? *Culture* 10(3–4): 1–5.

Alexander, J. C. 1998a. *Neo-functionalism and After*. Oxford: Blackwell.

Alexander, J. C. (ed.) 1998b. *Real Civil Societies: Dilemmas of Institutionalization*. London: Sage.

Alexander, J. C. 2003. *The Meanings of Social Life. A Cultural Sociology*. Oxford: Oxford University Press.

Alexander, J. C. 2004. *Cultural Trauma and Collective Identity*. Berkeley: University of California Press.

Alexander, J. C. 2006a. *The Civil Sphere*. Oxford: Oxford University Press.

Alexander, J. C. 2006b. Cultural pragmatics: social performance between ritual and strategy. In J. C. Alexander, B. Giesen and J. L. Mast (eds), *Social Performance. Symbolic Action, Cultural Pragmatics, and Ritual*. Cambridge: Cambridge University Press, pp. 29–90.

Alexander, J. C. and Colomy, P. 1990. *Differentiation Theory and Social Change*. New York: Columbia University Press.

Althusser, L. 1972. *For Marx*. New York: Pantheon (originally in French, 1965).

Althusser, L. and Balibar, E. 1970. *Reading Capital*. London: New Left Books (originally in French, 1968).

Cohen, P. 1968. *Modern Social Theory*. London: Heinemann.

Colomy, P. 1997. Jeffrey C. Alexander's neofunctionalism. In J. H. Turner (ed.), *The Structure of Sociological Theory*. Belmont, CA: Wadsworth-Thomson, pp. 43–59.

Durkheim, E. 1982. *The Rules of Sociological Method, and Selected Texts on Sociology and its Method*. London: Macmillan (originally in French, 1895; reprinted, 1992).

Durkheim, E. 1984. *The Division of Labour in Society*. Basingstoke: Macmillan (originally in French, 1893).

Elias, N. 1978. *What is Sociology?* New York: Columbia University Press (originally in German, 1970).

Geertz, C. 1973. *The Interpretation of Cultures: Selected Essays*. New York: Basic Books.

Giddens, A. 1977. *Studies in Social and Political Theory.* London: Hutchinson.

Giddens, A. 1979. *Central Problems in Social Theory: Action, Structure and Contradiction in Social Analysis.* London: Macmillan.

Giddens, A. 1981. Agency, institution and time-space analysis. In K. Knorr-Cetina and A. V. Cicourel (eds), *Advances in Social Theory and Methodology: Towards an Integration of Micro- and Macro-Sociologies.* London: Routledge, pp. 161–75.

Giddens, A. 1984. *The Constitution of Society. Outline of the Theory of Structuration.* Cambridge: Polity.

Homans, G. 1961. *Social Behavior: Its Elementary Forms.* New York: Brace and World.

Knorr-Cetina, K. and Cicourel, A. V. (eds) 1981. *Advances in Social Theory and Methodology: Towards an Integration of Micro- and Macro-Sociologies.* London: Routledge.

Kuper, A. (ed.) 1977. *The Social Anthropology of Radcliffe-Brown.* London: Routledge & Kegan Paul.

Kuper, A. 1978. *Anthropologists and Anthropology; The British School 1922–1972.* London: Penguin.

Latour, B. and Woolgar, S. 1986. *Laboratory Life: The Construction of Scientific Facts.* Princeton, NJ: Princeton University Press.

Levine, D. N. 1995. *Visions of the Sociological Tradition.* Chicago, IL: University of Chicago Press.

Luhmann, N. 1982. *The Differentiation of Society.* New York: Columbia University Press.

Luhmann, N. 1990. *Essays on Self-Reference.* New York: Columbia University Press.

Malinowski, B. 1944. *A Scientific Theory of Culture.* Chapel Hill: University of North Carolina Press.

Marcuse, H. 1968. *One-dimensional Man.* London: Verso.

Merton, R. K. 1968. *Social Theory and Social Structure.* New York: The Free Press (enlarged edition).

Münch, R. 2000. *Ethics of Modernity: Formation and Transformation in Britain, France, Germany and the United States.* Lanham, MD: Rowman & Littlefield.

Münch, R. 2001. *Nation and Citizenship in the Global Age: From National to Transnational Ties and Identities.* New York: Palgrave.

Parsons, T. 1937. *The Structure of Social Action; A Study in Social Theory with Special Reference to a Group of Recent European Writers.* New York: McGraw-Hill.

Parsons, T. 1951. *The Social System.* London: Routledge & Kegan Paul.

Parsons, T. 1960. Pattern variables revisited: A response to Robert Dubin. *American Sociological Review* 25(4): 467–83.

Parsons, T. 1966. *Societies: Evolutionary and Comparative Perspectives.* Englewood Cliffs, NJ: Prentice-Hall.

Parsons, T. 1977. *The Evolution of Societies*. Englewood Cliffs, NJ: Prentice-Hall.

Radcliffe-Brown, A. R. 1952. *Structure and Function in Primitive Society*. London: Cohen and West Limited.

Radcliffe-Brown, A. R. 1958. *Method in Social Anthropology*. Chicago, IL: University of Chicago Press.

Rocher, G. 1974. *Talcott Parsons and American Sociology*. London: Thomas Nelson (originally in French, 1972).

Sztompka, P. 1986. *Robert Merton: An Intellectual Profile*. London: Macmillan.

3

The Enigma of Everyday Life

Symbolic Interactionism, the Dramaturgical
Approach and Ethnomethodology

In the previous chapters we discussed two theoretical traditions which tend to focus upon macro-sociological issues, dealing with those societal entities that transcend the routines and contingencies of our daily life. In a sense, this picture dominated the sociological scene in the 1950s, and probably added to an increasing, though fragile, sense of self-assurance amongst sociologists. Whereas social psychology was thought to deal merely with the empirical study of interactions between individuals, to sociology was attributed the pivotal task of unmasking latent functions or hidden societal structures stretching over long periods of time. Back in the early nineteenth century, Auguste Comte, never missing an opportunity to express his feelings of grandeur, christened his own child, *la physique sociale* or *la sociologie*, as nothing less than the queen of sciences. During the heyday of structuralism and functionalism, and after having lost part of its dominance, sociology considered itself still to be the head of the social sciences. Soon, however, even that title had to go.

The pretension to supremacy disappeared once sociologists were forced to recognize the sociological importance of a number of studies which were traditionally considered only to be relevant to social psychology. Three schools are significant here, all distinctly American, but each conceptually very different from the other. The first school, often referred to as 'symbolic interactionism', goes back to pragmatism in philosophy and, in particular, to the work of the American philosopher G. H. Mead (1863–1931); other influences include Georg Simmel (1858–1918) and G. H. F. Hegel (1770–1831). The second school, the so-called 'dramaturgical approach', centres around Erving Goffman's (1922–82) writings. Mead, Simmel and Durkheim had a significant impact on Goffman's thought. The third school, headed by Harold Garfinkel (1926–), answers to the unfortunate name of 'ethnomethodology'. It is philosophically rooted in, inter alia, Alfred Schutz's phenomenology and the later Wittgenstein.

If macro-sociology lost its monopoly in the 1960s, it did not happen all at once. Once the ideas of symbolic interactionism, the dramaturgical approach and ethnomethodology became widespread within the sociological community, they received mixed and extreme responses. For some, the new creeds represented innovative and challenging alternatives to the hypothetic co-deductive and structural-functionalist 'dogmas' of the day. But others saw the new approaches as trivial, as stating the obvious, or as new wine in old barrels. More extreme critics challenged their alleged subjectivist and individualistic biases as nothing less than heresy from a sociological point of view. At the time, there was no decisive winner in this battle, but attitudes have since changed. Some of the concepts and methods introduced by these new approaches have gradually filtered through. This gradual acceptance is demonstrated by their usage in attempts in the 1980s to develop a grand theory of society. Anthony Giddens's structuration theory relied heavily on Goffman's dramaturgical approach and ethnomethodology, and Jürgen Habermas's theory of communicative action made use of symbolic interactionist notions (see chapters 5 and 7).

In the 1990s these attempts at grand theoretical syntheses gradually gave way to more focused, less ambitious undertakings. In addition, the traditional emphasis on large-scale institutional features of modern societies (the social system, the state, social class, etc.) was replaced by the study of the more loosely defined features of contemporary societies. Global migrations, transnational identities, virtual communities and political consumerism are but a few examples of the plethora of exciting new topics that interest social scientists today. In the final section of the chapter, we discuss one such topic – trust – in order to illustrate how the work of Garfinkel and Goffman still inspires current micro-sociological analyses of human action today (for example, the work of Randall Collins), as well as how interactionism and microstructural analysis can be productively combined with rational choice theory, as is demonstrated in the work of Russell Hardin.[1]

G. H. Mead and symbolic interactionism

As mentioned above, symbolic interactionists depended on Mead's work. Although some would argue that they use a particularly idiosyncratic reading of it, an exposition of Mead's social psychology acts as an important stepping-stone towards understanding the full scope of symbolic interactionism. The term itself was only coined by Herbert Blumer in 1937 – after the death of Mead, who was a contemporary of

Durkheim and Weber – and the movement was not in full swing until the 1960s.

Mead studied at Oberlin College, Harvard, Leipzig and Berlin, and taught most of his life alongside John Dewey in the philosophy department of the then newly founded University of Chicago, a position he got by invitation of Dewey (who resigned from Chicago in 1904 and was offered a position in Columbia the following year). Mead and Dewey became close friends, regularly exchanging ideas; this explains, to some degree, the similarities of their respective philosophies. However, where Dewey's influence was prominent in philosophy and education, Mead's work was to be remembered especially for its contributions to core issues in social psychology and sociology. While Dewey was very prolific and, at an early age, already the rising star of American philosophy, Mead, although an inspiring teacher, was arguably a less productive writer. He never completed a book or monograph and only published his first fully developed article at the age of 40. He only gained wider renown posthumously through the publication of a number of books based on his lectures. Amongst these 'student notes', *Mind, Self and Society* (1934) has been particularly important for our understanding of the relationship between language, social interaction and reflectivity. Less widely known, but still of some interest to sociologists, is the enigmatic and vast *The Philosophy of the Act* (1938), which links insights from evolutionary theory with Mead's own 'social behaviourism'. For those interested in the philosophical problem of time, there is the even more obscure *The Philosophy of the Present* (1959), Mead's somewhat muddled attempt to integrate evolutionary biology, Bergsonian philosophy, the theory of relativity and his own social psychology. Finally, there is his sketchy *Movements of Thought in the Nineteenth Century* (1936), which, amongst other things, attempts to show the growing importance of time in science and philosophy. Of these four volumes, *Mind, Self and Society* is undoubtedly the most accessible, although there are the inevitable ambiguities to be expected from a book not directly written by the author.

Although partly borrowed from nineteenth-century German philosophy, Mead's views, as expressed in *Mind, Self and Society*, were very much ahead of their time. For instance, by elaborating upon the social nature of the self and meaning, he anticipated some of the pivotal ideas in Wittgenstein's *Philosophical Investigations*. Long before the adequacy of positivist epistemology became an issue for the social sciences, Mead expressed doubts on the validity of J. B. Watson's behaviourism for social psychology, and developed an alternative scenario in which the notion of reflective self-monitoring plays a central role.[2] It comes as no surprise that those contributors to social psychology, such as Rom Harré and Paul Secord, who attempted to create a counterweight to the imperium of positivist and quantitative methods, drew heavily, not only upon the widely acclaimed 'later' Wittgenstein, but also upon Mead (Harré and Secord 1972).

One of Mead's core concepts is the self. The self is a feature of human beings, and of human beings only. It implies the capacity to be an object to oneself from an outsider's perspective (1934: 136ff.). While writing this paragraph, for instance, we take up the attitude of the imaginary reader and thereby look upon alternative ways of expressing ourselves before choosing one of them. Strongly opposing the Cartesian picture of a 'solitary' self, one of Mead's central claims is that the self cannot but be a *social* self, bound as it is with social interaction and language (ibid.: 1, 48–51, 140, 222ff.; 1964: 105–13, 243). It is fair to say that there are two ways in which Mead's concept of the self is a *social* self, although the distinction is not one drawn by himself. Let us call them the 'symbolic' and the 'interactionist' dimensions of the social self, for reasons which will soon become clear (see Baert 1992: 56–7). The interactionist dimension is the more straightforward of the two. It refers to people's capacity to adopt the attitude of others. It is indeed by seeing ourselves from the perspective of the imaginary reader that we are able to reflect upon the meaning of alternative ways of expressing ourselves.

The self is social not only because of its interactionist dimension, but also because of its dependency on the sharing of symbols, in particular language, with other selves. Here, the symbolic dimension comes into play. To take up the above example again, it is precisely because we and our imaginary reader share knowledge of the English language that we are able to anticipate what the meaning of our writings would be for that person. Whenever signs are shared, Mead uses the terms 'significant gestures' and 'significant communication' (1934: 61ff., 81ff.). Interaction amongst animals is limited to non-significant communication. The barking of one dog to another might elicit the latter's reaction, but that reaction is never anticipated by the first dog. Although our examples hitherto have been limited to language, Mead's symbolic world also involves 'non-verbal gestures' and 'non-verbal communication'. Greeting somebody, nodding, table manners, winking at somebody or ignoring that person – these are all examples of non-verbal communication. They are not dissimilar to verbal communication in that they also involve the self and its attendant reflectivity, and rely upon a background knowledge of shared meaning for a successful outcome.

Obviously, the self ties in with self-reflection and what are currently called self-control and self-monitoring. By self-reflection, a term occasionally employed by Mead himself but left undefined, social psychologists refer to the ability of individuals to reflect upon their own circumstances, on the meaning and effects of their own (imaginary, possible or real) actions, on their beliefs about themselves, and on their beliefs about their beliefs. Self-control or self-monitoring are terms of more recent origin, not explicitly used by Mead, but clearly implied in his writings on the self. As it is now commonly used, self-control refers to the ability of individuals to direct their own actions on the basis of self-reflection; self-monitoring is that form of self-reflection directed towards self-control (see, e.g., Mischel and Mischel 1977). To consider again the example of writing, self-monitoring implies that one reflects upon the meaning of alternative ways of expressing oneself and then chooses from amongst these alternatives. The picture thus provided is very different indeed from John B. Watson's behaviourism – the dominant argument in American psychology at the beginning of the twentieth century. Watson's view was unsubtle, if not crude, even by behaviourist standards: human actions were to be seen as analogous to animal behaviour, to be explained and predicted through a stimulus-response mechanism. Watson excluded concepts that are not immediately observable, such as mind or self. Mead's social psychology is very much directed against this extreme form of external determinism. People are different from animals because they have selves. The fact that the self is not immediately accessible to observation is not sufficient for it to be banned from scientific analysis. The self and reflectivity go hand in hand, and reflectivity implies that people's actions cannot be explained, let alone predicted, by a simple stimulus-response mechanism.

It is not uncommon for authors to become well known to the public for some of their less penetrating or less well-developed notions, and Mead is not an exception to this unfortunate pattern. His distinction between the 'I' and the 'me' occupies a central role in the secondary literature, although it remains ill-defined throughout *Mind, Self and Society* (1934: 173–8, 192ff.). The distinction is reminiscent of Henri Bergson's dynamic and static self, and it is not unlikely that, in this context, Mead was directly influenced by the French philosopher, since, as can be inferred from some of his articles and lecture notes, he was well acquainted with Bergson's work (see, e.g., Mead 1907; 1936: 503–10). On one reading, the 'me' stands for the societal, conservative components of the self, and the 'I' refers to its idiosyncratic, innovating aspects. If the 'me' sets the limits of the game through rules about which moves are allowed and which are not, the 'I' refers to the unpredictable nature of any move. But on another reading, the difference between the 'I' and the 'me' is that the latter is by definition an object to the former. The 'I' can never be observed. Whenever one tries to catch the 'I', whenever one attempts to observe it, it vanishes, for that which one observes cannot but be the 'me'. Whenever the 'I' acts, it instantly transforms into the 'me' and is thus inevitably lost in the past. One can recall it, but only as the 'me'.

The interactionist dimension of the self has so far been discussed in terms of an individual's ability to take up the attitude of *single* others. However, one of Mead's central assertions in *Mind, Self and Society* is that people, looking at themselves from the perspective of other individuals, often take up the attitude of the 'generalized other' (1934: 152–64; 1964: 245–7, 284ff.). This refers to a collective whole, which transcends the idiosyncratic features of its individual members. While writing, we see ourselves from the perspective of an imaginary reader insofar as he or she is representative of a larger community of English language readers. By taking up the attitude of the generalized other, one takes into account rules and conventions which belong to a larger community, not merely to isolated individuals. The generalized other thus points at the societal nature of the 'me' component of the self. However, this should not compel us to believe that the generalized other is merely constraining the 'I'. It is not *in spite of*, but *because of* a set of commonly shared rules and conventions that a creative 'I' is able to come into being. If there were no language, the creative poet would have no resources. Change presupposes structure – there can be no creation *ex nihilo*.

Mead's writings are not free from criticism. Given that Blumer's symbolic interactionism very much relied upon Mead's social psychology, we will deal with Mead's relevance for sociology when we discuss Blumer. We will now assess the validity of some core philosophical argumentations which Mead presented. Mead's central philosophical position is the notion that the self is social, but he was unclear as to what this meant exactly. Going through his writings, it is possible to attribute two separate meanings to this notion. First, he made the strong claim that society and shared symbols are a necessary (and maybe sufficient) condition for the emergence of the self. Second, he made the weaker claim that it is fruitful, for the purposes of social psychology, to conceive of the self in relation to society and shared symbols. Mead's writings have shown convincingly the validity of the weaker claim, but they fail to provide any substantial support for the stronger anti-Cartesian thesis. At times, he seemed to assume mistakenly that evidence in support of the weaker claim necessarily implies evidence in support of the stronger claim.

There are similar ambiguities in his philosophical critique of behaviourist psychology. First, he presented an internal criticism. He seemed to claim in particular that the importance of reflectivity in human conduct makes for the inherent unpredictability of human behaviour to the extent that behaviourism fails to make the accurate predictions which it sets out to make. Second, he presented an external critique. The argument here is that, by neglecting the self, behaviourism cuts out that which is essential to human interaction. Taking the self into account leads to an enriched understanding of human conduct. Mead backed his external critique rather well, though not his internal critique. He did show successfully that his notion of the self leads to a more sophisticated understanding of the interface between individual and society. But nowhere in his writings can be found conclusive evidence or argumentation to support the statement that, due to the self, behaviour is inherently unpredictable.

As mentioned earlier, Mead's notion of a creative social self was directed against the dominant views of the day. It was Watson's determinism which had to be defeated, not by regressing into an introspective subjectivism, but by going beyond a Cartesian dualism of mind and body, and beyond an opposition between society and the individual. If behaviourism was always at the back of his mind, a similar mainstream argument was, half a century later, the target of the new school of symbolic interactionism. Symbolic interactionism emerged as a reaction against the dominant sociological practices of the day – against the alleged obsession with quantitative methods and structural-functionalist explanations (see chapters 1 and 2). Durkheim's heritage, and particularly his positivist methodology, was now considered too burdensome for the social sciences, whose subject area, because of its very nature, resists a positivist strait-jacket.

Herbert Blumer (1900–87) was one of the instigators of the rebellion and, incidentally, also responsible for coining the term 'symbolic interactionism'.[3] He had been a student at Chicago, taught there for a while, and then moved to Columbia where he became a central counterpart to and critic of Merton's functionalism and Lazarsfeld's quantitative sociology. Blumer had been a student of Mead's, and was of the opinion that the sociological community had much to learn from him. Then followed a long journey of rediscovery – not only of Mead, but also of Dewey and the origins of American pragmatism. As so often with rediscoveries, however, it was a somewhat coloured one, directed towards Blumer's ambitions for a new paradigm of sociology and inevitably reflecting his own ideas as well as those of Mead. Although it is an endearing feature of Blumer that he attributed so many of his own ideas to his mentor, and was sometimes justified in doing so, it has nevertheless unintentionally led to a slightly distorted reading of Mead.

Blumer's research programme is best approached through *Symbolic Interactionism*, a collection of essays in which he spelled out the core propositions of his theoretical argument. Four ideas are central to his version of symbolic interactionism. First, he followed Mead in stressing that individuals have selves and therefore a capacity for 'self-interaction' (Blumer 1969: 62–4). Self-interaction comes into play whenever people make indications to themselves – whenever they address themselves and respond to the address before acting in public. Self-interaction enables them to evaluate and analyse things in order to plan ahead. So the individual's behaviour is not to be seen as a mere response to the environment; neither is it the outcome of need-dispositions, attitudes, unconscious motives or social values. Through interacting with themselves, people are able to anticipate the effects of alternative lines of conduct and thus to choose amongst them.

Second, Blumer deviated from Mead's social behaviourism in adding a sociological dimension, alluding, like Parsons, to Hobbes's problem of order. Parsons's answer to Hobbes's dilemma is essentially a Durkheimian one, referring as it does to the internalization of central social values; for Blumer, the persistence of established social patterns is contingent upon people's recurrent use of identical forms of interpretation (ibid.: 65–8). One's interpretative scheme is, in its turn, dependent on confirmation by consistent interpretative schemes by others. By thus opening the path for a cognitive account of social order, Blumer anticipated Garfinkel's ethnomethodology. He went further than that, however. Compared to Garfinkel, he is more wary of portraying social life as nothing but social order, insisting that people regularly redefine each other's acts, possibly leading to new objects, new interactions or new types of behaviour.

Third, people act towards their environment on the basis of the meaning they attribute to it. For Blumer, meaning is not intrinsic to objects, neither is it a mere expression of the individual's mind (ibid.: 68–70). Following the American pragmatic tradition, Blumer argued that the meaning of an object for an individual emanates from the individual's tendency to act towards it. Thus, a person's readiness to use a pencil as something to write with gives the object the meaning of what we call 'a pencil'. It follows that each object can have various meanings – potentially an infinite number of them. Grouse are not the same to a grouse-shooter as they are to an animal rights campaigner. And they are different objects again for a discerning gourmet who chooses them as his or her main course, or for a bird-watcher or a scholarly ornithologist. This tendency to act in a particular way is, in its turn, constituted, maintained and modified by the ways in which others refer to that object or act towards it. Within the household, for instance, numerous expectations by husband and children obviously reinforce a particular meaning of womanhood.

Fourth, Blumer used the term 'joint action' to refer to a 'societal organization of conduct of different acts of diverse participants' (ibid.: 17, 70–7). Examples of joint actions are a marriage, a lecture, a tennis match or a church service. Like Durkheim's concept of social fact, which should not be seen as the mere outcome of psychological phenomena, Blumer's 'joint action', although made up of the component acts, is different from each of them, and from their aggregate. In other respects, however, Blumer's symbolic interactionism differs substantially from the view spelled out in Durkheim's *Rules of Sociological Method*, or it at least contrasts with a number of views that have traditionally been attributed to Durkheim. Durkheim's notion of social facts as *external* led to a picture of repetitive and pre-established forms of social life that are independent of an interpretative process. Blumer, instead, insisted that joint actions, however stable, are formed out of the component acts, and hence dependent on the attribution of meaning. So even in the most repetitive of joint actions 'each instance of such joint action has to be formed anew. The participants still have to build up their lines of action and fit them to one another through the dual process of designation and interpretation' (ibid.: 18). Despite this, Blumer came closer to Durkheim's claim about the externality of social facts when he argues that people, while attributing meaning, draw upon pre-existing frames of interpretation. This Durkheimian notion allowed Blumer to allude to the historical dimension of joint actions. Each form of joint action, whether old or new, grows out of previous joint actions. As for Mead, there is no *tabula rasa* possible in Blumer's portrait of the social world.

Sociologists and social theorists have remained critical of Mead's social behaviourism and Blumer's symbolic interactionism. Underlying their scepticism is often the assumption that any substantial theoretical contribution to the study of society ought to take account of two core insights. First, there is the Durkheimian view that sociology should focus on the way in which people's conduct is constrained by social structure. Second, there is the Weberian position that sociologists should be sensitive to the unintended effects of purposive action. The critique of Mead and

Blumer has often been that they do not account for either social structure or unintended effects, and thus that, however fruitful their work
might be as a contribution to social psychology, they fail as a social
theory. Our view is that the critique is partly justified, and we will explain
why.

Let us first consider the Durkheimian notion, and assess Mead's and
Blumer's work in this light. There is no ambiguity in the case of Blumer:
he deliberately avoided reference to structure. However, things are more
complicated in the case of Mead. Contrary to the accepted view, we
believe that Mead's writings do *not necessarily* neglect social structure; it
simply depends on how one wishes to define structure. If one decides to
follow the more recent trend in social theory to conceive of structures as
rules and resources (see, e.g., Giddens 1993), Mead's notion of the self and
its attendant concept of the generalized other indeed imply the concept
of structure. After all, to adopt the arguments of others implies the internalization of the community's implicit shared rules. Notwithstanding this
fact, insofar as Mead's writings do recognize structure, they exhibit a one-
sided, if not an impoverished, understanding of it. In Mead's work, the
generalized other appears mostly as a medium which allows for (rather
than precludes) agency, and as enabling (rather than constraining).
Remember that, from a Meadian perspective, it is precisely because of the
'me' components of the self that the creative 'I' comes into being. There
is no hint of the Durkheimian insight that structures, as unacknowledged
conditions, constrain and determine people's actions (cf. Durkheim 1982:
50ff.; see also chapter 1). From a Durkheimian view, language or mental
frameworks can limit people's capacities to imagine what are possible
forms of life or possible life choices. Moreover, even if certain choices are
thought of as theoretically possible, the internalized generalized other is
constraining in that it links particular imaginary choices with particular
effects (see chapter 1).

Mead and Blumer have also been criticized for neglecting the concept
of unintended consequences. Here again, critiques are partly justified.
Mead and Blumer did occasionally mention that individuals are regularly
faced with novel or unanticipated events, which lead to the emergence of
reflectivity (Maines et al. 1983: 163ff.; Mead 1929). Moreover, in his writings on pragmatic philosophy, Mead also referred to the phenomenon of
trial and error of scientific activities in which scientists learn from their
mistakes (1936: 264–91, 507ff.; 1959: 13ff.). Nevertheless, nowhere in
Mead's or Blumer's work can be found a systematic attempt to see some
of these unanticipated events or 'mistakes' as unintended or unforeseen

effects of previous actions. Again, from the point of view of sociology, though not social psychology, this is a serious lacuna.

There are other ambiguities in Mead's and Blumer's work, which make it less useful for sociological purposes. Take, for instance, the notion of reflectivity, one of the key notions in symbolic interactionism. Mead and Blumer used this concept in at least two different ways. One is what might be called 'reflectivity of the first order', which involves tacit knowledge and self-reflective monitoring. Here, people reflect upon their actions, imaginary or real. When we speak, for instance, we reflect upon imaginary ways of expressing ourselves. This reflectivity of the first order is obviously prominent in *Mind, Self and Society* and *Symbolic Interactionism*, but occasionally both Mead and Blumer seemed to suggest a very different type of reflectivity, alluding to people's capacity to reflect not just upon their actions, but upon the underlying structural conditions of these actions. This 'reflectivity of the second order' ties in with explicit and discursive knowledge.[4] In Mead's and Blumer's work, both types of reflectivity blur into one. For sociological purposes, however, the distinction is indispensable. Reflectivity of the first order is central to our daily interactions, embedded as they are in routine practices and interwoven with the unintentional reproduction of structures.[5] Reflectivity of the second order is characteristic of 'high modernity' and, if developed by more than the single individual and part of a public-collective discussion, becomes a potential source for deliberate maintenance or deliberate change (see also Baert 1992).

How, from a sociological point of view, does Blumer compare to Mead? First, it is ironic that, whereas Blumer tried to demonstrate the sociological significance of Mead, he failed to take on board some of the latter's crucial sociological insights. Mead recognized the central role of the generalized other in reflectivity. It is due to shared meaning that people are able to anticipate the effects of alternative lines of conduct. The generalized other is absent in Blumer's picture, and that is a major weakness. Second, compared to Blumer, Mead's work erroneously presents a view of society that is too consensual, which may be reminiscent of more traditional orders, but surely inadequate for grasping more advanced societies. Blumer avoided presenting this picture, and rightly so. Some shared meaning might be necessary for any society to operate smoothly, but society today is characterized by the mutual coexistence of distinct cultural forms. There is certainly not just one set of implicit rules and procedures. Third, compared to Mead's purely philosophical enterprise, Blumer's strength lay in the way in which he was able to link his theory with issues of research methodology, as can be inferred from his criticisms of survey research and from his writings on the role of qualitative research methodology within a symbolic interactionist frame of reference. Loyal to the dynamic features of Mead's theory of the self and society, Blumer stressed the dynamic nature of social life – the continuous readaptation to an ever-changing environment – a feature that a number of contemporary methods failed to capture.

Erving Goffman's dramaturgical approach

Goffman's decision to study sociology was not a straightforward one. Initially, he specialized in the natural sciences, then he dropped out of university, toyed with the idea of going into films, and only later decided to take up postgraduate work in sociology and anthropology at the University of Chicago. By then, Chicago had built up a considerable tradition of empirical social research; Everett Hughes and Blumer were amongst the inspiring teachers there. After graduating and publishing the widely acclaimed *The Presentation of Self in Everyday Life* (1969), Goffman taught for 10 years at the University of Berkeley, where he collaborated closely with Gregory Bateson. Amongst other things, Bateson and his group studied the phenomenon of mental illness, and there are, undoubtedly, similarities between their approach and Goffman's account of the mentally ill. Goffman subsequently moved to the University of Pennsylvania, where he developed a keen interest in the work of a group of sociolinguists. Again, this interest led to intense collaboration, and Goffman's writings increasingly dealt with the sociological dimensions of speech and conversation. His last book, *Forms of Talk* (1981), is a compilation of essays dealing with this topic, and conversational analysis often draws on Goffman's later work.

Goffman's work is sometimes referred to within the context of symbolic interactionism, and there are obvious reasons for linking the two. Both made a conscious attempt to avoid explaining human conduct in terms of system imperatives. Both saw as their object of study the interaction patterns between individuals. Both emphasized that these individuals have the ability to reflect upon their actions, and thus to manipulate their environment. However, there are also clear differences. Compared with Blumer's ambitious claims, for instance, Goffman consciously avoided the development of a consistent theoretical frame of reference (something he has often been criticized for). Also, in some respects, Goffman's work is even closer to Garfinkel than to Blumer, in particular when he referred to the way in which social order and predictability are skilful accomplishments of the individuals involved. Goffman's work, idiosyncratic and innovative as it was, cannot be written off as a mere appendix to symbolic interactionism, and it is worth elaborating upon its major themes.

Goffman has always been rather critical of the tendency to categorize or classify an author's work. This might explain why he hardly ever acknowledged major intellectual influences on his own work. Two influences are, however, beyond doubt: Simmel and Mead. Let us first deal with the German sociologist Georg Simmel. His attention to the 'unnamed or unknown tissues' of social life struck a chord with Goffman. First, like Simmel, Goffman portrayed daily life as a highly complex enterprise in which human beings employ tacit and practical knowledge as they go along. Analogously to Simmel, and anticipating some of Garfinkel's central assertions, Goffman referred to the seen-but-unnoticed character of most of our mundane activities (see also Manning 1992). Second, Simmel's analysis of modern culture demonstrated the extent to which the anonymous character of modern life, rather than leading to an ethos of cynical manipulation, made for the emergence of interactions which are heavily dependent on complex mechanisms of secrecy and mutual trust. Simmel's starting point is that for interaction between modern, urban individuals to be possible, they need a minimum of information about each other. However, even as each individual attempts to obtain information about others, so must the information which others receive from that individual be controlled (Simmel 1950: 307–78). Goffman presented a similar view. People are constantly monitoring themselves, masking bits of their selves and accentuating other aspects. The way we dress, the way we speak, our gestures – all these are meant both to convey and to conceal who we are.

This brings us to Mead's influence. Mead and Goffman both portray a dynamic self, actively intervening in the world. Like Mead, Goffman accentuated the extent to which people are reflective beings, able to monitor their actions and, thus, to manipulate their surroundings. Remember that Mead acknowledged that people share meaning, and are therefore able to anticipate the effects of alternative imaginary courses of action. Goffman's portrait of social life assumes this Meadian framework. The existence of what Mead called a generalized other is indeed a *sine qua non* for the successful masking and presenting of the self. Without shared meaning, the subtle mechanisms of concealment and revelation would break down.

Goffman's interest was in 'encounters'; that is, face-to-face interactions where people are constantly in the physical presence of others. Encounters can involve 'unfocused' or 'focused' interaction, the distinction being mainly a matter of absence versus existence of mutual awareness amongst the participants involved (Goffman 1963: 24ff.; 1972a: 7–13). Reminiscent of Mead's account of the self and role-taking, Goffman argued that, in interaction, human beings are continuously attending to their own actions while adopting other people's views. A brief account of *The Presentation of Self in Everyday Life* will demonstrate how Goffman's analysis of encounters works.

Goffman analysed encounters by drawing upon metaphors from and analogies with the theatre, hence the reference to his work as dramaturgical. He was, of course, not the only one to do this. Shakespeare is renowned for portraying social life by means of role-playing. Ralf Dahrendorf's concept of '*homo sociologicus*' draws upon a similar picture. However, analogies with acting and the stage have often led to a picture of social life as somehow predetermined. This is surely not the case in Goffman's dramaturgical approach. In his view, it is fair to say, people do not merely follow a script, and insofar as they do, they are also the author of that very same script. Hence 'performances', Goffman's main topic of research, are defined by him as all activities by individuals which serve to *influence* the 'audience' within the encounter (1969: 28ff.). In his view, these performances are rule-governed, in that rules refer to tacit, practical codes with respect to appropriate behaviour.

The 'front' is that aspect of the performance which, in a 'general and fixed fashion', helps the audience to define the situation (ibid.: 32ff.). There are two important aspects to a front: the setting and the personal front. The setting, 'the scenic parts of expressive equipment', refers to background items which provide the scene and 'stage props' for the action to take place; for instance, *décor*. Whereas the setting is usually linked to a particular place, the 'personal front' refers to those items which are intimately linked to the performer and which therefore are likely to follow him or her around; for instance, body language or speech patterns. Personal front can be divided into 'appearance' and 'manner'. Appearance refers primarily to the social status of a performer, but it also indicates his or her 'temporary ritual state'; for instance, whether he or she is involved in work or in leisure, or how busy he or she is. Manner indicates which role the performer intends to play in the forthcoming interaction; for instance, an aloof manner might indicate a reduced commitment on the part of the performer. Normally, people expect some consistency between setting, appearance and manner, but sometimes this is not the case, which can lead to quite humorous situations – for instance, where somebody puts on a manner out of synch with his or her social status. It is characteristic of social fronts that they are abstract and general, applicable to different situations. In this context, Goffman gives the example of white labcoats commonly used in many professions, creating an aura of 'professionalism' and reliability (ibid.: 36–7).

In general, as they interact, people have to dramatize their activities in order to give the impression that they are performing well and that they have things under control. Sometimes the two are not compatible. A student who focuses on conveying to a teacher that he or she is listening might exert so much time and energy doing so that little of the teaching is absorbed. Part of this dramatization is that people, during their performances, tend to give expression to the 'officially accredited values of society', a habit obvious from examples of those who aspire to the lifestyle of their social or economic superiors (or at least what they believe that lifestyle to be). Sometimes people downplay their qualities, such as in the case of teenagers who, in the company of members of the opposite sex, may play at being rather naive and silly. In both these scenarios, people often have to conceal those actions or signs that are inconsistent with the yearned for standards.

Whereas the above might appear highly individualistic, Goffman introduces the concept of 'team' to refer to a group of people who cooperate to maintain a particular definition of a situation. Teams have certain characteristics in common (ibid.: 83–108). They imply loyalty and competence by each of the individuals involved, since a failure by one of them might be threatening for all. Goffman also introduces space into the analysis, the concept of region referring to any place which indicates the barrier between what is visible to the audience and what is not (ibid.: 109–40). Whereas performances take place in the front region, the back regions involve supporting or preparatory activities for the front region. The back region provides the means for an emotional outlet for the front region, an obvious example being the waiter who politely takes orders, but once in the kitchen expresses his contemptuous feelings for the customer. Goffman introduces the concept of 'impression management' to summarize the above mechanisms (ibid.: 203–30). Individuals tend to control the way in which they are perceived by others through a number of devices. There are, first of all, the 'defensive attributes and practices', including, for instance, 'dramaturgical loyalty', which means that team members have to be able to trust each other and to keep secrets. Second, there are the 'protective practices'. Here, through tact, it is the audience itself that helps the performers save their show. An example of this counterintuitive claim is the case where the audience voluntarily stays away from back regions, or where people display tactful inattention once confronted with embarrassing situations. A third type of device refers to the fact that performers have to be sensitive to any hints provided by the audience so that they can alter their behaviour accordingly.

In other works, Goffman elaborated upon the rule-governed nature of the social world, drawing a number of central distinctions: between symmetrical and asymmetrical rules, between regulative and constitutive rules and, above all, between substantive and ceremonial rules (1972b: 48–56ff.). Compared to asymmetrical rules, symmetrical ones imply reciprocal expectations. Whereas regulative rules provide people with behavioural guidelines in particular circumstances, constitutive rules provide the context in which regulative rules might apply. Whereas substantive rules direct behaviour with respect to those areas of life which seem to have significance in their own right, Goffman's interest was directed towards those rules which he coined 'ceremonial' and which are directed towards conduct in matters which have, at most, secondary significance by themselves. These rules, however trivial at first blush, are central to sustaining feelings of psychological security and trust. Goffman distinguished between two components of such ceremonial rules: demeanour and deference (ibid.: 56–95). The latter refers to the way in which people present themselves as reliable and able to be counted upon. The former refers to the way in which people sustain ontological security and trust by expressing appreciation through 'avoidance rituals' and 'presentational rituals'. Avoidance rituals keep intact the ideal spheres (Simmel's terminology) surrounding the individuals: silencing embarrassing episodes are one of them. Presentational rituals are positive tools for honouring individuals through, for example, salutations, invitations and compliments.

A central notion in Goffman's work is that of 'situational propriety', referring to the way in which the meaning of actions or concepts is dependent on the context in which they emerge (1963: 24, 193–7, 216–41). This notion ties in with a previous point in that, as human beings, we gradually learn practical and tacit knowledge which enables us to understand the meaning of actions within a particular context. Many manifestations of mental illness demonstrate situationally inappropriate behaviour in that the very same conduct might have been acceptable were the context a different one. The notion of practical and tacit knowledge also ties in with Goffman's concept of 'involvement', referring to the way in which people are able to give or withhold attention to others in a given situation. Involvement ties in with two other notions: accessibility and civil inattention. The former refers to our tacit knowledge with respect to the degrees of availability towards strangers and acquaintances, whereas the latter refers to our ability to acknowledge the presence of strangers, while avoiding prolonged attention through a sign of deference. Civil inattention is one of the ways in which strangers mutually reinforce feelings of trust and of relative predictability. This becomes especially obvious whenever civil inattention is not obeyed, often a sign of outright hostility on the part of the person who breaks the rule, and which results in the other party feeling uneasy and distraught.

For a long time, social theorists have neglected Goffman's work, for three reasons. First, some stated that, although he introduced a wide range of new concepts, his work lacks a consistent theoretical frame of reference. His work is descriptive. At best, the theory is implicit in it; at worst, the theory is absent. Second, some critics have stated that Goffman expressed nothing new. There are two sides to this critique. On the one hand, it is argued that a significant number of Goffman's insights had already been made by social scientists and novelists who preceded him. On the other hand, some objected to the fact Goffman's work states the obvious: it articulates what every socially accomplished person already practically knows. Third, it has been argued that Goffman's concept of the self is not a universal one. His framework is indicative of modern Western culture, 'other-directed' as it is, in which people cynically stage things, constantly calculating and manipulating their environment, and in which other individuals are treated as mere objects.

These criticisms are only partly justified. With regard to the first, it is not entirely fair to accuse Goffman of neglecting theory construction. Although it is the case that the main thrust of his approach is more descriptive than explanatory, his later work, *Frame Analysis*, provides ample evidence that he was interested in constructing 'general statements' on the structure of human behaviour (1974: xiv). In his view, the primary object of sociology is not culture or the class structure, but rather the structure and organization of ordinary actual behaviour (ibid.: 564). When social agents enter a certain situation, they are immediately confronted with the question, 'What is it that is going on in here?'. According to Goffman's frame analysis, we apply frameworks in order to make sense of reality. For instance, if one is at a bank, one has to behave like a customer, adjusting one's manners, linguistic skills and facial expressions accordingly. Goffman's aim is to unmask this socially concealed world of frameworks, keys and fabrications that, once unmasked, turns out to be established in its smallest details. *Frame Analysis* is a brilliant and detailed description of this concealed structure of social experience. From this point of view, *Frame Analysis* can be seen as Goffman's own concealed theoretical framework, certainly more inductive than deductive, more concerned with illustrating a point than demonstrating a hypothesis, but also more creative and original than most sociologists of his time.

With regard to the second criticism, it is not within the scope of this book to deal with the question of how much others adumbrated Goffman's ideas. An intellectually more challenging question is whether Goffman stated the obvious or not, and whether this affects the relevance of his work. In some respects, he did express that which is already 'seen-but-unnoticed'. Many of his observations are articulations of those trivial aspects of daily life which remain unnoticed by the individuals involved, but this does not make them insignificant for the purposes of social theory. Goffman has provided insights into the complex interrelationship between self-presentation, trust and tact, and there is a growing recognition amongst social theorists, such as Giddens and Randall Collins, that these notions are central to the production of social order and predictability in daily social interaction. Giddens and Collins overstate the case for Goffman by adopting a vague notion of social order. There are basically two meanings to order. One is politico-strategic order, referring to a relative absence of dissensus and disagreement concerning the distribution of scarce goods or power. The other is symbolic order, referring to a kind of agreement concerning the meaning of objects and actions, and, relatedly, to the co-ordination of everyday interaction. Goffman's work might be relevant for the explanation of symbolic order, though not for dealing with politico-strategic order, and it goes without saying that the latter does not follow from the former. So to say that Goffman's work provides insights into the production of order *in toto* is wrong. However, his writings certainly help to explain symbolic order and are thus relevant to social theory.

With regard to the last criticism, we wish to make three points. First, it is probably true that Goffman's view is deeply ingrained in modern Western culture. But *any* conceptual framework or analysis about society shares some presuppositions with the culture in which it arises. So this argument in isolation cannot be held against Goffman. Second, without question Goffman's examples are specific to the cultural settings which he was describing, but this does not imply *ipso facto* that his work is ethnocentric. As a matter of fact, a significant number of *concepts* which he employed can be and have been applied to understand other cultural settings as well. Third, it is not true that Goffman relied upon the notion of an atomistic, calculating self. For instance, the individuals portrayed have a strong emotional commitment towards their presentation of the self. Through tact, they help others with *their* presentation of the self – and they trust others to do the same. These individuals are far removed from cynical, manipulative individuals.

Let us summarize the above. For a long time, Goffman was considered a maverick, the *enfant terrible* of American sociology. He was seen as a novelist or impressionist. Only more recently has he been presented as a reluctant theorist. Isaiah Berlin famously described Tolstoy as somebody who 'was by nature a fox, but believed in being a hedgehog' (Berlin 1967: 4) – that is, while Tolstoy aimed to present a single organizing principle, his thought was actually extremely scattered and diffuse. Some have presented Goffman in opposite terms. They argue that while he conceived of himself as fascinated by the minutiae of daily existence, he could not help presenting a bigger picture. We are sympathetic towards this reading. But it should also be remembered that, unlike Blumer, Goffman himself did not wish to address core questions of social theory, and that general theory-building was not a priority of his. This leaves his writings open to various interpretations.

Ethnomethodology

The name 'ethnomethodology' was coined by Harold Garfinkel, who founded a new sociological school under that banner. Although some recent ethnomethodologists deviate slightly from Garfinkel's initial party line, his work remains very much associated with the school. Garfinkel originally carried out doctoral work at Harvard under the supervision of Talcott Parsons. Garfinkel had already developed some ideas in his doctoral dissertation (1952) which were to become prominent in his later work. He subsequently joined the sociology department at UCLA, where he inspired many postgraduates and built up a thriving research centre. The publication of his *Studies in Ethnomethodology* in 1967 led to a worldwide interest in the newly founded school. Other scholars were to follow the new creed; well-known ethnomethodologists include Deirdre Boden, John Heritage, Michael Lynch, Harvey Sacks and Don Zimmerman.

Symbolic interactionism and ethnomethodology share much in common. Both analyse patterns of daily interaction rather than broader social structures; both neglect longer historical spans; both emphasize the extent to which social order is a negotiated and skilful accomplishment of the individuals involved; both strongly oppose the Durkheimian notion that social facts have to be treated as things, analogous to physical objects; and both symbolic interactionism and ethnomethodology direct their attention instead to the sense-making practices in which people are involved – the way in which meaning is attributed to the social world.

However, symbolic interactionism and ethnomethodology arise out of different philosophical traditions. Remember that symbolic interactionism was very much indebted to Mead's reflections upon the interaction between self and society. The intellectual influences on Garfinkel and his followers are more varied. There is, first of all, the influence of Parsons, especially his account of Hobbes's problem of order. Second, there is the influence of Schutz's phenomenology, in particular his concept of *epoché* of the natural attitude. There is, third, Mead's influence on Garfinkel and other members of the school. Mead had an impact on ethnomethodologists, both direct and indirect (via Schutz). Finally, there is the influence of the later Wittgenstein, in particular his discussion regarding the relationship between meaning and shared rules. Within the limited scope of this book, we will concentrate only on Garfinkel's contributions to ethnomethodology. He was especially influenced by Parsons and Schutz, and less so by Mead and Wittgenstein. We will therefore concentrate on the formers' impact.

Garfinkel and ethnomethodology are often seen in opposition to mainstream sociology, in particular to Parsons's frame of reference. It is undoubtedly true that Garfinkel rebelled against some aspects of Parsons's work, but the two also share a number of features. Their similarities and differences are closely bound together. First, Parsons's voluntarist theory strongly opposed those positivist accounts which saw people's action as biologically determined or as passive recipients to their environments (1937: 3–470). In his action frame of reference, people attribute meaning to their surroundings, they have goals, they also have information about how to achieve these goals and they act accordingly (see chapter 2). Garfinkel likewise developed a view which conceived of individuals as exercising agency – not as mere products of social or biological factors. But Garfinkel presented a more 'cognitive' or 'reflective' account. He was interested in the tacit knowledge which people employ in order to make sense of reality, and, as such, affect reality. Whereas Parsons's action frame of reference played down the knowledgeability of people, Garfinkel attributed an important role to how people understand and reason (Garfinkel 1967: 3–103). From this follows Garfinkel and H. Sacks's (1970) notion of 'ethnomethodological indifference': while studying how people account for and produce reality, ethnomethodologists need to refrain from making judgements regarding the validity of people's sense-making practices.

Second, one of the recurrent questions in Parsons's writings is how social order is brought about. This question was first raised by Hobbes, and Parsons considered it to be one of the core questions of any substantial theory of society. He thought that utilitarian frameworks could not answer Hobbes's 'problem of order'. The solution, so he argued, needs to be found mainly in Durkheim's work and to some extent in Freud's (see, for instance, Parsons 1937: 708–14, 719–26). For Parsons, Durkheim has shown convincingly that the problem of order is resolved through the internalization of the central values and norms in the personality structure of the individuals involved. Values, which are internalized through socialization, have a lasting effect on both the ends of action and the means to achieve them. In general, people will not be able to adopt an instrumental orientation towards the values and norms which they have internalized. The internalization explains need-dispositions which cause people to act (see chapter 2). Garfinkel dealt with exactly the same question: how does social order come about? He found Parsons's answer unsatisfactory, however, and instead paid attention to the shared common-sense procedures by which people constantly interpret their surroundings. After all, 'ethnomethodology' literally alludes to the methods or procedures by which ordinary members of society make sense of and act upon their everyday lives (Garfinkel 1974). From this angle, it became possible to see social order as contingent upon continuous interpretative acts by the individuals involved.

There is one obvious way in which Garfinkel differed from Parsons. Unlike most of current American sociology which was empirical and rather compartmentalized, Parsons was an incurable grand theorist, who occasionally carried out empirical research, but whose prime aim was to develop an overarching theory which would embrace a multitude of disciplines in the social sciences. Garfinkel, on the other hand, dealt with only a few questions, and he and his team carried out numerous empirical researches in order to answer those questions. Garfinkel and other ethnomethodologists recognized the empirical bent as central to their work. Examples of Garfinkel's researches are the well-known breaching experiments, his work on the 'accomplishment of gender', and his analysis of the 'documentary method of interpretation' (1963; 1967: 76–185). All of these play a fundamental role in Garfinkel's intellectual development.

Besides Parsons, Garfinkel found most of his theoretical inspiration in the work of the banker-cum-philosopher Alfred Schutz (1899–1959). Schutz opposed the neo-positivist tendency to postulate a unity of method between the social and the natural sciences, arguing that the former deal with an already 'pre-interpreted' world which begs for an interpretative methodology.[6] Schutz's attempt was to merge Edmund Husserl's phenomenology with sociological concerns, trying to grasp the way in which individuals understand and make sense of the surrounding social world. Schutz followed Husserl's phenomenology in attributing importance to the 'natural attitude' and its attendant common-sense knowledge. A number of features are characteristic of the sense-making practices of people in daily life activities, and these become prominent once juxtaposed with the scientific way of making sense of the world.[7] For instance, contrary to scientific rationality in which one's own biography is reduced to a minimum, common-sense rationality is perceived from a particular individual perspective, specific to time and space. Whereas scientific rationality always doubts the facticity of the social world, common-sense rationality rests mainly upon the *epoché* of the natural attitude, which implies that the social world should be taken for granted unless disruptions or new events occur. A suspension of doubt is deeply ingrained in our daily life. Through the medium of a 'stock of knowledge at hand', predominantly social in origin, people approach the social world in terms of 'familiarity and pre-acquaintanceship'. While interacting with each other, people assume 'the general thesis of reciprocity of perspectives'. Schutz went on to argue that, rather than remaining at the level of scientific rationality and imposing this onto the social world, sociologists should attempt to register the common-sense, practical rationality by which individuals make sense of and account for their surroundings. This idea was taken up by ethnomethodologists and acted as one of their pivotal methodological devices. Schutz's work and his distinction between different forms of rationality were, likewise, very prominent in Garfinkel's breaching experiments. These demonstrate the extent to which scientific rationality, once applied to ordinary daily situations, erodes the implicit presupposition of reciprocity of perspectives and eventually leads to disorganization, disruption and anomie.

For Garfinkel, what is crucial to Schutz's view is that, unlike scientists, people involved in everyday situations assume an undoubted correspondence between the world as it appears to them and the world as it is (Garfinkel 1963: 210–11; Heritage 1984: 52ff.). Furthermore, each individual expects other individuals to assume this correspondence and to act accordingly. In their daily lives, people draw upon an unquestioned 'stock of knowledge at hand' or 'common-sense understandings' through which they and their actions are typified. Typification ties in with the capacity of an individual to anticipate another's responses to his or her actions – a truly Meadian notion. Similar to Mead's notion of a 'world taken for granted', a person's stock of knowledge is taken to be 'self-evident' until 'further notice', until disruptions occur. Implicit in most daily interactions is also the 'et cetera' assumption – the assumption that we can reasonably expect things in the future to be as they were in the past. Garfinkel added the importance of Schutz's thesis of reciprocity of perspectives, alluding to both the 'assumption or idealization of interchangeability of standpoints' and the 'assumption or idealization of the congruency of relevances'. The former refers to the way in which any person takes for granted that others would see events in the same typical way if that person's here-and-now became theirs, and to the fact that others assume this as well. The latter refers to the fact that individuals assume that, in spite of their differences, they select and interpret the surrounding objects in an empirically identical manner. It also includes the fact that people implicitly assume that other people act in accordance with the same assumption (Garfinkel 1963: 212–13; Schutz 1962: 11ff.). This notion of intersubjectivity was to become one of the leitmotivs of ethnomethodology, as it was thought to be crucial for understanding the reproduction of social order. It is people's mutual expectations which make for the unintended reproduction of society.

Ethnomethodologists study the routines of daily life. Ethnomethods refer to the way in which, in daily life, ordinary citizens draw upon a complex network of interpretative procedures, assumptions and expectations through which they make sense of and act upon their surroundings (Garfinkel 1974). Garfinkel introduced the notion of 'reflectivity of accounts'. By this, he meant that people constantly make sense of their surroundings, and these sense-making practices are constitutive of that which they are describing (1967: 7–9). Ethnomethods are achieved through tacit and practical knowledge, rather than discursive or theoretical knowledge. That is to say, ordinary citizens do not have to know the rules or procedures explicitly. They *know* the rules only in the sense that they are skilful in acting in accordance with them, but this differs from knowing the rules theoretically in the sense of being able to state them discursively. The 'seen-but-unnoticed' character of our knowledge in daily interactions is exemplified in Garfinkel's famous analysis of 'Agnes', who was born as a male, but who in adolescence purposefully designed an idiosyncratic endocrinological configuration, and at the age of 19 decided to have a sex-change operation. After biologically 'becoming' female, Agnes still had a long way to go. She had to learn a complex set of new rules and procedures about how to behave and speak as a woman. Whereas girls would gradually 'learn' this through practice, Agnes developed a more discursive knowledge about 'how to go on' as a female, similar to somebody who is learning a foreign language. Agnes is a fascinating study of the construction of gender (ibid.: 116–85).

Indexicality is central here. The term 'indexical sign' was originally introduced by Charles Peirce and later developed by Y. Bar-Hillel, referring to the fact that the context in which a token is used provides meaning to that token. Analogously, Garfinkel used 'indexicality' and 'indexical expressions' to allude to the extent to which the meaning of objects, social practices and concepts depends on the context in which they arise (ibid.: 4–7). It follows that his notion of indexicality demonstrates striking similarities with Goffman's concept of situational propriety. Part of people's tacit knowledge is indeed a capacity to grasp the meaning of objects or practices within a particular context, and, moreover, to infer meaning by 'creating' or 'attributing' a context. However, the creation of meaning is not a one-sided process. Indeed, in a manner reminiscent of the notion of the hermeneutic circle, people draw upon the context or situation to attribute meaning to practices, but the latter also enable people to create or sustain their sense of the context. This 'mutual elaboration of action and context' is central to Garfinkel's documentary method of interpretation, which we will discuss shortly.

Garfinkel is especially known for his empirical research, in particular his breaching experiments and the so-called documentary method of interpretation. His breaching experiments were designed to explore the consequences of disrupting the routines of daily life (see, e.g., Garfinkel 1963). For example, students were asked to act as if they were lodgers at home. So the parents were confronted with children who acted according to rules and procedures which differed radically from what the parents used to expect from them. They were very formal with their parents, only spoke when spoken to, etc. The parents, who were unaware of the experiment, reacted with anger, discomfort and bewilderment. Garfinkel and his colleagues inferred two conclusions from these experiments. First, that people have a strong emotional allegiance towards the implicit rules and procedures upon which they continually draw. Second, they demonstrated the way in which the interpretative procedures are 'doubly constitutive' of the activities which they organize: the rules, expectations and assumptions not only make for the visibility of normal conduct in daily interaction, but also for the visibility of conduct which deviates from it. Once the rules are broken, people do not necessarily adjust their interpretative procedures, but instead tend morally to condemn the 'deviant' (Heritage 1987: 226–40).

Equally important is Garfinkel's concept of the documentary method of interpretation – a term borrowed from Karl Mannheim – and the related empirical research.[8] Analogously to the notion of the hermeneutic circle, Garfinkel's documentary method of interpretation alludes to a recursive mechanism in which people draw upon interpretative procedures to construct 'documentary evidences', which are, in their turn, employed to infer the interpretative procedures (1967: 77ff.). While people draw upon interpretative procedures which make sense of reality, the very same framework remains intact and is reproduced, even in cases where the reality concerned is potentially threatening for that framework. For instance, students were asked to attend a counselling session: in spite of the fact that the counsellors gave random answers to their queries, the students said afterwards that they had had a great time and that they learned a lot about themselves. Obviously, they did not realize that this was a 'false' setting. The reason is that they drew upon an interpretative framework with background expectations about the social situation to be encountered; this framework helped them make sense of the situation and in such a way that those expectations remained intact in spite of the fact that the situation was an 'obvious' potential threat to the very same expectations.

For a long time Garfinkel and ethnomethodologists were regarded as irrelevant for the purposes of social theory. The study of mundane activities was seen as relevant for the purposes of social psychology, not for social theory. Many social theorists today conceive of Garfinkel's ethnomethodology differently. They recognize that its strength lies in its ability to account for social order as a skilful accomplishment of knowledgeable people. There is a growing consensus that the minutiae of everyday interaction may be central to the explanation of social coordination and cohesiveness (see chapter 4) – there is certainly some truth in that defence. Garfinkel has indeed shown that individuals have a remarkably strong emotional commitment to their interpretative procedures and expectations, and that they are reluctant to reassess their validity when confronted with disruptions. Furthermore, whereas mainstream sociology has treated common-sense knowledge as an epiphenomenon, Garfinkel has illustrated how it needs to be seen instead as a worthwhile topic of investigation.

There are, nevertheless, weaknesses to Garfinkel's ethnomethodology. First, he claimed to have answered more adequately than Parsons the age-old question of how social order is brought about. However, as with Goffman, whether he is successful in doing so depends entirely on the meaning of 'social order'. Like Goffman, Garfinkel's strength lies in accounting for the production and reinforcement of shared meaning. Like Goffman, however, Garfinkel's framework cannot explain a relative lack of dissensus regarding allocation of scarce goods and power. Whether Garfinkel's view is superior to that of Parsons depends on which aspect of order is focused upon. However successful Garfinkel might be in accounting for symbolic order, Parsons's scheme seems more appropriate for explaining politico-strategic order.

Second, partly because Garfinkel focused on people's 'natural attitude of everyday life', he failed to account for transformations in the underlying social structure. His empirical analyses have shown that most daily life activities involve the continuous application of shared commonsensical knowledge, and that, once confronted with potentially disruptive experiences, people tend to design complex mechanisms which enable them to restore order. Despite this observation, Garfinkel seemed to ignore the potential that people had, once confronted with novel experiences, to reflect upon the underlying interpretative procedures, rules and expectations previously drawn upon. In *The Structure of Scientific Revolutions* (1970), Thomas Kuhn demonstrated how scientists, faced with the accumulation of anomalous results, have a public-collective reflection upon the underlying rules and assumptions of their paradigm, leading to substitution by a new set of rules and assumptions. All this is relevant for the main project of ethnomethodology. Ethnomethodologists set out to explain social order, while conceiving of the latter solely as an *unintended* accomplishment. However, the reproduction of structures can also be accomplished intentionally. Indeed, people's reflection upon the structures underlying their actions can lead to the *deliberate* maintenance of the very same structures.

Third, equally problematic is the absence of a substantial explanatory format in Garfinkel's work. He did not address the question *why* people become upset or outraged when rules or procedures are broken, or *why* they attempt to reinstate order when confronted with potential disruptions. In this sense, his ethnomethodological research is descriptive – begging for explanations, rather than providing them. This does not make

Garfinkel's work insignificant for the purposes of social theory. However, it does imply that, if his work is to be of any use at all to social theory, it needs additional social-psychological back-up.

Fourth, Garfinkel's tendency to neglect problems of power, prestige and asymmetrical relations is another problem, as they are likely to be constitutive of some of the mechanisms that he investigated. Take, for instance, the documentary method of interpretation and, in particular, the case of the students and the counselling session. The general aura, authority and prestige which surround the practices of the professionals are likely to be constitutive of the disposition of students somehow to suspend disbelief once they enter the counselling session, and they are also constitutive of the tendency of the students to sustain this suspension even if the advice provided is less than satisfactory. It is, therefore, indicative that in Hans Christian Andersen's tale 'The emperor's new clothes', it takes an innocent child, not properly socialized yet, to reveal that the emperor is naked. The adults in the story, obviously more susceptible to the asymmetry in social relations, are apparently more inclined to suspend disbelief in the face of authority.

Social rituals, emotions and trust: Collins and Hardin

Trust is central to Goffman's and Garfinkel's analyses of social life. Consider only the latter's conception of social order as a skilful and negotiated accomplishment of reflective individuals or Goffman's important notion of 'ceremonial rules', which sustain the individual's sense of psychological security and trust. In recent years, this concept has become one of the most popular buzzwords in the social sciences, even if not always in the most consistent manner (Misztal 1996: 2). A variety of disciplines and theoretical perspectives are engaged today in the study of the dynamics of interpersonal trust, long-term patterns of social trust, and its implications (mostly political, but also organizational). It should thus not come as a surprise that Randall Collins (1941–), a well-known contemporary intellectual heir of Garfinkel, Goffman and Mead, is one of the leading social theorists currently working on this area.

Ever since the publication of *Conflict Sociology* (1975), Collins has been developing a micro-sociology of human action. His chief contention is that the sociological analysis of large-scale structures should be founded upon a micro-sociological understanding of the world of emotions, morality and social interaction. For example, grand structures such as the economy should be translated into combinations of micro-events amenable to rigorous empirical analysis. Such a translation strategy, Collins argues, 'reveals the empirical realities of social structures as patterns of repetitive micro-interaction', i.e., the repetitive behaviour that 'takes place in particular factories, office buildings, trucks, etc.' (1981: 985, 995). What are, then, the main conceptual elements of Collins's micro-sociology?

First, the basic unit of sociological analysis is neither the individual nor the social structure, but the situation where people are face-to-face. From this point of view, social systems and structures are but the product of the aggregation of numerous, successive interactions over extended periods of time (Collins 1987). Second, and drawing creatively upon the work of Durkheim and Goffman, Collins suggests that these successive interactions in which participants mutually focus their emotions are to be treated as 'interaction rituals'. For a social interaction to be defined as an interaction ritual, four conditions have to be met: the bodily co-presence of two or more people; a boundary that separates insiders from outsiders; all participants have to share a mutual focus of attention; and all of them have to share a 'common mood or emotional experience' (2004: 48). Collins conceives of these elements as variables: any variation in their intensity provokes a similar variation in the effects of a given interaction ritual. There are four such effects: group solidarity, emotional energy (a feeling of exhilaration and enthusiasm which induces initiative), collective symbols which are the moral repository of the group and, finally, a feeling of morality that revolves around the respect for those group symbols. Consider a NBA match as an example of an interaction ritual. The team players are in close bodily contact; their clothes, songs and flags determine insider status; their attention is focused on the game; and the common mood is to win it. The fans supporting the teams are as much part of the ritual as the players themselves. The outcome is solidarity among groups of fans, exhilaration or disappointment (depending on the result of the match), sacred objects (star players such as Michael Jordan), and indignation towards bad sportsmanship, cheats and so forth. Third, Collins concludes that social relations depend on an underlying feeling of trust. Ritual solidarity and altruism are all instances of chains of motivation that push individuals from situation to situation. As this interaction ritual chain builds up over time, Collins argues, a macro-structure is formed. When fans come together to support their team, to refer back to the above example, feelings of group solidarity and interpersonal trust emerge, which over time give rise to a sense of collective identity. Here we see Collins using what Durkheim called 'the precontractual basis of social solidarity' (Durkheim 1985: 161), to provide his micro-sociological theory of interaction ritual chains with a radical character. It is a radical micro-sociology insofar as it claims that emotions and rituals, not strategic rationality, are the founding block of social life. As a social constructionist programme, Collins's theory of interaction ritual chains comes close to Alexander's strong programme of cultural sociology (see chapter 2).

In fact, Collins's work on trust is but one example in a growing literature on trust, social capital, personal networks and other related micro-sociological phenomena. Following the lead of Luhmann's path-breaking work on trust (1980), authors like Anthony Giddens and Ulrich Beck have studied trust in relation to broad societal changes in the context of their analyses of globalization, late modernity and risk (see chapters 5 and 8). Other authors explore the philosophical aspects of this issue (O'Neill 2002). And there are those who study trust (or the lack of it) from the point of view of its political implications. Here, Robert D. Putnam's *Bowling Alone* (2000) and Francis Fukuyama's *Trust* (1995) stand out as the most popular titles. In both cases, we are faced with the re-emergence of a classic argument by Alexis de Tocqueville. Without a trustworthy body of citizens there is no democracy: trust is the condition of civic participation which, in turn, is the condition of any free and democratic political regime. As with other theoretical developments, this recent increase of sociological interest in trust is associated with real-world events. The first one was certainly the transition to democracy by several East European countries in the wake of the fall of the Berlin Wall in 1989 and the subsequent demise of the Soviet Union (see, e.g., Sztompka 1999). The latest recovery of Tocqueville as a sociological classic is closely related to the need to identify the conditions that these countries (in particular, their civil societies) had to meet in order for their transitions to democracy to be successful. Another one is the 'civic malaise' detected by Putnam, Fukuyama and others in the United States at the turn of the twenty-first century. What these authors are arguing is that, from Tocqueville's visit to America in the 1830s through the better part of the twentieth century, a network of civil associations played an important role in combating the pernicious consequences of individualism in the United States. In the past few decades, however, there has been a noticeable decrease in civic participation. If trust is a necessary ingredient for cooperation and social order, then this decrease in social capital (a sort of civic virtue related to the social networks and the norms of trustworthiness that emerge from them) could be undermining the very bases of American democracy (see Putnam 2000: 19).

This assertion has been criticized from various angles. Although much could be said about the empirical validity of Putnam's thesis (is there really a decrease in civic participation or does it depend fundamentally on how you measure it?), what we wish to discuss here is a powerful criticism of its micro-sociological foundations. One of the protagonists of this criticism is Russell Hardin (1940–). He has put forth a conception of 'trust as encapsulated interest' (2002: 1): I trust you because you have an interest in fulfilling my trust. Since you value the continuation of our relationship, you have a rational incentive to take my interests into account, i.e., you *encapsulate* my interests in your own interests. Hardin goes as far as suggesting that such an interest in the continuation of the relationship should be conceived of as the rational and materialistic minimal core of most trust relationships. He uses an example from literature to illustrate his point. In Dostoyevsky's *The Brothers Karamazov*, we are told the story of a lieutenant colonel who, as commander of a unit out of Moscow, had an arrangement with a local merchant called Trifonov. The lieutenant colonel would lend substantial sums of the military's money to Trifonov under the condition of having it returned, along with a gift, by the time of every periodical audit of the books. When the day comes that the lieutenant colonel is unexpectedly relieved of his command, he asks Trifonov to return the last sum, 4,500 rubles, loaned to him. To his surprise, Trifonov refuses. Since the lieutenant colonel could not afford their illegal transactions to be made public, Trifonov ceased to have an incentive to be trustworthy. According to Hardin's encapsulated conception of trust, the lieutenant colonel should not be surprised at all at Trifonov's refusal. There are two central elements in this rational model of trust. The parties need an incentive to carry on being trustworthy and they need to know whether they can trust the other. At the moment he was told he was to be replaced, the lieutenant colonel should have realized that his partner in crime ceased to have an incentive to be trustworthy. Trifonov's interests *no longer encapsulated* his interests. From that moment on, their trusting relationship's days were numbered.

Let us use Dostoyevsky's imaginary relation of trust between the lieutenant colonel and the merchant Trifonov to illustrate the first two types of relations that are subsumed in Hardin's encapsulated-interest model of trust. The first is a 'one-way trust game' (2002: 14). It is a one-way trust relation because it is only the lieutenant colonel who has to trust Trifonov to return the loan; Trifonov need only act in his own interest. Moreover, if the game was to be played only once, Trifonov had no interest whatsoever in returning the money. If, however, the merchant can foresee two or more plays of the game beyond the current one, it always serves his interest to repay the money. The second type of trust relation is slightly more complex, as it involves a reciprocal relationship. An ongoing mutual trusting relationship is more stable than the previous one since, in this case, both parties have an incentive to be trustworthy. As long as future expectations of their relationship were motivating, the lieutenant colonel could trust Trifonov because it was in the merchant's interest to do what the lieutenant colonel trusted him to do, and vice versa. Finally, Hardin claims that his model of trust as encapsulated interest includes a third type of trusting relationship, namely the 'thick relationships' typical of family circles or close workmates. Actually, there are authors who suggest that it is only in such close communities that authentic trust can thrive (Williams 1988). Hardin disagrees. For him, we should apply the same rational choice account of trust to the case of thick relationships: they are the source both of incentives (of the trusted to fulfil the trust) and of knowledge (to allow the truster to trust). From this perspective, thick relationships, considered by some to be the condition for trust, become 'merely a special case of the encapsulated theory of trust' (2002: 22). According to this theory, there are three broad domains in which we experience trust relations. The first is that of interpersonal relations: all the three cases discussed above (one-way trust games, mutual trust relations and thick relationships) cover most of our trust relations at this level. The two other categories refer to trust relations sustained by institutions and to those that are mediated by other (non-institutional) third parties. Hardin's rational choice approach claims that trust is important only at the interpersonal level. In larger-scale contexts, trust is either unnecessary (institutions and governments often maintain order and cooperation through mechanisms without depending on trust) or even detrimental to cooperation (it can lead to closed networks; see Cook et al. 2005). Note the contrast between this conclusion and the neo-Tocquevillean view represented by Putnam, Fukuyama and others: while the latter see trust as an essential ingredient of social cooperation, rational choice proponents prefer to emphasize the various substitutes for trust that make it possible for individuals, conceived of as utility maximization social atoms, to live together in highly complex societies. The application of rational choice theory to the problem of trust is, of course, but a small instance of this influential paradigm. The next chapter is devoted to the discussion of its nature and limitations and its most recent lines of development.

Further reading

As far as the social sciences are concerned, Mead's major ideas appear in his *Mind, Self and Society*. From a social-psychological point of view, the articles 'A Behaviorist Account of the Significant Symbol' and 'The Genesis of the Self and Social Control' are important, and they are both available in Mead's *Selected Writings*. For an up-to-date introduction to Mead's work, see Carreira da Silva's *G. H. Mead. A Critical Introduction*. Blumer's reading of Mead is spelled out in a number of articles in his *Symbolic Interactionism; Perspective and Method*. For a challenging overview of symbolic interactionism, there is Rock's *The Making of Symbolic Interactionism*. For a more detailed in-depth account of the debates surrounding symbolic interactionism, an interesting collection of articles can be found in *Symbolic Interactionism*, two volumes edited by Plummer. Schutz's *magnum opus* is undoubtedly *The Phenomenology of the Social World*, but for those who want a less philosophical introduction to a phenomenologically inspired sociology, there is also, by Schutz in collaboration with Luckmann, *The Structures of the Life-World*. Garfinkel's style of writing is rather inaccessible and jargonistic, and therefore Heritage's *Garfinkel and Ethnomethodology* might be a *sine qua non* for understanding his *Studies in Ethnomethodology*. Leiter's *A Primer on Ethnomethodology* reads well, and is an excellent introduction to various concepts and themes in ethnomethodology; so too is Benson and Hughes's *The Perspective of Ethnomethodology*. With respect to Goffman, it is worth starting with his *The Presentation of Self in Everyday Life*, and then moving on to his *Asylums, Encounters, Stigma* and, finally, *Strategic Interaction*. Manning's *Erving Goffman* is a good introduction, linking Goffman to broader issues in social theory, though rather close to Giddens's interpretation. A more advanced secondary source on Goffman is *Erving Goffman; Exploring the Interaction Order*, edited by Drew and Wootton. Collins's most important later work is *Interaction Ritual Chains*, which is also one of his most readable books yet. On trust, Putnam's *Bowling Alone* is an accessible introduction. For the rational choice critique, see Cook et al.'s *Cooperation Without Trust?*.

References

Baert, P. 1992. *Time, Self and Social Being; Outline of a Temporalised Sociology*. Aldershot: Ashgate.

Benseler, F., Hejl, P. M. and Köck, W. K. (eds) 1980. *Autopoiesis, Communication and Society: The Theory of Autopoietic Systems in the Social Sciences*. Frankfurt: Campus Verlag.

Benson, D. and Hughes, J. A. 1983. *The Perspective of Ethnomethodology.* London: Longman.

Berlin, I. 1967. *The Hedgehog and the Fox: An Essay on Tolstoy's View of History.* London: Weidenfeld & Nicholson.

Blumer, H. 1969. *Symbolic Interactionism: Perspective and Method.* New York: Prentice-Hall.

Collins, R. 1975. *Conflict Sociology.* New York: Academic Press.

Collins, R. 1981. On the microfoundations of macrosociology. *American Journal of Sociology* 86(5): 984–1014.

Collins, R. 1987. Interaction ritual chains, power and property: The micro–macro connection as an empirically based theoretical problem. In J. C. Alexander, B. Giesen, R. Münch, and N. J. Smelser (eds), *The Micro–Macro Link.* Berkeley: University of California Press, pp. 193–206.

Collins, R. 2004. *Interaction Ritual Chains.* Princeton, NJ: Princeton University Press.

Cook, K. S., Hardin, R. and Levi, M. 2005. *Cooperation Without Trust?* New York: Russell Sage Foundation.

Drew, P. and Wootton, A. (eds) 1988. *Erving Goffman: Exploring the Interaction Order.* Cambridge: Polity.

Durkheim, E. 1982. *The Rules of Sociological Method, and Selected Texts on Sociology and its Method.* London: Macmillan (originally in French, 1895).

Durkheim, E. 1985. Precontractual solidarity. In R. Collins (ed.), *Three Sociological Traditions: Selected Readings.* New York: Oxford University Press (originally in French, 1893), pp. 161–74.

Fukuyama, F. 1995. *Trust. The Social Virtues and the Creation of Prosperity.* New York: The Free Press.

Garfinkel, H. 1952. The perception of the other: a study in social order. Unpublished PhD dissertation. Harvard University.

Garfinkel, H. 1963. A conception of, and experiments with 'trust' as a condition of stable concerted actions. In O. J. Harvey (ed.), *Motivation and Social Interaction.* New York: Ronald Press, pp. 187–238.

Garfinkel, H. 1967. *Studies in Ethnomethodology.* Englewood Cliffs, NJ: Prentice-Hall.

Garfinkel, H. 1974. On the origins of the term 'ethnomethodology'. In R. Turner (ed.), *Ethnomethodology.* Harmondsworth: Penguin, pp. 15–18.

Garfinkel, H. and Sacks, H. 1970. On formal structures of practical actions. In J. C. McKinney and E. A. Tiryakin (eds), *Theoretical Sociology.* New York: Appleton-Century-Crofts, pp. 338–66.

Giddens, A. 1984. *The Constitution of Society; Outline of the Theory of Structuration.* Cambridge: Polity.

Giddens, A. 1989. *The Consequences of Modernity.* Cambridge: Polity.

Giddens, A. 1992. *Modernity and Self-identity: Self and Society in the Late Modern Age.* Cambridge: Polity.

Giddens, A. 1993. *New Rules of Sociological Method*. Cambridge: Polity (2nd edn).

Giddens, A. and Turner, J. (eds) 1987. *Social Theory Today*. Cambridge: Polity.

Goffman, E. 1961. *Asylums*. Harmondsworth: Penguin.

Goffman, E. 1963. *Behavior in Public Places; Notes on the Social Organization of Gatherings*. New York: Free Press.

Goffman, E. 1964. *Stigma*. Englewood Cliffs, NJ: Prentice-Hall.

Goffman, E. 1969. *The Presentation of Self in Everyday Life*. Harmondsworth: Penguin.

Goffman, E. 1970. *Strategic Interaction*. Oxford: Basil Blackwell.

Goffman, E. 1972a. *Encounters; Two Studies in the Sociology of Interaction*. London: Penguin.

Goffman, E. 1972b. *Interaction Ritual: Essays on Face-to-face Behavior*. Harmondsworth: Penguin.

Goffman. E. 1974. *Frame Analysis. An Essay in the Organization of Experience*. Harmondsworth: Penguin.

Goffman, E. 1981. *Forms of Talk*. Oxford: Basil Blackwell.

Hardin, R. 2002. *Trust and Trustworthiness*. New York: Russell Sage Foundation.

Harré, R. and Secord, P. 1972. *The Explanation of Social Behaviour*. Oxford: Basil Blackwell.

Harvey, O. J. (ed.) 1963. *Motivation and Social Interaction*. New York: Ronald Press.

Heritage, J. 1984. *Garfinkel and Ethnomethodology*. Cambridge: Polity.

Heritage, J. 1987. Ethnomethodology. In A. Giddens and J. Turner (eds), *Social Theory Today*. Cambridge: Polity, pp. 224–72.

Kuhn, T. 1970. *The Structure of Scientific Revolutions*. Chicago, IL: University of Chicago Press (2nd edn).

Leiter, K. 1980. *A Primer on Ethnomethodology*. Oxford: Oxford University Press.

Luhmann, N. 1980. *Trust and Power*. New York: Wiley.

Maines, D. R., Sugrue, N. M. and Katovich, M. A. 1983. The sociological import of G. H. Mead's theory of the past. *American Sociological Review* 48(2): 161–73.

Mannheim, K. 1952. *Essays on the Sociology of Knowledge*. London: Routledge & Kegan Paul.

Manning, P. 1992. *Erving Goffman and Modern Sociology*. Cambridge: Polity.

Maturana, H. R. 1980. Man and Society. In F. Benseler, P. M. Hejl and W. K. Köck (eds), *Autopoiesis, Communication and Society: The Theory of Autopoietic Systems in the Social Sciences*. Frankfurt: Campus Verlag, pp. 11–32.

McKinney, J. C. and Tiryakin, E. A. (eds) 1970. *Theoretical Sociology*. New York: Appleton-Century-Crofts.

Mead, G. H. 1907. Review of Henri Bergson's *L'Évolution créatrice. Psychological Bulletin* 4: 379–84.

Mead, G. H. 1929. The nature of the past. In J. Coss (ed.), *Essays in Honor of John Dewey*. New York: Henry Colt, pp. 235–42.

Mead, G. H. 1934. *Mind, Self and Society. From the Standpoint of a Social Behaviorist*. Chicago, IL: University of Chicago Press.

Mead, G. H. 1936. *Movements of Thought in the Nineteenth Century*. Chicago, IL: University of Chicago Press.

Mead, G. H. 1938. *The Philosophy of the Act*. Chicago, IL: University of Chicago Press (reprinted 1972).

Mead, G. H. 1959. *The Philosophy of the Present*. Chicago, IL: University of Chicago Press.

Mead, G. H. 1964. *Selected Writings*. New York: The Bobbs Merill Company.

Mischel, W. and Mischel, H. N. 1977. Self-control and the self. In T. Mischel (ed.), *The Self: Psychological and Philosophical Issues*. Oxford: Blackwell, pp. 31–64.

Misztal, B. 1996. *Trust in Modern Societies. The Search for the Bases of Social Order*. Cambridge: Polity.

O'Neill, O. 2002. *A Question of Trust. The BBC Reith Lectures 2002*. Cambridge: Cambridge University Press.

Parsons, T. 1937. *The Structure of Social Action*. New York: McGraw-Hill.

Plummer, K. (ed.) 1991. *Symbolic Interactionism* (vols I and II). Aldershot: Edward Elgar.

Putnam, R. 2000. *Bowling Alone. The Collapse and Revival of American Community*. New York: Simon and Schuster.

Rock, P. 1979. *The Making of Symbolic Interactionism*. London: Macmillan.

Schellenberg, J. A. 1978. *Masters of Social Psychology; Freud, Mead, Lewin, and Skinner*. Oxford: Oxford University Press.

Schutz, A. 1962. *Collected Papers, Volume 1*. The Hague: Martinus Nijhoff.

Schutz, A. 1967. *The Phenomenology of the Social World*. Evanston, IL: Northwestern University Press (originally in German, 1932).

Schutz, A. and Luckmann, T. 1974. *The Structures of the Life-World*. London: Heinemann.

Silva, F. C. 2007. *G. H. Mead. A Critical Introduction*. Cambridge: Polity.

Simmel, G. 1950. *The Sociology of Georg Simmel*. Glencoe, IL: Free Press.

Sztompka, P. 1999. *Trust: A Sociological Theory*. Cambridge: Cambridge University Press.

Turner, R. (ed.) 1974. *Ethnomethodology*. Harmondsworth: Penguin.

Williams, B. 1988. Formal structures and social reality. In D. Gambetta (ed.), *Trust: Making and Breaking Cooperative Relations*. Oxford: Blackwell, pp. 3–13.

The Invasion of Economic Man

From Rational Choice Theory to
the New Institutionalism

Individualistic and economic approaches to social life were amongst the *bêtes noires* of Durkheim's sociological project. Part of the constitution of the new discipline of sociology was to distinguish it clearly from psychology and economics, not only in terms of subject-matter, but also in terms of theoretical approach. In opposition to individualistic approaches, society was considered to be an entity *sui generis* – not a mere aggregate of its component parts. Furthermore, rational calculative attitudes were seen as limited to particular spheres of social life, and, even in cases where these attitudes were prevalent, a precondition for their existence was identified in shared norms and values.

Sociology has long been dominated by this Durkheimian perspective. In its weak version, sociological reasoning is seen as alien to the picture of actors rationally pursuing their individual interests. A stronger version presumes that reason is, in John Wilmot's terms, 'an *ignis fatuus* of the human mind': that behind the surface level of rational action lies a deeper more fundamental level of unacknowledged social structures. That Durkheimian perspective, advocated in either of its versions, has permeated twentieth-century sociology; there is indeed a consensus amongst otherwise very different theorists such as Parsons, Dahrendorf, Garfinkel, Bourdieu and Giddens on the irreducibility of social life to economic logic (see chapters 1, 2, 3 and 5). Even Weberian action theorists, who have traditionally been hostile to holistic types of explanation, are keen to distance themselves from any form of economic reductionism. The emergence of rational choice theory in social and political science in the course of the 1980s has therefore been all the more surprising and revolutionary. Rational choice theory in the study of politics and sociology is nothing short of the invasion of economic man. It is the ultimate imperialist assault of economics on sociology – the subordination of *homo sociologicus* to *homo economicus*.

Of course, it could be argued that economic man has been expansionist in the past. After all, Hobbes's political theory relied heavily upon the view that the world is inhabited by rational, self-interested agents, and Adam Smith occasionally employed economic reasoning to account for political action. Furthermore, the utilitarian reforms of the early nineteenth century drew upon an economic logic postulating that, at all times and places, people tend to avoid pain for pleasure, and that institutions should be directed towards these utilitarian principles. Some rational choice theorists go even further and argue that Tocqueville's and Marx's methodologies adumbrated a rational choice perspective.[1]

However, only recently has the economic approach been employed in such a sophisticated way as to encompass so many different aspects of social life, ranging from church attendance and marriage to war situations and suicide patterns (see, e.g., Arrow 1951; Becker 1976; Coleman 1990; Downs 1957; Olson 1965). The sophistication and the broad applicability of current economic reasoning are both partly due to the emergence and development of game theory. Game theory aims at dealing conceptually with situations in which individuals make decisions while being aware that their choices may (and usually will) be affected by the choices of the other players (see, e.g., Kreps 1990). As to its sophistication, game theory has provided several fine counterintuitive insights: for instance, that, in certain situations, people might be worse off by acting in the pursuit of self-interest. The abstract nature of game theory lends itself to wide application, further encouraging its popularity.

In this chapter we deal with the economic approach and its usage in explaining non-economic phenomena. The first three sections help to set the stage. In the first section – which scholars already familiar with rational choice theory might wish to skip – we discuss the assumptions that underlie the economic approach. This involves outlining what advocates of the economic approach mean by rationality and rational behaviour. In the second section, we discuss game theory, which is often used by rational choice theorists. In the third section, we discuss the new institutionalism, especially as it is developed in political science. In the fourth section, we discuss some examples of rational choice applications in social and political science. We elaborate on the work of Downs, Olson, Becker, Coleman and Knight. Finally, in the fifth section, we set out to discuss the main limitations of the economic approach.

Before beginning, let us briefly elaborate on what we wish to discuss or, more importantly, what we will not discuss. This chapter obviously deals with the economic approach, or what is nowadays called 'rational choice theory' (henceforth, RCT). We use the term as it is commonly employed – that is, defined as a sociological theory which tries to explain social and political behaviour by assuming that people act rationally. However non-controversial, a number of consequences follow from this definition. First, we deal with the rational choice perspective as a theory which attempts to explain social and political phenomena, not economic behaviour. Some of the criticisms which we raise against RCT might also apply to its usage in economics, but we would prefer to leave it to economists to judge whether the points raised here are also relevant for their discipline. Second, RCT (at least according to our definition) is to be distinguished from philosophical reflections regarding rationality and rational choice. These philosophical views occasionally inform RCT, but the latter certainly does not incorporate all these philosophical reflections. Hence, our criticisms against RCT (*infra*) are not necessarily criticisms of Elster's or Hollis's philosophical writings (see, e.g., Elster 1979; 1983; 1986a; 1986b; 1989; Hollis 1988; 1994). Third, RCT is distinct from decision theory. Decision theory is a normative theory, in that it informs one about that which an individual should do if he or she were rational. RCT occasionally relies upon insights from decision theory, but we do not intend to focus on this, and will deal with it only insofar as our critique of the rational choice perspective necessitates it. Fourth, rational choice theorists develop *sociological* theories, and they aim to explain and predict behavioural patterns of groups of people. RCT should not be understood as a theory which simply explains or predicts individual behaviour. For instance, some rational choice theorists purport to explain and predict voting patterns – not each (or any) individual's vote.

Rational choice explanations

The myriad versions of RCT notwithstanding, most followers of the theory take on board the following key notions: the assumption of intentionality; the assumption of rationality; the distinction between 'complete' and 'incomplete' information, and, in the case of the latter, between 'risk' and 'uncertainty'; and the distinction between 'strategic' and 'interdependent' action. We will deal with each in turn.

First, rational choice theorists assume intentionality. Rational choice explanations are indeed a subset of so-called 'intentional explanations'. Intentional explanations do not merely stipulate that individuals act intentionally; rather they *account* for social practices by referring to beliefs and desires of the individuals involved. Intentional explanations are often accompanied by a search for the unintended (or so-called 'aggregation') effects of people's purposive action. Contrary to functionalist forms of explanations (see chapter 1), the unintended effects of social practices are not employed to explain the persistence of the very same practices. Rational choice theorists pay particular attention to two types of negative, unintended consequences or 'social contradictions': counterfinality and suboptimality. Counterfinality refers to the 'fallacy of composition' which occurs whenever people act according to the mistaken assumption that what is optimal for any individual in particular circumstances is necessarily simultaneously optimal for all individuals in these circumstances (Elster 1978: 106ff.; 1989: 95ff.). Take Sartre's example of deforestation: every peasant intends to get more land by cutting down trees, but this leads to deforestation and thus erosion, so that, in the end, the peasants have less cultivable land than at the outset (1960: 232ff.). Suboptimality refers to individuals who, faced with interdependent choices, choose a particular strategy, aware that the other individuals will do the same, and also aware that everybody could have obtained at least as much if another strategy had been adopted (Elster 1978: 122ff.). Take the example of Sartre's peasants again. Suboptimality occurs when a peasant is aware of the possibility of the aggregated outcome, but nevertheless realizes that, whatever the others decide, it is to his or her advantage to cut down trees. The so-called Prisoner's Dilemma, which will be discussed later, is a clear example of suboptimality with two people involved.

Second, besides intentionality, RCTs assume rationality. Rational choice explanations are indeed a subset of intentional explanations, and they attribute, as the name suggests, rationality to social action. By rationality, it is meant, roughly speaking, that, while acting and interacting, the individual has a coherent plan, and attempts to maximize the net satisfaction of his or her preferences while minimizing the costs involved. Rationality thus implies 'the assumption of connectedness', which stipulates that the individual involved has a complete 'preference ordering' across the various options. From such a preference ordering, social scientists may infer a 'utility function' which attributes a number to each option according to its rank within the preference ordering. For a person to be rational, his or her preference ordering needs to fulfil certain requirements. The principle of transitivity is an obvious example of such a precondition: the preference of X over Y and Y over Z should imply the preference of X over Z. In case both connectedness and transitivity are met, rational choice theorists talk about 'a weak ordering of preferences' (Arrow 1951: 13ff.).

Rational choice explanations account for an individual's behaviour by referring to the *subjective* beliefs and preferences of that individual – not by the *objective* conditions and opportunities faced by that individual. So it is possible for someone to act rationally while relying upon false beliefs vis-à-vis what are the best means to achieve his or her goals or desires. However, for someone to be called rational, he or she is expected to gather, within the boundaries of what is possible, enough information such that his or her beliefs are substantiated. Endlessly gathering information can be a sign of irrationality as well, especially if the situation has a certain urgency. For example, confronted with an imminent military attack, a prolonged examination of possible strategies would have disastrous consequences.

Third, there is the distinction between uncertainty and risk. We have so far assumed that people know with certainty the consequences of their actions, but in reality people often possess only partial information regarding the relationship between particular actions and consequences. Some theoreticians even take the position that there are no real-life settings in which people are able to draw upon perfect information because, as Edmund Burke spelled out two centuries ago, 'you can never plan the future by the past'. There is a distinction within 'imperfect information' between 'uncertainty' and 'risk' – a distinction first introduced by both J. M. Keynes (1921) and F. Knight (1921) – and RCT tends to treat choice under uncertainty as choice under risk. Faced with risk, people are able to attribute probabilities to various outcomes, whereas confronted with uncertainty they are unable to do this. Rational choice theorists tend to focus upon risk for one of two reasons: either because they argue that situations of uncertainty do not exist, or because they argue that, if they do exist, RCT might be unhelpful in accounting for people's actions. Faced with risk, RCT assumes that people are able to calculate the 'expected utility' or 'expected value' for each action. To grasp the meaning of the concept 'expected utility', one needs first, for each outcome, X_i, to multiply the utility, U_i, of that outcome with the probability, P_i, that it will occur. The expected utility then stands for the sum of these multiplications: $U_1.P_1 + U_2.P_2 + \ldots + U_i.P_i + \ldots U_n.P_n$ (with n standing for the number of possible outcomes).[2]

Fourth, there is the distinction between strategic and parametric choices. With the exception of the above two types of social contradiction (which are indicative of 'strategic or interdependent choices'), we have concentrated hitherto on 'parametric choices'. These refer to choices faced by individuals confronted with an environment independent of their choices. Suboptimality and counterfinality are examples of strategic choices in that individuals need to take into account choices made by others before deciding their own course of action. To give another example, people who buy and sell shares on the stock market tend to take into account the choices of others before making a decision themselves. As part of RCT, game theory deals with the formalization of interdependent or strategic choices. It constructs ideal-type models which anticipate the rational decision for each player in a game where other players also make choices and where each player needs to take into account the choices of the other. We elaborate on game theory in the next section.

Game theory

Hitherto we have presented a rough picture of what game theory stands for. Since it is crucial in modern rational choice explanations, it is now time to spell out its main features. A game consists of at least two players who develop strategies in order to obtain certain outcomes or rewards. Games consisting of two players are called 'two-person games'; games for more than two players are referred to as 'n-person games'. The reward to each player depends not only on his or her own strategy, but also on the strategies and rewards of all the others involved in the game. Likewise, the strategy of each player is dependent on the strategy of the others. With the preferences of each player for various outcomes or rewards as given, game theory attempts to predict the strategies of the players were they to act rationally on the basis of the information available. Obviously, there might be a discrepancy between that game theoretical anticipation and people's actual choices in experimental or life settings.

A distinction is often drawn between 'cooperative' and 'non-cooperative' game theory (Kreps 1990: 9ff.). The non-cooperative version is that which is commonly understood by game theory. It is assumed that people act within their own interests, and they only choose to cooperate with others if it furthers their individual interests. In cooperative games each individual pursues the best outcome for the group, and that choice does not necessarily coincide with the best strategy if mere self-interest were at stake. As RCT tends to treat people as maximizing their individual interests, and given that the cooperative version is a far less developed branch of game theory, we will in the following focus on non-cooperative game theory.

In some cases, called 'variable-sum' or 'non-zero-sum' games, the net total of the rewards of all players is dependent on the strategy of each player. This is not the case in 'constant-sum' or 'zero-sum' games: here the gain of one player implies an equal loss for the others. Whereas constant-sum games involve pure conflict and rarely occur in real life, variable-sum games involve either pure collaboration or a combination of conflict and collaboration. Variable-sum games which involve only collaboration are called coordination games, whereas the combination of conflict and collaboration is exemplified in the Prisoner's Dilemma, the battle of the sexes, the chicken game and the assurance game. We will elaborate on these shortly.

Within non-cooperative game theory, two types of game can be distinguished: 'strategic form' games and 'extensive form' games (ibid.: 9–25ff.). In the strategic form game (sometimes referred to as the normal form game) players are considered to choose strategies simultaneously. The extensive form game takes into account the sequence of choices and the information gathered by the players each time. Thus, synchronic analysis is typical for strategic form games, whereas extensive form games imply a diachronic analysis. It is technically possible for any extensive form game to be converted into a strategic form game. There could be good reasons for doing so: for example, the snapshot provided in the strategic form game is simple and lends itself easily to analysis. Things are more complicated the other way around: any strategic form game can be converted to an infinite number of extensive form games. Given that the underlying logic is roughly the same in both cases, we will here, for the sake of clarity, only consider strategic form games.

All this sounds rather complicated, but a few examples will demonstrate the simplicity of the basic assumptions of game theory. We will start with the Prisoner's Dilemma, an example of a variable-sum game with mixed conflict and collaboration. This is probably the most well known of all games, not only because of its relevance in various areas of social and political life, but also because of some of its counterintuitive implications. Imagine that you and somebody else have committed a crime together, you are both arrested, but the police fail to provide conclusive evidence against either of you. You are put in separate cells, and you are cross-examined by the police. You are told the following: 'You have two choices: you either confess or you deny any involvement in the crime. If you confess and your accomplice does not, you will go free and your accomplice will get a life sentence. If you confess and so does your accomplice, you will both get 20 years. If you both deny involvement in the crime, you will both get 5 years. Your accomplice has been set the same conditions.'

Now, to clarify the argument which follows, imagine that you care more about the length of your own sentence than that of your accomplice; assume, in fact, that your relationship with your accomplice is purely 'professional', and that you have not developed any special bond while being jointly involved in criminal activities. The same applies to your accomplice, whom you therefore have no reason to trust any more than he or she can trust you. The concerns of your accomplice are first and foremost with the length of his or her sentence, and only then with yours.

Assuming that you care more about your sentence than that of your accomplice, your choice is straightforward. After rational reflection, you decide to confess to involvement, because this will be the most advantageous choice *whatever* the choice of your accomplice. This is easily proven. Your accomplice has two possibilities: confession or denial. Take the case where your accomplice denies: your confession then allows you to go free, whereas your denial would have led to your imprisonment for five years. A similar argument applies were your accomplice to confess: in that case you will both get 20 years, whereas, had you denied, a life-sentence would be waiting for you. So whatever your accomplice decides upon, it is to your advantage to confess.

Remember, too, that your accomplice has been told the same story, and, assuming that he or she decides on a rational basis and that the length of his or her own sentence is the priority, the decision will the same as yours: confession. Now a situation has arisen where you both decide to confess, and this means that you both end up with 20 years. But notice that it would be better for both of you to deny since each of you would then serve only 5 years instead of 20. The Prisoner's Dilemma thus demonstrates that the rational pursuit of individuals can lead to unintended, suboptimal results. Notice also that your (or your accomplice's) awareness of this paradox does not help to alleviate the problem: it still remains advantageous for you to confess, whatever the choice of your accomplice, and vice versa. In other words, the suboptimal result, although unintended, is not necessarily unforeseen.

We take the opportunity to introduce some technical notions related to game theory: pay-off, dominant strategy and Nash-equilibrium. In table 4.1 the pairs in each box refer to the pay-offs for you and your accomplice, depending on the decision of each. A pay-off or utility number is a numerical indication of how desirable a particular outcome is for each player. The first number of each pair refers to the pay-off of the 'row' player (you in this case), the second number indicates the pay-off of the 'column'

Table 4.1 Prisoner's Dilemma

		accomplice	
		deny	confess
you	deny	3,3	1,4
	confess	4,1	2,2

player (your accomplice in this case). Say your pay-offs are either 1 (which stands for the undesirable life sentence), 2 (20 years), 3 (5 years) or 4 (free).

Now, some caution is needed here: in statistical terms, a utility number is an ordinal variable and nothing more than that. That is, what matters is merely that 4 is higher as 3, that 3 is higher than 2, and 2 higher than 1 – that is all there is to it. It is not the case that a score of 4, for example, is twice as desirable as a score of 2. Our example demonstrates this: it does not make sense to say that being set free is twice as good as being imprisoned for twenty years.

In terms of pay-offs the following picture emerges: if your accomplice confesses any involvement, you score 2 by confessing as well and 1 by denying; if your accomplice denies, you get the highest score by confessing and 3 by denying. The same argument applies to your accomplice. Hence, confessing is your 'dominant strategy'; it is also that of your accomplice. A dominant strategy is one that is beneficial to you *whatever* the other player decides. Some games do not provide a dominant strategy, but all have at least one Nash-equilibrium. A Nash-equilibrium (sometimes referred to as simply 'equilibrium') is a pair of strategies where each represents the best strategy, given the other's strategy (Nash 1950). In the Prisoner's Dilemma the Nash-equilibrium refers to the pair (confess, confess) – the dominant strategies of both you and your accomplice. However, the equilibria of some games do not consist of dominant strategies. In our example there is only one Nash-equilibrium, but certain games have multiple equilibria.

Hitherto we have only discussed a single instance of the Prisoner's Dilemma. However, what happens when one is confronted with the same partner in various such dilemmas through time? The answer, it seems, depends on whether the number of games is finite or not, and whether the players involved know how many games are being played. If the game is played ad infinitum, or if the players do not know how many times the game will be repeated, the 'tit for tat' strategy seems to be one of the more effective procedures (Axelrod 1984). According to this strategy, in general you cooperate unless the other player defects, in which case your next move will be defection as well. But if the game is played a finite number of times and if both players know the exact number of times, then it can be shown that the cooperative tit for tat strategy breaks down. The reason is that in the last round the usefulness of one's cooperative strategy is eroded because there will be no further games. One's last game then becomes like a single Prisoner's Dilemma, and the rational decision is therefore to defect rather than cooperate. However, this also means that one's decision in the last game is fixed and is not affected by any of the previous games. Therefore one's decision for the penultimate game will not be affected by the last game, since that choice is already fixed. So the same logic applies here as well, and so on ad infinitum. One ends up deciding to defect throughout the sequence of games. The principle employed here is that of 'backward induction': one imagines the last game and then moves towards the first game.

A second type of dilemma can be found in the coordination game – a variable-sum game with pure collaboration. This game differs from the previous one in that it is in the interest of the players to coordinate – hence the name. Imagine the situation where you and somebody else are taking a lift. There is enough space for both of you in the lift, but you cannot *enter* the lift simultaneously – somebody needs to go first. You are not particularly in a hurry, and you are quite courteous: therefore you do not mind if the other person goes through first. What you want to avoid, though, is for both of you to attempt to go through first, or for both of you to wait for the other. Let us assume that the game is again symmetrical in that the person coming from the opposite direction has similar preferences to you. Table 4.2 represents such a coordination game. There are two equilibria: (wait, go) and (go, wait). Any other combination is less preferable.

As there are two equilibria, it is prima facie not altogether clear what each player needs to do. But in reality coordination games tend to be repeated. Imagine that you encounter that tortuous situation with the same person every day. The first encounter might be embarrassing, but

Table 4.2 Coordination game

		other person	
		wait	go
you	wait	0,0	1,1
	go	1,1	0,0

Table 4.3 Battle of the sexes

| | | woman | |
		dinner	cinema
man	dinner	4,3	2,2
	cinema	1,1	3,4

it is likely that after a few encounters a certain rule or convention becomes established. You might, for instance, take turns – that is, if you went first yesterday you would expect the other person to go first today. Or you might follow the rule that the older person always goes first. As neither you nor the other person minds who goes first, the nature of the arrangement is not important. But however arbitrary, once established, it is in your favour and in the other person's favour to stick to it. The rule or convention makes for the relative predictability of social life, and it is in your and the other person's interest to keep to it.

Like the Prisoner's Dilemma, the battle of the sexes (see table 4.3) is an example of a variable-sum game, with mixed collaboration and conflict. Here again, it is in the interest of both players to coordinate up to a certain point. The game is exemplified through a common dilemma faced by couples – hence the provocative name. Imagine a couple planning their evening. They want to do different things, though not if it means doing it without the other. The man prefers to go out for dinner rather than go to the cinema, but he would rather be with the woman even if she insists on going to the cinema. The woman prefers to go to the cinema rather than to go out to eat, but she would rather be with the man than go to the cinema alone. The two equilibria are (dinner, dinner) and (cinema, cinema). Any other combination would be worse, because most important for both is to avoid being alone.

Game theory is relevant for understanding a number of sociological phenomena. We have only dealt with examples of the Prisoner's Dilemma, but the other games have applications as well. In reality, the players do not have to be individuals; they can, for example, be 'decision-making' bodies such as firms or governments. Two types of empirical application can be distinguished here. First, there are straightforward cases, where one is dealing with only two players. Second, there is the extended case where more than two (and often many) players are involved; the similarities with the original game are nevertheless striking enough to make the use of the analogy fruitful. To take an example of the first type, the arms race between two superpowers is often conceived as a Prisoner's Dilemma: even if it is preferable for each superpower to disarm completely, it is in the interest of each to be fully armed *whatever* the other one does. Hence the suboptimal result.[3] Or take two countries opting for protectionist policies since this is the best choice *whatever* the policy of the other country, although an agreement to abandon protectionism would be beneficial to both. Second, the extended version with a large number of players elucidates the so-called 'free-rider' problem. Free-riders are rational decision-makers who benefit from the efforts of others without making any effort themselves. An example might be students who fail to attend lectures, and who count on their colleagues to provide them with the necessary lecture notes. Another concerns those who prefer not to strike for a pay rise but who still benefit from the rise once it is achieved through the efforts of others.

The new institutionalism

Since the 1980s, a growing number of scholars began to feel that some of the presuppositions of RCT were too strict to adapt to the 'real world'. Their answer was to re-evaluate the role of institutions (March and Olsen 1984; 1989). In fact, this was more a recovery of an old theme than the discovery of a new topic. Modern political science, for instance, was born in the nineteenth century as the study of the state, the political institution *par excellence*. In economics, Thorstein Veblen's classic *The Theory of the Leisure Class* (1899) signalled the consolidation of institutional economics. From the 1950s onwards, however, the study of rational individual behaviour gradually came to replace the traditional emphasis on institutions. In political science as in economics, this marked the ascent of the *homo economicus* to near hegemony. But in recent years, this hegemony began to be challenged by means of a re-examination of the role of institutions, the so-called 'new institutionalism'. Some neo-institutionalist proposals adopt a RCT orientation, trying to adjust the latter's emphasis on individual strategies of utility maximization to institutional factors (such as political constitutions, for example). Others do not. In this case, a more historical and inductive methodology is often employed. In what follows, we focus on RCT neo-institutionalism and contrast it to more historically sensitive versions.

Institutions now stand at the heart of much theorizing and explanation in economics and political science, once the stronghold of radical methodological individualism (Pierson 2000: 475). The 'new institutionalism' is based upon two general assumptions. Individual choices, even strategically rational ones, are no longer analysed as context-free (Clemens and Cook 1999: 444–5; Immergut 1998: 25). Here we have the first proposition of the theory of 'new institutionalism': 'institutions matter' – i.e., they influence norms, beliefs and actions. The second proposition is that 'institutions are endogenous': their form and their functioning depends on the context in which they were created and in which they exist and evolve (Przeworski 2004: 527). In short, scholarly interest in economic and political institutions, in particular the state, has been growing steadily in the last couple of decades and marks a downturn in the influence of methodological individualism (see, for example, Evans et al. 1985; Jessop 1990).

Despite this common analytical core, three varieties of neo-institutionalists are usually distinguished. First, there is the rational choice new institutionalism (see, e.g., Knight 1992). It emerged in the 1970s out of a paradox. According to traditional RCT, the outcomes of the US Congress should be highly volatile and unstable as political agents have specific agendas and are asked to vote on a variety of issues. Reality, however, was very different. The outcomes were remarkably stable and predictable. In order to try to solve this paradox, rational choice political scientists turned their attention to the 'rules of the game', i.e. institutions. Assuming that people choose strategies that will maximize their utility, they found that it is crucial to study institutions since they constrain this expected-utility calculus by stabilizing social expectations (e.g., as a college student, one is expected to be smart, popular, attractive, etc.; similarly, as a citizen, one is expected to pay taxes, vote regularly, etc.). Institutions do this in two different ways. They provide critical information and they sanction certain kinds of behaviour. By doing so, institutions stabilize expectations and structure social action so that equilibrium outcomes can be reached. Going back to the example of the US Congress, a RCT neo-institutionalist analysis typically studies legislation (say, a particular economic rule) as an equilibrium outcome within a game. The rules of this game are the institutional features of the political decision-making process (in this case, the committee structure of the Congress). The passing of legislation is the outcome of the game. It is an equilibrium outcome insofar as it is the optimal result of the bargaining process between rational political agents. Focusing on this bargaining process, a RCT neo-institutionalist analysis seeks to identify the motivations of political agents in passing that particular piece of legislation (Calvert et al. 1989).

Second, the so-called 'historical institutionalism' goes even further. It does not merely study how the 'rules of the game' affect political choices.

The historical institutional approach operates with a broadened conception of institution which includes factors such as culture, norms and routines. Paul Pierson and Theda Skocpol (2002) have identified three features that distinguish the work of authors operating within this branch of neo-institutionalism. First, they tend to favour substantive, 'real world' agendas. Typical research questions for historical institutionalists include, for example, explaining why some countries are stable democracies while most others are not. Second, they usually resort to temporal arguments. The notion of 'path dependency', for instance, refers to the dynamics of self-reinforcing feedback processes in a political system – once an institutional path is created, political actors find it increasingly difficult to reverse their course. Third, historical institutionalists emphasize context and configurations. While rational choice scholars focus on the 'rules of the game' that provide equilibrium solutions of collective action problems, historical institutionalists analyse uneasy balances of power and resources. At this point, a crucial methodological difference between these two branches of the new institutionalism emerges. While the rational choice approach relies on a 'universal toolkit' that can be applied everywhere, historical institutionalism rejects such a deductive logic and tends to develop its hypotheses more inductively (Steinmo and Thelen 1992: 12). This is a serious and resilient epistemological divide that even the new focus on institutions has so far failed to supersede.

Third, a branch of new institutionalism has emerged in sociology around the same time as the previous two but independently from both. Organization theory, a sub-field of sociology that specializes in medium and large-scale organizations such as companies, unions or political bureaucracies, has played a key role in the development of sociological institutionalism. A crucial difference distinguishes this new sociological institutionalism from Weberian classical institutionalism. The latter emphasized the distinction between contexts of action in which instrumental rationality predominated (e.g. bureaucratic contexts) and those in which cultural and solidaristic types of rationality prevailed (e.g. the private or intimate realm). The new version flatly rejects this distinction. New sociological institutionalists like Paul DiMaggio argue that the adoption by modern organizations of certain institutional forms and organizational procedures can only be explained in cultural terms (DiMaggio and Powell 1991). The maximization of some transcendent means–ends efficiency, presumed by the old institutionalism to explain the adoption of certain procedures instead of others by modern organizations, fails to answer the question of why companies produce radically different prod-

ucts to adopt similar procedures. The answer suggested by the new institutionalists is that a company functions very much as any other social
institution. Forms and procedures are transmitted as cultural practices:
what different companies producing distinct products share is not some
general rationality but a specific 'corporate culture' that gives them their
institutional identity (and helps distinguish them from, say, a ministry or
a religious organization). In addition, Herbert Simon (1985) uses the
concept of 'bounded rationality' to emphasize the limits of human cognition (on this notion, see also chapter 5).[4] His point is straightforward.
Contrary to what is assumed by RCT, the scarcity of time and information
that characterizes social life prevents individuals from calculating their
preferences based on a full assessment of all alternatives and their consequences. It is unrealistic to assume the existence of such an objectively
rational behaviour. In real life, given all the cognitive constraints – human,
artificial or organizational – individuals at best 'intend' to be rational. The
key to understanding human behaviour, then, lies in the shortcuts of
bounded rationality. Coping devices such as reliance on standard operating procedures, by allowing individuals to overcome their cognitive
limitations, is what makes coordinated action possible. Given the individual's limited information capability, it is organizations that promote
rational behaviour within their organizational context – hence *'bounded
rationality'*. Still, there are those who criticize this approach for not
showing enough sensitivity to context. Peter Hall, in *Governing the
Economy* (1986), compares the influences that organizations of capital,
labour and state (companies, unions and ministries, respectively) have on
economic policy choices in Britain and France. He eventually rules out
using the notion of bounded rationality as it erroneously imposes the
same logic on the analysis of different kinds of organizations (capital,
labour and state). In his view, organizations have their own distinctive
logic. Each organization has its own bounded rationality; there is no such
thing as an abstract organizational bounded rationality. As we shall see in
the next chapter, Hall draws on this insight in his 'variants of capitalism'
approach, one of the most successful examples of the focus of historical
institutionalism on configurations of policies, formal institutions and organizational structures.

Let us now clarify the exact extent to which the 'new institutionalism' had indeed helped RCT to overcome some of its shortcomings. In
order to do this we contrast the RCT new institutionalism first with conventional RCT and then with the other new institutionalisms. By focusing
on the 'rules of the game', RCT institutionalists have introduced an

important corrective to conventional RCT analysis of legislatures, international arenas and certain market settings. Previously intractable collective action problems (like the stability of the outcomes in the US Congress) are now solved by including institutions in the analysis. In this regard, RCT institutionalism constitutes a significant progress in relation to conventional RCT. The picture, however, is less clear when one confronts RCT institutionalism with other variants of institutionalism. As a point of reference, consider the issue of the origins and development of institutions: how do institutions arise and persist over time? The typical answer suggested by RCT institutionalism is highly functionalist. It tends to explain the origins of institutions in terms of the effects for which they are responsible: for example, constitutional social and economic rights are supposed to have been included in constitutions because they benefit large segments of the population. In short, origins are deduced from consequences. Historical institutionalists are better equipped to deal with the issue of institutional origins. Favouring induction over deduction, historical institutionalists focus on the historical record to find out why political agents choose to include those rights in the moments of constitutional creation: constitutional choice is thus analysed not in terms of its future consequences but in its own terms, as a bargaining process between rational political agents. If RCT institutionalism successfully enlightens 'games under rules', historical institutionalism shows superior capacity in explaining the no less important 'games over rules'. Sociological institutionalists approach the issue of institutional origins in a yet another way. Instead of the functionalist explanations suggested by RCT institutionalism, authors like Yasemin Soysal emphasize the importance that concerns for social legitimacy assume in moments of institutional creation. Soysal's focus is on the adoption of immigration policies by European countries and the US. Through a detailed comparative analysis, she shows that immigration policies have been motivated not by an instrumental calculus of what would be most functional to the state, but by a political judgement on the part of national authorities of what is most legitimate and appropriate in the light of contemporary conceptions of human rights (Soysal 1994). The contrast between sociological institutionalism and the rational choice variant is clear. The latter focuses on an abstract conception of instrumentality: 'given the interests of the state, which policies are the most efficient?' The problem with this approach is that policies are often pursued irrespective of their obvious dysfunctional character. What then explains the adoption of policies that do not serve the material interests of those who implement it? The answer suggested by sociological institutionalists, that those policies enhance the social legitimacy of national authorities, is a significant corrective to RCT institutionalism.

In the past two decades, new institutionalism has become the dominant approach in political science. It is also increasingly popular among economists and sociologists. Despite its growing influence, new institutionalism is far from being a coherent school of thought, with several distinct branches. As we have seen above, the most important difference within neo-institutionalism is the contrast between RCT and historical institutionalism. Whereas the former studies institutions in terms of coordination mechanisms that generate equilibria, the latter sees institutions as embedded in concrete, historical processes. Still, an effort is being made to overcome the analytical space between thick historical descriptions and timeless models. Though certainly laudable, such an effort requires empirical demonstration. With this issue in mind, we now turn to some concrete applications of both RCT and new institutionalism.

Examples of rational choice and new institutionalism applications

We have selected for this purpose five books which have contributed to a more sophisticated economic approach, and which made for its wider acceptance in social and political science. Anthony Downs's *An Economic Theory of Democracy* (1957) was one of the first books to explore the applications of RCT to political phenomena. Mancur Olson's *The Logic of Collective Action* (1965) attempted to use the same argument for the understanding of organizations. Gary Becker's *The Economic Approach to Human Behavior* (1976) was a collection of essays attempting to demonstrate the wide applicability of the economic approach to a variety of phenomena, ranging from drug abuse to marriage. James Coleman's *Foundations of Social Theory* (1990) is a contribution to social theory from the perspective of RCT. Finally, Jack Knight's *Institutions and Social Conflict* (1992) illustrates rational choice institutionalism. We will deal with each in turn.

First, there is Downs's *Economic Theory of Democracy*. The assumption in this is that politicians and voters act rationally. The motivations of politicians are personal desires such as income, prestige and power derived from holding office. Since these attributes cannot be obtained without being elected, the actions of politicians are aimed at maximizing political support, and their policies are merely a means towards this end. Voters establish a preference amongst competing parties based on a comparison between the 'utility income' from the activities of the present government and the 'utility income' if the opposition parties had been in office. Their choice is also dependent on the electoral system. In a two-party system the voter simply votes for the party which he or she prefers. In a multi-party system, however, the voter needs to take into account the preferences of others. For instance, if the preferred party has no chance of winning, then the voter opts for another party that might possibly keep the least preferred party out of power. Governments can gain votes by spending and lose votes by raising taxes. They will continue to spend until the marginal vote gain from their spending activities equals the marginal vote loss as a result of the taxes they had to impose to finance them. Vote gain and loss depend on the utility incomes of all voters and the strategies of opposition parties. Downs's work signalled a breakthrough for the economic approach in some areas of political science.

Second, we will turn to Olson's *Logic of Collective Action*. What Downs managed to do in political science, Olson did for organizational theory. Olson deals with those organizations that further the *common* interests of their members. For example, all members of a union have a common interest in better working conditions or higher wages (1965: 6ff.). He focuses upon 'public goods': that is, those that, having been provided for one or several persons in a group, cannot be withheld from the other members of that group (ibid.: 14ff.). The following problem then emerges. Assume that it is in the interest of all members of a large group to obtain the public good. Obtaining the public good, however, takes time and energy, so it is in the interest of each member not to contribute his or her effort, but to leave it up to the others to do so. Once the public good is obtained, it is available to all anyway. Furthermore, in large groups, one person's effort often does not make much difference. But if everybody operates on that basis, then nobody will obtain the public good. So, although it is in the interest of everybody to pursue the good, the group does not necessarily achieve this. All this explains why large groups tend to employ incentives and negative sanctions to make people contribute towards obtaining the public good (ibid.: 22–52).

Third, Becker's *Economic Approach to Social Behavior* is a collection of articles with a bold and provocative introduction. Underlying this work is the belief that what distinguishes economics from related disciplines is not the subject-matter, but its approach (1976: 3–5). Becker's aim is to demonstrate that what he calls the 'economic approach' is extremely powerful in that it can be applied to a wide variety of phenomena. Others have shown the usefulness of that approach for explaining economic life, but Becker sees it as his task to show the applicability of the economic approach to a wide range of non-economic behaviour. He is the clearest exponent of 'economic imperialism' in that he goes as far as saying that the economic approach 'provides a valuable unified framework for understanding *all* human behavior' (ibid.: 14). Becker sees the following assumptions as central to the 'economic approach'. First, people's preferences are relatively stable, and they do not differ substantially between various categories of the population, or between different cultures or societies. Second, people exhibit maximizing behaviour on the basis of an optimal amount of information. Third, markets exist which facilitate the coordination of the actions of the people involved and for the mutual consistency of their behaviour (ibid.: 5–7, 14). The strength of Becker's work lies in the technical sophistication of the modelling in his empirical work.

Fourth, there is Coleman's *Foundations of Social Theory*. Like Parsons's *Social System*, Merton's *Social Theory and Social Structure* and Giddens's *Constitution of Society*, Coleman's book aims at developing a treatise in general social theory (see chapters 2 and 5). Like Merton, Coleman backs up his theory with empirical research, which aims to demonstrate the usefulness of his research programme. Like Parsons and Giddens, Coleman attempts to transcend the traditional opposition between the macro- and micro-levels of society (1990: 6ff.). His contribution to social theory therefore operates at three levels: it aims at explaining how the properties of the system level affects the individual level; it attempts to account for what happens at the individual level; and it deals with how people's action affects the system level (ibid.: 8ff.). The basic idea is simple. Culture generates particular values in the people involved, which make them act in the pursuit of these values, and, while doing so, they affect society. The further elaboration of this proposition is complex and takes almost 1,000 pages. Especially important for this survey is Coleman's notion of purposive and rational action. In his view, people do not merely act intentionally, they also choose actions or goods which maximize utility (ibid.: 14). He provides two reasons for this assumption. First, a theory which assumes that people maximize utility has higher predictive power than a theory which simply postulates intentionality. Second, assuming that people maximize utility adds to the simplicity of the theory (ibid.: 14–19). Equally important, though, is Coleman's notion that purposive action affects the macro-level. He pays special attention to the role of unintended effects. People act purposefully, but they might produce results which they did not intend or which they did not foresee. Sometimes these effects might even counter the initial intentions (ibid.: 19ff.).

Fifth, there is Jack Knight's *Institutions and Social Conflict*. Unlike Coleman's *Foundations*, it is not a treatise of general social theory. It does propose, however, a deductive theory of institutional emergence and development. In this regard, Knight's rational choice institutionalism differs from the more historically inclined versions. He uses historical examples as illustrations of his arguments, not as the founding block of his theoretical model. He is not so much interested in long-term processes of social and political change as he is in developing a theory that explains the origins of norms. We say 'norms' because for Knight institutions are norms. Social institutions – norms, but also rules or rights – are mechanisms that stabilize social expectations through rewards and sanctions (1992: 2–3). Examples include all sorts of social organizations from families to companies or political legislatures. How do such institutions come about and endure? Knight's sophisticated version of RCT institutionalism tries to overcome the well-known drawback of conventional RCT institutionalism: functionalist reasoning. He does that by resorting to conflict theory. In his view, institutions reflect, and are the by-product of, social conflicts between individuals with asymmetrical power and resources. Take the institution of 'family' in ancient Rome (ibid.: 136–7). The resource advantage historically enjoyed by Roman men over women is reflected in the rules regulating Roman families. These rules were instruments of those in superior bargaining positions, namely Roman men. The result of these distributional conflicts is outcome equilibria that systematically favour the most powerful social agents. The formalization of this reasoning is an elegant theory of institutional emergence. Given the power asymmetries between social agents, in games with multiple equilibria individual bargaining is resolved in favour of those with a relative advantage in substantive resources. Agents with fewer resources voluntarily choose equilibria favoured by actors in superior bargaining positions because they are limited by their own expectations of the other's behaviour. 'As this becomes recognized as the socially expected combination of equilibrium strategies', Knight concludes, 'a self-enforcing social institution is established' (ibid.: 143).

Problems with rational choice theory

It is not difficult to see the attraction of RCT for social and political scientists. First, in contrast with the complexity of the philosophical accounts of rationality, rational choice explanations in social and political science are remarkably simple. The core of Becker's and Coleman's accounts can be summarized in a few elementary lines. Second, some of the presuppositions of the rational choice explanations appear commonsensical and thus beyond dispute. One takes for granted that people act purposefully, that they act knowingly, though produce unanticipated effects. Third, some of the results of rational choice applications are nevertheless counterintuitive. Take, for example, the insight that what is rational for each individual is not necessarily rational for all simultaneously. Fourth, RCT fuels the hope that a united social science is feasible. For two centuries sociologists and economists have been speaking different languages. RCT would allow for renewed communication across the disciplines.

Whatever the attraction, the problems with RCT are probably too severe for it to be considered as a viable alternative to 'sociological' reasoning. We will discuss five major problems: the tendency of rational choice theorists to develop *post hoc* explanations; their mistaken assumption of a culturally free notion of rationality; the fallacy of the so-called 'internalist' rational choice theorists; the fallacy of 'externalism'; and rational choice theorists' highly restricted use of history.

We will deal first with the issue of *post hoc* reasoning. Rational choice theorists tend to make sense of social practices by attributing rationality to them *ex post facto*. Indeed, they often conceive of their task as demonstrating the fact that social practices which are prima facie irrational are actually rational after all (see, for instance, Coleman 1990: 18; Becker 1976: 13–14). The more that practices appear to be irrational, the more significant the attempt to show that they are in fact rational. For instance, however irrational at first sight, some social psychologists, like Brown, use game theory to demonstrate that panic behaviour is rational after all (Brown 1965; see also Coleman 1990: 203–11). Sociological examples include the attempts to show that marriage patterns and criminal behaviour operate according to an economic logic (Becker 1976: 39–88, 205–50). Notice the analogy with early functionalism (see chapter 2). Whereas the functionalist tendency was to attribute social rationality retrospectively to practices which are prima facie irrational, rational choice explanations attempt to make sense of practices by attributing individual rationality *ex post facto*. Not dissimilar to the early functionalist tendency to legitimize existing practices, RCT is often invoked as a *deus ex machina*, suggesting that people live in Leibniz's or Voltaire's 'best [or at least the most rational] of all possible worlds'.

However, there are severe problems related to this *post hoc* theorizing. From the mere fact that these practices *can be* moulded into a rational narrative, it does not follow that, in this instance, RCT has been empirically validated or corroborated. For most, if not all, practices can be reconstructed in that way, especially given that rational choice theorists tend to attribute the preferences and beliefs which suit their theory to their research subjects. Rational choice theorists indeed often rely upon *ex post facto* reasoning to immunize their theory against potential falsifications. First, confronted with the fact that people do not always adjust their behaviour to new opportunities, rational choice theorists tend to argue that 'because adjustment is not costless, it may be rational to postpone it until one knows for certain that the change is a durable one' (Elster 1986b: 24). Second, confronted with the fact that people often contribute more to the achievement of collective goods than is predicted by the theory, rational choice theorists tend to argue that the individuals involved simply overestimate the impact of their actions (Hardin 1982: 115ff.). Third, there is the well-known 'paradox of voting'. Given that voting takes time and that each vote is unlikely to be decisive, RCT would expect people not to make the effort to vote. But a significant number of people *do* vote. Rather than treating this as a falsification, rational choice theorists tend to mould this counterintuitive phenomenon into a rational narrative as well. It was argued that people vote because they overestimate the impact of their vote or because voting provides them with some psychological satisfaction not accounted for by early rational choice theorists like Downs. They get psychological satisfaction from expressing allegiance to a political system or from contributing to a potentially successful enterprise (Coleman 1990: 290ff.; Hinich 1981; Riker and Ordershook 1973: 62; Schwartz 1987).

In short, the problem with this form of *post hoc* theorizing is twofold. First, it rests upon *post hoc* assumptions which are empirically not validated (for example, the assumption that people overestimate the impact of their actions). Second, it accommodates mutually exclusive observations (for instance, adjusted and unadjusted behaviour; cooperative action and defection; non-voting and voting), and is thus non-falsifiable. While rational choice theorists tend to situate themselves within a falsificationist tradition (see chapter 8), they fail to acknowledge that *post hoc* reconstructions do not serve as empirical corroboration of the theory.

The second problem is that most rational choice theorists tend to ignore or efface cultural diversity. First, some of the theorists do so rather obviously by making the contentious claim that preferences are stable across cultures (Becker 1976: 5ff.). This fits rather well with their tendency to attribute preferences to the subjects involved without checking empirically whether this attribution is justified. (If preferences are stable, then researchers can indeed trust themselves in attributing preferences to others.) Various unsatisfactory justifications are given for assuming that preferences are stable. The oddest one is the claim that economics knows little about preference formation, and that this is a sufficient reason for assuming preferences to be invariant (ibid.: 5). The absurdity of this logic is striking: the weakness of the approach (its inability to account for how people's preferences are formed) is used as its justification. A more convincing reason for assuming preferences to be fixed is that it adds to the simplicity of the model. Besides empirical testing, rational choice theorists often use the criterion of simplicity to judge between rival theories (e.g. Coleman 1990: 19). But although it could indeed be argued that simplicity is desirable, it should not be adopted at any cost, especially if doing so implies making empirically unsubstantiated or even false assumptions. And this is often the case here. In some areas of economics, preferences might be relatively invariant, but in many others they are not. Simply assuming that they are (and, in some cases, discounting the empirical counter-evidence) represents a lack of intellectual honesty.

Second, there is the more far-reaching presupposition in RCT that, confronted with the same situation and assuming constant preferences, there exists a single, culturally free 'rational course of action'. For instance, rational choice theorists introduce the notion of people's 'rational belief', without fully taking into account that the cultural context in which these people find themselves affects what counts as a rationally founded belief and what does not. The problem for RCT is that it deals with beliefs about the relationship between action and outcome which necessarily rely upon culturally embedded notions, for instance, regarding causality or agency. It is a mistake to reduce causality or agency, as RCT does, to only one of those notions. Take, for instance, two people, A and B, who observe that action x tends to be followed by outcome y. A holds a regularity notion of causality, and person B holds a realist view (see, e.g., Bhaskar 1979; Cartwright 1989; Hacking 1983). A might assume that the observation is sufficient (and necessary) evidence to conclude that x causes y; B does not. But it would be erroneous to say that A's belief is more rational than B's belief, or vice versa, simply on the basis of the particular notion of causality which A and B hold, especially given the fact that, even in academic literature, there is no consensus regarding the superiority of one notion over the other. (This is not to say that A or B might not have better arguments for defending his or her notion.)

It is important to mention that this second argument can also be used against decision theory. Let us remind the reader that, as a normative theory, decision theory indicates what, in a particular instance, is the rational course of action to take. It does not assume that people act as such (neither does it assume that people do not act in that way). Our previous objection to RCT (the argument against *post hoc* theorizing) does not affect the validity of the normative theory. In contrast, however, the argument that RCT rests upon a mistaken notion of culturally free rationality does not merely threaten RCT, but also the normative theory.

The third problem refers to the distinction between acting as if one is rational on the one hand, and acting because one is rational on the other. Rational choice theorists often defend their theories by showing that they are confirmed by empirical findings. It is important to understand exactly what they mean by the notion of corroboration or empirical confirmation. To justify their framework, they typically refer to the fact that the model, which is inferred from that framework, allows for accurate predictions about people's actions and the effects of their actions. Underlying this reasoning is the epistemological assumption that the validity of a theory depends on its predictive power.

Congruence between the model and reality is, however, not sufficient to corroborate the rational choice theories that form the basis of that model. First, recent developments in the philosophy of science undermine the notion that the strength of a theory depends on its predictive power (see chapter 8). Given that social systems tend to be open systems, corroboration and falsification of a theory are less relevant because they might be due to other generative mechanisms which potentially intervene (see Lawson 1989). Second, there is a distinction between acting rationally on the one hand, and acting *as if* one is rational on the other. From the observation of a congruence between the model and reality (and the attendant predictive power of the theory), it might be legitimate to infer that people generally act in accordance with the basic principles of rationality. But it would be erroneous to conceive of that congruence as empirical evidence that people generally act rationally. For individuals to act *as if* they are rational does not necessitate any rational decision process remotely similar to the one attributed to individuals by RCT. Take, for instance, a rival theory T′ according to which the individuals involved tacitly acquire skills and practices, and these skills and practices result in outcomes that appear to be rational on average. If M is the model derived from RCT, and M′ is the model derived from the rival theory T′, then M is identical to M′ because RCT and T′ differ only in whether they account for human action in terms of conscious calculation or of tacit knowledge. But this means that the very same empirical evidence which was used to support RCT can equally well be used to support the rival theory T′: if M proves to yield accurate predictions, then M′, being identical to M, does as well.

Some rational choice theorists might, of course, reply that their particular version of RCT is an 'externalist' one (see, e.g., Becker 1976; Friedman 1953; Posner 1980). Contrary to internalists, externalists abandon the intentionality requirement. Becker, for instance, states that his economic approach 'does not assume that decision units are necessarily conscious of their efforts to maximize or can verbalize or otherwise describe in an informative way reasons for the systematic patterns in their behaviour' (1976: 7). This externalist position introduces a theoretical argument which says that people in general act rationally, and that they do so *either* because they have tacitly acquired skills or practices (which are found to have a rationale) *or* because the skills or practices are the outcome of conscious calculation.

There are two problems with this counter-argument. First, given that the requirement of (necessarily) conscious calculation has been abandoned, this externalist position (T″) becomes remarkably similar to rival arguments such as T′, and it is no more justified to call say T″ a 'rational choice perspective' than it is to describe T′ as such. The only justification for doing so might be that T″ leaves open the *possibility* that people's skills and practices are the product of rational calculation, whereas T′ sees it exclusively in terms of tacitly acquired knowledge. Moreover, once one leaves the realm of artificial theories (such as T′), one realizes that rival theoretical arguments (which draw upon tacit or practical knowledge) do not even exclude the possibility of intentionality; they simply deny the regularity or typicality of its occurrence. Take, for instance, Bourdieu's perspective on social theory (1977; 1990; see also chapter 1). Bourdieu postulates that people's *habitus* is adjusted to the objective conditions in which they are situated, and that the *habitus* is not typically acquired consciously. He would not exclude the fact that the *habitus* is occasionally arrived at consciously; he would simply deny that it is the norm. We do not wish to argue that the explanatory format provided by Bourdieu and the one provided by the externalists are completely identical, but that they are not substantially different with regard to the issue of whether it is possible that the practices are the product of conscious calculation. Stated concisely, there are no obvious reasons that justify calling the externalist viewpoint – but not Bourdieu's – a rational choice perspective. But it is plainly nonsensical to call Bourdieu's theory a RCT, and it follows that it is equally absurd to call the externalist view a RCT.

Second, the explanatory power of the externalist argument is weak. Let us clarify this by invoking the Weberian notion that both 'causal adequacy' and 'adequacy of meaning' are a *sine qua non* condition for the validity of a social explanation. Whereas causal adequacy is fulfilled if, and only if, the explanation provided is supported by observed regularities, adequacy of meaning is fulfilled if, and only if, the explanation provided makes intelligible the observed regularities. Given that the social sciences deal with open systems, we would not attribute such significance to regularity conjunctions as Weber did. Neither do we wish to commit ourselves to his further specifications regarding how adequacy of meaning can be fulfilled through *Verstehen* (interpretative understanding). However, it is difficult to deny his general view that adequacy of meaning is essential to explanation in social and political science. To explain is indeed to make observed phenomena intelligible. And it is exactly on this score that the externalist view falls short. However high they might score on adequacy of causality, externalists are weak on adequacy of meaning because they do not wish to commit themselves to explaining *how* the observed patterns come about.

It is then not surprising that those who position themselves in the externalist camp tend to invoke intentionality and related notions (such as knowledge and foresight) once they discuss the results of their research. Take, for instance, Becker (a self-declared externalist) who argues that people live an unhealthy lifestyle not out of ignorance of its consequences, but because other things are more important to them than maximizing their lifespan. Smoking heavily or working hard 'would be unwise decisions if a long life were the only aim, but as long as other aims exist, they could be *informed* and in this sense "wise" ' (1976: 10; emphasis added). If one stuck to an externalist view (to which, theoretically, Becker subscribes), notions such as 'aims', 'informed decisions' and 'wise decisions' should be excluded. But given, at the level of adequacy of meaning, that externalism is weak, self-declared externalists have only two options. Either they stick to the externalist doctrine, and then they fail to say anything other than that people generally act as if they are rational; or they slip back into internalism when they discuss their results. It is no wonder that most, like Becker, are driven towards the second option (in spite of its difficulties, mentioned earlier).

Turning now to the limitations of rational choice institutionalism, it can be said that RCT faces great difficulties in mobilizing the past in order to explain the present and predict the future. One advantage of historical institutionalist studies is their ability to incorporate slow-moving causal processes in their analytical framework. Some institutional changes can take several decades to unfold: for instance, changes in pension systems are translated into effective public spending only two or three generations later. Game theory, however, generally requires that all the relevant actors, preferences and pay-offs are established and fixed at the beginning of the game. It is therefore unable to follow the historical unfolding of such processes of institutional creation and change (Munck 2001). Furthermore, game theory is particularly suited for explaining relatively simple and micro-level situations. When confronted with more complex settings, as is usually the case at the meso- or macro-levels of institutional analysis, game theory quickly runs into problems. One last difficulty lies in the inability of RCT to produce cumulative, comparative-historical knowledge. Recall the aforementioned example of rational choice study of American politics as the analysis of choices of politicians under the organizational constraints of Congress. Instead of tackling increasingly broader research questions, RCT tends to redefine politics in ever more diminutive terms. Thus American politics becomes the study of the decision-making procedures of Congress. The reason for this difficulty in producing cumulative knowledge lies in the reliance of RCT on game theory, a theoretical approach that leads it relentlessly back to an emphasis on the micro-level.

Further reading

For a simple introduction to RCT and its applications to social and political science, we recommend chapter 2 of Hindess's *Choice, Rationality and Social Theory*, and Becker's introduction to *The Economic Approach to Human Behavior*. It is worth bearing in mind that Becker is an advocate of RCT and Hindess is not. We would then suggest Elster's introduction to his edited volume *Rational Choice*: it is an excellent state-of-the-art compilation of advanced philosophical issues related to RCT. Introductions to the philosophy of the social sciences from the perspective of rational choice are Elster's *Nuts and Bolts for the Social Sciences* and Hollis's *The Philosophy of Social Science*. Standard works on RCT and its applications for empirical research are Becker's *The Economic Approach to Human Behavior* and Coleman's *Foundations of Social Theory*. Most books on game theory are written by and for economists, and Kreps's *Game Theory and Economic Modelling* is one of the best introductions. Worth reading is Olson's *The Logic of Collective Action*, one of the first systematic applications of RCT to empirical topics in politics and sociology. A further attempt to apply this approach to a broad range of empirical phenomena can be found in Boudon's *The Unintended Consequences of Social Action*. Abel's *Rational Choice Theory*, Elster's *Rational Choice* and Moser's *Rationality in Action* are edited collections with seminal articles on rational choice. Hindess's *Choice, Rationality and Social Theory* is a well-balanced and readable critique of RCT. A more convincing critique is Green and Shapiro's *Pathologies of Rational Choice Theory*. March and Olsen's *Rediscovering Institutions* provides a fine introduction to the new institutionalism. One of the best examples of RCT's neo-institutionalist analysis is Knight's *Institutions and Social Conflict*.

References

Abel, P. (ed.) 1991. *Rational Choice Theory*. Aldershot: Edward Elgar.

Arrow, K. 1951. *Social Choice and Individual Values*. New Haven, CT: Yale University Press.

Axelrod, R. 1984. *The Evolution of Co-operation*. New York: Basic Books.

Becker, G. S. 1976. *The Economic Approach to Human Behavior*. Chicago, IL: Chicago University Press.

Bhaskar, R. 1979. *The Possibility of Naturalism*. Hemel Hempstead: Harvester.

Boudon, R. 1982. *The Unintended Consequences of Social Action*. London: Macmillan (originally in French, 1977).

Bourdieu, P. 1977. *Outline of a Theory of Practice*. Cambridge: Cambridge University Press (originally in French, 1972).

Bourdieu, P. 1990. *The Logic of Practice*. Cambridge: Polity (originally in French, 1980).

Brown, R. 1965. *Social Psychology*. New York: Free Press.

Calvert, R., McCubbins, M. and Weingast, B. 1989. A theory of political control and agency discretion. *American Journal of Political Science* 33: 588–611.

Cartwright, N. 1989. *Nature's Capacities and their Measurement*. Oxford: Clarendon Press.

Clemens, E. and Cook, J. 1999. Politics and institutionalism: explaining durability and change. *Annual Review of Sociology* 25: 441–66.

Cohen, G. A. 1982. Reply to Elster on Marxism: functionalism and game theory. *Theory and Society* 11: 483–95.

Coleman, J. 1990. *Foundations of Social Theory*. Cambridge, MA: Harvard University Press.

DiMaggio, P. and Powell, W. (eds) 1991. *The New Institutionalism in Organizational Analysis*. Chicago, IL: University of Chicago Press.

Downs, A. 1957. *An Economic Theory of Democracy*. New York: Harper.

Elster, J. 1978. *Logic and Society; Contradictions and Possible Worlds*. Chichester: John Wiley and Sons.

Elster, J. 1979. *Ulysses and the Sirens*. Cambridge: Cambridge University Press.

Elster, J. 1983. *Sour Grapes: Studies in the Subversion of Rationality.* Cambridge: Cambridge University Press.

Elster, J. 1985. *Making Sense of Marx.* Cambridge: Cambridge University Press.

Elster, J. (ed.) 1986a. *Rational Choice.* New York: New York University Press.

Elster, J. 1986b. Introduction. In J. Elster (ed.), *Rational Choice.* New York: New York University Press, pp. 1–33.

Elster, J. 1989. *Nuts and Bolts for the Social Sciences.* Cambridge: Cambridge University Press.

Evans, P., Rueschemeyer, D. and Skocpol, T. (eds) 1985. *Bringing the State Back In.* Cambridge: Cambridge University Press.

Friedman, M. 1953. *Essays in Positive Economics.* Chicago, IL: University of Chicago Press.

Giddens, A. 1984. *The Constitution of Society: Outline of the Theory of Structuration.* Cambridge: Polity.

Green, D. P. and Shapiro, I. 1994. *Pathologies of Rational Choice Theory: A Critique of Applications in Political Science.* New Haven, CT: Yale University Press.

Hacking, I. 1983. *Representing and Intervening: Introductory Topics in the Philosophy of Natural Science.* Cambridge: Cambridge University Press.

Hall, P. A. 1986. *Governing the Economy.* Oxford: Oxford University Press.

Hardin, R. 1982. *Collective Action.* Baltimore, MD: Johns Hopkins University Press.

Hindess, B. 1988. *Choice, Rationality and Social Theory.* London: Unwin Hyman.

Hinich, M. J. 1981. Voting as an act of contribution. *Public Choice* 36: 135–40.

Hollis, M. 1988. *The Cunning of Reason.* Cambridge: Cambridge University Press.

Hollis, M. 1994. *The Philosophy of Social Science.* Cambridge: Cambridge University Press.

Immergut, E. 1998. The theoretical core of the new institutionalism. *Politics and Society* 26(1): 5–34.

Jervis, R. 1978. Co-operation under the security dilemma. *World Politics* 30(2): 167–214.

Jessop, B. 1990. *State Theory.* Cambridge: Polity.

Keynes, J. M. 1921. *A Treatise on Probability.* London: Macmillan.

Knight, F. 1921. *Risk, Uncertainty and Profit.* Boston, MA: Houghton Mifflin.

Knight, J. 1992. *Institutions and Social Conflict.* Cambridge: Cambridge University Press.

Kreps, D. 1990. *Game Theory and Economic Modelling.* Oxford: Clarendon Press.

Lawson, T. 1989. Abstraction, tendencies and stylised facts: a realist approach to economic analysis. *Cambridge Journal of Economics* 1(13): 59–78.

March, J. and Olsen, J. 1984. The new institutionalism: organizational factors in political life. *American Political Science Review* 78(3): 734–49.

March, J. and Olsen, J. 1989. *Rediscovering Institutions: The Organizational Basis of Politics.* New York: Free Press.

Merton, R. 1968. *Social Theory and Social Structure*. New York: The Free Press (enlarged edn).

Moser, P. K. (ed.) 1990. *Rationality in Action; Contemporary Approaches*. Cambridge: Cambridge University Press.

Munck, G. 2001. Game theory and comparative politics: new perspectives and old concerns. *World Politics* 53(2): 173–204.

Nash, J. 1950. The bargaining problem. *Econometrica* 18: 155–62.

Olson, M. 1965. *The Logic of Collective Action*. Cambridge, MA: Harvard University Press.

Parsons, T. 1951. *The Social System*. London: Routledge & Kegan Paul.

Pierson, P. 2000. The limits of design: explaining institutional origins and change. *Governance: An International Journal of Policy and Administration* 13(4): 475–99.

Pierson, P. and Skocpol, T. 2002. Historical institutionalism in contemporary political science. In I. Katznelson and H. Milner (eds), *Political Science: State of the Discipline*. New York: Norton, pp. 693–721.

Posner, R. A. 1980. The ethical and political basis of the efficiency norm in common law adjudication. *Hofstra Law Review* 8: 487–551.

Przeworski, A. 2004. Institutions matter? *Government and Opposition* 39(4): 527–40.

Riker, W. H. 1992. The entry of game theory into political science. In E. R. Weintraub (ed.), *Toward a History of Game Theory: Annual Supplement to Volume 24 of History of Political Economy*. Durham, NC: Duke University Press, pp. 207–24.

Riker, W. H. and Ordershook, P. C. 1973. *Introduction to Positive Political Theory*. Englewood Cliffs, NJ: Prentice-Hall.

Sartre, J.-P. 1960. *Critique de la raison dialectique*. Paris: Gallimard.

Schwartz, T. 1987. Your vote counts on account of the way it is counted. *Public Choice* 54: 101–21.

Simon, H. 1957. A behavioral model of rational choice. In *Models of Man, Social and Rational: Mathematical Essays on Rational Human Behavior in a Social Setting*. New York: John Wiley and Sons.

Simon, H. 1985. Human nature in politics. *American Political Science Review* 79: 293–304.

Soysal, Y. 1994. *Limits of Citizenship: Migrants and Postnational Membership in Europe*. Chicago, IL: University of Chicago Press.

Steinmo, S. and Thelen, K. 1992. Historical institutionalism in comparative politics. In S. Steinmo, K. Thelen and F. Longstreth (eds), *Structuring Politics: Historical Institutionalism in Comparative Analysis*. Cambridge: Cambridge University Press, pp. 1–32.

Veblen, T. 2008 [1899]. *The Theory of the Leisure Class: An Economic Study of Institutions*. Oxford: Oxford University Press.

Weintraub, E. R. (ed.) 1992. *Toward a History of Game Theory; Annual Supplement to Volume 24 of History of Political Economy*. Durham, NC: Duke University Press.

Sociology Meets History
Giddens's Theory of Modernity

Sociology and modernity

As modernity gradually replaced older forms of social and political organization, new scientific disciplines emerged to make sense of this epochal-changing phenomenon. Sociology and modernity are thus closely related projects. No wonder then that social theorists have always been particularly concerned with the origins and implications of modernity. Classic theorists, especially Weber, but also Marx, Tönnies and Durkheim, were particularly concerned with the historical dimension of this problem. What were the conditions for the emergence of capitalism in Western Europe? What allowed the birth of modern science in this part of the world? Why were 'modern times' closely related with the rise of the territorial nation-state, with an unprecedented conception of universal citizenship and a bureaucratic apparatus regulated by an instrumental rationality? Few contemporary social theorists have dedicated so much effort to re-examining the relationship between sociology and modernity as Anthony Giddens (1938–) has done. As we shall see, his theory of structuration and his writings on 'late modern' social and political forms are among the most influential sociological writings of the late twentieth century. Giddens's ideas will be contrasted with other sociological accounts of modernity. We choose four theorists whose work on modern social and political forms shows greater historical sensitivity than Giddens's. Modern revolutions, those epoch-changing phenomena that signal the birth of political modernity, have been the object of attention of Charles Tilly and Theda Skocpol. Michael Mann has developed an ambitious social theory of the sources of social power, with particular attention to its modern configurations. We conclude with the recent proposals by one of the discipline's elders, Shmuel N. Eisenstadt, for a 'multiple modernities' research programme. The sensitiveness to long-term historical change and global cultural diversity, however, needs not to be in confrontation with sociological reflections on modernity such as Giddens's. As we try to show, the sociological discourse on modernity faces a double challenge. As a discourse that is the product of the object it studies, social theory needs to engage in a critical self-reflection.[1] The other no less daunting challenge is that of coming to grips with modernity both as an historical epoch and a societal condition. Our first topic of discussion is Giddens's structuration theory. We begin with some introductory remarks on his career.

Although Giddens has been one of the main contributors to Anglo-Saxon social theory since the early 1970s, he was initially trained as a psychologist. He subsequently switched to sociology for his postgraduate work, but in some respects he remained loyal to his initial interest in psychology. Whereas most social theorists before Giddens would 'snub' Goffman or Garfinkel for dealing with 'trivial' matters of day-to-day life, one of Giddens's recurring themes has been that grand theory can learn a great deal from the empirical study of these routine practices (see chapter 3). Furthermore, his structuration theory is heavily supported by an in-depth reading of Sigmund Freud's work, and of E. H. Erikson's and E. V. Sullivan's ego-psychology. R. D. Laing's notion of ontological security occupies an important role in structuration theory, and Giddens's more recent works on modernity deal explicitly with a number of psychological issues such as intensified forms of reflectivity.

Giddens transferred to sociology for his Master's degree at the London School of Economics. The LSE was one of the main centres for sociology in England at the time – Oxford and Cambridge were still reluctant to accept the social sciences as a full academic discipline. Sociology was in the ascendant, though, especially in the newer universities such as Leicester, where Giddens joined the Sociology Department as a lecturer in 1961, initially teaching mainly social psychology. Leicester was a lively, cosmopolitan department, and Giddens's senior colleagues included Norbert Elias, Ilya Neustadt and Percy Cohen. At a remarkably late age, with the appearance of *What is Sociology?*, Elias was to become one of the forerunners of a theoretical assault on the empire of Parsonian functionalism – a position which Giddens was to inherit soon after (Elias 1978). During that period in Leicester, Giddens wrote a number of articles with substantial bearing on empirical research. In general, the 'earlier' Giddens seemed less preoccupied with grand social theoretical issues, although his articles on suicide and his edited book *The Sociology of Suicide* (1971a) were not devoid of conceptual considerations.

Another (though less clear-cut) example of this earlier phase is his *Class Structure of the Advanced Societies* (1973; revised edition 1981a), which deals with substantive issues that are related to the problem of class and class formation in modern society. However, in many respects this work already belongs to what might be called a later stage in Giddens's intellectual development. It involves a critical commentary on theoretical issues in the work of the classics of the social sciences, and it aims (although tentatively) at developing his own social theory. Giddens introduces the now well-known concept of 'structuration' in this book, linking it with a discussion of the extent to which classes are produced and reproduced through social practices.

The beginning of Giddens's second phase more or less coincides with his move from Leicester to Cambridge University, where he started as a university lecturer in 1969 and 15 years later became Professor of Sociology, with a fellowship at King's College. From around 1970 onwards, Giddens's writings demonstrate an increasing interest in grand theory, focusing upon a few classical social theorists, mainly Marx, Durkheim and Weber. His first book is a critical analysis of the work of these authors (1971b). He also wrote introductory books on Max Weber (1972) and Émile Durkheim (1978). Although these works do not lack originality, especially in their critical evaluation of the authors discussed, their aim is to elucidate sociological classics rather than to elaborate a new systematic frame of reference for understanding social life.

This changed with the appearance of *New Rules of Sociological Method* (1976; revised edition 1993). The reference in the title to Durkheim's *Rules of Sociological Method* is, of course, not accidental. Giddens's aim is nothing less than to develop a non-positivist conceptual framework and methodology for the social sciences, through the analysis of hermeneutic authors such as Gadamer, Schutz and Wittgenstein. *New Rules of Sociological Method* is indicative of the third phase in Giddens's writings. Although he still rigorously discusses other authors, exegesis has now become secondary, and his principal aim is to establish the contours of his own contribution to social theory (1977; 1979; 1982). Through his discussions of a wide variety of different intellectual traditions (from functionalism to Habermas), Giddens gradually introduces his structuration theory. Although the two volumes of *A Contemporary Critique of Historical Materialism* (1981b; 1985) deal with aspects of Marx's theory of history, they are also mainly directed towards the development of his own theory. This third phase came to a close with *The Constitution of Society* (1984), which is, as its subtitle suggests, considered to be Giddens's *magnum opus* in grand social theory.

Giddens's fourth phase is marked by a radical break from his previous works. Whereas his earlier books focus on general social theory, he now deals with the sociology of culture and, in particular, with problems related to modernity and detraditionalization. This new phase was initiated by lectures given at Stanford University and at the University of California, Riverside in the late 1980s, and led to the publication of *The Consequences of Modernity* (1990), in which Giddens explores the pivotal features of high modernity and their relationship with the so-called postmodern condition. The formation of the territorial nation-state, the modern political institution *par excellence*, is another topic of interest in this phase of his career (see Giddens 1985). He went on to develop related themes, focusing on concurrent changes at the level of the personality structure (1991; 1992).

The publication of *Beyond Left and Right* (1994) presumably heralds a fifth phase. This work deals with the possibility of a new social democratic political agenda, in order to cope with the challenges brought by globalization. Giddens has always shown a keen interest in politics, but since the early 1990s he has become increasingly active in the British Labour Party. Some of the ideas in *Beyond Left and Right* inspired the British Prime Minister, Tony Blair, and influenced his policies. Giddens's allegiance to the progressive centre-left has survived Blair's departure: *Over to You, Mr Brown – How Labour Can Win Again* (2007), one of Giddens's latest policy-oriented book, offers advice in areas such as welfare reform to Blair's successor, Gordon Brown. Giddens also wrote *The Politics of Climate Change* (2009), which argues for an ecological orientation in politics. In general, Giddens's interest has moved beyond purely academic activities towards more practical issues. Between 1997 and 2003, he served as Director of the London School of Economics, a position that entailed a broad involvement with educational policy matters in Britain and abroad.

In what follows we will focus on Giddens's third phase. That is, we will especially deal with his particular contribution to sociological theory – the so-called 'structuration theory'. Structuration theory is a general theory aiming to explore the interaction between social structure and human agency. It emerged in the late 1970s and early 1980s as a theoretical alternative to both structural-functionalist and interactionist perspectives (see chapters 1, 2 and 3). Although it is only associated with the work of Giddens, it would be mistaken to conceive of the theory as an isolated intellectual product. Indeed, some of the central notions of structuration theory were simultaneously developed by other authors. For instance, Giddens's argument shows striking similarities with Bourdieu's theory (see chapter 1).

Giddens's structuration theory

Giddens attempts to link different temporal levels of analysis. At one end of the spectrum there is Alfred Schutz's *durée* of day-to-day experience, referring to the repetitive and routine nature of our daily activities. At the other end of the spectrum is Fernand Braudel's *longue durée* of institutional time, referring to the relatively invariant structures which stretch over long periods of time. In between these two spans of what Claude Lévi-Strauss would call reversible time is the lifespan of the individual. Its irreversibility is captured by Heidegger's *Dasein* and its attendant notion of the finitude of people's existence – its *Sein zum Tode*. Giddens's work aims at linking these different temporal spans and thus demonstrates how, for instance, reproduction at the level of Schutz's *durée* contributes to reproduction at the level of Braudel's *longue durée*. One of the upshots of this is that Giddens's structuration theory aims at transcending the traditional micro–macro divide within sociology. In social life these three temporal spans intersect, and this has to be accounted for (1984: 34–7; 1981b: 19–20).

A second opposition which Giddens attempts to overcome is that between what he calls 'institutional analysis' and the 'analysis of strategic conduct'. Both types of analysis are arrived at through 'methodological bracketing'. Institutional analysis is achieved by bracketing strategic action. It investigates the recursive model of reproduction of structures, and it does not treat people as knowledgeable or purposive individuals. The study of strategic action, on the other hand, is achieved through placing the institutional realm under an *epoché*. It studies how people draw upon rules and resources for the continuation of their activities. Here, people are treated as active agents who know a great deal about social life. Whereas social theory has been divided between strategic and institutional analyses, Giddens's structuration theory aims at attributing equal status to both types of analysis. Neither is more important than the other; both are necessary for a full understanding of the workings of society (see, e.g., 1984: 288ff.).

Within this broader context, Giddens's structuration theory becomes understandable. One of his key notions refers to the so-called duality of structure, which postulates a particular relationship between social structure and human agency. The duality of structure, of which more in due course, allows Giddens to bind the different temporal levels, and to attribute equal status to strategic and institutional analysis. Before elaborating on this, we first need to clarify Giddens's conceptualization of human agency and, relatedly, his notion of power. We will then move on to his account of social structure and related terms.

Giddens relies upon Heidegger when he insists that action – or agency – does not refer to a 'series of discrete acts', but to a 'continuous flow of conduct'. Indeed, Giddens defines action as 'a stream of actual or contemplated causal interventions of corporeal beings in the ongoing process of events-in-the-world' (1979: 55). Note that this definition uncouples agency from intentionality: 'agency refers not to the intentions people have in doing things but to their capability of doing those things in the first place' (1984: 9). It follows that action ought to be seen as 'purposive' – not 'purposeful'. That is, people might lack clear intentions in everyday life, but they nevertheless regularly attend to their actions and to the actions of others. To say that people are agents is to acknowledge that they are always able to act otherwise: in any situation, people could either intervene or refrain from doing so. In short, Giddens's notion of agency implies that people are able to transform things, and that a fortiori the future is not pre-given (1993: 78–82). In Giddensian parlance, this 'transformative capacity' is power.

It is worth briefly elaborating upon Giddens's concept of power, and to contrast it with alternative notions of power. Power is sometimes conceived of as the ability of an individual to achieve his or her will, often (though not necessarily) against others. It is occasionally seen as the property of a collectivity, as linked with interest or as inherently oppressive. For Giddens, none of these conceptualizations will do. Power is intrinsic to agency: it refers to the individual's capability to intervene causally in a series of events. Two important points follow from this definition. First, power is not to be seen any longer as simply an impediment to freedom or emancipation. Instead, it becomes the very medium through which freedom is to be achieved (1984: 14–16; 1985: 7; 1993: 118). Second, all relationships of dependence provide resources which allow the subordinated to influence the superiors. However unequal the relationships are, there is always a 'dialectic of control' (1984: 16).

Giddens's account of structure is different from that of functionalist or structuralist-functionalist authors. Whereas they tend to conflate structure and system, Giddens goes out of his way to distinguish one from the other (see chapters 1 and 2). The latter refers to the patterning of social relationships across time and space, while the former refers to a set of social rules and resources which are recursively implicated in interaction. Similar to Saussure's distinction between language and speech, structure, marked by the 'absence of the subject', is located outside space and time, existing only in a virtual way as memory traces, to be implemented in spatially and temporally located interaction. Giddens draws heavily upon Wittgenstein's discussion of rules, defining them as implicit techniques or 'generalizable procedures' that are implemented in the enactment or reproduction of social practices (ibid.: 21). Giddens distinguishes two types of rule and two types of resource. Rules either constitute the meaning of things, or they relate to the sanctioning of conduct. Resources can be either authoritative or allocative. Allocative resources refer to control over objects, and are traditionally focused upon by Marxist authors who tend to reduce domination to ownership or control of property (ibid.: 31ff., 258ff.). Authoritative resources allude to types of transformative capacity, generating command over people. Authoritative resources are discussed by scholars like Foucault, and they refer to the organization of time and space, the body and life-chances (ibid.: 33; see also Craib 1992: 46–7; see also chapter 5).

Giddens is very careful in distinguishing various aspects of 'structure', and his terminology becomes rather complex. An exhaustive account of all his 'structure-related' concepts is impossible to provide here. Nor is such an account necessary for grasping the main line of his argument. So we will introduce only those terms that are really central to his view of institutional analysis. 'Structure' in the singular is to be distinguished from 'institutions', and from 'structural properties' of social systems. In Giddens's terminology, institutions are not organizations. Institutions refer to regularized practices stretching over long periods of time and across space: for instance, marriage. Structural properties are precisely the institutionalized features of social systems, providing their 'solidity' across time and space. Division of labour is an example of a structural property in a capitalist society (1984: 16–25). Structural principles are the most deeply embedded structural properties implicated in the reproduction of societal totalities: they indicate, for instance, the extent to which the state and the economy are separated, or the degree of time–space distantiation. The study of structural principles is the most abstract level of social analysis, and it enables Giddens to distinguish between different types of society: tribal, class-divided and class societies. Whereas in tribal societies time–space distantiation is low and kinship networks and tradition are important, in class-divided societies the city becomes a 'storage container' of military and political power. In class societies, power is concentrated in the nation-state, and time and space become commodified (ibid.: 185ff.).

Structures, as rules and resources, are understood by analytically distinguishing between three 'modalities'; that is, 'lines of mediation' between social interaction and social structure. These modalities are communication of meaning, application of sanctions and use of power (see table 5.1). The analysis of strategic conduct conceives of people as knowledgeable individuals who draw upon these modalities in order to proceed in their daily interaction. First, insofar as social interaction deals with 'communication' of meaning, individuals draw upon 'interpretative schemes' which, at the level of social structure, can be treated as 'semantic rules'. Second, the application of sanctions in interaction implies that people draw upon 'norms' which, at the level of social structure, can be analysed as 'moral rules'. The third modality ties in with people's transformative capacity. The use of power in interaction implies that people draw upon 'facilities' which, at the structural level, can be analysed as 'resources' involving structures of domination. Although analytically separate, in reality these modalities or lines of mediation intersect (ibid.: 28–30).

We can place an *epoché* upon reflexively monitored social conduct, and thus embark upon institutional analysis. Analogous to the distinction between different modalities, various institutions and structural properties can be distinguished: S stands for signification, D for domination and L for legitimation (see table 5.2). In reality, all three tend to play some role. For instance, while legitimation is undoubtedly central to the working of legal institutions, signification and domination are not entirely negligible either. Analogously, while domination is vital to the functioning of political and economic institutions, the latter also rely upon signification and legitimation.

Table 5.1 The dimension of the duality of structure

Interaction	Communication	Sanction	Power
(modality)	Interpretative scheme	Norm	Facility
Structure	Signification	Legitimation	Domination

Based on Giddens 1979:82; 1984:29

Table 5.2 Institutions and structural properties

Signification	Institutional Order
S-D-L	Symbolic orders/modes of discourse
D (auth)-S-L	Political institutions
D (alloc)-S-L	Economic institutions
L-D-S	Law/modes of sanction

Based on Giddens, 1979:107; 1984:33

It is now possible to specify more precisely what Giddens means by duality of structure, and to situate this notion within the intellectual field at the time. For those readers who are familiar with biology, there is a homology or structural identity between his notion of duality of structure, on the one hand, and Maturana's and Varela's theory of autopoiesis and self-reproducing systems on the other. Although Giddens's and Maturana's terminologies are different, the similarity between the two theories is striking, and Giddens himself acknowledges the influence of these developments in biology on his work. Both his and Maturana's theories draw attention to the mechanisms by which systems or structures ensure their own reproduction (1989: 204). Giddens's notion of duality of structure is basically that structures, as rules and resources, are both the precondition and the unintended outcome of people's agency. What does this mean precisely? We have already mentioned that, in Giddens's view, people draw upon structures in order to proceed in their daily interaction. Now, Giddens adds that, while drawing upon the structures, people cannot help but reproduce the very same structures. So structure allows for agency, which in its turn makes for the unintended reproduction of the very same structures. In other words, structures are recursively implicated in the process of social reproduction. It follows from the notion of duality of structure that there is a close relationship between the different temporal levels of social life. The 'reversible time' of institutions is, after all, both medium and effect of the social practices embedded in the 'continuity of daily life' (1984: 36ff.). It also follows from the duality of structure that a *tabula rasa* does not exist within the social realm. Any transformation, however radical, can only take place by drawing upon (and reproducing) the structural properties which are available. This explains why Giddens discards G. Gurvitch's notion of 'de-structuration'. Like Sartre, Gurvitch mistakenly opposes structure and freedom, and therefore attributes sociological significance to the notion of de-structuration. Any change, Giddens insists, goes hand in hand with structuration (1979: 70–1).

Giddens's duality of structure is easily exemplified by analogy with the use of language. As they speak, people necessarily draw upon the syntactical rules of the English language, but their utterances help to reproduce the very same structural properties. This example also demonstrates the extent to which Giddens's recursive model conceives of the reproduction of structures as an *unintended* outcome of social practices. For instance, individuals do not speak with the intention of reproducing the English language, but their speaking does contribute unintentionally to the reproduction of that language. The same applies to other forms of rule-governed behaviour: for instance, as they interact, individuals draw upon local rules of politeness and appropriateness, and in doing so they unintentionally reproduce them. Structures are unintended consequences of our practices, and they feed back into our practices as unacknowledged conditions of further acts. But contrary to functionalism and its attendant notion of societal needs, these unintended consequences should not be conceived as explanations for the persistence of practices (1977: 294ff.; 1984: 26–7).

Let us contrast this view on structure with a Durkheimian one (see chapter 1). There is the *locus classicus* in *Rules of Sociological Method*, where Durkheim defines social facts as general, external and constraining. Social facts are general because they apply to all people within a community: for example, the rules of English vocabulary and grammar are shared by all English speakers. Social facts are external in that they antedate people's existence: for instance, people necessarily draw upon a language which existed before they were born. Social facts are also constraining: for instance, our language puts limits on our thought. The concept of social facts was integral to Durkheim's attempt to demonstrate the extent to which society is an entity *sui generis*, and, *mutatis mutandis*, the extent to which sociology should be seen as independent, not to be reduced to other disciplines. In general, Durkheim, drawing upon a naturalist philosophy of the social sciences, adheres to a dualism between structure and agency in which the former somehow 'acts' upon the latter. Giddens demonstrates the paradox involved in this view with respect to the relationship between action and structure:

> the more that structural constraint is associated with a natural sciences model, paradoxically, the freer the agent appears – within whatever scope for individual action is left by the operation of constraint. The structural properties of social systems, in other words, are like the walls of a room from which an individual cannot escape but inside which he or she is able to move around at whim. (1984: 174)

Giddens attempts to overcome this Durkheimian dualism between structures and actions. First, he sees structures as memory traces which are constantly instantiated in social practices, and structures are as such *internal* to our actions (ibid.: 25). The persistence of structures is dependent on these regular instantiations. If we were to cease speaking English, then that language would somehow cease to exist. Second, Giddens sees structures as not merely constraining, but also enabling (ibid.: 25). In this sense, his approach demonstrates affinities with a Meadian or symbolic interactionist argument (see chapter 3). For instance, it is not *in spite of* language that we are able to think or intervene, but it is precisely *because of* the existence of language that we are able to do so. 'Structure thus is not to be conceptualized as a barrier to action, but as essentially involved in its production' (1979: 70).

Giddens's concept of the duality of structure rests upon the notion of knowledgeability, tacit knowledge and practical consciousness. One of his basic assertions is that people are 'knowledgeable agents' who know a great deal about social life, albeit not necessarily in an explicit way. Take the example of language again. We know how to speak our language in the sense that we know practically how to speak in accordance with the rules of grammar. This does not mean that we have to know our native language in any explicit manner in order to speak properly. On the contrary, our native language use tends to rest upon tacit, implicit forms of knowledge. We know how to do it, how to go on. We do not necessarily know which rules we draw upon. The same applies to other forms of rule-governed conduct. We know how to behave in public, without having to explain discursively the rules that we draw upon. What Schutz calls the 'stocks of knowledge' or what Giddens calls 'mutual knowledge' is not immediately accessible to the consciousness of the people involved. Replacing the traditional psychoanalytic distinction between the ego, super-ego and id, Giddens argues for his 'stratification model of action', according to which practical consciousness is to be distinguished from discursive consciousness or the unconscious. The distinction between the two levels of consciousness is not an impermeable one (one easily leads into another), whereas their separation with the level of unconscious motives or cognition is. In this context, people's knowledgeability is not only bounded by the unconscious, but also by the unacknowledged conditions and unintended consequences of their actions.

For Giddens, practical consciousness ties in with routines and with the reversible time of our daily activities, and it is here that he draws upon ethnomethodology and Goffman (see chapter 3). There are also similarities with, for instance, Garfinkel's work. In Garfinkel's breaching experiments, people draw upon cognitive frameworks which allow them to interpret reality such that the cognitive frameworks remain intact, even in cases where reality is potentially disruptive to the very same cognitive frameworks. Here we encounter a recursive model analogous to the duality of structure. But there is more to Giddens's interpretation of

Garfinkel. Giddens sees evidence in Garfinkel's experiments with trust that many of our social rules are deeply intertwined with a sense of onto-logical security. We learn from these experiments that disruptions in the routine character of our daily activities lead to extreme forms of anxiety or anger. Giddens links this with a particular reading of Freud. Routines minimize unconscious sources of anxiety and thus sustain a sense of onto-logical security. It is therefore not surprising that disruptions to our rou-tines lead to the effects described by ethnomethodologists.

Giddens's duality of structure is central to his account of the problem of integration. Integration, so he argues, is in need of a radically new approach. In general, it involves 'reciprocity of practices (of autonomy and dependence) between actors or collectivities' (1984: 28). However, previous theories fail to distinguish between 'social integration' and 'system integration'. Social integration refers to the reciprocity between individuals in contexts of co-presence. System integration, on the other hand, deals with the reciprocity between groups or collectivities across extended time–space intervals. System integration implies that structures 'bind' time and space, in that people's tacit knowledge enables society to proceed across longer temporal spans and across space. It follows from the duality of structure that social integration is essential to system inte-gration. Indeed, any face-to-face interaction unintentionally leads to the reproduction of structures, and eventually contributes to the binding of time and space.

This is not to say that all system integration can be reduced to social integration. There are other types of unintended consequence, not accounted for in the duality of structure, which are essential to system integration. Giddens distinguishes here between 'homeostatic causal loops', 'self-regulation through feed-back' or 'reflexive self-regulation'. All are crucial to system integration. Homeostasis refers to the operation of 'causal loops' whereby a series of variables affect each other, and the first variable in the series is affected by the last one such that the former is restored to its initial state. This is exemplified by the poverty cycle of material deprivation, in which the latter leads to poor education, which leads to low-level employment, which then leads to continued material deprivation. Functionalism tends to limit system integration to homeo-stasis, and it tends to disregard self-regulation through feedback and reflexive self-regulation. Self-regulation through feedback differs from homeostatic systems in that directional change takes place. For example, better education for the poor might lead to improved employment pros-pects, so that the poverty cycle is broken. Reflexive self-regulation refers to processes where people's knowledge about the social world is incorporated in their actions. For example, politicians might acquire knowledge about the intricacies of the poverty cycle and act upon that knowledge (Giddens 1979: 78–9).

It should be clear from the discussion of social and system integration that time–space intersections are crucial to social life. However, the spatio-temporal characteristics of 'modern' societies are radically different from those of 'traditional' societies. First, in modern societies time and space become independent, abstract, standard yardsticks against which things are measured. This particular notion of space and time is often treated as if it were universal, but it certainly is not. For example, time-reckoning in most traditional societies took place exclusively with reference to other 'socio-spatial markers' or regular natural events (Giddens 1990: 17–21). Second, modernization is characterized by 'time–space distantiation', that is, the extension of social systems across time and space. This phenomenon is due to, for example, centralization, intensified forms of surveillance, and efficient communication systems. Indicative of time–space distantiation is the increasing 'disembedding' of social interactions. Disembedding mechanisms remove social relations from the immediacy of a local context. Giddens distinguishes two types of disembedding mechanisms: 'symbolic tokens' and 'expert systems'. Symbolic tokens are 'media of interchange' which transcend time and space. There are various types of symbolic tokens, but money is an obvious example. Expert systems are systems of specialized knowledge and professional expertise which make possible the adequate functioning of our daily life. There are, for example, several expert systems which make for relatively safe flying. Sophisticated technical competence and expertise are involved in the making of the plane, the construction of the airport, the air traffic control, and so on. Note that trust is central to both symbolic tokens and expert systems. People tend to have 'faith' in money without a cognitive appreciation of its workings. Likewise, they generally trust expert systems without really understanding the knowledge involved. Trust is thus a central feature of modernity (ibid.: 4–35).

Ever since the publication of *New Rules of Sociological Method* and especially since *The Constitution of Society*, structuration theory has been the subject of fierce debate and criticism. In what follows, we discuss what we consider to be the more problematic areas in structuration theory. In a sense, Giddens's strengths also reveal his weaknesses. It is in fact difficult to find logical gaps or contradictions in his theory of structuration. Whenever pressed on a particular aspect of social life, he appears able to point out successfully the extent to which this issue can be accommodated within the parameters of the theory. However, he is able to avoid criticisms and to 'absorb' reality within his work precisely because of the nature of the theoretical construction provided. Core parts of Giddens's theory of structuration constitute a mode of theorizing about which we have been warned ever since the appearance of Karl Popper's *Logic of Scientific Discovery* (see chapter 8). In contrast to other grand theorists, Giddens on the whole abstains from providing bold conjectures – quite a few of the basic statements actually verge on the tautological. It is difficult to argue against his notion that people's knowledgeability is always bounded by unacknowledged conditions and unforeseen consequences – how could it be otherwise? Many aspects of Giddens's carefully worked-out theory are simply immune to refutation, being as self-evident as logical formulae. Furthermore, even when he deals with more substantive issues such as long-term change, he remains rather cautious, referring to the relatively uncontroversial notion of time–space distantiation.

Giddens's avoidance of risk goes hand in hand with his tendency to set up straw men, only to destroy them. In contrast to his own cautious nature, Giddens's straw men live dangerously insofar as they cannot but be proven wrong. His portrait of functionalism, for instance, is a stereotypical and out-dated one, failing to tackle more sophisticated versions, such as Alexander's neo-functionalism, Luhmann's system theory or Cohen's consequence laws (see chapter 2). The main target throughout his critical analysis of functionalism is Merton, especially the latter's unfortunate discussion of latent and manifest functions. Even when explicitly asked to comment in a debate surrounding contemporary interpretations of Marx (focusing on the differences between Jon Elster's rational choice perspective and Cohen's interpretation in terms of consequence laws), Giddens does not really tackle the functionalist arguments involved, but takes the opportunity to reiterate his own position within social theory (Giddens 1982). Similarly, his criticisms of evolutionism fail to take into account recent, more sophisticated developments in the area of analogies between biological and social evolution (e.g. Bhaskar 1981; Harré 1981; Wright 1989). Ironically, Wright points out that once a less stereotypical definition of evolutionism is adopted, Giddens's own theory of history in terms of space–time distantiation falls within that category.

More problematic than this, however, is that structuration theory, at least in its archetypal version, takes time into account only insofar as it reveals the production of social order. It rightly rejects the 'common-sense' (and functionalist) conflation of time with change (and order with synchronic analysis), but it tends to move towards the other extreme, subscribing to a conservative and recursive model of society (see also Archer 1990: 77–8). Although structuration theory provides a different answer from the 'normative integration model' of Durkheim and Parsons, it tends to focus on the same question of how social order (as opposed to change) comes about. This ties in with a tendency on the part of structuration theory to overemphasize what Mouzelis (1989) calls the 'natural/ performative' relationship drawing upon 'first-order' concepts. By emphasizing the accomplished reproduction of society through tacit knowledge and practical consciousness, structuration theory is especially appropriate for understanding the routines of daily life. What tends to be neglected, however, is the possibility of the emergence of explicit or discursive knowledge, and its role in the process of deliberate change and maintenance of social structures. Once confronted with novel experiences which do not fit in with their taken-for-granted world, people might adopt a more distanced, theoretical attitude towards the structures which were hitherto taken for granted, and they might act in accordance with that knowledge. Even those who wish solely to explain the reproduction of structures cannot ignore the importance of people's ability to develop discursive, theoretical knowledge of previously tacit rules and assumptions. As we already pointed out in our discussion of Bourdieu (see chapter 1), it is misleading to conceive of the reproduction of structures as merely an unintended accomplishment via tacit knowledge and practical consciousness. It regularly happens that people's articulations and discursive awareness are constitutive of reproduction.

The problems with structuration theory become even more obvious once modernity is made the focus of attention. Giddens himself sees modernity as the breaking with routines, as the capacity of people to reflect upon their conditions and as their ability to bring this knowledge to bear on future actions. However, these are features which are hardly compatible with structuration theory, since the latter emphasizes the production of social order through the mechanisms of practical consciousness and tacit knowledge. It is therefore no surprise that in Giddens's texts on modernity the core of his structuration theory is absent. The concepts which he introduces (such as 'institutional reflexivity') are independent of structuration theory, and are not derived from it. The reason for this is precisely that structuration theory is not well placed to grasp modernity and that modernity in itself makes the inadequacies of structuration theory apparent. This point will be resumed in our final remarks.

Time is of the essence: Tilly, Skocpol, Mann and Eisenstadt

As we have just seen, Giddens's treatment of time is ambivalent. On the one hand, he can be credited for paving the way to a new era of Weberian historical interpretation by means of his historically sensitive reconsideration of the sociological classics (1971b). On the other, his theory of structuration does not incorporate time in a satisfactory way. There are a number of recent proposals aimed at filling the gap between abstract theorizing and attention to history. In what follows, we will focus on four such examples: Charles Tilly's writings on collective action, Theda Skocpol's analysis of social revolutions, Michael Mann's work on the sources of social power, and S. N. Eisenstadt's 'multiple modernities' paradigm. We will discuss each in turn.

Following the footsteps of George Homans,[2] Barrington Moore (1966), and Stein Rokkan (1975), Charles Tilly (1929–2008) worked in history and sociology. As an attempt to bridge the chasm between historical particularism and social-scientific abstract models (e.g. 1981: 32), Tilly's historical sociology is particularly instructive in how it incorporates time into theory building. By combining statistical techniques to test sociological hypotheses with archival research to study history, Tilly is able to develop an innovative theory of collective action. He argues against a tradition within sociology that treats mass popular protest as a sign of psychological disturbances. From Durkheim and Tarde to Parsons and Smelser, there is an intellectual tradition that tends to interpret the unsettling social consequences of the shift towards modernity in terms of 'mobs', 'disorders' and 'mass movements'. Tilly, in contrast, believes these notions to be 'top-down words', the 'words of authorities and elites for actions of other people – and, often, for actions which threaten their own interests' (1978: 227). He adopts instead a bottom-up approach, according to which mobilization, collective action and even revolutions are an integral and no less legitimate part of modern social life. In this light, for instance, a riot ceases to be a pathological sign of social disaggregation and becomes an inevitable by-product of the struggles between different social groups pursuing their conflicting interests. This 'new social history' from below is amenable to formalization. In the case of collective action, Tilly proposes a model with five major components. First, the 'interests' which are at stake when one group interacts with another: 'who gains and who loses what?'. Second, the group's 'organization': 'to what extent does the way the group is organized affect its capacity to act on its interests?'. Third, 'mobilization' concerns the process by which the group acquires resources (as varied as weapons, votes, goods or simple labour power) needed for action. Fourth, 'opportunity' refers to the relationship between the group and the world around it: changes in that relationship can sometimes mean a threat to the interests of one group and a new chance for another. Fifth, when people act together in pursuit of common interests, we have 'collective action', the product of changing combinations of interests, organization, mobilization, and opportunity (ibid.: 7).

What is the subject-matter of such an analysis of collective action? Tilly distinguishes three intersecting areas: the basic analytical unit is the 'group', i.e., a particular population with some common structure and shared beliefs; the starting point of the analysis can also be an 'event', such as a particular revolution or a series of riots in a certain region; finally, 'social movements' (e.g., the women's movement) can also be the subject-matter of collective action analysis (ibid.: 9–10). Equipped with this model, collective actions such as the Stamp Act resistance in Philadelphia and New York in the late eighteenth century can be analysed in such a way that generalizations can be drawn from it. Formalizing this event would entail mapping the interests of the participants, estimating the state of opportunity and threat with respect to those interests, checking their mobilization levels, and identifying the extent to which these variables accounted for the character and intensity of their collective action. Tilly further distinguishes between short-term and long-term analyses. From a short-term perspective, the groups involved in the Stamp Act resistance are seen as undertaking their action purposively: they seek to realize their interests with the means at their disposal within the limits set by their relationship to the world around them. In the case of very large social changes (say, industrialization or state-making), Tilly turns from purposive to causal models: those long-term changes simultaneously affect the interests and the organization of the competing groups (1990: 14–15). The link between these two time scales is similar to that of pictures and a film. In the short-run snapshots, we have strategic interaction. But as these short-run portraits accumulate over time, the social scientist should integrate them into a 'continuous account of the process by which collective action changes and flows' (1978: 231). As soon as time enters the analysis, today's political repertoires of collective action are put into perspective. For the Stamp Act protesters, the demonstration itself had not yet entered the repertoire. Similarly, the strike was not yet available as a legally recognized type of collective action for workers. A theory of collective action needs to acknowledge the contingent character of political repertoires, while aiming at generalizations that allow one to compare different contexts, identify chains of causality and offer explanations of the phenomenon in study. The resolution of this tension between history and theory is the ultimate aim of Tilly's work.

Although Theda Skocpol (1947–) certainly agrees with this last goal, her understanding of how one should reconcile history and theory is different from Tilly's. Whereas Tilly's theory of collective action focuses on the interests, ideas and beliefs of the actors as explanatory tools, Skocpol's analysis of social revolutions privileges a structural analysis that revolves around the 'state'. In *States and Social Revolutions*, she proposes to bridge the gap between history and theory that plagues contemporary approaches by means of a 'comparative historical analysis' aimed at developing, testing and refining 'causal explanatory hypotheses about events or structures integral to macro-units such as nation-states' (1979: 36). She focuses on three social revolutions: the French Revolution of 1786–1800, the Russian Revolution of 1917–21 and the Chinese Revolution of 1911–49. Her claim is that, despite their many differences, these three cases of successful social revolution all share similar causal patterns. Rejecting Tilly's 'voluntaristic' approach to collective action, Skocpol maintains that these social revolutions were the product of cross-pressures between two sorts of phenomenon (1979: 16). First, there were external challenges. In the decades prior to the social revolutions, the old-regime states faced intense rivalry at the international level, which included waging war against more modernized adversaries. Second, internal divisions also played an important role as the emergent middle classes clashed with the landowning elites leading to repeated domestic political conflicts. There is thus a pattern shared by all three cases – in France, Russia and China social revolutions were preceded by widespread peasant revolts that undermined and eventually destroyed the power of the dominant classes. One could thus ask whether the causal arguments Skocpol developed for these cases could be extended into a general theory of revolutions; her answer is an unequivocal 'no' (ibid.: 288). Changing world-historical circumstances and different political histories make it difficult if not impossible to extend her descriptive generalizations into a proper social scientific explanation. For instance, the world scene in the late eighteenth century provided the French Revolution with a radically different context from those in which the revolutions in Russia and the China took place. Still, as Skocpol's more recent line of historical institutionalist work attests (see chapter 4), she believes that a better understanding of the structures and conjunctures at play in the three periods of revolutionary crisis can be attained and eventually contribute to a cumulative conception of science (see Pierson and Skocpol 2002: 713–18).

States and Social Revolutions definitely left a lasting mark on the discipline.[3] It inspired an entire generation of historically inclined sociologists to study large-scale social and political phenomena. Three decades after its publication, it has rightly acquired the status of a classic sociological text. As with any other text, especially classics, numerous criticisms have been levelled against *States and Social Revolutions*. We begin by contrasting Skocpol's perspective with Tilly's proposal and then present one such critique. While Skocpol explicitly criticizes Tilly's conception for its 'idealism', it has to be said that her structural analysis can itself be criticized for the opposite reason. Collective action appears in Skocpol's analysis as an explanatory variable, not as a phenomenon requiring explanation. As a result, 'dominant classes', 'peasant classes' and 'organized revolutionary vanguards' emerge as faceless entities that are supposed to explain the socioeconomic and political conditions that led to the social revolutions. However, we are not provided with any explanation whatsoever concerning their motives and organizational mechanisms. As we have seen above, this is the very aim of Tilly's theory of collective action. Turning now to a possible criticism of Skocpol's work, it is highly questionable to claim, as Skocpol does, that strengthened states – more centralized and with efficient modern bureaucracies – have emerged from all three social revolutions (1979: 285). The demise of the Soviet Union, for instance, has been attributed in large part to the overwhelming bureaucratic inefficiency of that regime. A harsh critic of Skocpol's thesis that revolutions were to be understood as processes of bureaucratic rationalization is the British sociologist Michael Mann, to whom we now turn.

Michael Mann (1942–) critically engages Skocpol in the second volume of *The Sources of Social Power*, his *magnum opus* and one of the most ambitiously conceived sociological treatises of the past few decades. He focuses on the case of post-revolutionary France. In his view, while it is undisputable that French revolutionaries modernized and bureaucratized state administration, this does not mean that the size or scope of total administration increased at all. Also, the performance of the revolutionary state was far from the efficiency image it projected. For instance, its fiscal record was pathetic, unable to collect more than 10 per cent of the taxes it demanded. For most of the nineteenth century, France had not one administration but several ministries, in which personal discretion prevailed over the abstractness and universality one associates with modern bureaucracy. Mann writes: 'So the French Revolution, like the American, promised more bureaucracy than it delivered. . . . Skocpol and Tilly emphasize bureaucratization and state power; I emphasize their limits' (1993: 463).

One could add to that that Skocpol, Tilly and the later Giddens can all be said to illustrate the recent empirical turn in social theory (see chapter 8). By contrast Mann's lifelong aim has been that of producing a theory with an equivalent degree of abstractness and generality to Parsons's structural functionalism. Unlike Parsons, however, Mann rejects a conception of human societies as social systems founded upon consensus on shared beliefs and expectations. Mann's alternative consists in claiming that society is not a totality, neither is it a system. Instead, he offers us an analytical point of entry to deal with the 'impure and "promiscuous"' (ibid.: 10) complexity of social life in the form of a model of the overlapping and intersecting networks of power that constitute society. Mann distinguishes four sources of social power: ideological, economic, military and political power (IEMP). Unlike Parsons's AGIL model (see chapter 2), Mann's IEMP model does not refer to an abstract social system, divided into subsystems or dimensions. Rather, it is a formalization of the major social networks present in concrete human societies from the beginning of historical record to the present. Let us now see in detail how Mann conceptualizes the sources of social power and its institutional forms; this will be followed by a brief analysis of two books in which he applies this 'developmental account of an abstraction, power' (1986: 538) to concrete historical phenomena such as fascism and ethnic cleansing.

The starting assumption of Mann's IEMP model is that social life can best be conceived of as a drama in which social actors struggle, sometimes to the death, to control ideological, economic, military and political power organizations. The exercise of general power over a territory is made through a combination of four specific types of power. 'Ideological power' refers to the social power that the control of an ideology brings to those groups and individuals who monopolize it. Mann has two distinct examples in mind here: religions and secular ideologies such as liberalism, socialism and nationalism. The importance of these meaning-producing movements lies in their ability to control a crucial human need, namely to find meaning in life, be it in a religious ritual or in a political rally. 'Economic power' is particularly important, as it concerns the need to produce in order to subsist: no human society can survive for very long without extracting, transforming, distributing and consuming natural resources. The struggle for the control of economic power is thus a crucial feature of social life. Going beyond Marx, Mann argues that the organizational forms of economic power include not only social classes, but also social sections and segments. For instance, any given social class is composed of several sections (say, a skilled trade), whereas a segment is here used as a group whose members are drawn from several classes (say, the social segment 'patron-client' includes members of at least two different social classes). Mann's analysis is thus more fine-grained than conventional social class analysis, dealing better with the multi-causal and multi-level character of most social phenomena. 'Military power' refers to how the modern nation-state has a monopoly of violence. This source of social power is relatively recent. Until the nineteenth century, armies were often controlled by noblemen (as in the Middle Ages) or had a substantial autonomy from the political power. As indicated above, general power is exercised through a combination of all four types, which enjoy a relative autonomy from each other. The last type, 'political power', refers to the power exerted by the state (on the 'return of the state', see chapter 4).[4] The regulation by a central administrative bureaucracy of the nation-state's territory has proved to be an essential ingredient in modern human history.

Mann labels his theory of the state as 'institutional statism', a part of his more general 'organizational materialism' (1993: 52). His theory of the state comes in two stages. First, Mann tries to provide an institutional definition of the state. In order to do so, he reinterprets Weber's conception of the state from a neo-institutionalist perspective (see chapter 4). He is thus able to identify several organized actors in domestic and foreign policy, the two main areas of intervention of the state. Second, he seeks to counter the tendency of institutionalist analysis to proliferate organizational complexity by resorting to a functionalist analysis. He does this by developing a 'polymorphous theory of "higher-level state crystallizations"' (ibid.: 54). What does this mean? The idea is that every state is polymorphous, i.e., it is composed of multiple institutions. Over time, these institutions tend to crystallize. Thus realist scholars tend to claim that modern states have crystallized as security-pursuing states, whereas Marxist ones usually argue that they have crystallized as capitalist states. Mann's approach offers a synthesis of these perspectives. In his view, there are four basic 'higher-level crystallizations' – 'capitalist, militarist, representative, and national' (ibid.: 81) – none of which has ever enjoyed a hegemonic status.

Mann has recently applied this social theoretical framework to the analysis of concrete historical phenomena. In *Fascists* (2004), he offers us an exemplary combination of historical in-depth research and general social-scientific analysis. He comes very close to actually bridging the gap between history and sociology. First, he engages in a comparison of the trajectories of fascist movements in Germany, Italy, Spain, Austria, Hungary and Romania. Second, he provides insightful single country inter-regional comparisons. Third, he combines these with analyses of the successive phases of the developmental process of each fascist movement (ibid.: 1–30). Mann is thus able to make a relevant contribution to the literature on authoritarian regimes: he shows that in all six cases there is a prevalent core fascist constituency, i.e., a social basis of support that made it possible for fascist regimes to emerge and consolidate. Rather than being supported by the lower middle class, as it is usually assumed, Mann demonstrates that a heterogeneous social set comprising soldiers, veterans, civil servants, teachers and members of an ethnic majority living in a disputed territory provided fascism with its social basis of support. Furthermore, Mann shows that in Nazi Germany a segment of civil society (namely, small-town, Protestant, middle-class associations) provided key support to Hitler's regime (ibid.: 177–206). This finding seems to confirm Alexander's thesis in *Real Civil Societies* (1998) on the ambivalent character of civil society (see chapter 2), while questioning Putnam's assumption that civic participation is necessarily connected with liberal democracy (see chapter 4). Another application of Mann's social theory is *The Dark Side of Democracy* (2005), a monumental study of ethnic cleansing. Oddly enough, though, Mann's analysis of ethnic cleansing is not limited to democratic regimes, either in formation or established. Most of the book is not about democracies at all. Mann discusses at length the Armenian genocide, the Holocaust, the communist cleansing, the former Yugoslavia and Rwanda. Unlike what is suggested by the title, ethnic cleansing emerges as the dark side of nationalism. Despite this incongruity, Mann is able to identify a set of necessary conditions for ethnic cleansing to occur (ibid.: 1–33). These include (1) a divided elite from which a segment becomes radicalized; (2) a core constituency composed chiefly of young males, which is mobilized in support of the radical segment of the elite; (3) several ethnic groups, with competing claims on territory and the state; and (4) a crisis situation that dramatically enhances a sense of insecurity amongst the elite. Generalizing from several case studies, Mann suggests that, typically, ethnic cleansing occurs when three factors come together: there is a radicalized segment of the elite, it is in control of the state and it mobilizes its social basis of support to carry out the killings in response to the intensification of the crisis situation. Mann is thus rejecting two established explanations of ethnic cleansing: that it requires massive social support and that is a state-planned endeavour. On the contrary, he claims, murderous ethnic cleansing, a distinctively modern phenomenon, has been the work of a relative few and it is far from being a carefully implemented state policy planned long in advance.

As to the shortcomings of Mann's work, we would like to highlight its Eurocentric character. Such a criticism, of course, refers not so much to Mann's most recent applied research as to his general social theory as laid out in the multivolume *The Sources of Social Power* (1986; 1993). In particular, we find Mann's explanation of the 'rise of the West' in the modern era – primarily linked to the spread of political state power – somewhat unconvincing. Western Europe is treated as a coherent whole, quite a contentious perspective, and phenomena like the rise of towns (Tilly and Blockmans 1994), the Reformation (Gorski 2003) or the scientific revolution are dismissed by Mann as possible explanations for the emergence of Western modernity. More importantly, Mann's account lacks a comparative perspective. One can only properly explain the rise of the West if the analysis includes a comparison with non-Western societies. As authors like Jack Goody (e.g. 1996) have long emphasized, the understanding of any given civilizational unit requires a global comparative perspective. This is exactly the ultimate aim of Eisenstadt's 'multiple modernities' programme, our next topic of discussion (see, e.g., Roniger and Waisman 2002).

Shmuel N. Eisenstadt's (1923–) long and distinguished career merits a few introductory remarks. To begin with, he is perhaps the most historically erudite sociologist since Max Weber. In the course of more than half a century of work on sociological theory, comparative-empirical analysis and in-depth case studies, Eisenstadt has provided the discipline with numerous and important contributions (e.g. 1963; 1986; Eisenstadt and Curelaru 1976). In what follows, we focus on his recent sociological approach to comparative civilizations. As a macro-sociological theory, it represents an alternative to the mainstream modernization theories. Eisenstadt began his career as a follower of Parsons, but in the course of the 1960s he grew increasingly critical of Parsons's evolutionism, turning instead to Weber as his main source of inspiration (1968). It is important to clarify how Eisenstadt positions himself within the Weberian sociological tradition if one wishes to understand his latest work. His notion of 'multiple modernities' rejects not only the Parsonian theories of modernization and of convergence of industrial societies, but also the classical sociological analysis of Marx, Durkheim and even Weber (2006: 199). Eisenstadt's point is that reality proved Parsons's evolutionism wrong. Instead of the expected convergence of individual societies towards a common model of 'modern society', with the United States playing the self-reassuring role of the 'pioneer', actual developments around the globe indicate that different societies have modernized along different lines of institutional development. While all societies are becoming 'modern', the precise meaning of 'modern' and its institutional expressions vary enormously. In Eisenstadt's own words, modernity

> has indeed spread to most of the world, but did not give rise to a single civilization, or to one institutional pattern, but rather to the development of several modern civilizational patterns, i.e. of societies or civilizations which share common characteristics, but which yet tend to develop different even if cognate ideological and institutional dynamics. (Ibid.: 200)

Eisenstadt's macro-sociological theory of comparative civilizations identifies five major factors shaping the institutional contours of the 'multiple modernities'. First, the contours of modernities have been changing as a result of the internal dynamics of the various institutional arenas (political, economic, technological, etc.) of each society. Second, modernities have been shaped by the political struggles between different states. Third, the shifting hegemonies in different international systems (say, the British Empire for most of the nineteenth century and America's influence in the twentieth century) have also contributed to shaping the institutional contours of modernities. Fourth, the confrontation between modernity and non-Western civilizations (such as the Islamic, Hinduist, Buddhist, Confucian, and the Japanese) is yet another relevant shaping factor. Fifth, the confrontations resulting from the promises of modernity (steady and continuous economic development, political liberal democracy, social equality, scientific progress) and its actual concretizations (cyclical economic crises, liberal democracy as the political regime of only a few developed countries, growing global inequalities, ethical and environmental limits to scientific activities) activate the consciousness of the contradictions inherent in the cultural programme of modernity (ibid.: 207–8). Weber already identified such a contradiction: the contradiction between 'the creative dimension inherent in visions leading to the crystallization of modernity, and the flattening of these visions, the "disenchantment" of the world, inherent in growing routinization and bureaucratization' (Eisenstadt 2002: 8).

One of Eisenstadt's favourite examples to illustrate the crystallization of these multiple modernities is Japan (1996). From the Meiji Restoration in the second half of the nineteenth century, which introduced the

Western programme of modernity into Japanese society, to the current institutional configuration of modern Japan, Eisenstadt offer us a detailed account of this specific modernity. In particular, he emphasizes the function performed by constellations of elites, their power relations with other sectors of society, the impact of international factors and Japan's incorporation in the modern international system as the key explanatory variables of the Japanese process of modernization. As the relevant variables change in different parts of the world, so does the institutional configuration of modernity. Hence, the cultural programme of modernity, which initially emerged in Western Europe, has been appropriated and reinterpreted by other civilizations in a constant process of interaction. One major advantage of this 'multiple modernities' research programme lies in its ability to avoid what Bernard Yack (1997) has aptly described as the 'fetishism of modernity' – that is, the widespread assumption that 'modernity' should be conceived of as a coherent monolith, disregarding its actual immense diversity and contradictions. There is no 'modernity' in the singular, if this supposes a unified and harmonious whole. Rather, there are as many 'modernities' as there are different modern institutional configurations. In this sense, Eisenstadt's notion of multiple modernities is a promising step in clarifying the empirical and analytical implications of a non-fetishist understanding of modernity. There are, however, difficulties with this proposal.

The most important one concerns the use of the plural in the expression 'multiple modernities'. If by modernity one means a whole epoch in world history, or a societal condition expressed in a set of institutional forms, or even something as elusive as a 'time orientation' (Therborn 2003: 294), it is still not clear on what empirical grounds one can speak of modernities, in the plural. One wonders whether Eisenstadt and his colleagues are putting too much emphasis on the differences between modern societies and downplaying the differences between these and their pre-modern predecessors. Take the example of Japan. Eisenstadt's thesis is that modern Japan has more in common with *pre-modern* Japan than with, say, *contemporary* Germany, for he assumes that there is greater variance between civilizational lines than across time (see also Schmidt 2006: 81). We doubt that such a thesis would resist serious empirical scrutiny: are the institutional arenas that define Japan and Germany as modern societies really that different? Are science, technology and the economy in these two countries so different to the point that one could speak of, for example, a 'German science' as being fundamentally different (following different principles and arriving at different results) from a

'Japanese science'? This can hardly be the case. A valid alternative has been developed in the emerging field of political economy and neo-institutionalist studies (see chapter 4), where there is a growing literature on 'variants of capitalism' (Hall and Soskice 2001). Even though one is dealing with the same basic phenomenon – capitalism – this model allows one to distinguish its specific institutional configurations: as different members of the same family, the German 'variant of capitalism' can be distinguished from the Japanese one. Similarly, instead of talking about 'multiple modernities', one should rather analyse different 'variants of modernity' (Schmidt 2006: 82; see also Silva 2008: 9–29), whose historical paths of development are characterized by successive 'entanglements'.[5] Despite these shortcomings, one thing seems certain. Whether operating with the notion of 'multiple modernities', 'entangled modernities' or 'variants of modernity', the most recent work on comparative historical sociology provides abundant reasons to discard Giddens's Eurocentric view of modernity. Contrary to what we are told in his best-seller *The Consequences of Modernity*, modernity is not a societal model that emerged in seventeenth-century Europe and which subsequently became worldwide in its influence (1990: 1). As Eisenstadt and his associates have shown, one can be modern in radically different ways. In addition, as Goody (2006) has demonstrated, most of what we, Westerners, tend to think as distinctively 'Western' is in fact imported from other civilizations. Ethnocentric thinking is the price one pays for ignoring the vast history of cultural borrowings. In a fundamental sense, then, authors like Eisenstadt show that history and sound comparative work allow us to take critical distance towards our beliefs and prejudices (see also Skinner 1988: 287). Meeting the challenge of coming to grips with modernity as both an historical epoch and a societal condition thus becomes a step closer.

Further reading

For a brief introduction to structuration theory, we recommend the concluding chapter of Giddens's *New Rules of Sociological Method*, chapter 2 of his *Central Problems in Social Theory*, the introduction to his *The Constitution of Society*, and Cohen's chapter in Giddens and Turner's edited volume, *Social Theory Today*. For an introduction to Giddens's views on modernity, we would suggest the opening chapter of his *Modernity and Self-Identity*. A very solid, although uncritical, introduction to Giddens's structuration theory can be found in Cohen's *Structuration Theory: Anthony Giddens and the Constitution of Social Life*. One of the best introductions to historical sociology is *Vision and Method in Historical Sociology*, a collection of essays edited by Skocpol. Tilly's classic *From Mobilization to Revolution* is an interesting and accessible entry point to his work. As to Tilly's most recent work, we recommend *Cities and the Rise of States in Europe, AD 1000 to 1800*, a collection of essays edited by him and Wim Blockmans. Skocpol's classic *States and Social Revolutions* remains compulsory reading for anyone interested in historical sociology. The introduction and the chapter devoted to the theory of the modern state in the second volume of *The Sources of Social Power* are an accessible entry point into Mann's ideas. Also useful is Hall and Schroeder's collection of essays dedicated to Mann's social theory, *An Anatomy of Power*. The introductory chapter on the 'sociology of the fascist movement' in Mann's *Fascists* is one of the best available applications of the comparative historical method. The collection of essays, *Multiple Modernities*, is a good introduction to Eisenstadt's and his followers' most recent work on comparative historical sociology.

References

Alexander, J. C. (ed.) 1998. *Real Civil Societies: Dilemmas of Institutionalization.* London: Sage.

Archer, M. 1982. Morphogenesis versus structuration: on combining structure and action. *British Journal of Sociology* 33(4): 455–83.

Archer, M. 1988. *Culture and Agency: The Place of Culture in Social Theory.* Cambridge: Cambridge University Press.

Archer, M. 1990. Human agency and social structure: a critique of Giddens. In J. Clark, C. Modgil and S. Modgil (eds), *Anthony Giddens: Consensus and Controversy.* London: Falmer Press, pp. 73–84.

Bernstein, R. J. 1989. Social theory as critique. In D. Held and J. Thompson (eds), *Social Theory of Modern Societies; Anthony Giddens and his Critics.* Cambridge: Cambridge University Press.

Bhaskar, R. 1981. The consequences of socio-evolutionary concepts for naturalism in sociology: commentaries on Harré and Toulmin. In U. J. Jensen and R. Harré (eds), *The Philosophy of Evolution.* Brighton: Harvester Press, pp. 196–209.

Bryant, G. A. and Jary, D. (eds) 1991. *Giddens' Theory of Structuration.* London: Routledge.

Callinicos, A. 1985. Anthony Giddens – a contemporary critique. *Theory and Society* 14: 133–66.

Cohen, I. 1987. Structuration theory and social *praxis*. In A. Giddens and J. Turner (eds), *Social Theory Today.* Cambridge: Polity, pp. 273–308.

Cohen, I. 1989. *Structuration Theory: Anthony Giddens and the Constitution of Social Life.* Basingstoke: Macmillan.

Craib, I. 1992. *Anthony Giddens.* London: Routledge.

Eisenstadt, S. N. 1963. *The Political Systems of Empires.* New York: Free Press.

Eisenstadt, S. N. (ed.) 1968. *Max Weber on Charisma and Institution Building.* Chicago, IL: University of Chicago Press.

Eisenstadt, S. N. 1978. *Revolution and the Transformation of Societies.* New York: Free Press.

Eisenstadt, S. N. 1986. *A Sociological Approach to Comparative Civilization: Theoretical Development and Direction of a Research Programme.* Jerusalem: Hebrew University Press.

Eisenstadt, S. N. 1996. *The Japanese Civilization in Comparative Perspective.* Chicago, IL: University of Chicago Press.

Eisenstadt, S. N. (ed.) 2002. *Multiple Modernities,* New Brunswick, NJ: Transaction Publishers.

Eisenstadt, S. N. 2006. Multiple modernities in the framework of a comparative evolutionary perspective. In A. Wimmer and R. Kössler (eds), *Understanding Change. Models, Methodologies, and Metaphors.* Basingstoke: Palgrave Macmillan, pp. 199–218.

Eisenstadt, S. N. and Curelaru, M. 1976. *The Form of Sociology – Paradigms and Crises.* New York: Wiley.

Elias, N. 1978. *What is Sociology?* New York: Columbia University Press (originally in German, 1970).

Giddens, A. (ed.) 1971a. *The Sociology of Suicide.* London: Cass.

Giddens, A. 1971b. *Capitalism and Modern Social Theory: An Analysis of the Writings of Marx, Durkheim and Max Weber.* Cambridge: Cambridge University Press.

Giddens, A. 1972. *Politics and Sociology in the Thought of Max Weber.* London: Macmillan.

Giddens, A. 1977. *Studies in Social and Political Theory.* London: Hutchinson (reprinted, 1979).

Giddens, A. 1978. *Durkheim.* London: Fontana.

Giddens, A. 1979. *Central Problems in Social Theory: Action, Structure and Contradiction in Social Analysis.* London: Macmillan (reprinted, 1993).

Giddens, A. 1981a [1973]. *The Class Structure of the Advanced Societies,* 2nd edn. London: Hutchinson.

Giddens, A. 1981b. *A Contemporary Critique of Historical Materialism. Volume 1: Power, Property and the State.* London: Macmillan.

Giddens, A. 1982. Commentary on the debate. *Theory and Society* 11: 527–39.

Giddens, A. 1984. *The Constitution of Society; Outline of the Theory of Structuration.* Cambridge: Polity (reprinted, 1993).

Giddens, A. 1985. *A Contemporary Critique of Historical Materialism. Volume 2: The Nation-State and Violence.* Cambridge: Polity (reprinted, 1992).

Giddens, A. 1987. *Social Theory and Modern Sociology.* Cambridge: Polity.

Giddens, A. 1989. Structuration theory: past, present and future. In C. Bryant and D. Jary (eds), *Giddens' Theory of Structuration.* London: Routledge, pp. 201–21.

Giddens, A. 1990. *The Consequences of Modernity.* Cambridge: Polity (reprinted, 1994).

Giddens, A. 1991. *Modernity and Self-Identity; Self and Society in the Late Modern Age.* Cambridge: Polity.

Giddens, A. 1992. *The Transformation of Intimacy; Sexuality, Love and Eroticism in Modern Societies.* Cambridge: Polity (reprinted, 1993).

Giddens, A. 1993 [1976]. *New Rules of Sociological Method,* 2nd edn. Cambridge: Polity.

Giddens, A. 1994. *Beyond Left and Right: The Future of Radical Politics.* Cambridge: Polity.

Giddens, A. 2007. *Over to You, Mr Brown – How Labour Can Win Again.* Cambridge: Polity.

Giddens, A. 2009. *The Politics of Climate Change.* Cambridge: Polity.

Giddens, A. and Turner, J. (eds) 1987. *Social Theory Today.* Cambridge: Polity.

Goody, J. 1996. *The East in the West.* Cambridge: Cambridge University Press.

Goody, J. 2006. *The Theft of History.* Cambridge: Cambridge University Press.

Gorski, P. S. 2003. *The Disciplinary Revolution. Calvinism and the Rise of the State in Early Modern Europe.* Chicago, IL: Chicago University Press.

Hall, J. and Schroeder, R. 2006. *An Anatomy of Power: The Social Theory of Michael Mann.* Cambridge: Cambridge University Press.

Hall, P. A. and Soskice, D. 2001. *Variants of Capitalism: The Institutional Foundations of Comparative Advantage.* Oxford: Oxford University Press.

Harré, R. 1981. The evolutionary analogy in social explanation. In U. J. Jensen and R. Harré (eds), *The Philosophy of Evolution.* Brighton: Harvester Press, pp. 161–75.

Homans, G. C. 1941. *English Villagers of the Thirteenth Century.* Cambridge, MA: Harvard University Press.

Homans, G. C. 1961. *Social Behavior: Its Elementary Forms.* New York: Harcourt, Brace & World.

Jensen, U. J. and R. Harré (eds) 1981. *The Philosophy of Evolution.* Brighton: Harvester Press.

Mann, M. 1986. *The Sources of Social Power. Volume I: A History of Power from the Beginning to AD 1760.* Cambridge: Cambridge University Press.

Mann, M. 1988. *States, War and Capitalism.* Oxford: Blackwell.

Mann, M. 1993. *The Sources of Social Power. Volume II: The Rise of Classes and Nation-states, 1760–1914.* Cambridge: Cambridge University Press.

Mann, M. 2004. *Fascists.* Cambridge: Cambridge University Press.

Mann, M. 2005. *The Dark Side of Democracy: Explaining Ethnic Cleansing.* Cambridge: Cambridge University Press.

Moore, B. 1966. *Social Origins of Dictatorship and Democracy. Lord and Peasant in the Making of the Modern World.* Boston, MA: Beacon.

Mouzelis, N. 1989. Restructuring structuration theory. *Sociological Review* 37: 613–35.

Pierson, P. and Skocpol, T. 2002. Historical institutionalism in contemporary political science. In I. Katznelson and H. Milner (eds), *Political Science: State of the Discipline*. New York: Norton, pp. 693–721.

Rokkan, S. 1975. Dimensions of state formation and nation-building: a possible paradigm for research on variations within Europe. In C. Tilly (ed.), *The Formation of National States in Western Europe*. Princeton, NJ: Princeton University Press.

Roniger, L. and Waisman, C. (eds) 2002. *Globality and Multiple Modernities. Comparative North American and Latin American Perspectives*. Brighton: Sussex Academic Press.

Schmidt, V. 2006. Multiple modernities or varieties of modernity? *Current Sociology* 54(1): 77–97.

Silva, F.C. da 2008. *Mead and Modernity. Science, Selfhood, and Democratic Politics*. Lanham, MD: Lexington Books.

Skinner, Q. 1988. A reply to my critics. In J. Tully (ed.), *Meaning and Context: Quentin Skinner and his Critics*. Cambridge: Polity, pp. 231–88.

Skocpol, T. 1979. *States and Social Revolutions. A Comparative Analysis of France, Russia, and China*. Cambridge: Cambridge University Press.

Skocpol, T. (ed.) 1984. *Vision and Method in Historical Sociology*. Cambridge: Cambridge University Press.

Therborn, G. 2003. Entangled modernities. *European Journal of Social Theory* 6(3): 293–305.

Thompson, J. B. 1989. The theory of structuration. In D. Held and J. Thompson (eds), *Social Theory of Modern Societies; Anthony Giddens and his Critics*. Cambridge: Cambridge University Press, pp. 56–76.

Tilly, C. 1978. *From Mobilization to Revolution*. Reading, MA: Addison-Wesley Publishing Company.

Tilly, C. 1981. *As Sociology Meets History*. New York: Academic Press.

Tilly, C. 1990. *Coercion, Capital, and European States, AD 990–1992*. Cambridge, MA: Blackwell.

Tilly, C. and Blockmans, W. (eds) 1994. *Cities and the Rise of States in Europe, AD 1000 to 1800*. Boulder, CO: Westview Press.

Wright, E. O. 1989. Models of historical trajectory: an assessment of Giddens' critique of Marxism. In D. Held and J. Thompson (eds), *Social Theory of Modern Societies; Anthony Giddens and his Critics*. Cambridge: Cambridge University Press, pp. 77–103.

Yack, B. 1997. *The Fetishism of Modernities: Epochal Self-consciousness in Contemporary Social and Political Thought*. Notre Dame, IN: University of Notre Dame Press.

6

The History of the Present
Foucault's Archaeology and Genealogy

Michel Foucault (1926–84), one the most influential thinkers of the later twentieth century, began his career in the 1940s at the renowned Parisian École Normale Supérieure. Amongst his teachers were the Hegelian philosopher Jean Hyppolite, the philosophers of science Georges Canguilhem and Georges Dumézil, and the structuralist Marxist Louis Althusser. Marxism, existentialism and, later, structuralism were the dominant strands of thought during Foucault's formative years at the École Normale, and his work can be seen as very much in opposition to Sartrean Marxism. Like that of his friend Gilles Deleuze, Foucault's *oeuvre* was significantly marked by Nietzsche's influence; like Deleuze, Foucault strongly opposed the humanistic tenets of existentialist Marxism, the adherence of the latter to a Cartesian concept of the self, its penchant for constructing a grand narrative and the pivotal role it attributes to praxis (Foucault 1990a: 3–16).

After the École Normale, Foucault taught at the University of Uppsala in Sweden, followed by a short spell as Director of the French Institutes of Warsaw and Hamburg, after which he returned to France. Meanwhile, he had published *Maladie mentale et personnalité* (1954), a scholarly work about mental disorder, remarkably non-Foucauldian in style and spirit. In 1961 he published his doctoral dissertation, *Folie et déraison: histoire de la folie à l'âge classique* (*Madness and Civilization*) – the now well-known study of the history of the relationship between madness and reason from the Middle Ages, focusing on the way in which reason and unreason become differentiated with the advent of modernity and the extent to which this differentiation was accompanied by the medicalization of madness (1989a). Although *Madness and Civilization* was well received in academic circles, and its literary and allegorical style applauded, it did not reach a wider audience. The book did, however, provide Foucault with sufficient academic renown to be offered a chair in philosophy at the University of Clermont-Ferrand.

La Naissance de la clinique (*The Birth of the Clinic*) followed in 1963 (1989c). In a similar vein to *Madness and Civilization*, but influenced more explicitly by structuralism, this book is an 'archaeological' study of medical perception, dealing with the relationship between medical knowledge and the emergence of the human sciences. We will expand on the method of archaeology later in this chapter; it suffices here to say that it aims at uncovering underlying assumptions that are dominant over a long period of time. The birth of the 'science of man' (*sciences de l'homme*) was also a central theme in *The Order of Things* (*Les Mots et les choses*) (1989d [1966]). Heavily influenced by the structuralist vogue, this is an archaeological history of the rules of organization and formation which structure the modes of intellectual frameworks. Its publication led at once to Foucault's spectacular breakthrough onto the French intellectual scene. Shortly afterwards, however, he left France to teach at the University of Tunis, thus missing the events of May 1968. He returned one year after these upheavals to the newly founded University of Vincennes, and published at the same time *The Archaeology of Knowledge* (*L'Archéologie du savoir*) (1989b). This work can be seen as a methodological commentary on his previous books, his equivalent of Durkheim's *Règles de la méthode sociologique*, with the author elaborating upon, inter alia, his intellectual position and locating himself with regard to structuralism and other intellectual developments.

In 1971, Foucault left the turmoil of Vincennes to take up the chair of the history of systems of thought at the Collège de France. The contrast could not have been sharper. At the time, Vincennes was in a state of perpetual chaos, whereas the Collège de France was, and still is, the French equivalent of All Souls College, Oxford: with no students and hardly any teaching obligations, it is the archetype of an academic ivory tower. Interestingly enough, it was during this period that Foucault again became actively involved in politics, consistent with his concept of local struggle and its attendant role for the intellectual. In 1975 he published *Surveiller et punir* (*Discipline and Punish*), a history of punishment and imprisonment, probably his most influential work abroad, though less well received in France (1977a). Although drawing upon Nietzschean genealogical rather than his own earlier archaeological methods, *Discipline and Punish* brings together a number of themes in Foucault's earlier work, in particular the role of the emerging social sciences in the formation of new disciplinary techniques.

A similar genealogical analysis and an analogous critique of psycho-analysis is central in the three volumes of *The History of Sexuality* (*L'Histoire de la sexualité*) (1979; 1990b; 1992). One of his main targets here is psycho-analytic discourse and its attendant 'repression hypothesis'. Rather than a liberating force, psychoanalysis is indicative of, and grew out of, the confessional procedures which are so central to modern society. More volumes on the history of sexuality were planned, but Foucault died suddenly in 1984. By then, he had acquired the reputation of the *enfant terrible* of French academia. He had secured a committed string of followers who admired his literary style and his new approach to history, and an equally committed consortium of enemies who maintained that he was nothing but a charlatan, shallow but shrewd in playing up to the media and into the latest Parisian fashion.

Some of these criticisms rely upon a superficial reading of Foucault's writings. As a matter of fact, many secondary sources fail to do justice to his work, and even the more sympathetic readings tend not to acknowledge the radical nature of his intellectual project. They evaluate his work by using traditional standards. Many commentators on Foucault are even unaware of the extent to which their criticisms are external ones. That is, they fail to recognize that Foucault has a different agenda from traditional social theory and history. In this chapter, we will focus on the distinctiveness of Foucault's project, and evaluate his work in that light.

A new conception of knowledge acquisition

The best starting point to elucidate Foucault is to contrast him with a mainstream view in sociology and social theory. Since the birth of the social sciences, there has been a consensus within social scientific and philosophical circles regarding the nature of social scientific knowledge. First, it is assumed that one's social scientific knowledge aims at depicting, explaining or understanding a 'world out there'. This world is different from and exists independently of one's theoretical presuppositions. Second, the type of knowledge involved is *ipso facto* not self-referential. That is, it is not the aim of social scientific knowledge to reveal or understand the presuppositions that are the medium through which that knowledge is arrived at. Third, this type of knowledge should aim at explaining unfamiliar phenomena by drawing upon analogies with phenomena that are familiar. To put it more bluntly, this type of knowledge attempts to eradicate the unfamiliar by turning it into the familiar (see chapter 8).

Much has, of course, been said about the differences between various philosophies of the social sciences. We do not wish to question the many dissimilarities between, for instance, positivism, realism or falsificationism regarding the demarcation between science and non-science, the nature of explanation or the notion of causality (see chapter 8). Despite these dissimilarities, the three characteristics mentioned above are shared by a significant number of philosophies of social science. Some philosophies might be more *explicit* in promoting one or more of these assumptions (for instance, the first and the third assumption are among the *idées maî-tresses* of realism), but most subscribe at least *implicitly* to all three positions. More importantly, most empirical researchers in the social sciences carry out their studies in line with the three assumptions. It is therefore appropriate to talk about a 'traditional consensus' in sociology.

Now, we argue that Foucault presents an alternative to the traditional consensus. He presents a form of knowledge about the social world which is first and foremost 'self-referential'. That is, it is not primarily (and certainly not merely) directed towards reconstructing a world out there, but rather ultimately directed at revealing our own previously held assumptions. A related fact is that his principal target is the familiar, not the unfamiliar. More precisely, rather than drawing upon analogies with the familiar to explain the unfamiliar, his writings aim at creating distance, revealing and threatening what was hitherto taken for granted. In what follows, we will demonstrate that this type of knowledge acquisition runs throughout Foucault's work, and, given that he is a historian, we will reveal the consequences of that conception of knowledge when applied to the discipline of history. We hope thereby to point out some misreadings of Foucault, and to defend him against misguided criticisms.

Scholars familiar with Foucault might object to the way in which we identify one methodological theme running through his work. It has indeed often been pointed out that an 'epistemological break' or discontinuity distinguishes Foucault's earlier archaeology from his later genealogy (see, e.g., Sheridan 1990; Smart 1988: 41ff.). Just as it is commonplace to talk about an early and a mature Marx, or about an early and a later Wittgenstein, so scholars similarly refer to archaeology and genealogy in Foucault. There are undoubtedly convincing arguments for seeing the two periods as radically different. The philosophical views which influenced them are, after all, clearly distinct: archaeological methods are very much embedded in French structuralist thought, whereas genealogy is heavily indebted to Nietzsche's writings. Hence Foucault, as an archaeologist, shares the scientific and objectivist pretensions of fellow-structuralists, whereas Foucault as a genealogist leads the way to post-structuralist thought. Our position is, however, that by dividing Foucault's work into archaeology and genealogy his critics fail to recognize the methodological continuity throughout his work. If commentators acknowledge continuity, then this tends to be merely thematic. For instance, some argue that although Foucault fails to discuss *explicitly* the concept of power in his earlier work, it is nevertheless a continuous theme (a view expressed by Foucault himself). We wish to show instead that the types of knowledge acquisition involved in the early and the later Foucault are not as radically different as is sometimes suggested, and thus more methodological continuity can be attributed to his work than is customarily assumed. First, we will discuss his archaeological work, then we will elaborate upon his genealogical writings. Finally, we summarize the similarities with regard to the issue of knowledge acquisition.

First, however, we need to add one more qualification. It is well known that Foucault made several attempts to distance himself from particular labels such as 'structuralism' (1989b: 15ff.; 1989d: xiv; see also chapter 1). Surely, given the Parisian cultural 'field', in which claims to originality are crucial to one's reputation, it is understandable that Foucault, like other French prima donnas, did not wish to be too closely associated with other intellectual trends. It would be a mistake, however, to think of Foucault as a mere *enfant terrible* working outside any intellectual setting. Despite his attempts to argue that archaeological methods are developed without resort to structural analysis, it is our conviction that the latter is indispensable for making sense of the former. This is not simply to say that Foucault's archaeological methods *in toto* are structuralist. For instance, his notion of language as an event or act is indeed far removed from, if not in contradiction to, the structuralist notion of *langue* as structure. What we wish to say, rather, is that the two perspectives do share a significant number of assumptions, and that pointing out their differences does not add significantly to the understanding of archaeology. Even if it is true that Foucault does not *consciously* use structuralism in his archaeology, it is perfectly legitimate (and, ironically enough, entirely in line with Foucault's own archaeological methods) to call archaeology structuralist because, first, structuralist analysis is a *sine qua non* for making sense of archaeology; second, structuralism became prominent during Foucault's formative years; and, third, several of Foucault's teachers were well acquainted and sympathetic towards the new structuralist movement. Foucault's originality does not rely upon his ability to create ideas and concepts *de novo*. Rather, it lies in his ability to combine successfully different intellectual strands, and, of course, in his capacity to direct them towards a self-referential type of knowledge acquisition.

Archaeology

In general, Foucault's earlier historical writings rely upon what he calls archaeological methods. These underlie most of his publications in the 1960s, amongst which his *Madness and Civilization* and *The Order of Things* are best known. In *The Archaeology of Knowledge*, Foucault sets out to elucidate his methodology and to situate it within the recent intellectual developments in France. His archaeology is influenced by a wide variety of intellectual traditions, two of which are worth recalling. First, there is the (already mentioned) influence of the French structuralist movement in general and French structuralist history (the Annales School) in particular (see chapter 1). Second, there is the impact of French philosophy of science on Foucault's archaeology (see 1989b: 3–30).

Let us first start with structuralism and the structuralist historical research of the Annales School. For the sake of clarity, it is necessary to distinguish between two strands in structuralist social science (see chapter 1). One strand attempts to account for social systems by drawing on analogies with linguistic systems. This 'linguistic' strand often relies upon Saussure's (or Jakobson's) insights about meaning and its relation to *langue*. Social life is seen as an amalgam of signs; the meaning of each sign is arbitrary, and depends on each sign being different from other signs currently in use. This linguistic strand is represented in, for example, Barthes's *The Fashion System* (1983). The early Foucault also draws upon this type of structuralism, but the Annales School does not, and as we wish first to deal with its influence on Foucault, we will, *ad interim*, omit the linguistic strand.

This leads us to the second form of structuralism, which attempts to demonstrate the extent to which people's thoughts and actions are moulded and constrained by underlying structures. This strand necessarily relies upon a realist philosophy of science; it assumes a 'stratified' conception of reality which attributes reality status not only to observed phenomena, but also to underlying structures which generate or cause the phenomena (see chapter 8).[1] This strand goes back to some of Durkheim's writings, and it is this kind of Durkheimian structuralism which has been taken up by members of the Annales School. They oppose what Braudel calls the '*courte durée*' or '*histoire événementielle*' (1966: preface), the latter referring to the history of events or the history of great men or women who have shaped our past. Against this narrative approach to history which is so typical of the *histoire Sorbonniste*, Braudel and others argue for the importance of structuralist types of historical enquiry. Reacting against the positivist tendencies of French historiography, structuralist historical research aims to uncover the *longue durée*; that is, the relatively stable, unacknowledged, constraining structures which stretch over long periods of time. Beyond the level of events, individual choices and other vicissitudes lie deeper, more stable layers of underlying structures. Some of these structures are physical, for instance geographical or climatological constraints. Some scholars are more interested in mental constraints, focusing, for example, on the extent to which particular epistemological frameworks have dominated particular epochs.

Foucault's archaeological work is very much indebted to French structuralist history, as he also attempts to unravel the latent structures which have stretched over long periods of time (1989b: especially 3–17). When he mentions the 'archaeological' level of analysis, he is in fact referring to the rules of formation which stipulate the conditions of possibility of what can be said within a particular discourse during a relatively long timespan. For instance, he brings to light particular discourses about madness and sanity which were common for centuries, and similarly he detects 'epistemes' which dominated science and philosophy. Both discourses and epistemes refer to the implicit and shared rules which operate 'behind the backs' of individuals and which are a *sine qua non* for the formation of statements. These rules specify which statements can be made and which are true or false (ibid.: especially part 2).

As acknowledged by Foucault in *The Archaeology of Knowledge*, his work also makes use of conceptual tools which were introduced by French historians of science such as Bachelard and Canguilhem. These scholars oppose a continuous conception of history, and they introduce the notion of discontinuity or rupture to distinguish various scientific epochs and to underline their differences (ibid.: especially 3ff.; see also Bachelard 1984 and Canguilhem 1978). Foucault contrasts the 'new history' with previous types of history in which the task of the historian was to *efface* discontinuity – to mould it into a narrative of continuity:

> For history in its classical form, the discontinuous was both the given and the unthinkable: the raw material of history, which presented itself in the form of dispersed events – decisions, accidents, initiatives, discoveries: the material, which, through analysis, had to be arranged, reduced, effaced in order to reveal the continuity of events. Discontinuity was the stigma of temporal dislocation that it was the historian's task to remove from history. (1989b: 8)

So, under the old type of history, discontinuity was at best an embarrass-
ment for the historian at work – a failure, maybe a sign of lack of craftsmanship. In the new type of history, with which Foucault identifies
himself, discontinuity, rather than being an obstruction, becomes essential
to the practices of the historian:

> One of the most essential features of the new history is probably this
> displacement of the discontinuous: its transference from the obstacle to
> the work itself; its integration into the discourse of the historian, where it
> no longer plays the role of an external condition that must be reduced,
> but that of a working concept; and therefore the inversion of signs by
> which it is no longer the negative of the historical reading (its underside,
> its failure, the limit of its power), but the positive element that determines
> its object and validates its analysis. (Ibid.: 9)

Foucault recognizes the twofold nature of this statement. On the one
hand, it means that the historian uses the notion of discontinuity as an
instrument for approaching reality. Discontinuity is a tool which allows
the historian to divide up domains or periods. On the other hand, it means
that the historian assumes that discontinuity is part of reality (ibid.).

Foucault merges structuralist notions with this concept of discontinuity, and his archaeological method thus aims at pointing out two phenomena. First, he searches for underlying structures, which are relatively
unacknowledged by the individuals involved, and which are relatively
stable over long stretches of time. Second, he looks for those radical transformations in history which separate the periods of relative stability –
those ruptures which call an end to an epoch and which herald a new
longue durée. Foucault's view of history indeed suggests long periods of
permanence, each of which is dominated by a particular framework or set
of practices. These periods are separated by relatively short intervals
(often spanning only a few decades) in which the shift from the old structure to the new is accomplished. There are thus two 'rhythms' in Foucault's picture of history: the very slow rhythm of the *longue durée* (which
reflects the influence of structuralist history) and the accelerated rhythm
of *rupture* (which reveals very much the influence of French history of
science). Note that Foucault does not always show much interest in
explaining how these radical transformations came about. He occasionally
justifies his lack of interest in that question by arguing that the methodological problems involved are severe (1989d: xiii).

It is at this stage important to go back to the influence of structuralism
on Foucault's writings, in particular the influence of the linguistic strand.

Central to the linguistic strand is a holistic theory of meaning (see chapter 1). According to this theory, the meaning of a sign is dependent on its differences from the other signs currently in use within that structure (see, e.g., Saussure 1959: 88ff., 110ff., 120–2). Now, combined with the above Foucauldian picture of discontinuous history, this holistic theory of meaning implies that the various structures, which follow each other through time, are not simply different, but incommensurable. Indeed, every rupture leads to the emergence of a radically different structure, and given that the meaning of signs is dependent on structure (in the way described above), meaning necessarily undergoes a profound change as well. That is why, when reading Foucault, one gets the impression that with every discontinuity an entirely different world is created. This explains Foucault's reference to Jorge Luis Borges's fictitious Chinese encyclopedia in the preface to *The Order of Things*. In that encyclopaedia animals are divided into:

> (a) belonging to the Emperor, (b) embalmed, (c) tame, (d) sucking pigs, (e) sirens, (f) fabulous, (g) stray dogs, (h) included in the present classification, (i) frenzied, (j) innumerable, (k) drawn with a very fine camelhair brush, (l) *et cetera*, (m) having just broken the water pitcher, (n) that from a long way off look like flies. (Foucault 1989d: xv)

Foucault emphasizes the extent to which this Chinese taxonomy relies upon rules and assumptions alien to us. For example, Borges's construction does not rely upon our distinction between 'the Same and the Other'. Likewise, Foucault's history, if successful, aims at presenting such bewildering discontinuities in thought and in practice throughout history.

We are now in a position to elaborate upon how Foucault's archaeology suggests a self-referential concept of knowledge, and how it draws upon the unfamiliar in order to account for the familiar. The different periods which he portrays are not only radically different from each other, they also contrast with the present day. As a matter of fact, they often stretch as far as the present day. So Foucault's portrayal necessarily involves a contrast between past and present. A number of consequences follow from this. The most obvious is that Foucault's work facilitates the awareness that, to put it epigrammatically, *the present has not always been.* That is, the portrayal of different periods allows one to become aware of the fact that some of the concepts or practices which are used today are not as universal or fixed as they might seem. For instance, reading *Madness and Civilization*, one is struck by the extent to which past definitions of madness and the ways in which the insane were then treated are alien to the conceptions, categorizations and practices of today. Second, through juxtaposition with the past, the present becomes visible. That is, structures tend to be taken for granted by the individuals who are subjected to them, and these structures are therefore unlikely to be visible to them. Juxtaposition with a different structure, whether real or imaginary, might lead to the making manifest of a previously latent structure. And this is exactly what Foucault does. His depiction of past epistemes, for instance, makes for the uncovering of contemporary conceptions surrounding epistemology or ontology. Third, it should now be clear that, in some respects, Foucault's archaeology implies the exact reverse of the realist conception of science. Realism argues that science attempts to make sense of unfamiliar phenomena by drawing upon analogies with phenomena which are familiar (see chapter 8). In contrast, Foucault's methodology attempts to draw upon knowledge about and dissimilarity with the unfamiliar (the distant past) in order to gain access to a 'familiar stranger' (the taken-for-granted present). Notice the extent to which the past, rather than a mere object of research or end-point, is a medium for access to the present. Fourth, given that Foucault's archaeology makes manifest the structures of today and shows that they are not universal, and given that structures exercise power mainly through their invisibility and through the fact that they are experienced as universal, his earlier work creates the possibility for the corrosion of the present. Once people become aware of the assumptions or rules upon which they have hitherto unconsciously drawn, and once they realize how radically different these were in the past, then the strength of these assumptions or rules is potentially undermined.

Genealogy

In the 1970s, Foucault abandons archaeology for genealogy. So *Discipline and Punish* and the three volumes of *The History of Sexuality* are offered as genealogical works. It has often been pointed out that, in this period, Foucault is very much influenced by Nietzsche. We think that is a fair description. This is not to say that Nietzsche did not exercise any influence on Foucault before 1970 (see 1989b: 12–14). Rather, the claim is that his influence becomes more explicit and systematic after that date. First, Foucault borrows Nietzsche's notion of genealogy – for instance, in the article 'Nietzsche, history, genealogy', where he explicitly acknowledges and quotes his mentor *in extensor* (1977b: 140–64).[2] Second, in this period,

Foucault, like Nietzsche, puts forward an anti-essentialist position. According to this nominalist position, the meaning of objects or practices varies according to the context in which they arise. This might explain why Foucault is reluctant to provide an explicit definition of newly introduced concepts such as power. Third, like Nietzsche, Foucault makes use of the concept of power, and this concept plays a dual role in his theory. As with Nietzsche, Foucault realizes that power struggles accompany the emergence of new meanings. Nietzsche, for instance, argues that the meanings of good and evil shifted radically with the advent of Christianity, and that this transformation of meaning was the product of a particular power struggle at the time. Foucault is also indebted to Nietzsche when he conceives of power as intertwined with knowledge; knowledge is not neutral to power, nor is it simply self-emancipatory. For instance, Foucault demonstrates in *Discipline and Punish* the extent to which the emerging social sciences and psychiatry, while disguised as liberating forces, were essential to the development of new, and more efficient, forms of social control (see especially Foucault 1980). Fourth, like Nietzsche, Foucault's genealogical history is opposed to any meta-narrative which would incorporate past, present and future. There is of course a storyline which runs through *Discipline and Punish* (and through *The History of Sexuality*, for that matter), but there is no overall theoretical scheme which necessarily unfolds itself through time.

We will now elaborate upon what we see as the cardinal features of Foucault's notion of genealogy. The genealogist goes back in time in order to show that at some point radically new meanings were allocated to concepts. It is then demonstrated that the emergence of these new meanings was due to power struggles or contingency. The new meanings were subsequently transmitted across generations, and so became part of the culture. These meanings gradually came to be experienced by people as self-evident, necessary, innocuous (if not honourable) and consistent.[3] Foucault's genealogy, on the other hand, aims at demonstrating that these meanings are neither obvious, necessary, harmless, honourable nor coherent. First, the self-evident nature of the current meanings is undermined by demonstrating that radically different meanings existed in the past. Second, against any form of causal-mechanical view or teleology is the genealogist's attention to 'the accidents, the minute deviations – or conversely, the complete reversals – the errors, the false appraisals, and the faulty calculations that gave birth to those things that continue to exist and have value for us' (1977b: 146). Consequently, the genealogist breaks with any presentist view which assumes a necessary unfolding of laws or wheels of history: 'the things which seem most evident to us are always formed in the confluence of encounters and chances, during the course of a precarious and fragile history' (1990a: 37). Third, current meanings are shown to be less harmless or honourable than is assumed by demonstrating that they are interrelated with power struggles. The starting point for a genealogist is that belief systems or ethical systems appear innocuous or, stronger, ought to be held in respect; after all, they deal with matters of truth and morality. The genealogist shows that, contrary to that appearance, belief and ethical systems are very much implicated in power struggles (1977b: 142ff.). Fourth, lack of coherence is shown by demonstrating how new meanings coexist with old ones. It would indeed be a mistake to assume that old meanings are completely erased by new ones as if a *tabula rasa* were possible. In Foucault's own words: 'We should not be deceived into thinking that this heritage is an acquisition, a possession that grows and solidifies; rather, it is an unstable assemblage of faults, fissures, and heterogeneous layers that threaten the fragile inheritor from within or from underneath' (ibid.: 146).

Before elaborating on how Foucault uses genealogy in *Discipline and Punish*, let us briefly enlarge on his concept of power. Power is, after all, central to genealogy: remember that power struggles accompany and explain the emergence of new meanings. Foucault himself introduces the concept rather late. Reminiscent of Molière's Mr Jourdan who suddenly realizes that he has been speaking prose all his life, Foucault stated in an interview in 1977: 'When I think back now, I ask myself what else it was that I was talking about, in *Madness and Civilization* or *The Birth of the Clinic*, but power' (1980: 115). In discussing power, he draws upon a counterfactual argument: it comes into play whenever people are made to do something which they would not have done otherwise. However, Foucault insists that his examination does not aim to provide a 'theory' of power, rather an 'analytics' of power (1979: 82). The analytics of power refers to a description of the domain occupied by relations of power, and to the identification of the tools which are necessary for the analysis of that domain. Despite this 'instrumental' stance, Foucault's discussion of power is theoretical in various ways.

First, he very much rebels against what he sees as the two dominant theoretical positions with respect to power: a 'judicial-liberal' and a Marxist conception. Foucault argues that both conceptions restrict power to its economic dimension. In Marxist writings, for instance, power appears as a commodity, directed towards the maintenance and reproduction of economic relations. By contrast, Foucault's concept of power is explicitly non-economic (1990a: 104–5). Second, Marxists often rely upon what Foucault calls a 'descending' type of analysis. That is, power is seen as imposed on people from above. Foucault's methodological rules suggest an 'ascending' analysis of power. Here, the understanding of the local figurations contribute to the broader mechanisms at a macro-level (1979: 84–5). Third, Foucault argues that several macro-analyses tend to describe power in terms of 'possession': they talk about a class or the state possessing power and imposing it on its subjects. In Foucault's micro-physics of power, power appears instead as a strategy, emerging out of the relationships between people, transmitted through the subjects, rather than imposed on them. As nobody's particular property, power cannot be localized. It is therefore dispersed, not centralized in society; there is no locus of control, no centre of gravity (ibid.: 92–5).

Fourth, Foucault's rejection of power as something possessed by an individual or group ties in with his refusal to deal with the concept in terms of intentionality or decision. The function of power is compared to a chain in that it 'circulates' through a 'net-like' organization. The individual is not an 'elementary nucleus', a 'primitive atom' subjected to power. One of the pivotal features of power is that it identifies individuals who, instead of being the 'points of application' of power, become the 'vehicle' through which it is circulated (1980: 97–8). Fifth, related to the previous point, Foucault does not wish to accept a 'negative' reading of power. In a negative view, power is merely an impediment to agency. Take the history of sexuality, for instance. According to a negative concept, power only comes into play insofar as sex and pleasure are repressed or negated: 'power can "do" nothing but say no to them' (1979: 83). For Foucault, power does not merely operate in a negative fashion, it also constitutes things (and the latter are sometimes the vehicles for its replication); it creates, for instance, the 'individual' in the first place, or it creates sexual desires (1980: 120–4). Finally, in some structuralist writings, there is hardly any role for agency. Foucault insists, instead, that power relations always involve the possibility of resistance. They are intrinsically unstable and can be reversed (1979: 95ff.). Genealogy might help in overturning that 'hazardous play of domination'.

One of the criticisms levelled at Foucault's 'analytics' of power referred to its seemingly exclusive focus on the detailed texture of particular techniques and practices of power. In doing so, critics claimed, Foucault was neglecting the large-scale relations between groups, collective agents and institutions (Gordon 1991: 4). Foucault answered this criticism in his late 1970s lectures on 'governmentality' (1991). In these lectures, he tried to show the methodological continuity between a 'microphysics of power', such as the one he applied in the study of the disciplinary techniques at the origin of the modern penal system in *Discipline and Punish*, and a 'macrophysics of power', whose object is the techniques and practices employed in the governing of populations at the level of entire nation-states. In 1978, Foucault offered an annual course entitled 'Security, territory and population', part of a lecture series that had begun in 1970 and would last until his demise in 1984. In this particular course, he delivered a lecture on the topic of 'government rationality' (or 'governmentality', to use Foucault's neologism) where he tried to elucidate how power has been exercised in Western societies since early modern times.[4]

In our view, this lecture can be seen as a genealogical exercise. Foucault's explicit aim was to transform state power into a 'problematic', thereby questioning the self-evident or necessary character of the ways we think about politics. Foucault is not interested in identifying, as political philosophers usually are, the 'best form of government'. Rather, his aim is to study the questions 'How do we govern?' and 'How are we governed?', that is, to analyse the conditions under which specific political regimes came into being, are maintained and change. From the perspective of such an 'analytics of government', the power exerted by the modern nation-state, far from being the natural outcome of some historical process, should be seen as the outcome of 'a triangle, sovereignty-discipline-government, which has as its primary target the population and as its essential mechanism the apparatuses of security' (1991: 102).

Foucault's argument is clear enough. In medieval and early modern Europe, the rationale of political power was to ensure the continuity of the sovereign's power over the territories that compose his kingdom. In the early sixteenth century, however, the rationale of power suffers a dramatic change. The end of government is now the life (and death) of human beings constituted as a population. According to Foucault, this marks the birth of 'biopolitics'. In 1976, he had already hinted at this specific form of power exercised over persons as living beings when he introduced the notion 'biopower' in the final chapter of *The History of Sexuality*. But in this lecture he goes a step further and associates it with the theme of government. As a consequence, one can now see more clearly how the above-mentioned triangle constituted by sovereignty, discipline and government emerged and developed.

The historical origins of this triangle can be traced back to two opposing processes that occurred in sixteenth-century Europe. On the one hand, there was the movement towards the establishment of the territorial nation-state ('state centralization'), a historical process that has long caught the attention of historical sociologists, as we have seen in the last chapter. On the other hand, there was the totally different movement of 'dispersion and religious dissidence' brought about by the Reformation and Counter-Reformation (ibid.: 87–8). It is at this time that the doctrines of reason of state begin to emerge. This literature on government, which would span most of the next two centuries, represents nothing less than an epistemological revolution – with it, the 'art of government' acquires an autonomous type of rationality. The principles of government cease to be part and parcel of the divine order of the world, as the medieval divine right theories suggested. The state starts now to be conceived of as being governed by rational principles which are intrinsic to it. The organizing theme of the 'reason of state', in the sense that the state, like nature, is governed by an autonomous sort of rationality, is singled out by Foucault as the first sign of the emergence of the modern governmental rationality, or governmentality (ibid.: 97).

By this Foucault wishes to describe the ways we think about political power and government. The questions that come associated with governmentality thus include who can govern, who and what is governed, and how governing is possible in the first place. Government is seen as a practice or, as he puts it, an 'art' insofar as it involves a number of techniques and procedures. Foucault's 'macrophysics of power' proposes to reconstruct the historical path of development of this specifically Western form of governmental rationality. This reconstruction, however, does not assume the form of a series of successive developmental stages, as evolutionary accounts often do. Foucault's alternative is to conceive it as a relation between three forms of power – sovereignty, discipline and government – whose object is the population. Hence the term *bio*politics.

Biopolitics came into being as the 'art of government' of the sixteenth and seventeenth centuries gradually gave way, in the course of the eighteenth century, to a 'political science'. The primary object of biopolitics is human beings constituted as a population. This is a regime of political practices concerned with matters of life and death, with health and illness. In order to attain this goal, the state makes use of political economy, a new science whose purpose is to assist the intervention of the government in that specific sector of reality that is the economy. Sanitation, housing and working conditions are but some aspects of the intervention of the biopolitical power. Likewise, the school, the prison and the factory are but some of the institutions through which the behaviour of individuals could be observed, monitored, shaped and controlled.

If the population is the government's finality, its rationality comprises a triadic relation between different forms of power. Let us now see how Foucault describes the history of governmentality. As a result of the change in character of the art of government between the sixteenth and the eighteenth centuries, sovereignty ceases to be a purely juridical and political affair to become a political economic one. A country's sovereignty is no longer about only maintaining territorial integrity; it involves also providing a legal foundation to its biopolitical activities (e.g. the welfare of the population and the improvement of its condition). As for discipline, Foucault has no doubts. With the rise of biopolitics the need for the development of disciplinary technologies and practices increases significantly. A politics concerning the administration of life, especially at the level of entire populations, requires the 'management of population in its depths and details' (ibid.: 102). Finally, the third vertex of the triangle, government, acquires a whole new meaning when it comes to signify the government of a population. It now becomes an 'economic government' (ibid.: 92–5). Its interventions in the field of economy and population acquire an economic character in two different senses: from a fiscal point of view, it needs to be financially viable; and from the perspective of its internal organization, it has to follow an economic logic. It is worth quoting Foucault's genealogical account of governmentality in full:

> The ensemble formed by the institutions, procedures, analyses and reflections, the calculations and tactics that allow the exercise of this very specific albeit complex form of power, which has as its target population, as its principal form of knowledge political economy, and as its essential technical means apparatus of security. (Ibid.: 102)

So far we have dealt with the theory behind Foucault's notions of genealogy and power. Let us now return to genealogy, and show how Foucault uses it in *Discipline and Punish*. He argues that up until the late eighteenth century punishment was a public and gruesome spectacle, symbolizing the strength of the sovereign and directed towards the body of the victim (1977a: 3–69). He goes to some length to show that, rather than being simply a barbarous system, the form of punishment has its own logic – logic that is as sophisticated and internally coherent as ours. Be that as it may, this practice led to much disorder, because the person to be executed had, in the face of death, nothing to lose, and, confronted with an enormous audience, considerable power. It was not uncommon for someone in this situation to speak openly against the sovereign or the regime, and for the audience then to side with the condemned (ibid.: 57–69).

Confronted with these problems of the 'society of spectacle', policy-makers and intellectuals thought of more 'efficient' forms of exercising social control. This inspired the utilitarian reforms at the beginning of the nineteenth century, which set in motion a 'disciplinary' society, in which conceptions of punishment were radically transformed. The spread of disciplinary power aims at a regular, systematic training and monitoring of the body (ibid.: 135–69). As early as the eighteenth century, the *philosophes* had already expressed their hostility on humanitarian grounds towards the old penal system. Jeremy Bentham's new system, however, bore hardly any resemblance to that which they had in mind. The consequence of his system was anything but the reform of criminals; its effect was to implement more efficient forms of social control which could be (and were) applied outside the penal system.

Characteristic of the emerging disciplinary society was the emphasis on incarceration, 'hierarchical observation', 'examination' and 'normalization' (ibid.: 170–94). The panopticon is Foucault's example *par excellence* of hierarchical observation in the nineteenth century. The panopticon implies a particular organization of space such that at any time the inmates are unable to know whether they *are* being watched, and they know that they *might* be monitored. This system is supposed to lead to 'self-correction': knowing that they might be watched at any time, the inmates end up monitoring themselves (ibid.: 170–7, 195–228). Besides hierarchical observation, disciplinary power implies an emphasis on what Foucault calls 'normalization'. That is, elements of behaviour are rewarded or punished depending on whether they adhere to or deviate from the postulated norm. On the basis of this penal accountancy, people are ranked depending on the extent to which they conform to standards (ibid.: 177–84).

The combination of hierarchical observation and normalization culminates in the notion of the 'examination'. The successful implementation of the examination ultimately depended on the development of sophisticated procedures for documentation and classification. The emerging 'science of man' made possible such procedures. Hence, the social sciences, although prima facie directed towards self-emancipation, played a crucial role in the transformation into a 'disciplinary' society. However much this society of 'surveillance' was bound up with social control, the new system gradually appeared as obvious, coherent and benevolent. So, by the late twentieth century, the disciplinary regime has permeated many realms of society:

> The judges of normality are present everywhere. We are in the society of the teacher-judge, the doctor-judge, the educator-judge, the 'social worker'-judge; it is on them that the universal reign of the normative is based; and each individual, wherever he may find himself, subjects to it his body, his gestures, his behaviour, his aptitudes, his achievements. The carceral network, in its compact or disseminated forms, with its systems of insertion, distribution, surveillance, observation, has been the greatest support, in modern society, of the normalizing power. (Ibid.: 304)

So genealogy undercuts the present in a number of ways. First, like archaeology, it erodes the present through juxtaposition with the past. The present is made manifest, and found not to be universal: 'history serves to show that-which-is has not always been' (1990a: 37). Foucault opens *Discipline and Punish* with a significant contrast: a detailed account of the gruesome public execution of Damiens in 1757, followed by the rigid time-schedule of a prison regime 80 years later (1977a: 3–7). The juxtaposition of public spectacle and prison system reveals the assumptions of both. The reader is struck by how different the public spectacle of former times is from the penal system of today; meanwhile, the assumptions of the latter system are revealed. Second, genealogy undercuts present meanings by demonstrating the accidents which accompanied their initial emergence. For instance, the misfortunes and unintended outcomes of the old penal regime led to the call for a different system (ibid.: 73ff.). 'What reason perceives as *its* necessity, or rather, what different forms of rationality offer as their necessary being, can perfectly well be shown to have a history; and the network of *contingencies* from which it emerges can be traced' (1990a: 37). So, these forms of rationality 'reside' upon human practice and human history, and 'since these things have been made, they can be unmade, as long as we know how it was that they were made' (ibid.: 37).

Third, genealogy leads to a certain loss of innocence, since that which is hitherto experienced as innocuous is shown to be very much tainted by power struggles. Foucault sets out to show in *Discipline and Punish* that, rather than being solely emancipatory, the social sciences are not just implicated in, but essential to the emergence of a disciplinary society. Likewise, however benevolent its intentions, the carceral system is shown to be characteristic of this disciplinary regime (1977a: 293ff.).

Fourth, genealogy undermines particular justifications of the present. Present belief systems or practices are often legitimized by indicating that they are a continuous progression from the past. Genealogy aims at demonstrating that both the assumption of continuity and the notion of progress are erroneous. Past practices and concepts appear so distinct that they cannot be moulded into a continuous narrative. Every system creates its own internal logic and justification, and it is impossible to provide an independent yardstick to judge between, for instance, different regimes of power. This explains why, after the hideous details of the execution of Damiens, Foucault takes on the difficult task of showing the internal logic of that system. And it also explains why Foucault points out that the present penal system ties in with the spread of disciplinary techniques and hence is not simply an advance in humanitarianism (compared to the *ancien régime*): 'Humanity does not gradually progress from combat to combat until it arrives at universal reciprocity, where the rule of law finally replaces warfare; humanity installs each of its violences in a system of rules and thus proceeds from domination to domination' (ibid.: 151).

Fifth, genealogy undermines the apparent coherence of present belief or normative systems. That which appears to be a unitary, consistent system is shown to be heterogeneous and to consist of disparate layers of meaning. This is partly because, as we mentioned earlier, previous meanings are never completely erased. In practice, however, Foucault does not always seem to be successful in applying this fifth principle. Indeed, one recurrent criticism of *Discipline and Punish* points out that, contrary to the apparent black-and-white picture painted by Foucault, the 'society of spectacle' is still prevalent today – a criticism essentially in line with the notion of genealogy. But on other occasions Foucault seems to be more sensitive to the multilayered nature of reality. The science of man might portray itself as singularly self-emancipatory, but it is shown in *Discipline and Punish* to have other features as well (ibid.: 192ff.; 1980: 107ff.).

Evaluation and current developments

It has traditionally been said that Foucault's archaeological and genealogical periods are radically different from each other; just as it is commonplace to distinguish Picasso's Blue period from his Pink period, so are Foucault's archaeology and genealogy contrasted. We have suggested instead that we look at Foucault in a different way, and be sensitive to the continuity in his work. We have tried to show that through all of his work Foucault relies upon a concept of knowledge acquisition which is self-referential and which draws upon the unfamiliar to gain access to the familiar. This account exposes the significance of this concept of knowledge acquisition when applied to the study of history. Within the *contours* of the traditional consensus, the historian aims at explaining past events. That explanation can only be relevant to the present insofar as the observed regularities are not merely restricted to that period, and are thus a stepping-stone towards law-like generalizations. In contrast, once a Foucauldian self-referential concept has been adopted, the historian is in search of the present, and the past is his or her gateway towards that present. The very same act of revealing the present also undercuts that present. In Foucauldian parlance, history becomes a 'history of the present' in that he sees his own task as describing 'the nature of the present, and of "ourselves in the present"', in the light of the fact that the present 'is a time which is never quite like any other' (1990a: 36).

This way of looking at Foucault has a number of advantages, two of which are worth mentioning here. First, it allows us to conceive of his work as a coherent whole. Not only does it allow us to see the link between archaeology and genealogy, it also enables us to make intelligible several themes or ideas which would otherwise appear marginal (or unrelated) to the main project of his work. Take Foucault's notion of the role of the intellectual. It is well known that Foucault argues against what he sees as a 'traditional' conception of the intellectual. For Foucault, that traditional conception assumes that the intellectual is a messianic figure, who preaches from above, and who incites political action in the name of truth. It is also well known that Foucault substitutes this for the more modest conception of what he calls the 'new' intellectual: that is, someone who provides expertise and technical knowledge to assist in local struggles (1980: 62). We grant that it is possible to account for Foucault's rejection of the traditional notion of the intellectual without taking on board our main argument as given above. It could, for instance, be argued that his position against the traditional intellectual is a necessary corollary of his postmodern hostility towards meta-narratives or totalizing systems. But making sense of Foucault's proposal for the *new* intellectual becomes more difficult without relying upon the view elaborated in this chapter. It is indeed difficult to conceive of what the 'advisory' role of the new intellectual consists, as long as one remains within the realm of a traditional concept of knowledge acquisition. Our argument is that the tools provided by the new intellectual are exactly those we have stressed in this chapter: they are revelations about and alterations of one's own presuppositions. Foucault himself acknowledges this in his discussion of the 'ethics' of the new intellectual by distinguishing the mere academic from the academic who is also an intellectual:

What can the ethics of an intellectual be . . . if not . . . to make oneself permanently capable of *detaching oneself from oneself* (which is the opposite of the attitude of conversion)? . . . To be at once an academic and an intellectual is to try to manipulate a type of knowledge and analysis that is taught and received in the universities in such a way as to alter not only others' thoughts, but also *one's own*. This work of altering one's own thought and that of others seems to be the intellectual's *raison d'être*. (1990a: 263–4; emphasis added)

Second, this way of looking at Foucault helps to explain what appear, from the perspective of the traditional consensus, to be peculiarities, omissions and weaknesses in his work. For example, many critiques focus on his lack of interest in *explaining* discontinuity. He does indeed demonstrate radical shifts in, for instance, epistemes or systems of punishment, without always properly explaining how the changes were brought about. However, this is only problematic so long as one imposes on him *ab extra* a traditional conception of knowledge acquisition. Once it is acknowledged that Foucault adopts a self-referential conception, it is clear that the explanation of discontinuity does not necessarily fall within the scope of his enterprise. (This is not to say that explaining discontinuity *ipso facto* falls outside his enterprise.) Rather than merely accounting for why particular changes have occurred in the past, Foucault's main aim is to elucidate and undercut present belief and ethical systems. Once the traditional consensus has been abandoned in favour of the self-referential one, one cannot but be sympathetic towards his omissions. If our view on Foucault's concept of knowledge acquisition is correct, then these criticisms simply miss the point. They criticize him for failing to accomplish something which he did not set out to obtain in the first place, and which, from his perspective, should not necessarily be aimed at anyway.

This is not to say that Foucault's writings are entirely without flaws. There *are* problems with his work, and we will now elaborate on two of the more important lacunae. They concern his relativist position in his archaeological work and the notion of power in his genealogical period. We have already touched upon Foucault's relativism in his earlier work. We argued that it relies upon two assumptions: a structuralist theory of meaning and a notion of discontinuity. If *ex hypothesi* the meaning of a concept is to be derived from its relationship with the absent totality within a language game, discourse or episteme, and if a radical discontinuity between different language games is assumed, then indeed the notion of 'incommensurability' between different language games seems to follow. This is, we think, the most plausible defence of the relativism in Foucault's archaeology. However, under close scrutiny, things become more complicated. There is, first and foremost, the obvious point made by so many that Foucault's relativist claim, like any such statement, is necessarily applicable to itself, and thus disarms itself. Even setting aside this problem of relativism in general, however, Foucault's particular version of it fails because he does not provide criteria which could justify why he considers certain language games to be discontinuous or not. More importantly, any such decision regarding the criteria is an arbitrary one. It might, of course, be argued that there is discontinuity between language games if, and only if, their underlying rules are sufficiently distinct. But there remains then an arbitrariness regarding which underlying rules are to be selected. Also, there remains the question of how much difference amounts to incommensurability. Surely, the selected discourses and epistemes still have a large number of underlying assumptions in common (there is, after all, no *tabula rasa* in the social realm).

Equally problematic is Foucault's notion of power. Remember that he argues that it is a mistake to conceive of power as merely negative. It is not just repressive or an impediment; it is also constitutive. It is productive in that it creates. Given the broad spectrum provided, it is hardly surprising to find Foucault subsequently concluding that power is everywhere (1979: 93). We would agree with Layder's overall criticism that 'Foucault's notion of power is rather elastic and defies any definite pinning down. As a result of the vagueness or fuzziness that surrounds his notion of power, Foucault is able to evade or fend off potential criticism by stretching his notion to cover all eventualities' (1994: 107). A concept which hardly excludes anything is a highly suspect one. Why stretch the concept of power beyond the boundaries of our daily use of the concept, and why neglect fine distinctions drawn by other theorists? Concepts, such as the Parsonian concepts of influence, socialization and internalization, suddenly fall under the imperialist heading of the catch-all Foucauldian concept of power or domination. Foucault's tendency to conceive of power so broadly is not as innocuous as it might appear at first sight, since from this position it is only a small step to argue that existing power relations will necessarily be replaced by new power relations, and previous systems of domination by later systems of domination.[5]

Foucault continues with the idea that 'power relations are both intentional and nonsubjective' (1979: 94), but his exposition of the relationship between purposive action and unintended effects is confusing. His argument is that 'there is no power that is exercised without a series of aims and objectives. But this does not mean that it results from the choice or decision of an individual subject' (ibid.: 95). So far so good, but this is then followed by the methodological dictum not to 'look for the headquarters that preside over its rationality; neither the caste which governs, nor the groups which control the state apparatus, nor those who make the most important economic decisions direct the entire network of power that functions in a society' (ibid.). It is obvious that this methodological advice does not follow from the previous statement about the incongruence between intention and effect. The fact that people want one thing and end up with another is not a sufficient reason for abandoning the study of the *relationship* between the wanting and the effect (on the contrary, it probes that question), and understanding that relationship is only possible by taking into account the purposive act in the first place. A related point is that although Foucault is essentially correct in pointing out the importance of the local or 'micro'-dimensions of power, state power (and monopoly over the use of power) can still be a necessary condition for the emergence of techniques of surveillance and so on (see Poulantzas 1978 and Layder 1994: 106–8).

Foucault's statement that 'where there is power, there is resistance' is vague (1979: 95). Does it mean that power always entails resistance or merely that it entails the possibility of resistance? The latter is hardly a bold conjecture, while the former begs further explanation. Why should power necessarily imply resistance, especially if power is so loosely defined in the first place? Surely, if power is conceptualized such that it also incorporates those cases where individual wants are unconsciously influenced (that is, Foucault's 'positive' concept of power), then it seems even more unlikely that power always entails resistance. Foucault himself argued in an interview:

> [I]f power were never anything but repressive, if it never did anything but to say no, do you really think one would be brought to obey it? What makes power hold good, what makes it accepted, is simply the fact that it doesn't only weigh on us as a force that says no, but that it traverses and produces things, it induces pleasure, forms knowledge, produces discourse. (1980: 119)

A similar argument can be found in *The History of Sexuality* (1979: 86), but it goes without saying that this position weakens Foucault's claim concerning the necessary link between power and resistance.

Despite these difficulties, Foucault's ideas have proved to be very inspiring for social scientists around the world. Judith Butler's path-breaking 'performative' conception of gender (1990; 2005; see also chapter 2 for the recent social theoretical upsurge of interest in 'performance') and David Garland's 'sociology of punishment' are two such examples. In what follows, we focus on the latter's work, which has become a central reference in criminology in the past couple of decades. A critical reader of Foucault, David Garland (1955–) has tried to go beyond the author of *Discipline and Punish* by putting a greater emphasis on cultural and institutional factors (see chapters 3 and 4). In his view, Foucault's great contribution was to have thematized punishment as a key topic in social theory (one would have to go back to Durkheim to find another major social theorist interested in this theme). Foucault, however, employed an excessively instrumental and functionalist approach to punishment (Garland 1990: 157–75). Garland's alternative is a conception of punishment as a 'social institution': punishment should be studied as any other social institution (say, the family or the market) since the practices of punishment help define the identity of the society in which it takes place. In other words, punishment, far from being a detached dimension of social life in modern societies, is part and parcel of their normative self-understanding. Penal practices help define what is right and what is wrong, normal and abnormal, legitimate and illegitimate. Punishment, therefore, regulates social life on two distinct levels: first, it directly regulates behaviour considered to be socially harmful; second, it provides an interpretive framework that allows the population in general to make moral judgments (ibid.: 252). More recently, Garland has joined authors like Zygmunt Bauman (1998) and Loïc Wacquant (2006) in trying to explain the sharp rise in incarceration rates in contemporary Western countries. In *The Culture of Control*, Garland associates the recent changes in the policies of crime control to a profound societal shift. At the heart of the shift is the dismantling of the welfare state, and of the social rights culture associated with it. One consequence of the neo-liberal attack on the welfare state has been the erosion of the 'penal-welfarism' that had dominated criminal justice practice since the late nineteenth century. Today's 'tough on crime' measures such as 'Three strikes and you're out' would be unthinkable just a few decades ago. If until the 1970s the focus had been on rehabilitating the criminal and avoiding incarceration at all cost, today the policies of crime control have become intensely politicized and victim-centred, and possess a highly expressive and punitive character (Garland 2001: 142–3). According to Garland's discussion of punishment in the United States and Britain, what he calls the 'reactionary thematization' of late modernity has led to the dissolution of the 'solidarity project' of the 'inclusive welfare state society' of the post-war period (ibid.: 199, 165). In his own words, '[i]f penal-welfare conveyed the hubris and idealism of twentieth-century modernism, today's crime policies express a darker and less tolerant message' (ibid.: 199).

The influence of Foucault's ideas is not limited, of course, to criminology and social theoretical accounts of punishment. Take his work on power, governmentality and biopolitics. Even though Foucault wrote relatively little on these topics, his insights on how modern politics are inextricably connected with the biological existence of human beings are a central reference in this field. The Foucauldian thesis that modernity signals a break in human history – politics become 'biopolitics' as political power begins to regulate the life of populations – has inspired a whole generation of critically oriented authors (Foucault 1979: 143). A case in point is the Italian philosopher Giorgio Agamben (1942–), to whom we owe the most sophisticated theoretical development of Foucault's ideas on biopolitics. In *Homo Sacer*, Agamben extends Foucault's thesis that modernity is a biopolitical age (originally meant to describe the advent of the modern age in the eighteenth century) to the analysis of the concentration camp and of the totalitarian regimes of the twentieth century. To Agamben, the 'camp' is the hidden paradigm of modernity, where the politics of life (eugenics) swiftly gave way to politics of death. When that occurs, biopolitics become 'thanatopolitics' (i.e. the political management of death and destruction). The notion that sovereignty is exercised over the body politic suddenly acquires a literal sense. As Agamben explains, it is over the *bodies* of the citizens that the modern sovereign, in alliance not only with the 'jurist, but also with the doctor, the scientist, the expert and the priest' (1998: 21) exercises his power. Zygmunt Bauman agrees with Agamben's diagnosis. In his important *Modernity and the Holocaust*, Bauman shows how the elimination of foreign and impure bodies goes hand in hand with the purification of the body politic (see chapter 8).

In a more empirically oriented way, Nikolas Rose (1947–) has also been drawing on Foucault's notion of biopolitics in order to enquire into the medical and ethical aspects of the new biomedicine. Contrary to Agamben and Bauman, however, Rose (1996) believes there is a clear break between our 'advanced liberal' modern societies and the modern societies of the first half of the twentieth century. The latter were dominated by what Foucault called the 'good shepherd' mentality; that is, the paternalistic welfare state sometimes had to take difficult decisions, like eliminating those individuals bearing a defective constitution in order to protect the fitness of the flock as a whole. Today, however, this pastoral power is no longer administered by the omnipotent welfare state. Drawing on his field experience (e.g. Rabinow and Rose 2006), Rose suggests that today's regime of biopower is better described as a plural and contested area in which a multitude of social actors participate, including ethics committees, professional associations, researchers, self-help organizations and insurance and biotech companies (Rose 2006: 9–39). At the centre of Rose's agenda one finds one of Foucault's central preoccupations: the body. In Rose's view, selfhood is becoming increasingly somatic – that is, the human body has become the privileged site of experiments with subjectivity. From tattoos and body-piercing to plastic surgery, from diets to fitness and vitamins, a 'somatic individuality' is emerging as the distinctive feature of our age (Novas and Rose 2000). Such an emerging somatic self, far from being passive in the face of their biological fate, takes a very active stance towards it. With the aid of the new biomedicine, increasingly customized and individualized, somatic individuals are more aware of their biological identities. It is in this context that the anthropologist Paul Rabinow (1996), himself a renowned Foucault scholar, talks about 'biosociality'. Individuals come together and collectively demand legal protection, recognition and respect for their biological identities: for instance, family members of those with breast cancer or Alzheimer's disease join groups and organizations not only to see their rights respected, but also to make claims on how research should be conducted and directed (see, e.g., Burke 2008). Rabinow's and Rose's interest in biopolitics leads them to a newly defined interest in the social and political implications of capitalism. For them, biopolitics has become bioeconomics and this, in turn, has allowed the emergence of somatic individuals for whom personhood is expressed in terms of corporeality. Consumers of medical techniques, somatic individuals engage in a vital politics whose arenas are their own bodies down to the molecular level. A new ethics of life is thus emerging, one in which recognition and respect for life itself is the object of adjudication.

Though significant, Foucault's influence on contemporary critical theorizing does not stand alone. Critical theory today also draws from a very different kind of critical reflection on liberal capitalist modernity. We refer to the Frankfurt School of critical theory, a broad neo-Marxist intellectual movement concerned with the economic, political, scientific and psychological consequences of modern developed societies. Sometimes these two strands of critical theorizing clash. Such was the case with the early

1980s debate between Habermas and Foucault on modernity, with the latter being accused by the former of throwing the baby out with the bath water: the critical potential of modernity should not be neglected at risk of jeopardizing the very notion of critical thinking. Despite the profound differences that such moments bring to the fore, contemporary critical theorists share a broad mistrust of liberal modernity, with its distinctive instrumental type of rationality, free market ideology and juridical conception of democratic politics. In the next chapter, we turn to the critical social theories developed by the current representatives of the Frankfurt School, Jürgen Habermas and Axel Honneth.

Further reading

Perhaps because it is not as subtle as some of his other works, *Discipline and Punish* is one of Foucault's most accessible works and therefore worth starting with. We would then suggest his article 'Nietzsche, genealogy, history' (in *Language, Counter-memory, Practice*), which provides a good introduction to his methodology and his indebtedness to Nietzsche. *Madness and Civilization*, *The Birth of the Clinic* and *The History of Sexuality* deal with the history of, respectively, madness, medicine and sexuality. Issues related to science are dealt with in *The Order of Things* and *The Archaeology of Knowledge*. There is a huge amount of secondary literature on Foucault, but, as a simple introduction, Smart's *Michel Foucault* will do. An excellent summary of each phase in Foucault's work can be found in Sheridan's *Michel Foucault: The Will to Truth*. A good commentary on Foucault's notions of governmentality, biopolitics and genealogy is Dean's *Governmentality*. A more challenging attempt to link Foucault with other theoretical developments, in particular Marxism, can be found in Smart's *Foucault, Marxism and Critique* and Poster's *Foucault, Marxism and History*. Foucault's philosophy of the present and Habermas and Taylor's critique of Foucault's account of the Enlightenment are discussed in an excellent chapter of Hiley's *Philosophy in Question*. Habermas deals with Foucault in *The Philosophical Discourse of Modernity*, Taylor's argumentations can be found in his 'Foucault on freedom and truth' (*Political Theory*) and Nancy Fraser's criticisms are summarized in the article 'Foucault on modern power: empirical insights and normative confusions' (*Praxis International*). On the new developments of Foucault's ideas, one should read Garland's *The Culture of Control* and Rose's *The Politics of Life Itself*, in particular the final chapter 'Somatic ethics and the spirit of biocapital'.

References

Agamben, G. 1998. *Homo Sacer: Sovereign Power and Bare Life.* Stanford, CA: Stanford University Press (originally in Italian, 1995).

Bachelard, G. 1984. *The New Scientific Spirit.* Boston, MA: Beacon Press (originally in French, 1934).

Baert, P. 1996. Realist philosophy of the social sciences and economics: a critique. *Cambridge Journal of Economics* 20: 513–22.

Barthes, R. 1983. *The Fashion System.* New York: Hill and Wang (originally in French, 1967).

Bauman, Z. 1998. *Globalization: The Human Consequences.* Cambridge: Polity.

Braudel, F. 1966. *La Méditerranée et le monde méditerranéen à l'époque de Philippe II.* Paris: Armand Colin.

Burke, L. 2008. 'The country of my disease': genes and genealogy in Alzheimer's life writing. *Journal of Literary Disability* 2(1): 63–74.

Butler, J. 1990. *Gender Trouble: Feminism and the Subversion of Identity.* London: Routledge.

Butler, J. 2005. *Giving an Account of Oneself.* New York: Fordham University Press.

Canguilhem, G. 1978. *On the Normal and the Pathological.* Dordrecht: Reidel (originally in French, 1943).

Dean, M. 1999. *Governmentality. Power and Rule in Modern Society.* London: Sage.

Foucault, M. 1954. *Maladie mentale et personnalité.* Paris: PUF. (2nd revised edn, retitled *Maladie mentale et psychologie*, 1962).

Foucault, M. 1971. Orders of discourse. *Social Science Information* 10: 27–30.

Foucault, M. 1977a. *Discipline and Punish: The Birth of the Prison.* London: Allen Lane (reprinted, 1991; originally in French, 1975).

Foucault, M. 1977b. *Language, Counter-memory, Practice,* ed. D. F. Bouchard. Ithaca, NY: Cornell University Press.

Foucault, M. 1979. *The History of Sexuality. Volume I: An Introduction.* London: Penguin (reprinted 1990; originally in French, 1976).

Foucault, M. 1980. *Power/Knowledge; Selected Interviews and Other Writings 1972–1977,* ed. C. Gordon. Hemel Hempstead: Harvester Wheatsheaf.

Foucault, M. 1989a. *Madness and Civilization; A History of Insanity in the Age of Reason.* London: Routledge (originally in French, 1961).

Foucault, M. 1989b. *The Archaeology of Knowledge.* London: Routledge (originally in French, 1969).

Foucault, M. 1989c. *The Birth of the Clinic: An Archaeology of Medical Perception.* London: Routledge (originally in French, 1963).

Foucault, M. 1989d. *The Order of Things: An Archaeology of the Human Sciences.* London: Routledge (originally in French, 1966).

Foucault, M. 1990a. *Politics, Philosophy, Culture; Interviews and Other Writings 1977–1984,* ed. L. D. Kritzman. London: Routledge.

Foucault, M. 1990b. *The History of Sexuality. Volume 3: The Care of the Self.* London: Penguin (originally in French, 1984).

Foucault, M. 1991. Governmentality. In G. Burchell, C. Gordon and P. Miller (eds), *The Foucault Effect. Studies in Governmentality.* Chicago, IL: University of Chicago Press, pp. 87–104.

Foucault, M. 1992. *The History of Sexuality. Volume 2: The Use of Pleasure.* London: Penguin (originally in French, 1984).

Fraser, N. 1981. Foucault on modern power: empirical insights and normative confusions. *Praxis International* 1(3): 272–87.

Garland, D. 1990. *Punishment and Modern Society: A Study in Social Theory.* Chicago, IL: University of Chicago Press.

Garland, D. 2001. *The Culture of Control. Crime and Social Order in Contemporary Society.* Oxford: Oxford University Press.

Geuss, R. 1994. Nietzsche and genealogy. *European Journal of Philosophy* 2(3): 274–92.

Gordon, C. 1991. Governmental rationality: an introduction. In G. Burchell, C. Gordon and P. Miller (eds), *The Foucault Effect. Studies in Governmentality.* Chicago, IL: University of Chicago Press, pp. 1–51.

Habermas, J. 1987. *The Philosophical Discourse of Modernity.* Cambridge: Polity (originally in German, 1985).

Hiley, D. R. 1988. *Philosophy in Question; Essays on a Pyrrhonian Theme.* Chicago, IL: University of Chicago Press.

Layder, D. 1994. *Understanding Social Theory.* London: Sage.

Novas, C. and Rose, N. 2000. Genetic risk and the birth of the somatic individual. *Economy and Society* 29(4): 484–513.

Phillip, M. 1985. Michel Foucault. In Q. Skinner (ed.), *The Return of Grand Theory in the Human Sciences.* Cambridge: Cambridge University Press, pp. 65–82.

Poster, M. 1990. *Foucault, Marxism and History: Mode of Production versus Mode of Information.* Cambridge: Polity.

Poulantzas, N. 1978. *State, Power, Socialism.* London: New Left Books (originally in French, 1978).

Rabinow, P. 1996. Artificiality and the Enlightenment: from sociobiology to biosociality. In *Essays on the Anthropology of Reason.* Princeton, NJ: Princeton University Press, pp. 91–111.

Rabinow, P. and Rose, N. 2006. Thoughts on the concept of biopower today. *Biosocieties* 1: 195–217.

Rose, N. 1996. Governing 'advanced' liberal democracies. In A. Barry, T. Osborne and N. Rose (eds), *Foucault and Political Reason.* London: UCL Press, pp. 37–64.

Rose, N. 2001. The politics of life itself. *Theory, Culture & Society* 18(6): 1–30.

Rose, N. 2006. *The Politics of Life Itself: Biomedicine, Power, and Subjectivity in the Twenty-First Century.* Princeton, NJ: Princeton University Press.

Saussure, F. de 1959. *Course in General Linguistics*. London: Peter Owen (originally in French, 1915).

Sheridan, A. 1990. *Michel Foucault; The Will to Truth*. London: Routledge.

Skinner, Q. (ed.) 1985. *The Return of Grand Theory on the Human Sciences*. Cambridge: Cambridge University Press.

Smart, B. 1983. *Foucault, Marxism and Critique*. London: Routledge.

Smart, B. 1988. *Michel Foucault*. London: Routledge.

Taylor, C. 1981. Foucault on freedom and truth. *Political Theory* 12: 152–83.

Wacquant, L. 2006. *Prisons of Poverty*. Minneapolis: University of Minnesota Press (originally in French, 1999).

The Spread of Reason

Habermas's Critical Theory and Beyond

Jürgen Habermas (1929–) studied philosophy, history, psychology and German literature at the universities of Göttingen, Zurich and Bonn. After completing his doctorate on Friedrich Schelling in 1954, he became a journalist, before taking up a position as Theodor Adorno's assistant at the Institute for Social Research, Frankfurt, in 1956. He subsequently taught at Heidelberg for a couple of years and then became professor of philosophy and sociology at the University of Frankfurt. He became co-director of the Max Planck Institute in 1971, and returned to the Johann Wolfgang Goethe University of Frankfurt 11 years later to take up the chair in sociology and philosophy. Since the early 1970s, Habermas has become a leading figure in philosophy and social theory, writing widely on core themes within the field. In spite of his dense style of writing, the high level of abstraction and occasionally the vast knowledge which he presupposes of the reader, his influence today vastly transcends the German-speaking world. Habermas is known especially as one of the most prominent twentieth-century exponents of 'critical theory'. Critical theorists, such as Adorno, Max Horkheimer and Habermas, do not simply wish to account for or explain the social world. They intend instead to evaluate both the potential and the problems of modern society, and their ultimate aim is to contribute to people's self-emancipation.

Like Karl Popper, Habermas is convinced that knowledge progresses through open discussion and criticism. In this respect, he also practises what he preaches. He has indeed been embroiled in several political and academic debates, some of which arose out of his writings, and most of which have led him to reassess and redefine his previous ideas and concepts. Amongst the most memorable debates are his encounters with positivist and falsificationist philosophers of science, supporters of the German philosopher Martin Heidegger, the hermeneutic philosopher Hans-Georg Gadamer, the system theorist Niklas Luhmann, the student movement in Germany and the post-structuralist or postmodernist movement in France.[1] There are very few philosophers or theorists who have shown such a persistent interest in differing views. There are even fewer who have been so willing, as Habermas has been, to take counter-arguments on board. As a result, Habermas's philosophy is far from static; it is constantly evolving.

Habermas's *Habilitationsschrift* was published as *Structural Transforma-tion of the Public Sphere* (*Strukturwandel der Öffentlichkeit*) in 1962.[2] It depicts the emergence and spread of a 'public sphere' of open debate in the eigh-teenth century, and it also deals with the gradual decline of that cultural pattern in advanced capitalist society. Contrary to Habermas's later works, this book is remarkably easy to read. It is, however, truly Habermasian in that it already reveals his fascination with the communicative dimen-sions of a liberal democracy. For Habermas, the 'public sphere' expresses a 'discursive will-formation' or free uncoerced debate amongst equals, and the latter was to become central to his notion of a critical theory. His interest in open, unconstrained debate led eventually to his notion of communicative rationality based on an in-depth reading of American pragmatic philosophy (which Habermas referred to as 'radical democratic Hegelianism').

Shortly after the publication of his dissertation, a number of articles and essays were translated and published under the title *Towards a Rational Society: Student Protest, Science, and Politics* (originally two books: *Protest-bewegung und Hochschulreform* and *Technik und Wissenschaft*). This book comments on, amongst other things, the student movement in Germany and the increase and dispersion of instrumental rationality in various aspects of life (1987d). Underlying his earlier work is the notion that, in the political arena, what Mannheim called 'substantial rationality' has been substituted by 'functional rationality'. This means that ultimate values have become less of a guiding force for political practices than they were before. Instead, politics is increasingly geared towards avoiding technical problems which threaten the equilibrium or the adequate functioning of the social and economic system. The ideas in the two earlier books are obviously not far removed from his mentors, Adorno and Horkheimer.

Habermas's originality shows itself first at the level of methodology and philosophy of the social sciences. In *Theory and Practice* (*Theorie und Praxis*), *Knowledge and Human Interests* (*Erkenntnis und Interesse*) and *On the Logic of the Social Sciences* (*Zur Logik der Sozialwissenschaften*) attention is focused on the epistemological foundations of critical theory. Habermas advances a critical account of both functionalism and system theory, attempts to situate critical theory in relation to hermeneutics and positiv-ist epistemology and distances himself from some positivist tendencies in the Marxist theory of society (see chapter 8). There is an obvious link with his earlier work: technical rationality goes hand in hand with those types of analysis that are indebted to a positivist or functionalist framework. But Habermas does not entirely reject the views of his opponents. Some insights of system theory are incorporated into his general social theory, and however suspicious he might be of 'empirical-analytical' modes of knowledge, they do remain an essential ingredient in his reconstruction of critical theory.

During the first half of the 1970s Habermas paid attention to a number of substantive issues. In *Legitimation Crisis* (*Legitimationsprobleme im Spät-kapitalismus*) he directs his attention towards societal problems related to the advent of modernity. He deals in particular with different types of crisis under advanced capitalism, in particular crises of motivational commitment and normative integration. Then followed *Communication and the Evolution of Society* (*Zur Rekonstruktion des Historischen Materialismus*), an attempt to provide a contemporary reassessment of Marx's theory of history, and to deal with the homology or structural identity between personality development and changes at a social level. Gradually, however, Habermas's interest turned towards the accomplishments of the linguistic turn in philosophy, and by the mid-1970s he had worked out the cornerstones of his theory of universal pragmatics – the prelude to his theory of communicative action.

In 1981 Habermas published his *magnum opus*: two volumes of *Theorie des Kommunikativen Handelns* (*The Theory of Communicative Action*). This is a *tour de force* in grand social theory, in which, amongst other things, he reworks the concept of rationality while overcoming some of the shortcomings of an originally Cartesian philosophy of consciousness (*Bewusstseins-philosophie*) and its attendant subject–object conception of cognition (1987c; 1991). Habermas's notion of communicative rationality and his criticisms of Marx are not unrelated. Marx paid exclusive interest to the concept of 'labour', and Habermas insists that linguistically mediated interaction is as vital to social reproduction and evolution as is labour. So the concept of labour needs to be supplemented with the notion of 'interaction'. Whereas labour ties in with instrumental reason, interaction refers to communication geared towards mutual understanding (1987a: 25–63). Likewise, Habermas's concept of communicative rationality (central to his attempt to develop a critical theory) is embedded in linguistically mediated interaction.

Having been exposed to various criticisms, Habermas has retreated from some of the more extreme positions in *The Theory of Communicative*

Action. Despite this, it is fair to say that he is still committed to the broad outline of the theory. Indeed, his more recent contributions share roughly the same assumptions. *The Philosophical Discourse of Modernity* (*Der Philosophische Diskurs der Moderne*), for instance, consists of a staunch defence of the project of the Enlightenment against anti-modernist, postmodernist and post-structuralist authors such as Nietzsche, Heidegger, Foucault, Derrida and Jean-François Lyotard (see chapter 6). For Habermas, these critiques of the Enlightenment have basically failed to recognize its emancipatory potential. Enlightenment thinkers stood for open debate and criticism, and thus for communicative rationality. More recently, Habermas made yet another substantial contribution to ethics and legal theory, first with *Justification and Application* (*Erläuterungen zur Diskursethik*) and later with the massive *Between Facts and Norms* (*Faktizität und Geltung*). His mature work in legal philosophy is again very much in line with the theoretical outline of his theory of communicative action.

Influences and early writings

The early Frankfurt School, of which Adorno and Horkheimer were the most eminent members, was founded in the early 1920s, and dissolved approximately ten years later because of the radically changing political scene in Germany at the time. Adorno et al. embarked upon an ambitious project aimed at reconstructing Marxist social theory while taking on board some Weberian and Nietzschean insights. They considered Marx too much enmeshed in, and thus not critical enough towards, the project of the Enlightenment. The members of the Frankfurt School left their home country in the mid-1930s for safer regions (in particular the United States), but a number of them, including Adorno, returned after the Second World War. Habermas, originally a student of Adorno and later his assistant, is considered to be the main successor of that generation – a leading intellectual, whose work, although from varied sources, is still in some respects faithful to the spirit of the early Frankfurt School.

There are a number of continuities running from the Frankfurt School to Habermas's work. Some commentators argue that, because of its interdisciplinary nature, Habermas's *oeuvre* comes particularly close to the research conducted in the early years of the Frankfurt Institute of Social Research (Outhwaite 2009). More substantively, Habermas shares with Adorno and Horkheimer a concern with the extent to which the *Aufklärung*, in spite of its liberating potential, has led to the spread and dispersion of means–end rationality in the West (Habermas 1991: 339–99). Furthermore, the early Frankfurt School and Habermas are highly critical of the epistemological assumptions of positivist sociology. They emphatically deplore the technical nature of positivist knowledge (1987b: 51–122; 1987a: 71–90; see also chapter 8). Habermas obtains from Adorno et al. a conception of critical theory as geared towards the self-emancipation of human beings. In this view, social scientific knowledge ought to help lift up past social and psychological restrictions.

Amongst the differences with, for instance, Adorno is that Habermas's penchant for developing a 'grand social theory' in a traditional mould is at odds with the former's criticisms of identity thinking. Adorno coined the term 'identity thinking' to designate any attempt to impose a unitary system of concepts and general definitions onto the particularity and idiosyncrasy of objects (Adorno 1973: 146–61). This ties in with yet another difference: whereas Adorno's view of rationality is still deeply embedded in the philosophy of consciousness, Habermas prefers to ground reason in the intersubjective context of daily linguistic usage. Whereas for Adorno the only safe haven for reason against the spread of instrumental rationality resides in the aesthetic realm, Habermas opts for a dialogical notion of reason. Also, whereas the Frankfurt School, following Weber, portrays a single and irreversible direction towards increasing instrumental rationality (*Zweckrationalität*) in the West, Habermas points out the twofold and selective nature of that rationalization process. For Habermas, one aspect of this process is indeed the alleged means–end rationality; another is the extension of judicial liberties and communicative rationality. The latter is worth defending (cf. Adorno and Horkheimer 1973: 1–119 with Habermas 1987b: 106–30). Finally, whereas the early critical theorists seem to reject bourgeois society *in toto*, Habermas argues that there are some formal features of bourgeois political institutions which are worth preserving. By contrast with Horkheimer and Adorno, Habermas indeed demonstrates how his notion of communicative rationality is already presupposed in the main institutions of our liberal democracy, and *mutatis mutandis* how an immanent critique of contemporary society becomes feasible (see also Dews 1986: 101ff.; Wellmer 1985: 52ff.; McCarthy 1985: 176ff.; Honneth 1987: 356–76).

Habermas is also widely acquainted with the broader German philosophical tradition. During his university training, he became familiar with Immanuel Kant, Hegel, Schelling, Johann Gottlieb Fichte, Marx and Georg Lukács. Amongst sociological influences are Marx's historical materialism, Durkheim's theory about the transition from mechanical to organic solidarity, Weber's theory of rationalization, Parsons's notion of social differentiation and Garfinkel's ethnomethodology. Further influences include the American pragmatism of Peirce, Dewey and Mead, Gadamer's hermeneutics, post-Wittgensteinian 'ordinary language philosophy' of Oxford's J. L. Austin, John Searle and Peter Strawson, and Jean Piaget and Lawrence Kohlberg's stage theory. Given the wide variety of Habermas's sources, it is remarkable that his own project is nevertheless unified thematically. Whether he is discussing Weber's concept of rationality or Mead's notion of a symbolically constituted social world, whether he is arguing against the excesses of logical-positivism or against the relativist inclinations of the French postmodernist wave, underlying his *oeuvre* one always finds a fierce belief in the project of the philosophy of the Enlightenment and in the principles of political liberalism. Most of his writings are centred around this deeply held conviction.

It should already be clear that, in some aspects, Habermas's project is not dissimilar to that of Giddens (see chapter 5). Indeed, they both attempt to integrate a wide variety of intellectual traditions in order to develop a post-empiricist, though explicitly non-relativist, contribution to social theory. Furthermore, both warn against the dangers of adopting a one-sided argument, whether it is so-called structure-related or actor-orientated. Each aims instead at linking different levels of social analysis and at overcoming previously held dualisms. Like Giddens, Habermas wants to transcend the opposition between the functioning at the system level on the one hand, and the workings at the symbolic, intersubjective realm on the other. In this respect, Habermas introduces two central concepts: the 'social system' and the 'life-world'. The life-world refers to the shared meanings and taken-for-granted nature of our daily activities. Habermas states that the life-world is central to social reproduction; by that he means that society is constantly made and remade through these routine practices. The life-world has, in particular, received close attention from 'internalist' viewpoints such as phenomenology and ethnomethodology (see chapter 3). The social system refers to the way in which social structures and functional imperatives constrain people's actions through the media of money and power. It has been the object of study from externalist perspectives such as structural-functionalism or system theory (see chapters 1 and 2). Whereas the life-world raises issues of communication, the social system relates to the forces and relations of production. Habermas's work pays attention both to the social system and to the life-world and aims to demonstrate their interplay. The life-world is dependent on the adequate functioning of the social system, especially the efficient use of resources and state-governed organization and coordination of activities. The social system needs properly socialized individuals and a certain degree of permanence at a cultural level. This is provided by the life-world (1976: 1–7; 1987c: 113–97).

For Habermas, critical theory should be seen as residing at the intersection between philosophy and science. Critical theory intends to uncover the structural conditions of people's actions, and it is ultimately directed towards transcending these conditions. Habermas goes to some lengths to define critical theory and to specify how it relates to other forms of knowledge. Relying partly upon Peirce's pragmatic philosophy and its attendant link between science and action, Habermas distinguishes in his earlier work three distinct forms of knowledge: empirical-analytical knowledge, hermeneutics and critical theory. These types of knowledge are related to three anthropologically distinct forms of a priori interests. Interests are understood as 'basic orientations' embedded in 'fundamental conditions' of reproduction and self-constitution of the human species (1987a: 196ff.).[3] Whereas the empirical-analytical or positivist approach ties in with technical control and prediction through nomological knowledge, hermeneutics seeks understanding within a context of intersubjective meaning. Finally, critical theory, as a combination of hermeneutics and empirical-analytical types of knowledge, is aimed at emancipation. It endeavours to question assumptions that previously have been taken for granted, and to remove psychological or social constraints and dependencies. Note that each of these interests is related to different means of social organization and media. Empirical-analytical types of knowledge have an affinity with 'instrumental action' or 'work', hermeneutics is relevant to 'language' or 'interaction', and critical theory deals with 'asymmetrical relations' or 'power' (ibid.: 308–15).

We will deal with each type of knowledge in turn. What Habermas calls empirical-analytical knowledge is basically a positivist notion of knowledge. Positivism is a broad term and includes, for instance, Comte's holistic thinking and his unilinear evolutionism on the one hand, and Mill's methodological individualism and his ahistorical approach on the other. Positivism is exemplified more recently in Hempel's or Nagel's deductive-nomological model. Originally an ambitious attempt to ban all metaphysics and religion, positivism now covers a large number of different assertions or themes. Amongst the latter are the assumptions that there is a unity of method between the social and the natural sciences; the notion that the social sciences ought to search for eternal law-like generalizations; the belief that the same format which allows phenomena to be explained also allows the prediction of the very same phenomena, and vice versa; a rejection of explanations which refer to subjective states of individuals such as motives or purposes; a predilection towards quantification; and a view of the social sciences as exclusively aimed at solving technical problems of society (see chapter 8). Habermas rejects the positivist claim that it is the only form of valid knowledge, and he also repudiates the positivist tendency to ignore the intersubjective and social dimension of scientific knowledge (ibid.: 71–90, 308–9). In his view, there is a residual positivism in Marxism insofar as it reduces social interaction to mainly (if not exclusively) a mechanical outcome of the productive forces (see also Bernstein 1978: 188–9; Giddens 1985a: 125ff.). Like Bourdieu and Giddens, Habermas recognizes that some hermeneutic insights are indeed relevant to the workings of the social world: people attribute meaning to their surroundings, and act accordingly (see chapters 1 and 5).

This brings us to the second type of knowledge. Hermeneutics, or the method of *Sinnverstehen*, postulates a qualitative difference between the methods of the social and the natural sciences. This argument goes back to Wilhelm Dilthey's appeal for a distinctive method of interpretative understanding (*Verstehen*) for the human sciences (*Geisteswissenschaften*). Dilthey clearly articulated the hermeneutic position in the so-called *Methodenstreit* at the end of the nineteenth century. According to him, whereas the natural sciences deal with questions like 'why?' and 'how?', the social sciences and history try to answer 'what?' questions. Although Dilthey initially presented an individualistic version of the method of *Verstehen*, in which re-enactment takes a prominent position, he later came to recognize the public-collective and linguistic features of this re-enactment process. Habermas argues that, due to its emphasis on descriptive analysis, Dilthey's hermeneutics is incapable of critically assessing the validity of statements. Furthermore, against Dilthey's assumption of a neutral or virginal re-enactment of the past and in line with Gadamer's notion of prejudice (*Vorurteilsstruktur*), Habermas argues that interpretations are only possible through the medium of implicit preconceptions. For him, the more recent developments within hermeneutics (for example, Schutz's sociological interpretation of Husserl's phenomenology, Peter Winch's interpretation of Wittgenstein's *Philosophical Investigations*, or Garfinkel's ethnomethodology) do not entirely overcome some of the shortcomings of Dilthey's work. Habermas finds more inspiration in the work of Gadamer, in particular his *Truth and Method*. Gadamer argues against the Enlightenment notion of value-free and theory-independent knowledge.

According to him, tradition and prejudice should not be seen as obstacles to the acquisition of knowledge, but rather as the precondition for the possibility of that knowledge. As the historicity of traditions is intrinsic to knowledge formation, knowledge is temporal and open to future reassessments. Understanding the world is not merely a one-way process – our very preconceptions are reconstructed in the encounter with the world. Most of these conceptual insights are taken over by Habermas, while he criticizes Gadamer for his alleged lack of a critical dimension. People's knowledge or interpretation, he argues, necessarily rely upon a number of implicit assumptions which are embedded in history and tradition, but it does not follow that different sets of assumptions are equally valid. What sociology needs in addition, Habermas continues, is a 'depth hermeneutics' which provides a yardstick enabling us to evaluate different traditions critically and to identify ideological distortions and their relationship with power relations (1987a: 140–60, 309–10; 1988: 89–170).

Habermas's depth hermeneutics falls under the third type of knowledge: critical theory. Critical theory rests upon a combination of causal explanation and *Sinnverstehen* and is ultimately aimed at self-emancipation. Self-emancipation takes place whenever people are able to challenge past restrictions which are a result of distorted communication (1987a: 310–11). Although Freud defined his theory in close association with the natural sciences, Habermas conceives of psychoanalysis as the example *par excellence* of critical theory. The hermeneutic dimension enters a psychoanalytic encounter whenever the psychoanalyst helps the patient to re-enact previously repressed memories and experiences. Habermas talks about 'depth hermeneutics' here, since the psychoanalyst attempts to move behind the surface meaning and to delve further at the level of repressed needs and wishes. One of the aims of this interaction is, of course, to reveal to the patient the previously hidden causal mechanisms which have hitherto influenced behavioural patterns; this then is the empirical-analytical dimension. However, the ultimate goal of the psychoanalytic encounter is the removal of these restrictions of the past, which Habermas calls the emancipatory dimension of psychoanalysis (ibid.: 220ff.). Another example of critical theory, but at a societal level rather than at a psychological one, is historical materialism. Like psychoanalysis, historical materialism is directed towards reflection and critical awareness.

Habermas's earlier writings, and in particular *Knowledge and Human Interests*, suffer from a number of weaknesses. First, as he later acknowledges himself, his earlier thought is still embedded in what he calls a Cartesian 'philosophy of consciousness' (or philosophy of the subject) in that it overlooks the social nature of communicative practices. Second, although Habermas demonstrates persuasively that psychoanalysis can be self-emancipatory for the *individual*, this does not imply, as he seems to assume, that psychoanalysis is a stepping-stone for a critical theory of *society*. Many doubts have since emerged regarding such potential for psychoanalysis (Pusey 1987: 74). Third, the early Habermas regularly conflates reflection upon socially induced constraints, on the one hand, and liberation from these constraints, on the other. When later pressed on this issue, he recognizes that self-reflection is a necessary, though not sufficient, condition for negating past restrictions. But in his early writings the two notions are not always properly distinguished. Fourth, Habermas uses the term 'reflection' with at least two different meanings. One refers to the Kantian concept of 'critique' as reflection upon the conditions of possibilities of knowing or acting. Another refers to the Hegelian emancipatory notion of *Bildung* as reflection upon hitherto unconscious or hypostatized constraints (see Bernstein 1985b: 12–15). Habermas later recognizes this ambiguity in these writings, calling the latter self-criticism and the former rational reconstruction. He devoted an important part of his work in the 1990s, including *The Theory of Communicative Action*, to the phenomenon of rational reconstruction. In this context, he relies upon what he calls 'reconstructive sciences', referring to Chomsky's generative grammar, Piaget's theory of cognitive development and Kohlberg's theory of moral development. These reconstructive sciences reveal the underlying rules of our pre-theoretical 'knowing how'. Habermas's theory of communicative action or universal pragmatics is itself such a reconstructive science. This theory allows him to follow Kant in his notion of reason, reflecting upon the universal conditions of its own functioning, while avoiding the a priori nature of Kant's enterprise (ibid.: 15ff.).

The theory of communicative action

This brings us to his seminal work on rationality. For Habermas, an action or a statement is rational if it can, in principle, be justified on the basis of an open debate with equal participation for each individual. This working definition can be used to address three aspects of the concept of rationality. One component is epistemological. Its leading question is whether or not each culture incorporates its own rationality. Habermas's conceptualization of rationality as procedural leads him to reject relativist notions such as those of Winch, who relies upon Wittgenstein's *Philosophical*

Investigations. A second component of rationality operates at the level of social theory. It deals with the rationality claims which are made in one's explanations of social conduct (see chapter 4). The third component, to which Habermas pays most attention, refers to the sociology of culture and particularly the cultural process of transition which the West has undergone since roughly the sixteenth century.

By focusing on this third component, Habermas reacts partly against Weber's notion of disenchantment (*Entzauberung*) and Adorno and Horkheimer's concept of instrumental reason. According to these authors, modern civilization is characterized by an increase in the logic of means–end rationality. As such, they are highly critical of the project of modernity. For Habermas, however, rationalization is not a single, but a twofold process. On the one hand, it indeed involves instrumental rationality, as it has been conceptualized by Weber and the Frankfurt School. Like them, Habermas is highly critical of excessive means–end rationality. On the other hand, there is undoubtedly a more positive component to the rationalization process in the West. Habermas decides to call this positive aspect of the Enlightenment 'communicative rationality'. Communicative rationality refers to the institutionalization of mechanisms of open criticism and defence. Whereas instrumental rationality links in with the imperative of the social system, communicative rationality refers to the level of the life-world. Communicative rationality becomes the cornerstone of Habermas's contribution to critical theory (1991: 1–141).

Central to Habermas's 'universal pragmatics' is the notion of competence. He argues that people possess specific practical skills which allow them to draw particular distinctions. One of these distinctions is between three types of action: 'instrumental', 'strategic' and 'communicative action'. Instrumental and strategic action are both orientated towards success, but while the former refers to a relationship with external nature, the latter deals with strategic situations between people. Strategic and communicative action are both social, but the latter is social action orientated towards reaching 'understanding' (*Verständigung*) with respect to all 'validity claims' (*Geltungsansprüche*) (ibid.: 328ff.). Obviously influenced by Popper, Habermas argues that people are able, in principle, to make an additional distinction between three different worlds: external nature, society and internal nature. Whereas the world of external nature refers to issues of a correct representation of facts, society refers to issues of moral rightness of social rules, and internal nature deals with issues of sincerity (ibid.: 236ff.). As will be obvious from what follows, the ability of people to make these various distinctions is central to Habermas's notion of communicative action.

One of Habermas's central claims is that the notion of rationality pre-supposes communication. To elaborate this argument, Habermas relies on speech act theory. He draws heavily upon Austin's distinction between illocutionary and locutionary speech acts. Austin introduces these terms to draw a distinction between saying something on the one hand, and doing something by saying something on the other. Following Austin, Habermas claims that every speech act can be divided up into a proposi-tional level and an illocutionary level. He combines this with his tripartite frame of worlds according to which there are three uses of language: cognitive, interactive and expressive. The cognitive use of language points to something in the objective world and draws upon constatives as a type of speech action. The interactive use refers to the social world, aims at establishing legitimate interpersonal relations and draws upon regulatives (like commands or promises). Finally, the expressive use refers to the subjective world, the intention or self-representation of the speaker, while drawing upon avowals. As will become clear in the following, these three uses of language tie in with three 'validity claims' (1979: 1–59; 1991: 286–328).

We are now in a position to elaborate on the core of Habermas's theory of communicative action. One of his pivotal assertions is that whenever people are involved in a conversation with one another four culturally invariant 'validity claims' are implicitly presupposed. These are 'intelligi-bility', 'truth', 'moral rightness' and 'sincerity'. Intelligibility (*Verständlich-keit*) refers to the presupposition that whenever one speaks, what one says has meaning and is not gibberish. As intelligibility is fulfilled within language use itself, it is not part of the subject-matter covered within Habermas's universal pragmatics. Truth (*Wahrheit*), the second validity claim, refers to the fact that, by saying something, there is the implicit idea that the 'factual content' of what is said is true. Moral rightness (*Rich-tigkeit*) refers to the implicit claim that, by saying something, one has the right to say it at a given moment within a given context. Finally, sincerity (*Wahrhaftigkeit*) is the implicit claim that, by saying what one says, one is not intending to deceive the other participants in the interaction.

The ability of people to differentiate between the three worlds ties in with the latter three validity claims. Truth belongs to the world of exter-nal nature; Habermas calls it the 'cognitive-instrumental sphere'. Moral rightness links in with the world of society; in Habermasian parlance, this is the 'moral-practical sphere'. Sincerity concerns the world of internal nature; Habermas calls it the 'evaluative or expressive sphere'. Although the validity claims are implicitly presupposed in communication, all are also potentially open to argumentation. Each validity claim is associated with a different form of argumentation. Theoretical discourse refers to the truth-validity of propositions or efficacy of actions; Habermas calls this form of discourse the 'cognitive use of language'. Practical discourse refers to the rightness of norms; Habermas coins it 'interactive use of language'. Aesthetic criticism and therapeutic critique refer to adequacy of value standards and truthfulness and sincerity of expressions; this is the 'expressive use of language' (1979: 59–68; 1973b: 1–40).

'Undistorted communication' differs from 'distorted communication' in that the people involved can openly defend and criticize all validity claims. This is especially the case in an 'ideal speech situation', which is an uncoerced debate between free and equal individuals, and as such it is entirely dominated by one principle: the 'force of the better argument'. Furthermore, all individuals involved have equal right to enter the discussion, and there is no repressed motive or self-deceit which might affect the outcome. The ideal speech situation is an ideal type in the Weberian use of the word, and one of Habermas's bold claims is that it is inherent in the nature of language. He refers to it as a 'counterfactual' ideal which can operate as a yardstick for critically evaluating and comparing real-life situations and as a critique of distorted communication (1970a; 1970b). Of the four validity claims, only truth and moral rightness can be redeemed in discourses which approximate an ideal speech situation. The intelligibility of a statement tends to be demonstrated by putting it differently, and sincerity can only be shown by subsequent actions. But truth and moral rightness can be redeemed in discourse. It follows that Habermas's notion of rationality and truth is a *procedural* one: his notion of rationality does not adhere to absolute foundations of knowledge, but to *procedures* of reaching knowledge (see also Giddens 1985b: 114–16). One of the upshots of this is that, analogous to Popper's rejection of a 'first philosophy', our knowledge is temporal – to be held until a better argument compels us to think otherwise. Contrary to, for example, Tarski's notion of a correspondence theory of truth, Habermas's consensus theory of truth refers to agreements reached on the basis of an open unrestrained debate amongst equals.

Hitherto, we have dealt mainly with the Habermasian notion of a rational 'conduct of life' (*Lebensführung*); but what about the differences between societies as to whether their 'form of life' (*Lebensform*) allows for such rational conduct? For Habermas, some societies are more predisposed to *Lebensführung* than others. In particular, the *Lebensform* of earlier civilizations seems less conducive to rationality. In this context, Habermas develops a theory of homology or structural identity between individual and societal development. For this he relies, in part, upon Piaget's work on the cognitive and moral development of children, distinguishing, as does Piaget, four stages of the child's development: the symbiotic, the egocentric, the sociocentric and the universalistic. Each phase leads to a 'decentring' of an egocentrically distorted view of the world. The child gradually learns to distinguish the objective, the social and the subjective realm. Before children enter the egocentric stage, they are unable to differentiate themselves from the environment, and it is only during the sociocentric stage that children gradually learn to distinguish physical and social reality. Finally, during the universalistic stage they learn to reflect critically upon their actions or values from the perspective of alternative arguments. This unilinear perspective ties in with Kohlberg's three stages of consciousness in ontogenesis: the pre-conventional, the conventional and the post-conventional (Habermas 1979: 69–129).

Consistent with his interpretation of, amongst others, Lévi-Strauss, Piaget and Kohlberg, Habermas argues that societal development goes through analogous stages to personal development. As opposed to modern world-views, mythical world-views do not allow people to distinguish between the external world, the social world and internal nature – they tend to conflate nature and culture, or language and the world. Analogous to individual development, there is a trend towards increasingly discursive rationality in the transition from mythopoietic, cosmological and religious cultures, to metaphysical and modern societies. Habermas adheres to a unilinear evolutionism in that he sees this trend towards increasing rationality as the inevitable and irreversible outcome of a collective learning process (ibid.: 69–177). Rationality becomes a possibility once a differentiation of the system and life-world takes place, plus a differentiation of the cognitive-instrumental sphere, the moral-practical sphere, the evaluative and the expressive sphere.

However, with the differentiation of the system and life-world, two problems occur. First, the maintenance of the economic and political dimensions of the social system might become eroded. This ties in with a 'motivation crisis' in the work sphere and a 'legitimation crisis' at the political level. Broadly speaking, Habermas's argument is that in advanced capitalism, politics is reduced to its pragmatic dimension; it is mainly in charge of macro-economic issues. However, if it fails to pursue its economic functions, it cannot rely upon legitimate authority, loyalty or commitment on the part of the citizens. Once politics is largely reduced to the solving of economic problems, recurrent economic crises are sufficient to erode its legitimacy (1976: 68–92; 1979: 178–205). Second, the system imperatives tend to instrumentalize the life-world, and this 'colonization of the life-world' leads to what Durkheim diagnosed as 'anomie' and Weber as a general loss of meaning. The subordination of the life-world to system imperatives is exemplified in Marx's theory of labour where the commodification of labour leads to the erosion of its life-world dimension. It is worth mentioning, however, that Habermas's theory of colonization differs significantly from the view of classical social theorists and their followers. He differs from Weber in that he does not conceive of the colonization of the life-world as part of an internal logic of modernization. In Habermas's view, the colonization of the life-world is not inevitable. This differs from a Marxist view in that Habermas's hope rests with the new social movements, and the latter do not operate within a traditional Marxist agenda. The new social movements are concerned with issues relating to quality of life and self-realization. Although these values are not incompatible with Marx's earlier writings, contemporary Marxists are reluctant to attribute such priority to these goals (1987c: 332–73).

Between facts and norms

After the publication of *The Theory of Communicative Action*, Habermas published copiously on moral philosophy, social theory and political analysis (see 1987b; 1990; 1993). In books such as *Moral Consciousness and Communicative Action* or *Postmetaphysical Thinking*, Habermas continues his move away from positive definitions of the 'good' or 'progress' (a noticeable feature of his early writings) towards a more proceduralist approach to morals (discourse ethics) and politics (procedural conception of deliberative democracy). Moral and political philosophy should thus focus on identifying the appropriate procedures and institutions that promote the elimination of particularistic (i.e. non-generalizable) prejudices and strategic interests. Habermas's last major theoretical treatise, *Between Facts and Norms*, is aimed at building the theoretical framework within which such procedures and institutions can be identified. To be sure, Habermas remains faithful to his strategy of theory construction. He first polarizes the multiple proposals of the debate; he then assesses both poles by identifying the strengths and weaknesses of each; and, finally, he presents his own proposal as a synthesis of the positive elements from each pole. A dialogical, rational and progressive strategy of theory construction is thus put into practice. In *Between Facts and Norms*, the theoretical poles constructed by Habermas are liberalism and civic republicanism. If the former has emphasized the role of individual rights at the expense of solidarity, the latter has endorsed a conception of popular sovereignty that needs to be translated into communicative terms if one wants to avoid the excesses of nationalism and ethnic particularism (see, e.g., 1996: 99). Habermas's alternative is a 'discourse theory of deliberative politics' (ibid.: 286). As hinted by the title, such a theory would supersede the tension between the facticity (e.g., the materialism of commercial law) and the validity (e.g., the idealism of constitutional law) internal to law. But this is not a purely juridical issue. The tension between 'facts and norms' is actually closely related to social theory. Consider, for instance, the system of rights. While it takes shape in constitutions (validity), it is implemented through various institutions (facticity). Habermas's ultimate aim is a critical social theory that resolves the tension between facts and norms *reconstructively*, i.e., through procedures and institutions, and not constructively, i.e., through substantive positive definitions of the good. Since Habermas no longer believes in 'epistemology as the *via regia*' (Dews 1986: 150) – i.e. as the primary form of justification of theory building – he adopts a conceptual strategy instead. As we have seen above, this strategy revolves around the communicative concept of reason. In what follows we discuss four of the most recent aspects of this building.

The first is related to Habermas's proposal (developed with his friend Karl-Otto Apel) for a discourse ethics (1990; 1998a; 2001a). As far as the level of abstraction is concerned, discourse ethics occupies an intermediary position in Habermas's intellectual edifice. The most general and abstract conceptual level is occupied by universal pragmatics, which aims at reconstructing the conditions for linguistic communication oriented to mutual understanding (1979; 1998b; see also Cooke 1994). Universal pragmatics, also known as formal pragmatics, is an interdisciplinary effort that draws from several disciplines, including pragmatics, semiotics and philosophy of language, among many others. At the less abstract level of the edifice one finds the theory of communicative action, a social theoretical enquiry into various types of rationality and behaviour.[4] Habermas's aim at this level is to show the relative superiority of communicative action, i.e., a type of communication oriented to mutual human understanding, in solving coordination and integration problems at the level of the lifeworld. Between these two levels there is discourse ethics. Briefly, it is an attempt to provide an answer for moral-practical problems from the perspective of communicative reason. It does not aim to achieve substantive results; it aims to justify the criteria of rationality and procedural norms derived from communicative reason. These include the rules and procedures of sincere, fair and open-minded communication. Discourse ethics is concerned with procedures, not results. To be valid, arguments need to meet three conditions: the speaker's intentions must be honest; the speaker has to make sure the argument is congruent with reality; the speaker cannot make use of particularistic prejudices. A brief reference to Habermas's 'U-principle' (universalization principle) might help us understand what is at stake here. The U-principle states that a moral norm is valid if, and only if, 'the foreseeable consequences and side effects of its general observance for the interests and value-orientations of *each individual* could be *jointly* accepted by *all* concerned without coercion' (1998a: 42). This is Habermas's version of Kant's famous categorical imperative. It differs from Kant's dictum insofar as it is meant to refer to actual discourses (Habermas calls them 'practical discourses'). It is not a mere thought experiment, but has a real foothold in social life. Imagine a heated 'practical discourse' on abortion. According to Habermas, the moral character of judgements such as 'the sacred character of life makes abortion an immoral practice' is determined not only by its intersubjective nature (it has to be the product of honest, open-minded participation in a debate), but also for having been able to gain a reasonable agreement from all those immediately affected. Here we see a possible limitation of Habermas's position: in the abortion debate, some of those affected are not born yet and might never be. Aware of this sort of difficulty, Habermas has sought empirical evidence to support discourse ethics in various fields, from social anthropology to the social psychology of Mead (see chapter 3). Discourse ethics, despite the vast array of criticisms it triggered, remains to this day one of the most influential proposals in contemporary moral philosophy.

The second aspect of Habermas's critical social theory that we wish to discuss is the model of democracy it proposes. Although the notion of democracy was already implicit in his early writings on the liberal public sphere, he did not properly theorize this conception before the publication of *Between Facts and Norms* (1996: 287–328). In this work, Habermas develops a procedural conception of deliberative democracy that, along with Rawls's case for the related notion of 'public reason' in *Political Liberalism* (1993),[5] has proved to be crucial in putting this model of democracy at the centre of the agenda of political theory since the early 1990s. The rise of deliberative democracy is closely related to the crisis of representative democracy that has been afflicting developed Western democratic regimes since the 1970s. The steady decrease of voter turnout posed serious questions over the democratic legitimacy of those regimes. One solution has been to promote other, complementary forms of political participation, in particular of deliberative nature. This was certainly the case for Habermas, for whom linguistic communication and direct forms of political participation have always been at the forefront of his intellectual and political interests. According to Habermas's version of deliberative democracy, citizens should regard the laws by which they have to abide as legitimate if, and only if, the democratic process has been procedurally organized so that its outcomes are products of a deliberative process of opinion- and will-formation. Following John Dewey's (1927) radical democratic ideas,[6] Habermas claims that the majority rule, if it is not preceded by political deliberation, is devoid of any substantive meaning (1996: 304). Electoral mechanisms such as voting are important to characterize a political regime as 'democratic' only insofar as they measure the outcomes of the unconstrained and mutually enriching political debates that constitute democracy as a way of life. An important element of Habermas's political thinking is the notion of the public sphere (ibid.: 329–87; see also Calhoun 1992; Crossley and Roberts 2004). In his view, without a vibrant public sphere democracy cannot survive for long. Take the crucial function of thematization, i.e. the choice of what is to be discussed. According to Habermas, thematization should pertain to the participants in the political public sphere, and not to the CEOs of some media company, if particular interests are to be eliminated from democratic opinion-formation.

The third aspect of Habermas's work we would like to present refers to his cosmopolitanism. Especially in the 1990s and 2000s, Habermas has devoted himself to analysing the social and political consequences of globalization and the so-called 'war on terror' in the Western political agenda (Habermas and Derrida 2004). A central concept at this stage of Habermas's career was the notion of 'constitutional patriotism' (*Verfassungspatriotismus*) (2001a). Given the tragic historical record of 'ethnic nationalism', Habermas prefers constitutional patriotism as a source of societal integration. His proposed solution for the problem of social cohesion in religious and ethnically plural societies such as ours – the contemporary formulation of the classical sociological 'problem of order' – is to unleash the emancipatory potential already present in constitutional democratic institutions. According to Habermas, the experience of living together under a democratic constitution, which protects the rights and interests of all, potentially gives all citizens a sense of political belonging, irrespective of their ethnic, religious or cultural background. Constitutional patriotism refers to this process of identification with the political-legal system of the democratic constitutional state. A favoured example of his is the European Union. One possible problem with this solution is, of course, that the clear-cut distinction between ethnic (thick) and civic (thin) modes of political allegiance tends to blur over time (see Markell 2000). Today's constitutional patriotism for the EU's legal and political system can very easily become tomorrow's aggressive pan-European nationalism. Despite its shortcomings, Habermas's cosmopolitanism has played an important role in recent debates on the possibilities of political regulation of globalization. For instance, his proposal for a 'postnational democracy' is an attempt to extend his procedural conception of deliberative democracy to the international level. It is more ambitious and democratic than Rawls's (1999) law of peoples, but less optimistic than David Held's (1995) proposal for a cosmopolitan democracy. It goes beyond Rawls's proposal insofar as it points to the need of having a democratically legitimate global political order. In contrast to Held, however, Habermas does tend to restrict deliberative democracy (but not constitutional patriotism) to the level of the nation-state. Beyond this level, Habermas contends, democratic self-legislation does not yet have the necessary political and legal conditions. He distinguishes between three different scales of governance. The first is the level of the nation-state, in which democracy as self-legislation can indeed take place under certain conditions. A second scale is transnational and, according to Habermas, in 'growing need of regulation and fair policies'. The most general scale of governance encompasses the whole globe but, at this level, the rule of international law is still far from having been 'constitutionalized' (2006a: 178). In short, Habermas's cosmopolitanism is still very much a conception in the making and one that has yet to provide a convincing answer to Kant's classical question of how 'perpetual peace' among nations can be secured in an increasingly globalized world.

The fourth and most recent aspect of Habermas's career deals with the re-emergence of religion. A 'methodological atheist' (2002: 129), Habermas positions himself between those who, like Rawls or Robert Audi, argue that religious reasons have to be translated into secular arguments if they are to enter public discussions, and those who contend that there is no need for such translation. As he explains in 'Religion and the public sphere', Rawls and Audi put an undue burden on believers: it should not be them but public officials and politicians who bear responsibility for the translation of religious claims into secular ones. But the opposite position of not requiring such a translation, held by authors such as Paul Weithmann and Nicholas Wolterstorff, entails even more serious consequences. This scenario could mean the blurring of the separation between state and church, jeopardizing the neutrality principle that supports democratic constitutional regimes. Habermas is very clear on this point. Even though he recognizes the immense influence of Christianity on Western political and philosophical modes of thinking (Ratzinger and Habermas 2006), he is adamant that 'all enforceable political decisions must be formulated in a language that is equally accessible to all citizens, and it must be possible to justify them in this language as well' (2006b: 12). In *Between Naturalism and Religion*, a collection of articles that was first translated into English in 2008, Habermas further develops his ideas on religion. His main argument is straightforward. Today's intellectual landscape is dominated by a central tension. On the one hand, in the past few decades we have witnessed staggering scientific advances in the areas of brain research and biogenetics. For instance, in 2003 the Human Genome Project determined the complete sequence of the DNA of the human species; and computerized pictures of the brain are nowadays commonplace, at least in hospitals of developed countries. On the other hand, religion has been revitalized to such an extent as to put in question conventional secularization theory. In philosophical terms, this return of religion often assumes the character of a fundamentalist critique of postmetaphysical Western modernity. Habermas's responses to the double challenge of scientific naturalism and religious fundamentalism are consistent with the central tenets of his thinking. Very much like the positivist behaviourism of the early twentieth century that motivated Mead's social conception of the self, Habermas detects the risk that a similar reductionism might be affecting today's neurosciences. Carried away by the impressive technological advances of our age, the tendency amongst contemporary neuroscientists to reduce human consciousness to chemical interactions in the human brain is as great, and misguided, as a century ago. Hence Habermas's plea for social scientists to demonstrate the cultural and normative dimensions of human consciousness to their colleagues in the life sciences. His message is clear. The human mind possesses a normative character that is no less important than its chemical and physiological counterpart. His response to the revitalization of religion is no less clear. Habermas suggests one should distinguish between dogmatist (or fundamentalist) religious positions and enlightened religions: contrary to the former, the latter have been important allies in the struggle for human rights and democratic forms of life (2008: 124). His methodological atheism places him closer to these enlightened religious forms, which marks an obvious departure from his earlier positions. He now openly criticizes the secularist ideology of naturalism for preventing enlightened religious views from participating in the political public sphere. In our view, the most significant aspect of this important collection of essays, however, concerns its partially autobiographical nature. In the opening essay, Habermas offers his readers a detailed and fascinating biographical digression. In it we are told how certain personal features might have played a crucial role in his interest in human linguistic communication (as a child he had surgery to his palate, which would result in a serious speech impediment). For someone who played a central role in as many debates as Habermas did for more than half a century, this revelation comes not so much as a surprise as a confirmation of his lifelong concern with the 'public sphere as a space of reasoned communicative exchanges' (ibid.: 12).

Evaluation and current developments

There is no doubt that Habermas's enterprise is a courageous one. At a time when the influence of liberal individualism is hegemonic in certain social sciences and a postmodern agenda still dominates in others, Habermas's work stands out for its attempt at finding new philosophical grounds for critical theory (see, e.g., Honneth et al., 1992). Despite the controversial nature of Habermas's work, its sheer breadth and depth are achievements in themselves. The latter accomplishments are probably unrivalled in the twentieth century. Habermas incorporates an impressive range of philosophies and sociological theories. He deals with a wide spectrum of issues, from traditional philosophical topics to the intricacies of contemporary politics. Given the enormous scope of his work and given the difficult tasks he sets out to achieve, it would be inconceivable for his project to be without any significant lacuna. We will not even attempt to provide here an exhaustive list of all the criticisms which have been levelled against his writings. It is simply too long, and Habermas has incorporated some of these arguments in his work anyway. We deal especially with his central writings on communicative rationality because they have been the most influential so far.

First, there is the rather tedious, though not insignificant, point that some aspects of his work lack a solid empirical grounding. Habermas's contribution to critical theory relies on a number of 'reconstructive sciences'. The latter have been regularly subjected to criticism on empirical grounds, and rightly so. For example, the empirical basis of Piaget's or Kohlberg's work does not remain uncontested, neither does Lévi-Strauss's *oeuvre* (see chapter 1). The lack of empirical support for these theories may jeopardize the core of his theory of communicative action, which in its procedure of rational reconstruction draws heavily upon them. A similar criticism applies to Habermas's theory of societal evolution, which he backs by his personal and selective reading of the work of other theoreticians of evolution (Weber, Marx and Durkheim, to name only a few), who in their turn often rely upon secondary sources. Habermas's reconstruction of others' accounts of evolution clarifies and illustrates his position very well indeed, but, as a defence of that very same position, it is inevitably unconvincing. This is certainly not to say that Habermas's theoretical frame of reference cannot be sustained by empirical evidence, but more research is needed to pass a judgement on this issue.

Second, there are problems with Habermas's statement that communicative action is orientated towards reaching understanding or agreement. It is, in Habermas's own terms, *verständigungsorientiertes Handeln*. However, the German word *'Verständigung'* is confusing since it incorporates both understanding and agreement. Of course, it could be argued that agreement presupposes at least a minimal form of understanding. If two people agree on something, then they necessarily must have some understanding of what it is they agree on. Understanding, however, does not presuppose agreement: if two people understand each other, it does not follow that they agree upon what has been understood (see also Roderick 1986: 158–9). This weakens Habermas's argument that communication presupposes the possibility of *Verständigung*. He might have compelling reasons for arguing that communication indeed requires as a condition the possibility of understanding, but this does not imply that there is such a tight link between the two as he thinks there is. This problem comes to the surface especially when communication takes place between individuals belonging to different cultures. This brings us to the third point, which follows.

Deeper criticism applies to the concepts of communicative rationality and of the ideal speech situation, as conceived and conceptualized by Habermas. Even if, hypothetically, one can imagine an ideal speech situation to exist, it is rather difficult to grasp how people would reach an understanding, let alone consensus, when radically different forms of life (and thus different underlying assumptions) are at stake. Under these conditions even Habermas's notion of 'the force of the better argument', however innocuous at first sight, appears problematic. The rules of valid argumentation themselves are indeed part of a cultural heritage and tradition, and therefore, in Habermas's own terms, open to debate and criticism. One enters a vicious circle here, since deciding upon the better argument is dependent on Habermas's 'force of the better argument', and this in turn will be decided upon by the force of the better argument, and so on, ad infinitum. Leaving these analytical problems aside, it is sufficient to notice that the ideal speech situation fails to serve its practical purposes in the confrontation between different cultural settings – especially obvious in the case of competing theoretical systems or paradigms in science.[7]

If Habermas is the most influential representative of the second generation of the Frankfurt School, Claus Offe and Axel Honneth are certainly among the most important of the third. To begin with, both are former students of Habermas. They have consistently pursued lines of research inaugurated by Habermas, or at least to which he had made a substantial contribution. Still, both Offe and Honneth have made original contributions of their own to the project of a critical theory of society. Let us start with Claus Offe (1940–). His main research interest is the welfare state. Offe has been one of Europe's leading social scientists on this topic since the 1970s. His analyses encompass the rise and fall of the literature on new social movements (1985), the demise of socialism, and the current challenges posed by economic globalization (2006). More than Habermas or Honneth, Offe has relied upon detailed empirical analyses to support his theses.[8] Endorsing a neo-institutionalist research strategy (see chapter 4), Offe aims at making Habermas's discourse ethics more amenable to empirical analysis. The fact that critical theorists like Offe draw on new institutionalism shows the extent to which this emerging methodological perspective is not exclusively associated with the individualist premises of rational choice theory. It also shows that the strand of critical theory that Offe represents is open to analytical perspectives other than those traditionally associated with the Frankfurt School, like Freud's psychoanalysis or Marxist class analyses. Offe's argument is straightforward. Habermas has rightly identified two elements that are necessary in order for a strong civic spirit to develop, namely constitutional guarantees (procedures) and civic courage (post-conventional moral judgements). However, the synthesis of these two elements in 'constitutional patriotism' does not by itself guarantee the development of 'solidarity', the steering media that critical social theorists wish to promote against 'money' and 'administrative power'. According to Offe, the constitutional and socialization (i.e. educational) conditions of a society may well be developed, but 'in the absence of corresponding institutions representing collective identities . . . the potential of moral capacities will still not be realized' (1992: 81). Here Offe has in mind the network of organizations that promote 'associative relations', i.e. non-governmental organizations and voluntary associations responsible for social representation and mediation of interests. 'Associative relations' are particularly important as they perform the catalysing function of activating the capacities for moral judgement. They do so, Offe explains, 'by generating as their by-product . . . the assurance of stability and conditions of trust' (ibid.: 83; see also chapter 3). Consider the example of the political public sphere that Habermas praises so highly.

Offe distinguishes between formal, representative democracy and direct, participatory forms of democratic life. The first is illustrated by a general election. In this case, the motivations behind the individual act of voting can be strategic and instrumental, as so much rational choice theory-oriented literature emphasizes. 'Under the institutional, contextual conditions of the political or associational public sphere' (ibid.: 85), on the other hand, motivations to justice and solidarity tend to predominate. Faithful to his lifelong interest in 'social movements' and other associative forms of democratic participation, Offe remains convinced that the critical potential of discourse ethics can only be unleashed under certain institutional conditions, namely those provided by 'associative relations'. In sum, Offe's latest contribution to a critical theory of society is an enquiry into the institutional arrangements of contemporary societies from the perspective laid out by Habermas's discourse ethics. It thus provides the kind of 'middle-range' theory that Habermas can be criticized for having failed to produce.

Axel Honneth's (1949–) contribution to the programme of a 'critical theory of society' is markedly different from Offe's. He does not believe that critical theory should grant a privileged status to 'social movements', or any other social group for that matter. Neither the proletariat, as so many Marxist-oriented authors believed for so long, nor the new social movements of the 1970s and 1980s can assist critical theory as a 'kind of empirically visible guiding thread for diagnosing normatively relevant problem areas' (Honneth and Fraser 2002: 120). In Honneth's view, the normative foundations of critical theory need to be located at a more fundamental level than that provided by any concrete social group. From this perspective, his project comes closer to that of Habermas. However, he is no less critical of Habermas's proposed solution than he is of Offe's. Honneth contends that Habermas's critical theory – founded on a search for perfect understanding – is flawed. In his view, preceding Habermas's quest is a yet even more fundamental and universal mode of human interaction: the 'struggle for recognition'. Over the past couple of decades, his aim has been to reconstruct such a fundamental level by means of a social theory of recognition.

After publishing several books that can now be seen as preliminary steps towards his theory of recognition, in 1992 Honneth published *Struggle for Recognition*, his *Habilitationsschrift* supervised by Habermas (the English translation was published in 1996). While Habermas's influence is unmistakable in this work (for example, the way in which Honneth conceives of American philosophical pragmatism as a form of Left Hegelianism), Honneth also distances himself from his former supervisor. Honneth resorts to the social psychology of Mead in order to supplement the model of recognition developed by the young Hegel (1996: 71). His claim is that the preconditions for successful self-realization in post-traditional societies were first identified by Hegel and then developed, on postmetaphysical terms, by Mead. In particular, he is interested in Mead's notion of the 'generalized other', the attitude of the social group that allows children to pass from the developmental stage of 'play' to that of 'game' (see chapter 3). Of the three types of relations of recognition identified by Hegel – love, right and solidarity – Honneth thinks that Mead's notion of the 'generalized other' helps to clarify the second one, legal recognition (ibid.: 80). In contrast to Hegel, however, Mead's analysis of the mutual relations of recognition covers neither the 'love relationship' nor the solidarity relationship. Modern societies have meanwhile changed dramatically over the course of the past 200 years, as a result of which, Hegel's and Mead's analyses are both out-dated. A case in point is the category of legal recognition. Both Hegel and Mead considered only 'liberal civil rights'. As Honneth points out, there has been in most developed countries an extension of human rights to encompass social and economic rights in the second half of the twentieth century. Until this period human rights included only political and civil rights (the right to vote, property rights, freedom of speech, etc.). With the ratification by the United Nations in 1966 of the International Covenant on Economic, Social and Cultural Rights a profound change occurred. Human rights now include a host of other more substantive, positive rights, such as the right to education and the right to the enjoyment of physical and mental health. As a consequence, Honneth argues, the legal prerequisites of self-recognition now include a substantive component, namely the specification of the conditions of their application (ibid.: 177).

More recently, Honneth has developed his theory of recognition in two different directions. First, in the 2005 Tanner Lectures he delivered at the University of California, Berkeley, later published as *Reification*, a strong case is made for the precedence of recognition over cognition. As we have seen, rational choice theory and related individualist perspectives begin with the assumption of a rational actor able to make choices in the world (see chapter 4). Honneth's aim is to show that this cognitivist premise is not as fundamental as it is purported to be. His central claim is that cognition is actually preceded by recognition. He recovers Lukács, Heidegger and Dewey to support his claim that the 'stance of empathetic engagement in the world . . . is prior to our acts of detached cognition' (2008: 38). In order to demonstrate further that recognition is prior to cognition in the realm of social activity, Honneth resorts to recent developmental psychological research to show that emotional identification is 'absolutely necessary to the taking over of another person's perspective, which in turn leads to the development of the capacity for symbolic thought' (ibid.: 43). He also draws on Stanley Cavell's notion of 'acknowledgement' to show that recognition precedes cognition in a conceptual sense. For example, when A says 'I am in pain' and B retorts, 'I know you are in pain', this is not an expression of cognitive knowledge but rather 'an expression of sympathy': it is only because B is able to acknowledge A's pain that a social relationship is possible in the first place (ibid.: 49). This, of course, does not preclude other possibilities. It is not difficult to imagine a case where someone says 'I know you are in pain' without it being an expression of sympathy. The extreme example would be the torturer. Still, the argument holds – it is necessary to have experienced pain to be able to think and talk about it.

Having produced several pieces of evidence to show the priority of recognition over cognition in human relations, Honneth introduces the notion of 'reification', his main point of interest in these lectures. This old idea, usually associated with the first generation of critical theorists, is recovered by Honneth to designate the process of 'forgetting' the fact that recognition precedes cognition. Reification as 'forgetfulness of recognition' is thus intended to capture a wide range of situations in which social actors, so one-dimensionally concerned with pursuing a goal, lose sight of other, possibly more important motives and aims. He gives the example of a tennis player so focused on winning that she forgets her opponent is her best friend (ibid.: 59). This is reification of other persons (or 'intersubjective reification'). But reification can come about in another way. One can be denied access to the fact of antecedent recognition by a series of 'thought schemata' that strongly diminishes our ability to see the situation beyond prejudices and stereotypes. Think of the tennis player who is so focused on winning the next tournament that she forgets she is also a woman whose rights have only recently been historically guaranteed. In this case, we are dealing with self-reification. Equipped with these two patterns of reification, Honneth's next and final step is to identify the social sources of the current processes of reification. Rejecting Lukács's sociological explanation of reification (that pointed to 'capitalist free-market society' as the source of all types of reification), Honneth argues that the two types of reification identified above have distinct social sources. The free market ideology that has dominated labour relations in advanced industrialized nations since the 1980s is, according to Honneth, the 'thought scheme' responsible for current processes of intersubjective reification. A good illustration of these processes is the booming sex industry, a sphere of labour in which the commodification of the human body is attaining unprecedented levels of social acceptability. Here we see the usefulness of Honneth's concept of intersubjective reification. This concept convincingly unmasks the contradictory nature of neo-liberalism, an unstable blend of moral conservatism and free market economic policies (ibid.: 81). Turning to self-reification, some institutionalized practices, like job interviews, promote simulated self-portrayals and are therefore obstacles to a proper relation to one's self. Is there anything more sadly ironic than trying to get your dream job at the expense of portraying yourself as you really are? In sum, Honneth's account of reification aims at providing contemporary social theory with tools that allow it to deal *critically* with rational behaviour that treats others (or oneself) as mere objects. In this way, the forgetfulness of recognition can be conceptually addressed.

The second direction in which Honneth developed his theory of recognition, as seen in *Disrespect*, is one in which he explores the systematic violation of the conditions of recognition. His critical social theory focuses on the social causes responsible for the distortion of social relations of recognition (2007: 72). If in *Reification*, Honneth is concerned with the process of forgetting that recognition precedes cognition, *Disrespect* discusses the circumstances under which recognition is denied. According to Honneth, critically orientated social scientists should direct their research efforts to a number of areas, each associated with a specific form of social recognition. Their research agenda should first include studies on practices of socialization, familial forms and relations of friendship. R. W. Connell's influential work on masculinities (1995) seems to illustrate what Honneth has in mind. Second, they should focus on the content and application of positive law: for example, how the legislation enacted by a certain country influences the life of those affected by it. And, finally, social scientists should focus 'on actual patterns of social esteem' (Honneth 2007: 75). Concerning this latter form of social recognition, Honneth is referring to the sphere of labour. Indeed, it is not difficult to see why unemployment jeopardizes social esteem: if one is prevented from pursuing an economically rewarding occupation, that person's social esteem of individual achievements and abilities will be seriously impaired. In the case of the second form of social recognition, Honneth argues for an expansion of the 'global recognition of human rights': it can 'no longer be pursued only by exercising diplomatic influence or putting economic pressure on certain nations; what is required is direct cooperation with internationally operating civil movements' (ibid.: 214). From this angle, Honneth seems closer to the enthusiasm of other contemporary critical theorists such as Seyla Benhabib (2004; 2008) on the prospects of a global emancipatory politics than to Habermas's more sober ideas.

More than a personal trait, this reflects Habermas's lifelong commitment to the ideal of a communicatively rational society, whose highly abstract nature nevertheless mirrors the territorial scale of the nation-state. This is a critical point. Peter Sloterdijk, perhaps one of Habermas's fiercest critics in Germany today, has actually based his project of a post-Frankfurt School critical theory upon the idea of a 'topological turn', that is, a move away from temporal towards spatial relationships. In addition, a central debate in social theory today concerns 'methodological nationalism' (see chapter 8). There is no reason to believe, however, that the exercise of rational critique undertaken by Habermas, Offe and Honneth necessarily disregards spatial issues. On the contrary, as this chapter shows, the latest generation of Frankfurt critical theorists is actively engaged in addressing the challenges posed by economic globalization, not least the political and ethical problems associated with the gradual decentring from the national scale (for example, how to guarantee the respect for human rights, traditionally enforced by constitutional democratic states, in transnational contexts). The critical social theories of Habermas and his younger colleagues Offe and Honneth are thus bringing the tradition of the Frankfurt School into the twenty-first century. Whether or not they leave as lasting an influence on Sociology as Habermas did remains to be seen.

Further reading

Those who wish for a historical introduction to the Frankfurt School can consult Held's *Introduction to Critical Theory*. For a fine analytical approach to the project of critical theory, we would suggest Geuss's excellent *The Idea of a Critical Theory*. For a brief, but comprehensible introduction to Habermas's work in general, Bernstein's introduction to his edited volume *Habermas and Modernity* and Giddens's contribution to the same volume (entitled 'Reason without revolution') are both a good start. Also recommended, though more difficult, is Dews's *Autonomy and Solidarity*, an edited collection of interviews with Habermas. Part III of Held's *Introduction to Critical Theory* discusses Habermas's work within the context of critical theory in general. McCarthy's *The Critical Theory of Jürgen Habermas* is an excellent introduction to his earlier work, but does not fully incorporate Habermas's theory of communicative action. The latter is summarized very well in Ingram's *Habermas and the Dialectic of Reason*. Habermas's universal pragmatics is critically evaluated in *Habermas: Critical Debates*, edited by Thompson and Held. Outhwaite's *Habermas* is a solid, well-balanced overview of Habermas's work and includes not only his writings on communicative rationality, but also his latest work on legal theory. *Habermas and Modernity*, edited by Bernstein, is an excellent series of articles dealing with Habermas's defence of the project of the Enlightenment. It is ironic that for someone who grounds critical theory primarily in communicative practices aimed at *understanding*, Habermas has been remarkably unsuccessful in addressing his audience in an intelligible, let alone accessible manner. However, his early books such as *The Structural Transformation of the Public Sphere* and *Towards a Rational Society* are more accessible, and so too are his most recent writings on globalization and the European Union. Honneth's *Disrespect* and *Reification* are easy to read and provide an excellent introduction to the intellectual agenda of the third generation of critical theorists.

References

Aboulafia, M. et al. (eds) 2002. *Habermas and Pragmatism*. London: Routledge.

Adorno, T. W. 1973. *Negative Dialectics*. London: Routledge (originally in German, 1966).

Adorno, T. W. and Horkheimer, M. 1973. *Dialectic of Enlightenment*. London: Allen Lane (originally in German, 1947).

Adorno, T. W., et al. 1976. *The Positivist Dispute in German Sociology*. London: Heinemann.

Baynes, K. 1992. *The Normative Grounds of Social Criticism. Kant, Rawls, and Habermas*. Albany: SUNY Press.

Benhabib, S. 2004. *The Rights of Others: Aliens, Residents, and Citizens*. Cambridge: Cambridge University Press.

Benhabib, S. 2008. *Another Cosmopolitanism*, ed. R. Post. Oxford: Oxford University Press.

Bernstein, R. J. 1978. *The Restructuring of Social and Political Theory*. Philadelphia: University of Pennsylvania Press.

Bernstein, R. J. (ed.) 1985a. *Habermas and Modernity*. Cambridge: Polity.

Bernstein, R. J. 1985b. Introduction. In R. J. Bernstein (ed.), *Habermas and Modernity*. Cambridge: Polity, pp. 1–32.

Calhoun, C. (ed.) 1992. *Habermas and the Public Sphere*. Cambridge, MA: MIT Press.

Connell, R. W. 1995. *Masculinities*. Cambridge: Polity.

Cooke, M. 1994. *Language and Reason: A Study in Habermas's Pragmatics*. Cambridge, MA: MIT Press.

Crossley, N. and Roberts, J. (eds) 2004. *After Habermas: New Perspectives on the Public Sphere*. Oxford: Blackwell.

Dallmayr, F. R. and McCarthy, T. A. (eds) 1977. *Understanding and Social Inquiry*. Notre Dame, IN: University of Notre Dame Press.

Dewey, J. 1984 [1927]. *The Public and Its Problems*. In J. A. Boydston (ed.), *John Dewey. The Later Works*. Volume 2: *1925–1927*. Carbondale: Southern Illinois University Press, pp. 235–372.

Dews, P. (ed.) 1986. *Autonomy and Solidarity: Interviews with Jürgen Habermas*. London: Verso.

Fahrenbach, H. (ed.) 1973. *Wirklichkeit und Reflexion: Festschrift für Walter Schulz*. Pfüllingen: Neske.

Geuss, R. 1981. *The Idea of a Critical Theory*. Cambridge: Cambridge University Press.

Giddens, A. 1985a. Jürgen Habermas. In Q. Skinner (ed.), *The Return of Grand Theory in the Human Sciences*. Cambridge: Canto, pp. 121–40.

Giddens, A. 1985b. Reason without revolution. In R. J. Bernstein (ed.), *Habermas and Modernity*. Cambridge: Polity, pp. 95–121.

Giddens, A. and Turner, J. (eds) 1987. *Social Theory Today*. Cambridge: Polity.

Habermas, J. 1970a. On systematically distorted communication. *Inquiry* 13(3): 205–18.

Habermas, J. 1970b. Towards a theory of communicative competence. *Inquiry* 13(4): 360–75.

Habermas, J. 1973a. Wahrheitstheorien. In H. Fahrenbach (ed.), *Wirklichkeit und Reflexion: Festschrift für Walter Schulz*. Pfüllingen: Neske, pp. 211–65.

Habermas, J. 1973b. *Theory and Practice*. Boston: Beacon Press (originally in German, 1963).

Habermas, J. 1976. *Legitimation Crisis*. Cambridge: Polity (originally in German, 1973).

Habermas, J. 1977. A review of Gadamer's *Truth and Method*. In F. R. Dallmayr and T. A. McCarthy (eds), *Understanding and Social Inquiry*. Notre Dame, IN: University of Notre Dame Press, pp. 335–63.

Habermas, J. 1979. *Communication and the Evolution of Society*. Cambridge: Polity (originally in German, 1976).

Habermas, J. 1987a. *Knowledge and Human Interests*. Cambridge: Polity (originally in German, 1968).

Habermas, J. 1987b. *The Philosophical Discourse of Modernity*. Cambridge: Polity (originally in German, 1985).

Habermas, J. 1987c. *The Theory of Communicative Action. Volume 2: Lifeworld and System: A Critique of Functionalist Reason*. Cambridge: Polity (originally in German, 1981).

Habermas, J. 1987d. *Toward a Rational Society; Student Protest, Science, and Politics*. Cambridge: Polity (originally in German, 1969).

Habermas, J. 1988. *On the Logic of the Social Sciences*. Cambridge: Polity (originally in German, 1970).

Habermas, J. 1989. *The Structural Transformation of the Public Sphere: An Inquiry into a Category of Bourgeois Society*. Cambridge: Polity (originally in German, 1962).

Habermas, J. 1990. *Moral Consciousness and Communicative Action*. Cambridge: Polity (originally in German, 1983).

Habermas, J. 1991. *The Theory of Communicative Action. Volume 1: Reason and the Rationalization of Society*. Cambridge: Polity (originally in German, 1981).

Habermas, J. 1993. *Justification and Application*. Cambridge: Polity (originally in German, 1989).

Habermas, J. 1996. *Between Facts and Norms. Contributions to a Discourse Theory of Law and Democracy*. Cambridge: Polity (originally in German, 1992).

Habermas, J. 1998a. *The Inclusion of the Other: Studies in Political Theory*, ed. C. Cronin and P. de Greiff. Cambridge: MIT Press (originally in German, 1996).

Habermas, J. 1998b. *On the Pragmatics of Communication*, ed. M. Cooke. Cambridge: MIT Press.

Habermas, J. 2001a. *The Postnational Constellation. Political Essays*, ed. M. Pensky. Cambridge: Polity (originally in German, 1998).

Habermas, J. 2001b. *On the Pragmatics of Social Interaction. Preliminary Studies in the Theory of Communicative Action*. Cambridge, MA: MIT Press (originally in German, 1984).

Habermas, J. 2002. *Religion and Rationality. Essays on Reason, God, and Modernity*, ed. E. Mendieta. Cambridge: Polity (originally in German, 1997).

Habermas, J. 2006a. *The Divided West*. Cambridge: Polity (originally in German, 2004).

Habermas, J. 2006b. Religion and the public sphere. *European Journal of Philosophy* 14(1): 1–25.

Habermas, J. 2008. *Between Naturalism and Religion: Philosophical Essays*. Cambridge: Polity (originally in German, 2005).

Habermas, J. and Derrida, J. 2004. *Philosophy in a Time of Terror: Dialogues with Jürgen Habermas and Jacques Derrida*, ed. G. Borradori. Chicago, IL: University of Chicago Press.

Habermas, J. and Luhmann, N. 1971. *Theorie der Gesellschaft oder Sozialtechnologie*. Frankfurt: Suhrkamp.

Habermas, J. and Rawls, J. 1997. *Débat sur la justice politique*. Paris: Éditions du Cerf.

Held, D. 1980. *Introduction to Critical Theory: Horkheimer to Habermas*. Cambridge: Polity (reprinted, 1990).

Held, D. 1995. *Democracy and the Global Order: From the Modern State to Cosmopolitan Governance*. Cambridge: Polity.

Hesse, M. 1982. Science and objectivity. In J. Thompson and D. Held (eds), *Habermas: Critical Debates*. London: Macmillan, pp. 98–115.

Holub, R. C. 1991. *Jürgen Habermas; Critique in the Public Sphere*. London: Routledge.

Honneth, A. 1987. Critical theory. In A. Giddens and J. Turner (eds), *Social Theory Today*. Cambridge: Polity (reprinted, 1990).

Honneth, A. 1991. *Critique of Power: Reflective Stages in a Critical Social Theory*. Cambridge, MA: MIT Press.

Honneth, A. 1995. *The Fragmented World of the Social: Essays in Social and Political Theory*. Albany: SUNY Press.

Honneth, A. 1996. *The Struggle for Recognition: The Moral Grammar of Social Conflicts*. Cambridge, MA: MIT Press (originally in German, 1992).

Honneth, A. 2007. *Disrespect. The Normative Foundations of Critical Theory*. Cambridge: Polity (originally in German, 2000).

Honneth, A. 2008. *Reification: A New Look at an Old Idea*, ed. M. Jay. Oxford: Oxford University Press.

Honneth, A. and Fraser, N. 2002. *Redistribution or Recognition? A Political Philosophical Exchange*. London: Verso.

Honneth, A. and Joas, H. 1988. *Social Action and Human Nature*. Cambridge: Cambridge University Press (originally in German, 1980).

Honneth, A. and Joas, H. (eds) 1991. *Communicative Action*. Cambridge: Polity (originally in German, 1986).

Honneth, A., McCarthy, T., Offe, C. and Wellmer, A. 1992. *Cultural-Political Interventions in the Unfinished Project of Enlightenment*. Cambridge, MA: MIT Press.

Ingram, D. 1987. *Habermas and the Dialectic of Reason*. New Haven, CT: Yale University Press.

Lukes, S. 1982. Of gods and demons: Habermas and practical reason. In J. Thompson and D. Held (eds), *Habermas: Critical Debates*. London: Macmillan, pp. 134–48.

Markell, P. 2000. Making affect safe for democracy? On 'constitutional patriotism'. *Political Theory* 28(1): 38–63.

McCarthy, T. 1984. *The Critical Theory of Jürgen Habermas*. Cambridge: Polity.

McCarthy, T. 1985. Reflections of rationalization in the theory of communicative action. In R. J. Bernstein (ed.), *Habermas and Modernity*. Cambridge: Polity, pp. 176–91.

Offe, C. 1984. *Contradictions of the Welfare State*, ed. J. Keane. London: Hutchinson.

Offe, C. 1985. New social movements: challenging the boundaries of institutional politics. *Social Research* 52(4): 817–68.

Offe, C. 1992. Binding, shackles, brakes: on self-limitation strategies. In A. Honneth et al. (eds), *Cultural Political Interventions in the Unfinished Project of Enlightenment*. Cambridge, MA: MIT Press, pp. 63–94.

Offe, C. 1996. *Modernity and the State: East, West*. Cambridge, MA: MIT Press.

Offe, C. 2006. Social protection in a supranational context: European integration and the fates of the 'European social model'. In P. Bardhan, S. Bowles and M. Wallerstein (eds), *Globalization and Egalitarian Redistribution*. Princeton, NJ: Princeton University Press, pp. 33–62.

Ottmann, H. 1982. Cognitive interests and self-reflection. In J. Thompson and D. Held (eds), *Habermas: Critical Debates*. London: Macmillan, pp. 79–97.

Outhwaite, W. 2009. *Habermas: A Critical Introduction*, Second Edition. Cambridge: Polity.

Pusey, M. 1987. *Jürgen Habermas*. London: Tavistock.

Ratzinger, J. C. (Pope Benedict XVI) and Habermas, J. 2006. *Dialectics of Secularization. On Reason and Religion*, ed. F. Schuller. San Francisco, CA: Ignatius Press.

Rawls, J. 1993. *Political Liberalism*. New York: Columbia University Press.

Rawls, J. 1999. *The Law of Peoples: With 'The Idea of Public Reason Revisited'*. Cambridge, MA: Harvard University Press.

Roderick, R. 1986. *Habermas and the Foundations of Critical Theory*. London: Macmillan.

Skinner, Q. (ed.) 1985. *The Return of Grand Theory in the Human Sciences*. Cambridge: Canto.

Thompson, J. B. and Held, D. (eds) 1982. *Habermas: Critical Debates*. London: Macmillan.

Wellmer, A. 1985. Reason, utopia, and enlightenment. In R. J. Bernstein (ed.), *Habermas and Modernity*. Cambridge: Polity, pp. 35–66.

A Brave New World?

The Empirical Turn in Social Theory

How distinctive is our age?

The world at the dawn of the twenty-first century is very different from what it used to be just a generation ago. The gloomy nuclear equilibrium of the Cold War gave way to an unpredictable new world order, where terrorism, nuclear proliferation and global warming seem to come together to announce a new era. The confidence in the progress of human-kind, founded upon the diffusion of the benefits of modernity (first and foremost technological and scientific, but also political, juridical and civilizational) has subsided. The way we describe the new world ahead of us bears some resemblance to the way our forefathers described the *fin de siècle* a century ago: rapid and unpredictable change, uncertainty and loss of confidence in the old truths. At least in the West, both the twentieth and the twenty-first centuries were preceded by relatively long periods of social and political stability, sustained economic growth and epistemic confidence. In *A Sociology of Modernity*, Peter Wagner identifies an 'early, restricted liberal, modernity in the Northwestern quarter of the world' (1994: 55) emerging between the late eighteenth and the mid-nineteenth centuries. This early liberal modernity would not last long. With the First World War, most of the Enlightenment hopes of steady and gradual social progress were shattered. However, the sceptical mood towards liberal capitalist modernity had begun long before, first with the Marxian political economic critique and later with Weber's critique of the modern tendency towards bureaucratization and instrumental rationalization. Wagner argues that there are structural similarities between this first crisis of modernity and the second one which is currently under way (ibid.: 175 ff.). They were both preceded by relatively long periods of confidence in the possibilities of modernity to realize its promises. In both cases, human-kind (especially in the West) seemed able to attain unlimited progress by means of the rational mastery of the problems of the world, social and natural alike. This is exactly what defines modernism: an unquestionable confidence in the human ability to know itself and the world, thus ruling both without reference to any other authority than human reason (Wagner 2001: 10). In both cases, a series of societal developments led to the dissolution of this Enlightenment confidence. Intellectuals had to make sense of a world in transition, a world where trust in the possibilities of modernity was replaced by the need to cope with the incertitude brought about by sweeping economic, cultural and social transformations. This is what, in broad terms, connects us today to the generation of Weber, Durkheim, Mead and Simmel – a shared understanding that, in times of profound epistemological uncertainty and rapid socioeconomic change, social sciences have to abandon traditional rigid schemes in favour of more processual and creative models.

Wagner's analysis is confined to the West.[1] If one broadens the scope of the analysis, the picture becomes much more nuanced and even contradictory. To make sense of this complex picture has been the aim of an increasing number of scholars in recent years. Of course, beyond the common interest in studying the condition of our age, there is not much that unites these authors. From the macro-sociology of Manuel Castells to Ulrich Beck's diagnosis of risk society, from Zygmunt Bauman's sociology of modernity to Saskia Sassen's political economy or the quasi-literary writings of Richard Sennett, contemporary social theory is less a common enterprise than a discursive medium through which different perspectives account for our world today.

Manuel Castells and the network society

Manuel Castells's (1942–) celebrated trilogy *The Information Age* is one of the most ambitious theoretical treatises on globalization written so far. Anthony Giddens even describes it on the cover of that trilogy as no less an intellectual triumph than Weber's *Economy and Society*. Before we analyse Castells's *magnum opus*, some brief remarks on his previous work are in order. Castells began his career in Paris in the late 1960s as a Marxist-oriented urban sociologist. His was a 'new' urban sociology, which by focusing on urban grassroots politics paid due attention to the emergent social actors of the time, the new social movements. The 'old' urban sociology was, in contrast, narrowly empiricist and lacked a proper 'theoretical object', a claim that revealed Castells's reliance upon Louis Althusser's scientific Marxism. With works like *The Urban Question*, *Monopolville* and *Luttes urbaines et pouvoir politique*, Castells became a central figure in the field of urban studies and local politics. *Dual City*, a detailed analysis of the widening gap between poor and affluent in post-industrial New York, which Castells co-edited with John Mollenkopf, already signals an interest on his part in economic globalization. The same can be said of *The Informational City*, one of the earliest attempts by Castells systematically to apply his notion of informationalism. But it is with the trilogy *The Information Age*, a 1,500 pages long diagnosis of the condition of the age in the macro-sociological tradition, published in the late 1990s, that Castells becomes one of the most influential interpreters of global issues of our time.

Whereas the first volume presents the rise of the network society, the second portrays the re-emergence of identity as a reaction to this societal development. In the third volume, Castells discusses how the dialectic between network and identity causes growing problems for the nation-state system as criminal global networks rapidly expand. If his earlier work is very much influenced by Marxism, his thinking today is much more indebted to network theory, Daniel Bell's theses on post-industrial society and Alain Touraine's ideas on the new social movements. Besides the holistic tendencies of his analysis and the priority it gives to economic and technological issues to the detriment of cultural ones, there is really not much Marxism left in Castells's work: networks, informationalism and flexibility are his current mottos.

Castells's thesis is that we live in the network society. This new society emerged as three interrelated processes that reinforced each other in the 1970s: the information technology revolution (an unintended consequence of the Cold War), the economic crisis of both welfare capitalism and state socialism, and the emergence of the new social movements. As a consequence of these processes, profound changes were felt in three domains: a new social structure (network society), a new economy ('informational capitalism') and a new culture (the internet culture of 'real virtuality') have all developed since the 1970s. In other words, the restructuring of capitalism since that time led to the emergence of the 'network society' in which 'information flows' are critical. The capitalist system of production no longer revolves around the production and commercialization of goods and services. Today, Castells claims, production is primarily 'informationalism' – that is, the control, manipulation and distribution of information as both a product and a means of organizing other products (1996: 14–15). He identifies five characteristics that distinguish 'informational capitalism', the emergent economic paradigm of our age: information becomes the fundamental economic good; information technologies dominate; economic systems organize themselves in global networks; relations of production become increasingly flexible; different technologies tend to converge. In the information age, economy, society and culture are governed by an all-encompassing 'network logic'. Castells has no doubts: 'Networks constitute the new social morphology of our societies and the diffusion of networking logic substantially modifies the operation and outcomes in the processes of production, experience, power and culture' (ibid.: 469).

In the second volume of *The Information Age*, Castells explores the consequences of this network logic for expressions of collective identities, especially in the form of social movements. His basic claim is that the network logic undermines the sense of identity of both individual and collective actors. Like Bauman and Sennett, Castells points to the decline of career employment as a sign of this societal trend. Jobs increasingly give way to 'projects' as the 'short term' replaces the 'long term' as the dominant economic temporality. Identity politics are thus a reaction to the diffusion of the new capitalist mode of organization (1997: 11). For Castells, social movements – from Islamic fundamentalism to Catalonian separatism and from Bolivia's electronic populists to the various types of feminisms – are attempts at identity construction in response to the global network mentality with its emphasis on the ephemeral. Castells's well-documented analysis shows how social movements today advance their agendas by subverting the network logic. A case in point is Mexico's Zapatistas, led by the legendary 'sub-commandant Marcos'. The Zapatistas have become an 'informational guerrilla movement' (ibid.: 79), successfully using the internet to gain the support of global public opinion in their war against the Mexican authorities. They have become an inspiration for innumerable other social movements around the world. Moreover, the Zapatistas have subverted the very notion of a 'project'. Instead of referring to an instrumental mode of economic organization, the idea of a 'project' has become a strategy of identity construction: it becomes a programme of social reconstruction aimed, in their case, at building bridges between the Indians, the poor and the educated urban middle classes so that new utopias can be created (ibid.: 286). The sense of solidarity that results from such projects is a powerful instrument for identity construction.

In the last volume of the trilogy, *End of Millennium*, Castells discusses at length the recent political events in a number of regional contexts in order to show the manifold expressions of the decline of statism and the concomitant rise of informationalism. He offers authoritative descriptions of the collapse of the Soviet Union, the process of European integration, the Asian Pacific economic surge led by development-oriented states, the emergence of global crime networks, and of the usually impoverished nations without states that he calls the 'Fourth World'. Interestingly, this volume is not so much a synthesis of the other volumes but a restatement or updating of the arguments presented in them. For instance, informationalism only provides an interpretive key in explaining the collapse of statism; it plays no explanatory role whatsoever in the rest of the book, something difficult to understand given Castells's earlier claim that this was *the* distinctive feature of our age. However, one of the most innovative aspects of *End of Millennium* is the way it interprets global crime. Informational capitalism puts a heavy burden on nation-states. Whenever these are unable to cope with that burden, as in Yeltsin's Russia, amongst the first things to disappear are the institutions responsible for securing law and order (1998: 180–8). As Castells notes, criminal organizations have been among the first collective actors to adapt to the new social order. The Russian Mafia and the Colombian drug cartels have been making effective use (digital money-laundering, for instance) of the current network logic and information technologies (ibid.: 201).

In more recent books, Castells has been pursuing specific aspects of the rise of the information age. *The Internet Galaxy*, for instance, is a study of the nature and influence of the internet as the technological basis for the form of organization *par excellence* of the information age, the network. In it, Castells depicts the internet culture as a four-layered hierarchical structure. First, there is the 'techno-meritocratic culture' of academics and scientists who believe that human progress is associated with the advancement of science. Second, there is a smaller 'hacker culture' (not to be confused with the criminal 'cracker culture', as often suggested by the media) composed of 'expert programmers and networking wizards' (2001: 41). Third, Castells identifies the virtual communitarian culture, formed by members of online communities like Facebook or Hi5: its very diverse composition mirrors the diversity of society itself. Fourth, there is the entrepreneurial culture of businessmen who saw in the internet a lucrative investment sector. This is one of the first attempts by a major social theorist to make sense of this astonishingly expanding phenomenon: between 1995, the first year of widespread use of the worldwide web, and 2010, the number of users will jump from 16 million to almost 2 billion (ibid.: 3). In *The Information Society and the Welfare State*, co-authored with Pekka Himanen, Castells discusses how a reformed Finnish welfare state manages to provide social protection while seizing the economic opportunities brought about by globalization. In one of his latest books, *Mobile Communication and Society*, Castells discusses the mobile communications revolution. His claim is that the cell phone, a technological apparatus of no less importance than the PC in the information age, is profoundly changing social life as it allows, for the first time in history, the possibility of global instant communication.

Three main criticisms can be levelled at Castells's theory of the network society. First, it is not so much an explanation as it is a description of the world today. Castells fails to flesh out the causal mechanisms behind the plethora of phenomena he so brilliantly describes. Take the use he makes of quantitative data in *The Information Age*. Two problems can be pointed out in this regard. He shows insufficient sensitiveness to the methodological limitations of resorting to international aggregate data, whose uneven reliability should make him less confident in making worldwide generalizations. Moreover, the quantitative data which he presents are sometimes redundant or unrelated to his arguments. It is one thing to suggest that there is a connection between changes in the public finances of most developed countries and the rise of social movements. It is certainly plausible to think that a diminished nation-state can facilitate the emergence of alternative projects of identity formation. But it is an altogether different thing to specify the causal mechanisms linking these two processes, and this Castells fails to do.

Second, given the amount of literature available about the limitations of modernization theory, it is hard to understand why Castells is so keen to follow this analytical perspective. His argument about the 'diffusion of the network logic' illustrates this difficulty. Instead of following the modernist view that globalization is a tidal wave embracing the planet, Castells would do better if he had subscribed, for instance, to the much more sophisticated 'variants of capitalism' approach developed by Peter Hall (see chapter 5). Were Castells to subscribe to this sort of more nuanced approach, his work would show more sensitivity to the complex processes of interaction and mutual redefinition between, on the one hand, global values and practices (say, human rights regimes) and, on the other, local incorporations of those values and practices. What Hall and his associates have been able to show is that these interactions between the global and the local level do not obey a homogeneous pattern of organization, as modernization theorists suppose. On the contrary, there are clear regional cleavages insofar as the incorporation and redefinition of global values and practices are concerned. Hence the notion of 'variants of capitalism' – it refers to one single phenomenon, whose scope is nowadays global, but whose specific configurations are clearly regional and sometimes even national (e.g. Japan). In our view, Castells's theory of the network society would gain much if it were to adopt a similar analytical orientation, whose global reach is compatible with greater awareness of sub-global patterns of organization.

Third, Castells underestimates place. His network society is a space of virtual flows and disembodied social relationships, where the culture of real virtuality reigns unchallenged. As a matter of fact, as authors like David Harvey suggest, the opposite seems to be true. Place is becoming all the more important as spatial barriers diminish. This is the great paradox of our age: '[T]he less important the spatial barriers, the greater the sensitivity of capital to the variations of place within space, and the greater the incentive for places to be differentiated in ways attractive to capital' (Harvey 1989: 298–9). The same idea has been explored with great success by Saskia Sassen, whose work we discuss below. For now it suffices to say that there are both theoretical and empirical reasons not to confuse globalization with deterritorialization. Some of the most successful theories of the global age deal with the growing importance of certain strategic places as global capitalism unfolds (e.g. Sassen's work on global cities). Likewise, the existing data on global values and practices from well-known international consortiums like the World Values Survey or the International Social Survey Programme consistently show variations by place to be no less significant than other variables, such as income, age, gender or religious affiliation (see, e.g., Clark and Hoffmann-Martinot 1998; Inglehart and Norris 2003).

In sum, Castells's main contribution to contemporary social theory is twofold. First, his earlier analyses on the city still constitute a reference for urban scholars worldwide. Second, his most recent writings on the network society, though more descriptive than explanatory, do provide a broad and informative perspective of our global world. It is no wonder, then, that since the late 1990s Castells has become one of the most requested social thinkers on global issues, working as an adviser to national governments, international bodies and private companies. The social influence of his theories is thus undoubted, as is his enthusiasm for the possibilities opened by the recent technological advances of our age, in particular the digital revolution triggered by the combined effect of the diffusion of personal computers and the internet. Our next author takes a markedly different stand on the consequences of the technological advances of the past few decades. Less optimistic than Castells, Ulrich Beck rose to international prominence with the translation into English in the early 1990s of his *Risikogesellschaft* (*Risk Society*), a widely influential book that focuses exactly on the negative, unintended consequences of our modern societies' reliance on technology. It is to Beck's work that we now turn our attention.

Ulrich Beck and risk society

There are two components to Ulrich Beck's (1944–) work: a substantive-empirical and a meta-theoretical dimension. The substantive-empirical component is straightforward: Beck wants to show the extent to which contemporary society is different from previous types of society. For him, society today differs from nineteenth-century society in a variety of ways. For instance, people no longer take institutions for granted but constantly *reflect on* and *choose* institutions. Previously, marriage and the family were given. Now, individuals can select from a variety of options, of which marriage is only one: they can remain single, they might wish to cohabit, or they might be in a relationship with someone who lives somewhere else (Beck and Beck-Gernsheim 2005). The meta-theoretical component of Beck's intellectual enterprise is more ambitious. He argues that these recent transformations are so vast that they necessitate a radical overhaul of our sociological apparatus. In spite of minor alterations over the years, the sociological tools which we currently employ are basically the same as those introduced in the late nineteenth and early twentieth centuries. They were very effective then; they allowed sociologists like Max Weber and Emile Durkheim to analyse the society in which they lived. However, these concepts and methodological strategies are no longer appropriate for exploring the social world today. If anything, they obfuscate what is so distinctive about the present situation. Beck wants to develop a new terminology and methodological strategy that fits the 'second modernity'. Similar to the way nineteenth-century sociologists had to invent a new vocabulary to analyse the radical transformations of society then, Beck insists that the current social changes demand a new frame of reference (Beck and Willms 2004: 11–61).

Until the publication of *Risikogesellschaft*, Beck was a relatively anonymous sociologist, specializing in the sociology of the family and work. When this book came out in 1986, it had an immediate impact on German social science. Since its translation into English in 1992, it has become a *cause célèbre* in the Anglo-Saxon world and has dictated the intellectual debate for a considerable time. *Risk Society* is not an ordinary academic book; it is quite eclectic in its oscillation between passages with a theoretical, speculative agenda and sections that read like political pamphlets with a strong moralizing tone. This book was first published in West Germany, and it reflects the concerns of many people in that society at the time. In the mid-1980s, West-Germany was, even by Western standards, a prosperous country with low unemployment figures and a high per capita GDP. Compared to the UK, where reform of the welfare system dominated the political debate, the main German political parties agreed on the desirability and feasibility of the welfare state. Other political issues, like immigration, had not yet emerged on the political scene, partly because immigration figures had remained low for a considerable period, and partly because the laws on citizenship at the time still denied many guest-workers the right to claim it. Only with the fall of the Berlin Wall and the extension of the European Union would immigration become a more significant political issue in Germany. This prosperity, together with the absence of other political concerns, provided a fertile climate for the rise of ecological awareness, which was indeed very strong in comparison with other parts of Europe. Beck's ecological views were prevalent in Germany at the time: there was a growing awareness that natural resources are limited and that unbridled industrialization would lead to catastrophic consequences for all. In addition, the electoral system (proportional representation) made it possible for the Green Party to become a significant political force. In short, Beck's central argument – that a society of scarcity had become a risk society – would be less meaningful to people living in, say, a poorer country, or one in which class divisions are more marked or in which other political issues are central. Likewise, the other thesis in the book – that individuals are becoming more individualized – might strike a cord with educated middle-class individuals living in a prosperous society, but perhaps less so with those who are less fortunate. Usefully for Beck's influence, the argument struck a chord in the US and in the UK, where the welfare state was being scaled back because of finance constraints, and many in the middle class saw themselves being deprived of 'social insurance' just as rising unemployment and global trade challenges exposed them to more income and employment risk.

Beck's argument centres round the notion of modernity. Modernity is characterized by the optimistic view that, with the help of technology and science, people will be able to control their natural surroundings effectively. This modern attitude has led to various negative, unintended effects, such as air and water pollution, toxins and global warming. Beck insists that these problems are new. Previous societies were confronted with various calamities and misfortunes, such as earthquakes, floods or droughts. But distinctive about these new quandaries is, first, that they are 'man-made': they are brought about by people's own attempts to control nature and to pursue profit (1992: 20–2). Beck argues that the nuclear reactor disaster at Chernobyl in 1986 was man-made as was 'mad-cow disease' (BSE); interestingly, he claims that floods and droughts these days are often man-made too, brought about as a result of climate change or interference with natural water flows and drainage. Second, these new dangers are to be distinguished from occupational hazards in that they affect a great many people (ibid.: 21–3, 34–5, 39–44). The growing gap in the ozone layer potentially affects all of us, regardless, say, of our nation-ality and class. It even affects future generations. These new hazards cross national borders and socioeconomic strata. However, their affect on industrialized nations and privileged sectors of society is generally less than it is on poorer areas: for instance, polluting industries find a haven in developing countries, and wealthier people live in cleaner neighbour-hoods. Third, the hazards today are not easily detectable (ibid.: 22–3). They are not immediately accessible to observation: how, for example, can we tell whether a soft drink contains carcinogenic ingredients? Even specialized research is unlikely to lead to conclusive results as to the dangers involved. Beck coined the term 'risk' to refer to any such (often for a long time undetectable) danger that humanity has brought upon itself. Hence the term 'risk society' to refer to how, in society today, people are constantly subjected to negative outcomes of previous attempts to control nature.

Note that Beck uses the term 'risk' in an unconventional fashion – quite differently from how economists employ it. Economists normally distin-guish between risk and uncertainty (see, e.g., Keynes 1921; Knight 1921). Both terms can be applied to situations in which individuals are con-fronted with incomplete information as to the outcomes of their actions, but whereas risk refers to situations in which people can attribute prob-abilities to the possible outcomes of their actions, uncertainty is limited to those in which individuals are unable to calculate these probabilities. Because they are calculable, risks (as defined by economists) are transfer-able and insurable. Beck's notion of risk is closer to economists' notion of uncertainty, because he accentuates that risks are often unanticipated and invisible, and that scientific research can rarely establish certainty as to their existence, probability, nature or magnitude. Risk society is actually a society of uncertainty, in which humanity has unwittingly caused prob-lems for itself, and in which no one, not even with the help of science, really knows the precise dangers to which they are subjected. Ignorance, rather than probabilistic knowledge, characterizes this type of society. One of the recurrent themes of Beck's work is indeed that current society differs from previous ones in that people are now confronted with systemic uncertainty (1995: 111–27; 1997: 161–77; 1999: 109–32; Beck and Willms 2004: 30–4).

Ignorance often underlies the actions of those who produce risks. This is particularly telling in the case of the 'boomerang effect'. By this term, Beck means situations in which, in the long run, people's self-interested actions, besides having negative effects on others, are also seriously detrimental for their own lives and livelihood. For instance, take Beck's own example of the use of artificial fertilizers and chemicals in German agricultural production (1992: 37–8). The use of these has grown substantially, and this has led to an increase in yields. But whereas the increase in yields has been around 20 per cent, this is nothing compared to the vast natural destruction caused by the fertilizers and chemicals. The farmers who used these means to increase their output now have to face the negative consequences of such methods: their own farmlands are not nearly as cultivable as they used to be, leading to a significant reduction in profit. Of course, intensive industrial agriculture can be destructive in a variety of ways, including for consumers: for instance, it leads to an increase in the levels of lead in milk, which is potentially harmful for children. But this type of agriculture obviously exhibits features of the boomerang effect in that farmers are eventually confronted with the disastrous effects of their own pursuit of profit. Ultimately, perpetrators become their own victims.

In *Risk Society* the substantive-empirical component of Beck's work is particularly striking. But there are already hints of meta-theory: he argues that a new logic is in play, one that demands new theoretical and methodological strategies. This meta-theoretical dimension has become much stronger in Beck's more recent work. He argues that social transformations now demand a different type of sociology with brand new concepts and methodologies. What are the changes that Beck identifies as the 'second modernity', and in which ways is sociology badly equipped to analyse them? First, Beck argues that various modern dualities are being eroded or blurred: for instance, the duality between life and death, between citizen and foreigner, and between culture and nature. Take the boundaries between culture and nature: gene technology and human genetics have blurred this distinction. Or take the opposition between life and death, which, because of technological transformations, is no longer as clear-cut as it used to be. It is not immediately obvious whether a person on a life-support machine is dead or alive. Medical experts and relatives of this person will be called in to negotiate these categories and make decisions. The erosion of these traditional dichotomies does not mean that they disappear altogether but that they are constantly debated and negotiated (Beck and Willms 2004: 27–8; 30–2).

Second, Beck notes that sociology often assumes that geographical proximity is essential to social interactions. However, because of recent developments in telecommunication (for instance, phones, email and satellite television), individuals are now able to interact in a meaningful way with others in faraway places. Social proximity no longer rests on physical proximity. This explains why immigrants can remain very much in touch with the politics, culture and sports of their home country and with family members left behind. They are in touch with and operate in different localities. Most people today live a 'dialogic existence': they have to straddle between different cultures and they have to resolve cultural differences (2006: 1–14; Beck and Willms 2004: 23–34; 68–9).

Third, for Beck, sociology often takes for granted that individuals are confronted with and determined by pre-existing social institutions and groups. Beck's point is best exemplified by Durkheim's view that social facts, the subject-matter of sociology, are both external and constraining. By this, Durkheim meant that sociology should study the extent to which people's actions and attitudes are determined by institutions and groups which pre-date them. But this Durkheimian view assumes that people have little say in what institutions or groups affect them. Beck argues that, under conditions of the second modernity, this view is unduly rigid. In the reflexive world of today, people often choose which groups they wish to belong to and which they want to avoid. Beck's notion of 'reflexive modernization' refers to this process: people no longer take for granted institutions, norms and practices, but they constantly reflect upon their validity and consider altering them or taking different options altogether (Beck et al. 1994; Beck and Willms 2004: 23–4, 29–33).

Fourth, contemporary society is, according to Beck, characterized by increasing 'individualization'. Individual biographies are no longer prescribed by society; people are regularly constructing their own narratives and their own notions of identity. Whereas in the first modernity people were still constrained by informal rules and conventions tied to class, gender and ethnicity, this is now less and less the case. For instance, in spite of legal changes, for a long time women's lives remained constrained by traditional roles and expectations. But these role-sets no longer have the same hold on women. Instead, women are more easily able to reflect on the type of life they want to lead, considering different options and acting accordingly. Of course, a woman might still lead the life of a house-wife, but the difference from the first modernity is that she *has to decide* this and that there are more categories to choose from – including those of part-time worker, home worker, unmarried partner, single parent – all of which challenge the previous duality between housewife and working wife. Note that individualization is accompanied by greater freedom but also by increased psychological pressure on people: they have to make decisions about their lives (Beck and Beck-Gernsheim 2001; Beck and Willms 2004: 62–108).

Fourth, Beck has argued in favour of what he calls cosmopolitanism in the social sciences (1999; 2005; 2006; Beck and Grande 2006; Beck and Sznaider 2006). Central to this cosmopolitan agenda is the rejection of 'methodological nationalism'. Beck contends that many sociologists take for granted that society is identical to the nation-state: they assume that societies can be studied as relatively autonomous entities (2000: 64–8; 2005: 21ff.; 2006: 24–33).[2] They acknowledge that nation-states are in competition with each other, and there might be economic exchanges between them. But they would insist that societies, as nation-states, are clearly demarcated entities. Beck's point is that recent transformations have made this methodological nationalism untenable. That is, the twenty-first century is the era of cosmopolitanism: 'modern' dualities, such as the global versus the local, and the international versus the national, have dissolved (1999: 1–18). The prime example is that, in com-parison with nation-states, multinational corporations are becoming increasingly more powerful. In the current global economy, corporations choose countries with low taxes and a good infrastructure. They have the power to withdraw and move somewhere else and they are therefore in a very strong bargaining position vis-à-vis the nation-state. Other exam-ples of this emerging cosmopolitanism are the growth of non-state actors (such as Amnesty International) and global social movements (such as Greenpeace) and the increasing importance of supranational actors (like the European Union or NAFTA). Finally, the production of risks is also indicative of current global interconnectedness: the Chernobyl disaster affected faraway places, and, more recently, bird flu travelled across dif-ferent continents. These examples indicate a clear discontinuity with pre-vious eras or epochs. Whereas previously it might have made sense for social researchers to focus on sovereign nation-states, recent develop-ments no longer make this methodological strategy tenable. In the era of cosmopolitanism, social research needs methodological cosmopolitanism, which implies, amongst other things, a concerted effort to study the 'transnational networks' that are being formed and which alter the nation-states themselves.

There are problems with the substantive-empirical component of Beck's argument. First, Beck overstates the distinctiveness of the second modernity. In particular, he overstates the extent to which class is no longer the prevailing category that it used to be. His argument is that, in the reflexive modernity of today, people are able to stand back from their class position and choose various lifestyles. But empirical research does not back this up, or at least shows that the issues are more complex than Beck suggests. Empirical evidence indicates that differences in consumption between the different social strata are at least as wide as they were in the past. For instance, different social classes still exhibit different patterns of food consumption. The nature of these differences has changed, but the gulf is still there. Previously, all strata were more or less rooted in their local national culture and exhibited differences within that culture. Today, those in the upper middle class exhibit more variety in food consumption, while those lower in the social strata do not experiment to the same extent. The former will try out Oriental, Middle Eastern or African food; the latter stick to their local cuisine. Class still matters, but it does so in different ways (Warde 1997). This brings us to the second point: some of the phenomena which Beck regards as characteristic of the second modernity are not as widespread as he claims they are. For instance, reflexivity and individualization are not equally prevalent amongst different social classes; they are particularly common amongst the educated upper middle classes. This shows again that class still plays a significant role, although differently from before. Take the case of consumption again. It is not the case that the whole population relates in a reflexive and cosmopolitan manner towards food consumption. On the contrary, this reflexivity seems to be the new prerogative of the upper middle classes; they exhibit what Beck calls dialogic existence. It is an important way in which they are able to differentiate themselves from other strata. The absence of such reflexivity among members of lower strata may be due to their lack of choice because of income constraints or their inability to choose because of limited education or awareness of alternatives – an empirical question that Beck's work tends not to address.

While we have indicated that there are some problems with the substantive-empirical side of Beck's argument, the meta-theoretical aspects of his work are equally problematic. Beck's argument is that the second modernity is so different from the first that sociology needs a radical overhaul. Instead, we need an entirely new type of sociology to grasp the true nature of the new modernity. Underlying this view is the assumption that there is a discontinuity between the first and the second modernity. They are not just different: they are *so* distinct that they call for different sociological terminologies and methodologies. Most contemporary sociology is still embedded in the late nineteenth century and is therefore inappropriate for understanding society today. Now, it is certainly true that new concepts can help identify the key aspects of society today, and Beck himself has contributed to this intellectual enterprise. This is no mean feat: an important part of the sociological imagination is to seize the present in imaginative ways and to show its uniqueness. However, less convincing is Beck's argument that a radically novel social *logic* is at play, one that demands a complete transformation of our theoretical and methodological strategies. Not only does Beck overstate the distinctiveness of society today, disregarding the extent to which the so-called first modernity already incorporated many of these changes, but also his own theoretical and methodological proposals are, in practice, not all that different from what previous generations of sociologists have put forward. They involve new concepts, but it is not entirely clear how they alter the fabric of sociology as such. Never shy of overstating the importance of his own endeavour, Beck has occasionally compared his task with Einstein's (Einstein's theory included Newtonian physics while building something radically different). But identifying new trends and coining new terms does not constitute a paradigm shift, a new research programme or a new sociology.

Zygmunt Bauman and liquid modernity

There are a few points in common between Beck and Zygmunt Bauman (1925–). Both have become known for their innovative take on modernity and for articulating the distinctiveness of the contemporary constellation in relationship to modernity. Both emphasize the extent to which the project of modernity can lead, and has led, to various negative unintended consequences. Both present a three-state model of societal evolution: whereas Beck distinguishes pre-modernity, modernity and reflexive modernity or risk society (1998: 19–31), Bauman identifies pre-modernity, modernity and postmodernity or liquid society. In both cases, the latest stage in the evolution of modern societies (Bauman's postmodernity and

Beck's reflexive modernity) is depicted as an epoch in which modernity has become aware of itself and its own limitations.

Bauman's earlier work explored the history of Marxist thought and the interplay between sociology and philosophical hermeneutics, but by the mid-1980s he started to develop a keen interest in what he called 'modernity' and 'postmodernity'. Standing in opposition to the pre-modern, modernity refers to both a philosophical outlook (the Enlightenment) and a societal organization (rational planning). The conceptualization of order marks a significant difference between the pre-modern and the modern eras. In modernity, order was no longer conceived as preordained; it was considered to be man-made and fragile. Importantly, Bauman argued that once it was believed that people, not God, created order, imperfections could no longer be tolerated. People could always do better, and with their newfound freedom came the moral obligation to improve on what they had achieved so far. Initially, modernity was accompanied by tolerance towards, and even encouragement of, diversity. Very soon, however, diversity was seen as antithetical to order. Ongoing attempts to reach perfection require planning, and planning is easier when faced with homogeneity. Bauman uses a garden metaphor to describe the notion of politics that accompanies this search for perfection and uniformity: politics is about taking care of 'cultured plants' that are essential to the utopia and to the weeding out of those features, institutions, practices or people that do not fit the grand scheme of things. This desirability of homogeneity and perfection easily slips into hostility towards cultural variety and, especially, towards ambivalence. Modernity tends to use neat categories or dichotomies ('in' versus 'out', 'native' versus 'foreigner', and so on) and exhibits particular intolerance towards those who cannot be categorized as such (1989: 56–60).

The shift towards modernity is also accompanied by increased instrumental rationality. This means that perfection, order and homogeneity can be accomplished with great efficiency. For Bauman, as for Weber, a bureaucracy epitomizes instrumental rationality. With its hierarchical structure, modern bureaucracies are highly efficient organizations partly because bureaucrats are trained and expected to follow adequately rules and orders from above. Bureaucrats have a reduced notion of moral responsibility, first because they are not taught to reflect on the rationale of the rules or orders that they follow – actually, this substantive rationality is actively discouraged in bureaucratic organizations. Second, because of the organizational structure in which they operate, bureaucrats are often a number of steps removed from the actual effects of their actions or decisions. Third, the organizational structure depersonalizes the decisions that are made by the bureaucrats. The language used in bureaucracies contributes to this depersonalization: devoid of their idiosyncratic feature, individuals become categories or numbers.

With this picture in mind, Bauman is keen to emphasize the dark side of modernity, the extent to which it can be, and indeed has been, implicated in atrocities and calamities on a grand scale. Following his wife's autobiographical account of life in the Warsaw ghetto and in concentration camps (1986), Bauman started exploring the relationship between modernity and Nazi massacres of Jews. In *Modernity and the Holocaust*, he suggests that, while the transition towards modernity was not a sufficient condition for the Holocaust, it was certainly a necessary condition. In this respect, Bauman challenges various widely cherished beliefs: that the Holocaust was a pre-modern, barbarian outburst, spurred on by deep-seated feelings of resentment and anger, incited by charismatic leaders who were reacting *against* bureaucratic rationality; that it was a specifically German product, engrained in the German psyche or spirit; or that it was mainly the product of widespread hatred towards the Jewish population. Against these views, Bauman points out that there were very few spontaneous eruptions of hatred towards Jews in Germany (even the *Kristallnacht* was carefully orchestrated); that the specific German context explains remarkably little in comparison with explanations that refer to the nature of modern society in general; and that the political and existential significance of the Holocaust goes far beyond the Jewish question and touches upon the very nature of the condition of modernity (1989: 1–30).

Bauman presents a convincing case as to why modernity contributed to the emergence of the Holocaust. The prevalence of modern, bureaucratic structures made for remarkably efficient organizations with literally amoral individuals, willing and able to pursue any goals, including inhumane ones, with unprecedented ease and competence. The individuals in such an organization are cogs in a well-oiled machine, faithfully following the orders from above, conveniently shielded from the consequences of their actions, and unwilling and unable to reflect on the objectives of the organization. For Bauman, rather than an emotional outburst, the Holocaust was the outcome of routine bureaucratic *modi operandi* and a cost-benefit analysis. Bauman sides with the functionalist school in arguing that the Holocaust was not planned from the outset, but emerged, by the early 1940s, as the most 'efficient solution' to the 'Jewish problem' (ibid.: 98–116). The assumption that mankind ought to be perfected fuelled the zealous and unrelenting weeding out of those institutions, practices or people that supposedly undermined the utopian order, and the Jewish people were seen as one of the major obstacles standing between the German race and utopia. Why did the Nazis target the Jewish population in particular? For Bauman, modernity's ingrained preoccupation with the drawing and maintenance of boundaries and its intolerance towards ambivalence made European Jews at the turn of the last century particularly vulnerable; they did not fit within neatly demarcated national and cultural boundaries. Under conditions of modernity, group identity ties in with nationhood, and the ambivalent nature of Jewish identity reminds everyone how arbitrary this equation is: after all, Jews appear as neither 'us' nor 'them' – neither hosts nor guests – hence, for instance, the widespread accusation in many countries that Jews were spying for other countries (ibid.: 61–82).

In *Legislators and Interpreters* and other writings, Bauman elaborates on the nature of intellectual production under conditions of modernity. With the emergence of the modern nation-state, intellectuals acquire a prominent role, helping to direct society and people in the direction of a more rational, ordered and altogether more perfect future (1992: 1–13). Valid knowledge is essential in the pursuit of this perfect blueprint. Indeed, valid knowledge allows for control and prediction, providing criteria for distinguishing between valid and invalid practices or courses of action. Many people hold on to erroneous beliefs because they are not properly educated and have to rely on tradition or religion. Intellectuals are able to step aside and steer clear of local traditions and prejudice. Because intellectuals have better access to superior or objective knowledge, they are like legislators, able to arbitrate in various disputes. They can arbitrate because they manage to design and follow correct procedures to obtain truth and moral or aesthetic judgement (1987: 2–5).

This contrasts sharply with the postmodern condition. In the course of the twentieth century, there is a distinctive shift from value rationality to instrumental rationality. Politics is no longer judged in terms of ultimate goals, but in terms of technical success in following prescribed methods. The legitimacy of political action no longer lies in the pursuit of a perfect blueprint, but in the solving of technical problems. In this new constellation, intellectuals have lost their previous legislative function, and postmodern notions of intellectual production reflect this loss. Postmodern philosophers reject the role of legislator on the grounds that any set of criteria is ultimately validated within a tradition. The modern notion of objective knowledge is a chimera because there is no neutral algorithm:

any attempt to provide such a set of superior criteria is embedded in a tradition or culture. Whereas modernity sees intellectuals as legislators, postmodernity sees them as interpreters, translating statements from one tradition to another. The postmodern intellectual no longer pretends to transcend language and culture, but facilitates communication between cultures with the help of sophisticated hermeneutic tools (ibid.: 4–6).

Bauman's distinction between legislators and interpreters echoes Richard Rorty's between epistemology and hermeneutics. In *Philosophy and the Mirror of Nature*, Rorty argues that the assumption of commensurability underlies any epistemology. To presuppose commensurability is to assume that it is possible to uncover a set of rules that enable us to judge between opposing knowledge claims. In contrast, hermeneutics helps bring about a conversation between different cultural traditions. Both epistemology and hermeneutics pursue consensus, but whereas the former believes that there is a common ground *prior* to the conversation, the latter rejects this assumption (1980: 315–33). For Rorty, foundationalism is deeply engrained in philosophy but it is also deeply flawed; philosophers would do better to embrace the conversational model provided by hermeneutics. In this respect, Rorty epitomizes Bauman's postmodern notion of intellectual production (see also Rorty 1991: 64ff.; 1999: 175–82), and indeed Bauman refers to him extensively (e.g., 1992: 19–20; 82–3).

For understanding the contemporary state of play, Bauman's analysis shows affinities with Lash and Urry's notion of disorganized capitalism (Lash and Urry 1987). Where the modern nation-state attempts to steer the economy, postmodern society promotes a deregulated economy. In *Liquid Society* and *Liquid Love*, Bauman argues that in the current neo-liberal climate individuals have become subject to unbridled market forces, constantly in need of being flexible and able to reinvent themselves whenever required. Under these circumstances social bonds have weakened dramatically, and Bauman uses the metaphor of liquidity to capture the transience of social relationships and institutions today. Opposed to 'solid modernity', Bauman's notion of 'liquid modernity' captures the fluidity of contemporary life. This means that people are often dislocated, developing short-term and unsatisfactory relationships, distressing and anxiety-provoking as this often is. There are striking similarities with Sennett's diagnosis of our times in his *The Corrosion of Character* (discussed in the final section of this chapter). Both authors underline the many sacrifices that people have to make in the continuous 'life-on-the-move' that is required in Western neo-liberal society.

Criticisms can be levelled at all these three broad themes in Bauman's work. First, there is his description of modernity. Bauman paints his world with such a broad brush that he has failed consistently to acknowledge the diverse ways in which the transition towards modernity has manifested itself in various societies (see chapter 5). Some commentators have rightly pointed out that Bauman's personal and professional experiences in Poland had considerable bearing on his later writings (Smith 1999; Tester 2001), and these experiences might explain his skewed representation of modernity. His depiction fits the way in which a *specific* variant of modernity manifested itself under *specific* circumstances, in Nazi Germany, Stalinist Russia and, significantly, its East European satellite states until the collapse of the Berlin Wall. These communist regimes tended to model themselves on a perfect blueprint of a utopian society, centred around order and homogeneity, and on the whole they relied on heavy bureaucratic structures for their execution and a clearly articulated ideology for their legitimacy. It is not surprising, then, that Bauman, who until middle age had lived his whole adult life in totalitarian socialist Poland, experiences modernity as such. But to infer from this that modernity *embodies* these characteristics is a serious leap, and one that does not survive close historical scrutiny. Different Western societies have modernized in different ways, and it is blatantly wrong to talk about a single modernity in the way in which Bauman does (see also Eisenstadt 2000; 2003; Huntingdon 1968; Moore 1967).

Second, Bauman's view of the Enlightenment is one-sided. Consider his account of the tight relationship between the modern nation-state and the intellectual-as-legislator. Of course, there are some links: for instance, the interest of the absolute monarchs in the ideas of *the philosophes* (Scott 1990), or the connection between American social science and state administration in the mid-twentieth century (Buxton 1985). But even in those isolated cases, historians question the closeness of the link. As a matter of fact, in the course of the nineteenth century, Enlightenment thinking became increasingly divorced from real-life politics (Koselleck 1959). The views of philosophers like Auguste Comte, who regarded their philosophy to be a stepping-stone towards the rational steering of society, fell on deaf ears: politicians and policy-makers were reluctant to use their services or draw on their doctrine (Lepenies 1987; Wernick 2001).

Third, Bauman's recent depictions of so-called 'liquid modernity' and 'liquid love' are even more problematic. His claim is that contemporary neo-liberal society is characterized by a lack of close, fixed ties and that this lacuna is problematic both for society and the individual. However,

Bauman makes factual assertions about the state of society today without proper empirical backing, let alone rigorous, focused research. His broad, sweeping statements about the state of society present a striking contrast with the analytical clarity and rigour of his earlier work. Whereas his earlier arguments on modernity and postmodernity are analytically tight and backed up by empirical evidence when needed, his later writings on the fluid state of society today are less so. The most questionable passages are those in which he writes about effects of the current political and economic climate for *all* members of society, independent of their place in the social ladder, their ethnic or religious identity or any other socio-logical variable that might be relevant. More illuminating are the passages in which he writes about specific sociological categories, like the unemployed or immigrant groups, but here it is particularly deplorable to see so few references to the interesting research that is available about these groups. Social theory needs to be supported by carefully designed empirical research, and Bauman's work on the liquid nature of contemporary society fails in this respect.

Saskia Sassen and the global city

One of the most influential thinkers on global issues today is Saskia Sassen (1949–). Sassen's political economy background allows her to back up her innovative theoretical claims with detailed empirical analyses. Her chief contribution to today's social theory is a model of globalization that enlightens often-neglected cultural, economic and political dimensions of this process. A case in point is the global network of urban megalopolis that she calls 'global cities'. In addition, the original character of Sassen's model leads her to enter the above-mentioned debate on 'methodological nationalism', inaugurated by Beck a decade ago. Sassen's original theorization of the processes of economic globalization and digitalization can be described as follows. The dominant interpretation of our global digital era suggests that technological advances such as the internet have been responsible for the emergence of a novel type of social formation: the network society. As we have seen, this is equated with a tendency for the disembedding of social life from the material world. Sassen's perspective, by contrast, emphasizes the growing importance of place in an increasingly globalized world. As authors such as Castells rightly point out the unprecedented character of phenomena like instant global communications, Sassen shows that these are only possible because of huge concentrations of built infrastructure. Whereas Castells et al. tend to focus on information outputs, Sassen calls our attention to the work of those who produce these outputs. In short, Sassen questions the dominant representation of the global information economy as placeless and argues instead that new types of spatialization of power have been emerging in the past couple of decades.

Sassen's recent work on global cities provides empirical footing to this argument. The city, of course, is not exactly a novel theme in sociological analysis. Classical theorists like Simmel (1950) and Wirth (1938) produced seminal accounts on cities as the prototypical milieu of modern life. But contemporary authors like Sassen try to unpack the role of the city in our globalized world. Only a few decades ago the prevalent view among political economists suggested that the idea of cities as important economic units was coming to an end. In books like *The Global City* and *Territory, Authority, Rights*, Sassen has countered this view and shown the centrality of metropolises like New York, London and Tokyo for the global capitalist system. The model of the global city rests upon a central proposition and a number of hypotheses. The proposition is that today's global economy encompasses a contradictory tension between, on the one hand, a tendency for geographic dispersal and mobility and, on the other, a tendency for the territorial concentration of resources to manage that dispersal. Sassen identifies five hypotheses.

First, the greater the geographical dispersal of economic activities, the greater the importance of central corporate functions: the more a company disperses its operations throughout the globe, the more complex are the managing, coordination and financing of that company's network of operations. Second, the more complex these central functions become, the more likely it is that global companies will 'outsource' them. These central functions are increasingly performed by highly specialized service firms (accounting, public relations, programming, etc.). Third, the more complex and globalized the markets of service firms are, the more its central functions are organized in concentrated urban economies. Certain cities are becoming extraordinarily intense information centres, concentrating in small territories a broad mix of talent, firms and expertise. Fourth, it is the services sector, highly specialized and networked, that becomes the key sector in global cities. Much more than, say, manufacturing that relies on large-scale production and transport infrastructure (factories and warehouses, roads and railways, etc.), it is the services sector that thrives in the technologically dense environment provided by the global city. Fifth, as the services sector becomes more global in reach (typically through a global network of affiliates) cross-border city-to-city transactions strengthen: as a result, Sassen suggests, a transnational urban system composed of several dozen global cities might be emerging (2007: 25–7). Global cities are the nodules of the worldwide network of flows of information: a hierarchy of such cities can be identified based upon their relative weight in the global economy (2001a: 171–96). From this perspective, cities like London, Tokyo or New York, with their ability to distribute and produce financial goods, are the kingpins of the global urban hierarchy.

Sassen's main finding is that global cities, despite the digital nature of their planetary interconnectedness, are also and foremost localities. Contrary to the virtuality of Castells's network society, Sassen shows in great detail the material and social conditions that explain the continuing pre-eminence of cities like New York. If it wasn't for the city's network of fibre-optic cable, and for the unusual concentration of both highly skilled professionals and a large supply of low-skilled workers, New York would never have been able to connect to distant points of production, consumption and finance, while ignoring the surrounding region. Without the enormous concentration of resources in small geographical locations, globalization could never had taken place, at least as we know it. This is what Sassen, the political economist, shows: place matters, especially in the globalized world (1998). Digital space, though essential to most global forms of activity, is nevertheless embedded in thick cultural, social, economic and subjective 'structurations of lived experience' within which we exist (2001b: 15). Take global capital markets. They are, Sassen observes, 'constituted through both electronic markets with a global span and locally embedded conditions – that is, financial centers and all they entail, from infrastructure to systems of trust' (2007: 18). In other words, it is important to recover place in any analysis of the global economy, especially place as constituted as a global city, because it forces one to acknowledge the crucial role played by locally rooted economies and work cultures, without which the global information economy couldn't work. Globalization is as much about disembedding and dematerialization as it is about new centres of power, concrete places that make use of the technological possibilities of our age and the huge concentrations of built infrastructure and labour to produce unprecedented amounts of wealth.

In works like *Globalization and Its Discontents* Sassen goes a step further and explores what she takes as the defining tension of today's global cities – the immense concentration of corporate and economic power of global capitalism and large concentrations of 'others' (i.e., illegal immigrants).

What is at stake here is more than a problem of economic inequality. Joining the radical democratic cosmopolitanism we discussed in the previous chapter (which includes authors like Benhabib, Held and others), Sassen claims that the global grid of cities is the most strategic place for the formation of transnational identities and communities. Traditional sources of identity, such as the nation or the village, no longer perform their function in global cities. Here, identities from all over the world meet, clash (sometimes in violent ways) and redefine one another. As a result of this unmooring and redefining of identities, a new politics is being forged that escapes the institutional control of the modern nation-state. Along with it, a new conception of transnational, cosmopolitan citizenship seems to be developing (1998: xxxii–xxxiii).

To understand better the implications of this claim, let us return for a moment to classic social theory. The close relation between city and citizenship, from medieval times to modernity, has long been studied. Weber, for instance, explored the historical conditions of the development of modern citizenship by tracing its origins to the medieval cities of Northern Italy and Central Europe (1962). Political modernity emerged as the centre of power was dislocated from the (local and regional) level of cities to the (national) level of the state. Modern constitutions are the clearest sign of this process of political modernization; they consecrate the twin notions of political sovereignty and national citizenship (the bundle of rights and obligations universally held by everyone inhabiting the territory upon which the state has sovereignty). Over a century ago, Weber recalled the early modern dictum that 'air of the city makes one free' to make the point that the historical origins of modern citizenship could be traced back to that specific European urban experience. Today, at the dawn of the twenty-first century, Sassen retorts that global cities are the birthplace of a new kind of post-national citizenship claims. If the nation-state is the political form *par excellence*, the emerging global grid of cities seems to be a new political arena where political claims can be demanded in novel ways (2006). Consider the largest political protest in human history, the demonstrations that took place worldwide on 15 February 2003 against the US invasion of Iraq: in *cities* around the world, more than 30 million people acted together to express their opposition to the imminent war. According to Sassen, events like this show that the global city is a strategic site for the formation of 'countergeographies of globalization that contest the dominant economic forms the global economy has assumed'. And she concludes: 'The national as the container of social process and power is cracked. This cracked casing opens up possibilities for a geography of politics that links subnational spaces, such as urban regions, and allows nonformal political actors to engage strategic components of global capital' (2001b: 19).

Sassen's reflections on globalization are not limited to its economic and political dimensions, however. She shows great interest, especially in her most recent work, in exploring the epistemological and methodological challenges that globalization poses to the social sciences. Her position is similar to Beck's critique of methodological nationalism, which we discussed above. Like Beck, Sassen is doubtful whether one can still rely on analytical categories that were developed under very different historical conditions from ours (2007: 23). Unlike Beck, however, she does not aim at rebuilding the entire discipline of sociology or economics because of this problem. Sassen's aim is more sober. Retaining the analytical bulk of social sciences (though a political economist, she shows a keen interest in disciplines like anthropology and geography), she wishes to explore alternative analytical categorizations in order to better study emergent empirical phenomena. A possible illustration is the realm of finance, a deeply digitalized activity with a global scope. But finance is a no less deeply localized activity, demanding buildings, airports, highly qualified human resources, etc. Modernist analytical forms, whose dichotomic mode of operation leads them to conceive of digital and non-digital as neatly separated realities, show great difficulty in analysing such hybrid phenomena. This is the reason why Sassen has shown interest in developing alternative analytical categorizations. A good example is the notion of 'imbrication'. By this she means the interpenetration of different orders of phenomena. To revisit the example of the finance sector, in this realm of activity the digital and the global are said to be 'imbricated' with the material and the local. In her own words: 'Digital space is embedded in the larger societal, cultural, subjective, economic, and imaginary structurations of lived experience and the systems within which we exist and operate' (2001b: 15). In our view, this attempt at overcoming what is usually called 'scalar thought' is perhaps Sassen's single most relevant contribution to today's social theory.

What is scalar thought and why is it so important to overcome it? Scalar thought assumes exclusive, hierarchical and a-historical relationships among different political levels or analytical scales (Sack 1980; 1986). For instance, in political science it is customary to study macro, meso and micro features of democracy and citizenship. At the macro level, research is conducted on political regimes, their institutions, economic determinants, ruling elites and patterns of supranational integration. At the meso level, political scientists evaluate continuity and change in social groups and movements that mobilize for political action. At the micro level, comparative research is conducted on individuals' social and political attitudes, values and behaviour. By concealing the fluid, multiple and overlapping forms of existence of these different analytical layers, this particular mode of thinking is responsible for many of the difficulties that social scientists currently face in studying new hybrid phenomena like globalization. Tracing a transnational process such as economic globalization without ignoring its territoriality and institutional grounding has led Sassen to question scalar thought's tendency to reify particular analytical scales. The national scale, for instance, actually encompasses 'a simultaneity of scales, spaces, and relations, some national in the historic sense of the word, some denationalized or in the process of becoming so, and some global' (2007: 42). We believe this thesis to be particularly important at a time in which global instant communications and transcontinental travel are rapidly becoming part of the everyday life of millions around the world.

Two criticisms can be levelled at Sassen's work. First, there is the relative neglect of culture, consumption and entertainment as crucial dimensions of global cities' dynamics. Economic globalization is not only about its financial aspects. The global city is as much a strategic site for corporate capital as it is a place of cultural consumption and of expressive lifestyles. Like Sennett, Sassen is still operating with the traditional opposition between capital and labour, while in fact one of the new distinctive features of our era is precisely a diminishing of class politics and a rise in salience of cultural issues, including personal and collective identity issues. Her account of the global city would certainly benefit from a broader, updated analytical framework that includes these emergent dimensions (Clark 2004; Florida 2002; 2005). Second, abstract theorizing is more important than Sassen suggests. Only an abstract and general theory can help flesh out the causal mechanisms between the several scales of action (e.g., between the actor's practices and the institutional milieus) and pay attention to large-scale phenomena and the *longue durée*. Theories from economics and political science come closest to this requirement. Also, between the concrete action of the individuals vividly described by Sennett and the structural approach of Sassen's or Castells's descriptions of the global age, we need more of what Merton (1957) called the 'middle-range' theories. At both levels of abstractness, theories perform an important role in guiding empirical research. The challenge that lies ahead is for social theory to actually become a discursive medium through which a plurality of proposals can come together and articulate concrete empirical findings from all analytical scales in order to corroborate or falsify theoretical accounts.

The obstacles facing such an endeavour should not be underestimated, though. It is difficult to standardize huge bodies of data from countries with disparate data-collecting resources. Disciplinary boundaries still pose obstacles to those researchers who work on cutting-edge themes, not to mention the ideological barriers that sometimes prevent real dialogue. So the obstacles to social theory today are, if anything, as great as they ever were. However, the need for social theorizing has only increased. Without sound theoretical lenses, it is increasingly difficult to make sense of the world. To guide the production and interpretation of the massive empirical data produced by social scientists around the world – from ethnographic reports to worldwide surveys – is the first and foremost mission of social theory. But other uses can easily be identified. At a time where the amount of information readily available through digital mass media is enormous, the need for cognitive tools that permit social actors to interpret that information has never been greater. Only then can people properly assess the limitations, biases and relevance of the information available and assess the opportunity it entails.

Richard Sennett and the fall of the public man

Of all the authors discussed in this book, Richard Sennett (1943–) is one of the easiest to read. His writings are so engaging that the boundary between fiction and social theorizing seems to blur.[3] What is unique is the way in which he blends together accounts of interviews with philosophical remarks, job statistics with ironical comments, and personal memoires with reflections on the condition of the age. One of the most acclaimed public intellectuals of his generation, Sennett has written profusely on the changing forms of selfhood and urban experience, and the personal costs of economic globalization. In *The Fall of Public Man*, perhaps his best-known work, Sennett makes a powerful case against the rise of the self-centred cultural mood that emerged as a consequence of the student revolts of the late 1960s. 'The reigning myth today', he writes, 'is that the evils of society can all be understood as evils of impersonality, alienation, and coldness' (1986a: 259). His point is that a narcissistic 'ideology of intimacy' has replaced the 'secular public culture' that dominated the best part of the twentieth century and is responsible for the sharp decay of civility in our time, i.e., 'the activity which protects people from each other and yet allows them to enjoy each other's company' (ibid.: 264). The more we focus on the depths of our intimate self, the less we are able to open ourselves to civilized relations with our fellow citizens. The cost of this ideology of intimacy has been enormous. We have lost the old humanistic sense of treating strangers as strangers, i.e., as individuals who are worthy of our respect for the sole reason that they are human beings. *The Fall of Public Man* came out long before today's reality shows, which indeed epitomize the hollowness of intimacy which is so central to Sennett's portrayal of the modern world.

The shared etymological root between 'city' and 'civility' did not pass unnoticed by Sennett. In books like *The Uses of Disorder*, *The Consciousness of the Eye* or *Flesh and Stone* he has explored this relation with great verve. He blames the infantilizing ideology of intimacy for people's lack of mastery over their own life, one of the central concerns of his analysis of urban experience. He is very critical of the purifying tendencies of so much contemporary urban planning, of which the exponential growth of gated communities is one of the most spectacular. Sennett argues that 'it is in the building of purposely diverse cities that society can provide men the experience of breaking from self-slavery to freedom as adults' (1992: xviii). A staunch defender of the public domain, he has repeatedly argued that people ought to realize the extent to which their lives are closely interwoven with the physical spaces, the buildings, parks and coffee houses, that make up the cities in which they live. If individuals begin to look at their cities in this way, the narcissism responsible for modern urban alienation can be replaced by a public culture in which anonymity goes hand in hand with community (1990; 1998a).

Faithful to his humanistic agenda, and perhaps influenced by his marriage to Sassen, Sennett's latest books have been devoted to the study of the consequences for the self and for family life of the new economy (2004; 2007). One good example is *The Corrosion of Character*, which sold tens of thousands of copies in Germany alone. Written in his usual engaging style, it revolves around a simple general argument. The free market economy of the early twenty-first century, with its obsessive emphasis on short-term goals and flexibility, is putting an unbearable pressure upon the personal lives of those associated with it. It begins in classic Sennett style. In the lobby of an airport, he meets Rico, the son of Enrico whom he had interviewed 25 years earlier for his *The Hidden Injuries of Class* (Sennett and Cobb 1972). Rico seems to embody his father's hopes: he is a successful consultant, happily married to Jeannette and a father of three, living in a suburb near New York. But, as we find out in the course of the book, there is a grimier truth lying hidden behind Rico's briefcase and expensive suit. 'Like Enrico, Rico views work as his service to the family; unlike Enrico, Rico finds that the demands of the job interfere with achieving the end' (1998b: 21). The personal fears that lurk behind the American Dream couple that Rico and Jeannette are meant to exemplify emphasize the dysfunctional nature of the free market economy. By bringing together two generations of interviewees, Sennett sets the perfect ground for his reflection on the personal consequences of the economic transformations of the last quarter of a century:

> It is the time dimension of the new capitalism, rather than high-tech transmission, global stock markets, or free trade, which most directly affects people's emotional lives outside the workplace. Transposed to the family realm, 'No long term' means keep moving, don't commit yourself, and don't sacrifice. (Ibid.: 25)

The new economy undermines the qualities of trust, loyalty, commitment and self-discipline. In turn, it exacerbates job insecurity as life experience is devalued to the detriment of youth. 'Flexibility equals youth, rigidity equals age', Sennett tells us, illustrating this with the case of Rose, the owner of his favourite bar in New York, the 'Trout'. A middle-aged New Yorker, Rose tried to swap careers, from running a bar to the advertising world, only to return disillusioned to the 'Trout'. Sennett concludes that it took courage for someone like Rose to 'risk something new, but uncertainty about where she stood combined with the denial of her lived experience sapped her nerve' (ibid.: 80). This type of critical note on the social consequences of the emerging global capitalist economy is a distinctive mark of Sennett's secular humanist agenda. In *The Craftsman*, his latest work, Sennett gives sequence to this agenda.

Travelling with his wife Saskia Sassen through the outskirts of Moscow just before the demise of the Soviet Union, Sennett came across an eloquent example of the material consequences of poorly motivated workers. The poor quality of construction of the housing blocks they visited back in 1988 reflected, Sennett suggests, limitations of one of modernity's moral imperatives to do outstanding work – to do it for the sake of community. The other is competition. Likewise, Sennett argues that by itself competition is not enough to guarantee quality work. Rejecting the triumphalism that some in the West felt about the superiority of this moral imperative, Sennett illustrates the limitations of competition with examples from jobs in the new economy. Resuming a line of argument he had already made in *The Corrosion of Character*, he suggests that the structure of rewards of most new economy companies simply does not motivate its workers as it is supposed to. 'We found', Sennett concludes, 'few among the technicians who believed that they would be rewarded for doing a good job for its own sake' (2008: 36). And this is exactly what this most recent book of his is about: 'craftsmanship', understood as the ethos of doing good work for its own sake.

Why is Sennett so interested in craftsmanship? The short answer is because it allows him to explore the connection between 'hand and head', an old pragmatist motto. In other words, Sennett's interest lies in a specific aspect of material culture, one that can be found in such disparate settings as the medieval guild or today's computer laboratory and that shares the same qualities of discipline and commitment in the pursuit of excellence. Craftsmanship is thus understood here as a basic human impulse, not an ancient way of life destroyed by the industrial and mass-production paradigm brought about by modernity. Not surprisingly, the time frame of Sennett's discussion is very broad. In his characteristic style, he entwines in his arguments (sometimes in the same passage) illustrations from Ancient Greece, the Middle Ages, the Renaissance and the present. A no less broad gallery of authors is invoked to support or illustrate his claims. And yet Sennett never loses his reader. In carefully crafted sentences, we are introduced to Rostropovich's legendary cello masterclasses in the 1950s and then transported to Stradivari's mid-eighteenth century workshop in the same line of argument. The craftsman is a universal category, to be found operating in all those disparate settings, and whose understanding enlightens human experience well beyond the manipulation of material objects. Sennett's claim is that 'the craft of making physical things provides insight into the techniques of experience that can shape our dealings with others' (ibid.: 289). Craftsmanship, in other words, expresses the continuum between the human body and social action.

The relevance of this continuum has also recently been emphasized by other contemporary pragmatists like Hans Joas. There is one major difference between Sennett's work and Joas's neo-pragmatist theory of human creativity though. Despite sharing the same radical democratic agenda and the same egalitarian conception of creativity (to be distinguished from the more elitist notion of genius), Sennett makes a claim to which other pragmatists, classical and contemporary alike, would have difficulty in subscribing. He claims that the tacit knowledge possessed by the craftsman is 'a, perhaps, *the*, fundamental human limit: language is not an adequate "mirror-tool" for the physical movements of the human body' (ibid.: 95). This is exactly the sort of dichotomy that philosophical pragmatism has been criticizing for over a century now. To suggest, as Sennett seems to do, that there is an insurmountable gap between language (i.e., scientific reasoning) and the world (in this case, the physical movements of the human body and the tacit knowledge they express), is to subscribe to a Cartesian and rationalistic logic totally at odds with the core principles of American philosophical pragmatism. The question is not whether language is an adequate mirror of reality or not (Sennett suggests it is not); the issue is to conceive of language as an integral part of reality just as our body is. As Dewey would put it, there is no 'tacit knowledge' of the craftsman as opposed to the 'pure or objective knowledge' of the social scientist – any and every form of knowledge is irreducibly social in nature. Let us now conclude with some additional comments on Sennett's overall contribution to today's social theory.

His talent as a public intellectual is undeniable. The interviews he offers reveal his vast erudition in such fields as urban planning, modern architecture, intellectual history and music. His writings are certainly among the best available to introduce social theory to a wider audience. Sennett's credentials as a social theorist, however, are more limited. These limitations are most clearly felt in the way he tries to incorporate American philosophical pragmatism into his own thinking. First, there are basic mistakes of interpretation. For instance, Sennett wrongly presents this theoretical tradition as a reaction to Hegel's work, when in fact pragmatism can be seen as an American outgrowth of Hegelianism.[4] Second, and most importantly, in works like *The Craftsman* Sennett subscribes to a conception of knowledge that can be traced back to Aristotle. According to this theory, one knows the world very much like someone watching a play in the theatre – the more accurate the knower's description of what her senses perceive, the more objective will be the knowledge she produces. Fittingly enough, Dewey used to deride this epistemological theory as a 'spectator theory of knowledge'. This is particularly relevant, as Dewey's 1934 *Art as Experience*, in which he explores this epistemological argument, is presented by Sennett as one of the books that influenced him the most in writing *The Craftsman*. Dewey (1934) makes the claim that what a work of art is cannot be confused with the object of art itself. Art exists in the process of experiencing art. There is no separation between the work of art and the individual who observes it, for it is the latter (by her own action) who gives meaning to the former. The spectator, in this view, is inextricably linked to the meaning of art. Dewey is thus rejecting the old Aristotelian conception of knowledge as the product of observation as pure reception: the human mind was depicted as a *tabula rasa* (Locke) that passively perceived the world around it. On the contrary, claims Dewey, knowledge is a problem-solving process in which we manipulate and change reality – i.e. we experiment with reality. There is no passivity on the part of the knower: to get to know something implies an active stance towards the world around us. Not a 'spectator theory of knowledge', but an 'experimental theory of knowledge' is what pragmatists advocate. It is thus difficult to understand Sennett's claim that language fails to *explain* craftsmanship since it cannot adequately *mirror* it. Were Sennett indeed one of the three main exponents of pragmatism in America today, as he claims to be (the others being Richard Rorty and Robert Bernstein), he could have never subscribed to such a spectator view of knowledge. It is not so much that he, even so, tried to write a book on the subject. The chief problem is the contradiction entailed for his social theoretical account of this facet of human behaviour. A social theory of craftsmanship, particularly a neo-pragmatist one as Sennett wishes to provide, cannot rely upon such a Cartesian epistemological basis. Unless he abandons such a contemplative and passive conception of knowledge production, Sennett's social theoretical account of craftsmanship will not be up to the task he set himself: 'Within the philosophical workshop of pragmatism', Sennett wishes to account for 'value of experience understood as a craft' (2008: 288). If the words he uses are thought to be mere reflections of the craftsman's actions, unable to capture their meaning, how is he supposed to provide such an account? The alternative has been laid out long ago by Dewey and reiterated and developed by later pragmatists. The meaning of craftsmanship – like that of art – lies in the process of experiencing it, which includes the social theorist's reflection translated into words. There are, of course, other epistemological perspectives, conceptions of knowledge and theories of truth outside the 'workshop of pragmatism'. In our concluding chapter, we discuss several contemporary epistemological doctrines in order to clarify the possible uses for social theory today.

Further reading

Sennett, especially in his latest writings, is very accessible. We recommend two books in particular: *The Fall of the Public Man*, which remains his main intellectual contribution, and the more recent *The Corrosion of Character*, an arresting portrait of the hidden consequences of neo-liberal capitalism. To understand Bauman, we would initially recommend that you resist reading secondary sources and probably start with *Modernity and the Holocaust*, because the book is very accessible and the argument is important. We would then suggest *Legislators and Interpreters*, which contrasts clearly with Bauman's view on modernity and postmodernity. Regarding secondary sources, it is worth consulting *Conversations with Zygmunt Bauman* and Smith's introductory book on Bauman. For Beck, his *Risk Society* is the obvious start to his theory about the second modernity. We would then recommend moving to the dialogue between Beck, Giddens and Lash in *Reflexive Modernization*. For those interested in Beck's theory of cosmopolitanism, we suggest first reading the introduction to *World Risk Society* and then his *Cosmopolitan Vision*. Castells's trilogy *The Information Age*, despite its size, is clearly written and one can read separate chapters on their own without much loss. As to Sassen, *The Global City* is her most important book even though it might be somewhat hard to follow. Her recent *A Sociology of Globalization* is more accessible.

References

Bauman, J. 1986. *Winter in the Morning: A Young Girl's Life in the Warsaw Ghetto and Beyond*. London: Virago.

Bauman, Z. 1973. *Culture as Praxis*. London: Routledge & Kegan Paul.

Bauman, Z. 1976. *Socialism: The Active Utopia*. London: George Allen & Unwin.

Bauman, Z. 1978. *Hermeneutics and Social Science: Approaches to Understanding*. London: Hutchinson.

Bauman, Z. 1987. *Legislators and Interpreters: On Modernity, Postmodernity and Intellectuals*. Cambridge: Polity.

Bauman, Z. 1989. *Modernity and the Holocaust*. Cambridge: Polity.

Bauman, Z. 1991. *Modernity and Ambivalence*. Cambridge: Polity.

Bauman, Z. 1992. *Intimations of Postmodernity*. Cambridge: Polity.

Bauman, Z. 1993. *Postmodern Ethics*. Cambridge: Polity.

Bauman, Z. 1995. *Life in Fragments: Essays in Postmodern Morality*. Cambridge: Polity.

Bauman, Z. 1997. *Postmodernity and its Discontents*. Cambridge: Polity.

Bauman, Z. 2000. *Liquid Society*. Cambridge: Polity.

Bauman, Z. 2003. *Liquid Love: On the Frailty of Human Bonds*. Cambridge: Polity.

Bauman, Z. and Tester, K. 2001. *Conversations with Zygmunt Bauman*. Cambridge: Polity.

Beck, U. 1992. *Risk Society: Towards a New Modernity*. London: Sage (originally in German, 1986).

Beck, U. 1995. *Ecological Politics in an Age of Risk*. Cambridge: Polity (originally in German, 1988).

Beck, U. 1997. *The Reinvention of Politics: Rethinking Modernity in the Global Social Order.* Cambridge: Polity (originally in German, 1996).

Beck, U. 1998. *Democracy without Enemies.* Cambridge: Polity.

Beck, U. 1999. *World Risk Society.* Cambridge: Polity.

Beck, U. 2000. *What is Globalization?* Cambridge: Polity (originally in German, 1997).

Beck, U. 2005. *Power in the Global Age.* Cambridge: Polity (originally in German, 2002).

Beck, U. 2006. *Cosmopolitan Vision.* Cambridge: Polity (originally in German, 2004).

Beck, U. and Beck-Gernsheim, E. 2001. *Individualization: Institutionalized Individualism and its Social and Political Consequences.* London: Sage.

Beck, U. and Beck-Gernsheim, E. 2005. *The Normal Chaos of Love.* Cambridge: Polity.

Beck, U. and Grande, E. 2006. *Cosmopolitan Europe.* Cambridge: Polity.

Beck, U. and Sznaider, N. 2006. Unpacking cosmopolitanism for the social sciences. *The British Journal of Sociology* 57(1): 1–23.

Beck, U. and Willms, J. 2004. *Conversations with Ulrich Beck.* Cambridge: Polity.

Beck, U., Giddens, A. and Lash, S. 1994. *Reflexive Modernization; Politics, Tradition and Aesthetics in the Modern Social Order.* Cambridge: Polity.

Brubaker, R. 1992. *Citizenship and Nationhood in France and Germany.* Cambridge, MA: Harvard University Press.

Buxton, W. 1985. *Talcott Parsons and the Capitalist Nation-State: Political Sociology as a Strategic Vocation.* Toronto: University of Toronto Press.

Castells, M. 1972. *Luttes urbaines et pouvoir politique.* Paris: F. Maspero.

Castells, M. 1977. *The Urban Question: A Marxist Approach.* Cambridge, MA: MIT Press (originally in French, 1972).

Castells, M. 1978. *City, Class, and Power.* New York: St Martin's Press.

Castells, M. 1989. *The Informational City: Economic Restructuring and Urban Development.* Oxford: Blackwell.

Castells, M. 1996. *The Information Age: Economy, Society and Culture. Volume I: The Rise of the Network Society.* Oxford: Blackwell.

Castells, M. 1997. *The Information Age: Economy, Society and Culture. Volume II: The Power of Identity.* Oxford: Blackwell.

Castells, M. 1998. *The Information Age: Economy, Society and Culture. Volume III: End of Millennium.* Oxford: Blackwell.

Castells, M. 2001. *The Internet Galaxy: Reflections on the Internet, Business, and Society.* New York: Oxford University Press.

Castells, M. and Godard, F. 1974. *Monopolville: Analyse des rapports entre l'entreprise, l'état et l'urbain à partir d'une enquête sur la croissance industrielle et urbaine de la région de Dunkerque.* Paris: Mouton.

Castells, M. and Himanen, P. 2002. *The Information Society and the Welfare State: The Finnish Model.* Oxford: Oxford University Press.

Castells, M. and Mollenkopf, J. (eds) 1991. *Dual City: Restructuring New York.* New York: Russell Sage Foundation.

Castells, M. et al. 2007. *Mobile Communication and Society: A Global Perspective.* Cambridge,, MA: MIT Press.

Chernilo, D. 2006. Social theory's methodological nationalism. *European Journal of Social Theory* 9(1): 5–22.

Chernilo, D. 2007. *A Social Theory of the Nation-State. The Political Forms of Modernity Beyond Methodological Nationalism.* London: Routledge.

Clark, T. N. (ed.) 2004. *The City as an Entertainment Machine.* Amsterdam: Elsevier.

Clark. T. N. and Hoffmann-Martinot, V. (eds) 1998. *The New Political Culture.* Boulder, CO: Westview Press.

Dewey, J. 1934. *Art as Experience.* New York: Perigee Books (reprinted, 2005).

Eisenstadt, S. 2000. Multiple modernities. *Daedalus* 129(1): 1–29.

Eisenstadt, S. 2003. *Comparative Civilizations and Multiple Modernities.* Leiden: Brill.

Favell, A. 2001. *Philosophies of Immigration: Immigration and the Idea of Citizenship in France and Britain.* Basingstoke: Palgrave.

Florida, R. 2002. *The Rise of the Creative Class: And How It's Transforming Work, Leisure, Community and Everyday Life.* New York: Basic Books.

Florida, R. 2005. *Cities and the Creative Class.* New York: Routledge.

Giddens, A. 1984. *The Constitution of Society: Outline of the Theory of Structuration.* Cambridge: Polity.

Giddens, A. 1993. *New Rules of Sociological Method,* 2nd edn. Cambridge: Polity.

Harvey, D. 1989. *The Condition of Postmodernity.* Oxford: Blackwell.

Huntingdon, S. P. 1968. *Political Order in Changing Societies.* New Haven, CT: Yale University Press.

Inglehart, R. and Norris, P. 2003. *Rising Tide: Gender Equality and Cultural Change Around the World.* Cambridge: Cambridge University Press.

Joas, H. 1993. *Pragmatism and Social Theory.* Chicago, IL: University of Chicago Press.

Joppke, C. (ed.) 1998. *Challenge to the Nation-State: Immigration in Western Europe and the United States.* Oxford: Oxford University Press.

Joppke, C. 1999. *Immigration and the Nation-State: The United States, Germany, and Great Britain.* Oxford: Oxford University Press.

Keynes, J. M. 1921. *A Treatise on Probability.* London: Macmillan (reprinted, 1948).

Knight, F. 1921. *Risk, Uncertainty and Profit.* New York: Houghton Mifflin.

Koselleck, R. 1959. *Critique and Crisis: Enlightenment and the Pathologies of Modern Society.* Cambridge, MA: MIT Press (reprinted, 1988).

Lasch, C. 1977. *A Haven in a Heartless World: The Family Besieged.* London: Norton (reprinted, 1995).

Lash, S. and Urry, J. 1987. *The End of Organized Capitalism.* Cambridge: Polity.

Lash, S. and Urry, J. 1994. *Economies of Sign and Space*. London: Sage.

Lepenies, W. 1987. *Between Literature and Science: The Rise of Sociology*. Cambridge: Cambridge University Press.

Luhmann, N. 1982. *The Differentiation of Society*. New York: Columbia University Press.

Luhmann, N. 1990. *Essays on Self-Reference*. New York: Columbia University Press.

Merton, R. K. 1957. *Social Theory and Social Structure*. New York: Free Press.

Moore, B. 1967. *Social Origins of Dictatorship and Democracy: Lord and Peasant in the Making of the Modern World*. London: Allen Lane.

Neumann, F. et al. 1953. *The Cultural Migration: The European Scholar in America*. Philadelphia: University of Pennsylvania Press.

Parsons, T. 1937. *The Structure of Social Action: A Study in Social Theory with Special Reference to a Group of Recent European Writers*. New York: McGraw-Hill.

Parsons, T. 1951. *The Social System*. London: Routledge & Kegan Paul (reprinted, 1979).

Porter, T. M. 2003. Genres and objects of social inquiry, from the Enlightenment to 1890. In T. M. Porter and D. Ross (eds), *The Cambridge History of Science. Volume 7: The Modern Social Sciences*. Cambridge: Cambridge University Press, pp. 13–39.

Rorty, R. 1980. *Philosophy and the Mirror of Nature*. Oxford: Blackwell.

Rorty, R. 1991. *Philosophical Papers. Volume 1: Objectivity, Relativism, and Truth*. Cambridge: Cambridge University Press.

Rorty, R. 1999. *Philosophy and Social Hope*. Harmondsworth: Penguin.

Sack, R. 1980. *Conceptions of Space in Social Thought: A Geographic Perspective*. London: Macmillan.

Sack, R. 1986. *Human Territoriality: Its Theory and History*. Cambridge: Cambridge University Press.

Sassen, S. 1998. *Globalization and Its Discontents*. New York: The New Press.

Sassen, S. 2001a [1991]. *The Global City. New York, London, Tokyo*. Princeton, NJ: Princeton University Press.

Sassen, S. 2001b. The city: between topographic representation and spatialized power projects. *Art Journal* 60(2): 12–20.

Sassen, S. 2006. *Territory, Authority, Rights: From Medieval to Global Assemblages*. Princeton, NJ: Princeton University Press.

Sassen, S. 2007. *A Sociology of Globalization*. New York: Norton.

Scott, H. M. (ed.) 1990. *Enlightened Absolutism: Reform and Reformers in Late-Eighteenth Century Europe*. Basingstoke: Palgrave Macmillan.

Sennett, R. 1986a [1974]. *The Fall of the Public Man*. London: Faber and Faber.

Sennett, R. 1986b. *Palais-Royal*. New York: Alfred A. Knopf.

Sennett, R. 1990. *The Consciousness of the Eye: The Design and Social Life of Cities*. New York: Norton.

Sennett, R. 1992 [1970]. *The Uses of Disorder. Personal Identity and City Life.* New York: Norton.

Sennett, R. 1998a. *The Spaces of Democracy. 1998 Raoul Wallenberg Lecture.* Ann Arbor: The University of Michigan Press.

Sennett, R. 1998b. *The Corrosion of Character. The Personal Consequences of Work in the New Capitalism.* New York: Norton.

Sennett, R. 2004. *Respect in a World of Inequality.* New York: Norton.

Sennett, R. 2007. *The Culture of the New Capitalism.* New Haven, CT: Yale University Press.

Sennett, R. 2008. *The Craftsman.* New Haven, CT: Yale University Press.

Sennett, R. and Cobb, J. 1972. *The Hidden Injuries of Class.* New York: Alfred A. Knopf.

Simmel, G. 1950. The metropolis and mental life. In K. Wolff (ed.), *The Sociology of Georg Simmel.* New York: Free Press, pp. 409–24 (originally in German, 1903).

Smith, D. 1999. *Zygmunt Bauman: Prophet of Postmodernity.* Cambridge: Polity.

Riesman, D., with Glazer, N. and Denney, R. 1952. *Lonely Crowd: A Study of the Changing American Character.* New Haven, CT: Yale Nota Bene (reprinted, 2001).

Tester, K. 2001. Introduction. In Z. Bauman and K. Tester, *Conversations with Zygmunt Bauman.* Cambridge: Polity, pp. 1–15.

Tocqueville, A. de 1850. *De la démocratie en Amérique.* Paris: J. Vrin (reprinted, 1990).

Wagner, P. 1994. *A Sociology of Modernity. Liberty and Discipline.* London: Routledge.

Wagner, P. 2001. *Theorizing Modernity. Inescapability and Attainability in Social Theory.* London: Sage.

Wagner, P. 2008. *Modernity as Experience and Interpretation. A New Sociology of Modernity.* Cambridge: Polity.

Warde, A. 1997. *Consumption, Food and Taste: Culinary Antinomies and Commodity Culture.* London: Sage.

Weber, M. 1962. *The City.* New York: Collier Books (originally in German, 1921).

Wernick, A. 2001. *Auguste Comte and the Religion of Humanity: The Post-Theistic Program of French Social Theory.* Cambridge: Cambridge University Press.

Wirth, L. 1938. Urbanism as a way of life. *American Journal of Sociology* 44(1): 1–24.

9

Conclusion
Social Theory for the Twenty-First Century

Social theory is an increasingly important intellectual endeavour in the social sciences today.[1] This greater importance, however, has not been attained without costs. The most significant cost is that the status of social theory vis-à-vis the social sciences has also become increasingly uncertain and needs to be reassessed. On the one hand, social theory has played a central role in the development of the social sciences in the past few decades. Initially mainly confined to sociology, debates within social theory have spilled over into other social sciences: many social scientists, including economists, geographers and political scientists, now engage with theoretical issues to a far greater extent than was previously the case. On the other hand, the precise role of theory in empirical research has become increasingly uncertain. Until recently the deductive-nomological model and its realist alternative were dominant ways of thinking about the relationship between theory and empirical research, but both have now been shown to be problematic. It is therefore important to reconsider the precise status of theory and to reassess what it can achieve and what it is for. In what follows, we present a neo-pragmatist proposal for the social sciences that puts self-knowledge at the centre of the intellectual stage.

The roles of social theory

Since the late 1970s, researchers in the social sciences and humanities have shown a growing interest in social theory. Social theory has managed to occupy the position of intellectual facilitator and catalyst in these domains. By this, we mean that it occupies the space in which cross-disciplinary debates are encouraged, channelled and coordinated, similar to the way in which, in the course of the twentieth century, mathematics became the language through which insights from one branch of the natural sciences reached other branches. In the past, of course, other disciplines like philosophy or history have fulfilled these roles in the social sciences, and there is no reason to assume that social theory will occupy this dominant and central position forever. For now, however, social theory is the main vehicle through which intellectual debates occur.

Social theory today performs yet another crucial function in the social sciences – it sets the agenda for what is to be studied, and how it should be studied. This can be easily demonstrated by the way in which intellectual developments within social theory have preceded and framed debates in the social sciences. For example, the issue of the public sphere was initially introduced within social theory (Habermas 1989; see also chapter 7), but has been explored across several disciplines, from media studies and gender studies to history (see, e.g., Dahlgren 1995; Landes 1988; Siltanen and Stanworth 1984). Another example is the debate around structure and agency, which, again, was initially a mainly theoretical discussion (see chapter 5), the fruits of which subsequently became incorporated in a number of social sciences, ranging from economics to political science (see, e.g., Lawson 1997; 2003; Marsh et al. 1999). Sometimes, however, developments in social theory are sparked by empirical research, though social theory remains the intellectual clearing-house – the medium through which these new ideas travel. For example, the post-humanist turn in science studies led to theoretical reflection on the nature of the social (Latour 1993; Law and Hassard 1999), which in turn inspired new research in social anthropology (e.g. Gell 1998). Likewise, the field of gender studies has initiated new theoretical reflections on gender, inequality and identity formation, some of which have influenced diverse disciplines from geography to international relations (see, e.g., Hooper 2000; McDowell 1999).

Initially, the allocation of a central role to theory coincided with the coming of age of the golden generation of twentieth-century European social theory. We are referring to a generation of intellectuals and academics, born between the world wars, that includes, for instance, Pierre Bourdieu, Niklas Luhmann, Jürgen Habermas, Michel Foucault and Anthony Giddens. The conditions in which they began to work has partly accounted for the central role their writings have come to play. First, they were productive during a period of expansion of higher education, a period also in which the social sciences in particular flourished. New research areas, such as gender and media studies, came on the scene, and those that already existed became stronger. Second, this generation of social theorists benefited from their association with sociology, which by the 1960s had become a major player in the academic field. It is not a coincidence that of the five social theorists mentioned, four occupied positions in sociology, Foucault being the exception. Third, the political orientations of these authors, and the way in which they incorporated those views in their work, fitted nicely into the progressive intellectual climate in academia at the time. With exceptions like Luhmann (who might be less easily classifiable in this respect), most social theorists regarded themselves as *critical* social theorists, who saw theory and social research as contributing to critical reflection on contemporary society. They differed greatly as to what ought to be criticized, what critique meant and how it could be achieved, but most subscribed to the view that theory or theory-driven research would tie in with a left or left-of-centre political agenda, whether it be a straightforward emancipatory or a decon-structionist one. Fourth, most of these theorists were trained in philoso-phy or were certainly knowledgeable of its recent developments, and they were able to translate 'the social turn' in philosophy into a coherent theoretical programme. By social turn, we refer to the way in which, in the course of the twentieth century, philosophers drew attention to the social nature of entities, which some had assumed to be self-evident, self-sufficient or fixed: for instance, the self, knowledge, rationality or aesthet-ics. This social turn provided fertile ground for the increasing authority of social theory.

Whereas this generation was initially linked to sociology, their writings quickly found resonance in other fields, such as social anthropology, geog-raphy and history. The opening up to other fields is probably even more striking now: it is rare nowadays to find European theorists who write exclusively for a sociological audience. It would be misleading, for instance, to portray Bruno Latour's actor-network theory or Axel Honneth's critical theory (see chapter 7) as primarily addressing sociologists. This is why it makes more sense to talk about *social* theory rather than *sociological* theory. Sociological theory suggests a discipline-bound form of theorizing – theory for sociological research. Sociological theory never existed in this pure form anyway. For instance, during the heyday of structural-functionalism, the application of this theoretical framework was not limited to sociology; social anthropologists were as committed to it as sociologists were (see chapter 1). But at least the disciplinary boundaries were clearer then, whereas theo-rizing now affects the social sciences in general – not just sociology.

Why social theory?

Given the current importance of social theory, one would expect clarity as to its precise role vis-à-vis the social sciences. But quite the opposite is the case. There is growing uncertainty as to what social theory can or should achieve, especially in relationship to the various social sciences it is supposed to serve. Ironically, there was more of a consensus on these matters during the period preceding the prominence of social theory. The problem for social theory today is that these earlier views about the relationship between theory and empirical research have been shown to be problematic. Two views, in particular, were widespread until two decades ago, but are no longer tenable. The first view conceives of theory, to use Carl Hempel's terminology (1965), in 'deductive-nomological' terms: as a set of laws and initial conditions from which empirical hypotheses can be derived. The second view sees theory in representational terms: as providing the conceptual building blocks for capturing or picturing the empirical world. The two views, the deductive and the representational one, are not necessarily mutually exclusive, and some authors subscribed to both. They are, however, analytically distinct.

The deductive-nomological view conceives of scientific theories as an explanatory endeavour, accounting for and predicting empirical phenomena. Proponents of this perspective include authors such as the aforementioned Hempel, Karl Popper and, to a certain extent, Imre Lakatos (who developed a sophisticated version of falsificationism). Empirical research is a testing device, like a judicial decision, informing the academic community about how valid the theory has proven to be. Philosophers have disagreed over the years as to the precise use of the empirical evidence in this judicial procedure. Initially it was thought that empirical confirmations increase the likelihood of the validity or probability of a theory, but then it was pointed out that we can never be sure about the truth or probability of a general proposition on the basis of a finite number of observations (however large that number). Popper and others argued that, logically speaking, while empirical confirmations cannot help us ascertain the validity or plausibility of a theory, one empirical refutation is sufficient to abandon a theory, so the creation of refutable theories and the process of trial and error became central to scientific discovery and progress (Popper 1959; 1991). In practice, given the theory-ladenness (and therefore fallibility) of empirical observations, it quickly became evident that one observation could never be sufficient to decide to abandon a theoretical framework or research programme. So a consensus was formed that only a large number of empirical refutations could justify switching to a new frame of reference. It is this Lakatosian version of falsificationism to which the majority of social scientists adhere and which constitutes the philosophical justification for their professional practices. The accumulated empirical evidence will help to decide whether or not to desert the research programme that is under investigation. If the counter-evidence is overwhelming, then a guilty verdict is inevitable and the research programme will have to be replaced (Lakatos 1970).

This notion of empirical research as a testing device has been criticized for a variety of reasons. First, Lakatosian falsificationism is an incoherent philosophical perspective, regardless of the scientific discipline on which we focus. Lakatos's philosophy is yet another failed attempt to present a neutral algorithm that would sum up scientific discovery and progress. Contrary to earlier falsificationism, this philosophical position seemingly solves the problem of the theory-laden nature of observations. But actually it does not. It does not because it still remains unclear how many empirical refutations would amount to a guilty verdict for the research programme on trial, especially given that each empirical observation is theory-laden and thus fallible and given that, as Lakatos himself points out, each observation relies on a set of auxiliary assumptions, the validity of which can be questioned.

Second, although sophisticated falsificationism has become an important justification for the practice of social science, scientific change has never operated on this basis, nor is it likely to ever do so in the future. It is difficult to identify any occasion where empirical research has led to the abandonment of a major research programme in the social sciences. Various pieces of empirical research inevitably present different and often mutually exclusive results so that the final verdict remains unclear. Researchers who supposedly investigate the cognitive validity of a particular research programme are often educated and formed within that perspective and exhibit loyalty towards it; when confronted with empirical counter-evidence, they blame auxiliary assumptions rather than the core of the research programme to which they are committed. Rational choice theory is a case in point (see chapter 4). There have been quite a few cases where empirical research seems to contradict the core assumptions of the theory but rational choice theorists tended to make *post hoc* adjustments which immunize the research programme against these allegations of empirical inadequacy.

Third, in the process of testing theories, researchers have to generalize from their specific research sample to the population as a whole. The problem with this inductive process is that a *specific* set of observational results (for instance, the relationship between socio-economic background and educational achievement in the UK today) are considered informative about an *infinitely* large population (for instance, the same relationship in *any* society, past, present and future). In other words, while social scientists hold onto a deductive-nomological view of theory construction, the actual testing relies on a highly problematic form of inductive reasoning by which statements about an infinite number of cases are inferred from a finite number of observations.

In the latter part of the twentieth century, the deductive-nomological view came under intense scrutiny, and gave way gradually to the representational model. According to the representational model, social research is a mapping device; research is successful if it manages to mirror the subject-matter as accurately and completely as possible. Social researchers act like social cartographers, charting the various aspects of the social realm precisely as they are and showing their connections. According to this view, social theory is essential to a truthful and comprehensive representation of the social; theory provides the necessary conceptual building blocks which allow for social cartography.

Social theorists who work in this vein develop an all-embracing ontology which allegedly covers the macro-, meso- and micro-dimensions of social life and the different time-spans (from the shorter temporal span of everyday life to the *longue durée* of historical time). They provide precise definitions for a whole range of concepts which are supposedly essential to the mapping of the social (social structure, agency, culture, and so on), and they investigate the precise nature of the intricate connections of these concepts. For example, Giddens's duality of structure (1984; see also chapter 5), Roy Bhaskar's transformational model of social action (1998) – according to which structure is both medium and unintended output of social practices – and Margaret Archer's morphogenic approach and its focus on the effects of different degrees of structural constraint on human action (1995; 1996) all attempt to conceptualize the precise relationship between society and agency. Research is then conceived as a mapping device, capturing the various dimensions of social life (see, e.g., Layder 1993).

Whereas in the previous model empirical research occupied a central role of arbitrage, this is no longer the case in this representational model. Empirical research is now no longer a testing device; it is no longer a judicial decision that informs us about the value of the theory. Instead, pieces of research have become mere instantiations of the ontological framework – ways of reminding us about the representational value of the theory. Research is about utilizing a theoretical frame of reference, showing that it is applicable in this specific instance. Research is successful if it manages to show that a specific area of research can be reformulated in terms of the theory.

This representational model is problematic for a variety of reasons. First, it relies on what John Dewey called the 'spectator theory of knowledge'. As we have seen in the last chapter, by this Dewey meant a view of knowledge that supposedly captures or mirrors the inner essence of the external world as completely and accurately as possible. It assumes a metaphor of vision: knowledge is about portraying or mirroring the world as it really is. Social cartography implies precisely that: it assumes that the knowledge obtained will somehow allow us to encapsulate the fundamental social nature of what is being investigated. Equipped with conceptual armoury, social researchers would be able to capture the world as it really is. But this metaphor of vision is misleading. As pragmatist philosophers have pointed out, knowledge does not involve a passive recording of external reality. Knowledge is an active coping with, not copying of, the world (Rorty 1980; 1982). This is particularly obvious in the case of social research where any act of description or interpretation necessarily relies on a set of presuppositions. The latter is a *sine qua non* condition of the former. Any reference to 'social reality' begs the question: social reality under which interpretative framework? Any allusion to observational social 'facts' begs the question: facts under which interpretative scheme?

Second, this representational model of social research leads to intellectual ossification because empirical research is no longer employed to challenge the theoretical framework that is being used. Instead, research is undertaken to demonstrate yet another applicability of that framework. We learn that the ontological frame of reference can be applied to yet another case, so this framework inevitably becomes reinforced. However, what precisely do we gain from learning that a particular social setting can be rephrased in terms of a given theory, especially given that most settings can be rearticulated in terms of any coherent theoretical framework? The answer is remarkably little. Whatever theory we use (whether the theory is derived from, say, Bourdieu or indebted to Bhaskar), we know in advance that the framework is the inevitable outcome of the empirical research which it was supposed to guide. In what follows, we will argue that the key to social research is not that it captures a previously hidden reality, but that it presents new innovative readings of the social. What is novel or innovative is relative to the common views which are currently held in the academic community and beyond.

Pragmatism and pragmatisms

The solution, we think, lies in abandoning these two diametrically opposed positions about the relationship between theory and empirical research. The deductive-nomological model sees empirical research as a grand inquisitor, informing the academic community about which theories are best and which are to be abandoned. The representational model denigrates empirical research, belittling it as a mere illustration or application of theories, simply a vehicle through which theories are articulated, reproduced and celebrated. This position easily leads to theoretical ossification because empirical research is employed to confirm – not challenge – the theoretical framework that is being adopted. However, the deductive-nomological model does not fare better. It only encourages theoretical change if we are confronted with a vast array of empirical refutations, and given the uncertainty as to what amounts to a valid empirical refutation and given the entrenched nature of research programmes, conceptual change is, in practice, limited. While the two positions are clearly different, both fail to realize how a confrontation with empirical phenomena can encourage us to adopt a new vocabulary, to take a new theoretical perspective on things. To appreciate how research and conceptual innovation can be linked, we need to adopt a very different philosophical outlook, which we call 'hermeneutics-inspired pragmatism'.

By pragmatism, we refer to the distinct philosophical tradition that was initially set in motion by Charles Peirce, later developed by William James and John Dewey, and further articulated by Richard Bernstein and Richard Rorty. This philosophical tradition is often portrayed as quintessentially American, and for very good reasons. Not only did the major pragmatists live and work in the US; their philosophical works emerged in response to distinctly American problems and concerns: they expressed distinctly American sentiments, hopes and anxieties. This is not to say that pragmatism is solely an American enterprise. Some European philosophers of the nineteenth century, like Henri Bergson and Friedrich Nietzsche, developed views which were remarkably close to those of pragmatism, as did the Oxford-based philosopher F. C. S. Schiller at the beginning of the twentieth century. Some of the older generation of American pragmatists studied in Europe, had regular intellectual exchanges with European intellectuals and were very much indebted to them. More recent exponents of pragmatist philosophy, like Rorty and Bernstein, engaged with and saw affinities with a number of continental European authors who were considered seriously out of line within the analytical tradition. The multiplicity of influences is not surprising, given that American pragmatism has always portrayed itself as non-doctrinaire, open and receptive to new ideas, in contrast with the boundary-consciousness of analytical philosophy and its general disdain towards much written in the German and French tradition.

If American pragmatism has been shown to be open to European philosophy, the latter has been less receptive towards the former. There are notable exceptions, such as Jürgen Habermas, whose critique of positivism and theory of communicative action drew on Peirce and the pragmatist tradition. All too often, however, pragmatism has been discarded as a parochial endeavour, too deeply ingrained in American society and its problems to appeal to a broader philosophical audience. Underlying our contribution is the conviction that this picture of pragmatism is deeply misleading (see, e.g., Silva 2008). By integrating American neo-pragmatism and phenomenology, we will demonstrate not only the bearing of pragmatism on contemporary philosophy of social science, but also the fruitfulness of a continued dialogue between the two traditions which on the surface look so different.

Before we proceed further, it is important to gain clarity as to the meaning of 'pragmatism' as opposed to the employment of the term in everyday language. People often equate 'pragmatism' with a 'pragmatic' attitude, according to which action ought not to be guided by a priori principles but primarily by an assessment of the actual constraints and opportunities of a given context. In foreign policy, the label 'pragmatism' refers precisely to this non-ideological stance, whereby political actors routinely seek to gauge and take advantage of what comes their way. Likewise, when social scientists label research as 'pragmatist', sometimes they mean that it does not follow rigid methodological principles and instead exhibits an eclectic or opportunistic choice and application of method. In those circumstances, we prefer to term this a 'pragmatic' attitude to distinguish it from the 'pragmatist' argument developed here. So a pragmatic stance implies that the choice of theories or techniques depends on the particular topic of investigation or situation at hand rather than on a well-articulated philosophical or theoretical position.

Our argument for a pragmatist stance has little in common with the methodological opportunism that characterizes a pragmatic attitude. First, we are not arguing that social researchers should pick and choose the theoretical framework or technique that somehow 'fits' or 'corresponds' best to the data or that seems opportune given the circumstances. We are actually sceptical of this view, not in the least because it draws on a problematic metaphor of vision, as if social research is meant to mirror the external social world as accurately as possible. Second, while a pragmatic attitude questions the usefulness of *any* philosophical account for social research, pragmatism questions the value of *some* philosophical debates, in particular about essences or ontology, and it also doubts the merit of *some* philosophical views, for instance, foundationalism. Pragmatism is sceptical of intellectual disputes if taking one or another position has no practical consequences for anyone (James 1907). For pragmatists, questions about inner essences or ontology are such scholastic enterprises because answering them in one way or another makes no practical difference.

What is the common ground which pragmatist philosophers share? What distinguishes the pragmatist outlook from those of other philosophical traditions? And which of the pragmatists' ideas have influenced our own agenda for the philosophy of the social sciences? To identify which ideas are shared by pragmatists is not a sinecure because pragmatism was, and still is, a heterogeneous entity. From the beginning, pragmatism entailed competing branches and antithetical positions, even to the extent that Peirce, who coined the term, later distanced himself from 'pragmatism' because he felt that some of the beliefs carried under this banner were so alien to his. It is ironic that some philosophers, whom we now regard as iconic figures of the pragmatist movement, occasionally invoked other labels to refer to themselves, with Peirce's 'pragmaticism' and Dewey's 'instrumentalism' being particularly poignant examples. More recently, Richard Bernstein, Donald Davidson, Nelson Goodman, Hilary Putnam and Richard Rorty have taken pragmatism into uncharted territories (such as literary criticism and critical theory). This has led commentators to question whether some of those contemporary developments can be as easily reconciled with earlier forms of pragmatism as the likes of Rorty would have us believe.

Nevertheless, it would be a mistake to infer from this that pragmatists have little in common. Most pragmatist philosophers – old and new – share a number of key ideas, which makes it possible to talk about a pragmatist movement. It is particularly important to illustrate a number of these ideas here because they underscore our perspective on the philosophy of the social sciences.

To start with, few commentators mention the humanist tendencies of pragmatism, which is surprising given how pervasive humanism is amongst classical and contemporary pragmatists and how essential it is to their intellectual project. James, Dewey and Schiller occasionally used the term to contextualize their own work, though they attributed different meanings to it (James 1911: 121–35; Rockefeller 1994; Schiller 1903; 1907). By humanism, we refer to a particular perspective according to which cognitive, ethical and aesthetic claims, including claims about those claims, are intertwined with human projects and are predominantly human creations. Not only ought those claims to be judged on their practical contribution to society, they are also social and cultural in nature, often entailing the cooperation of many individuals and drawing on a complex web of symbols and cultural codes. The social and cultural dimension of those claims has, in turn, a number of repercussions, of which the rejection of both foundationalism and objective knowledge are particularly important.

By foundationalism, we refer to the belief that philosophy can establish atemporal, universal foundations that secure aesthetic, ethical or cognitive claims. Historically, a significant number of philosophers conceived of their work as primarily a foundational enterprise. To be foundational in this sense, philosophy ought to be able to step outside history – outside culture or language – so as to adopt a 'neutral' position from which the right kind of prescriptions can be made. Most pragmatists take an anti-foundationalist stance. They believe that philosophical reflection cannot achieve this position of neutrality because it is, like other intellectual accomplishments, a *human* activity; and as a human activity, a *social* activity; and as a social activity, a *situated* activity (see, e.g., Bernstein 1991: 326ff.; Dewey 1938; Peirce 1877; 1878; Rorty 1982: xiiff.). This means that philosophical knowledge, like any other kind of knowledge, is always partial: it takes place from a certain vantage point. Pragmatists call for humility amongst philosophers, because, no matter what the amount of cleaning work they do, philosophy can never remove those human stains. As such, it cannot obtain the neutral stance which foundationalism requires.

A similar argument applies to other forms of knowledge, including scientific knowledge (Dewey 1929; James 1907). Scientific knowledge, too, is situated, partial, enacted from a particular viewpoint. Logical positivists spent a great deal of effort showing that scientific knowledge is superior to other forms of knowledge because it supposedly meets stringent criteria of objectivity. In this context, one talks about objective knowledge if it is not affected significantly by the attitudes and values of those who obtain this knowledge. In contrast, pragmatists insist that scientific knowledge is an intervention in the world and that, as an intervention, it is necessarily shaped by the interests or focus of the researchers involved.

This does not mean that knowledge is necessarily always subjective, if by subjective we mean that it fails to represent the external world accurately. In fact, pragmatists avoid using the label 'subjective' altogether; first, because it implies the possibility of objective knowledge in the way in which logical positivism postulated it; and second, because it mistakenly assumes that knowledge has something to do with the copying of the external world.

Descartes's method supposedly provided philosophical foundations that ensure infallible knowledge. In contrast, the pragmatist world is indicative of what Hilary Putnam (2004) called the 'democratization of inquiry': devoid of foundations, people are encouraged to reassess their views in the light of new empirical evidence. Various pragmatists might interpret this fallibilism differently. For the older generation of pragmatists, like Peirce, Dewey and Mead, scientific conjectures are empirically tested and, if necessary, replaced by superior scientific conjectures. It is the confrontation with new empirical phenomena that precipitates doubt, which only subsides once the old theory has been adjusted. Neopragmatists are less concerned with scientific discovery and change. They are more interested in how communities can adopt new vocabularies, redescribing themselves in the light of the new information provided. Rich, vital cultures are confident enough to exhibit openness towards uncomfortable experiences. As such, they are well equipped to redescribe and reinvent themselves. However, in both cases, anti-foundationalism goes hand in hand with a genuine fallibilist attitude whereby people are willing to question entrenched beliefs and replace them with more useful ones.

We already hinted earlier at the pragmatist rejection of the mirror view of knowledge (see, e.g., Dewey 1929; James 1907; Rorty 1980; 1999: 47–71). This mirror view conceives of knowledge in terms of passive and accurate recording of the essence of the external world. In this view, the external world is taken to be independent of human experience, waiting to be discovered. The mirror view is widespread both in philosophical and scientific circles, and it assumes an opposition between theory and knowledge on the one hand, and practice and action on the other. Knowledge is taken to be passive and instantaneous, whereas action is, by definition, active and proceeds through time. One of the upshots of this view is that knowledge should no longer be judged on the basis of its isomorphic relationship to the external realm, but on the basis of what kind of contribution it makes to our world. For too long, the dualism between theory and practice and its attendant preoccupation with accurate representation has led Western philosophers to ignore the practical difference knowledge can make. Pragmatism breaks with this dualism and takes seriously the notion of scientific engagement. In sum, our hermeneutically inspired pragmatist agenda for the social sciences comprises three central claims.

First, in the pragmatist tradition, methodological considerations are closely related to cognitive interests. By cognitive interests, we refer to the research goals that underlie the research process. It is a common mistake amongst social researchers to consider or debate methodological issues without specifying what they want to achieve. Those debates only make sense if the people involved in them want similar aims. Second, within the pragmatist spirit and its celebration of diversity, it is the task of philosophy to make us aware of the various objectives that may guide research and to promote cognitive interests which have been marginalized. Social research can pursue various cognitive interests: explanation (and possibly prediction); understanding; self-emancipation and critique; and self-understanding. Third, we wish to argue in favour of social research in pursuit of self-understanding. We are referring to research which makes manifest and which challenges the presuppositions of the community to which we belong. The modern notion of selfhood has individual connotations, but we are referring to collective forms of self-description and self-understanding. In our terminology, self-understanding refers to the way in which communities understand and correct themselves.

At this stage, it is worth elaborating on the link with Hans-Georg Gadamer's hermeneutics. Gadamer (1989) draws attention to the fact that while prejudice is a *sine qua non* condition for knowledge, the former is potentially affected by the latter. In layman's terms, while the presuppositions of individuals are the media through which they gain knowledge, this process of knowledge acquisition might also alter the very same presuppositions. However, Gadamer conceives of this complex association between prejudice and knowledge in terms of ontology. In contrast, we suggest we think of this relationship in methodological terms. By this, we refer to three directives. First, social researchers should realize that there is no such thing as unmediated access to the external world and that it is not worth pursuing this chimera. They ought to realize that their cultural presuppositions are a *sine qua non* condition for the research they conduct. Second, social researchers ought to be expected to be aware of the categories and assumptions that accompany their research and to make that knowledge publicly available. This reflectivity and its public availability make for more mature social research and more vibrant intellectual life. Third (and most importantly), a lot can be gained from conducting research that actively pursues this reflectivity. We are particularly interested in the methodological strategies that enable the pursuit of self-referential knowledge acquisition.

It is important to specify the precise nature of self-referential knowledge acquisition, or self-knowledge. Which modes of knowledge does this type of knowledge entail? It incorporates four such modes or components: conceptualization, critique, edification and imagination. First, self-referential knowledge implies a process of conceptualization or discursive formulation. It enables individuals to make explicit a number of presuppositions which they took for granted hitherto. Through confrontation with difference, people are encouraged to reflect on and put discursively their previously unquestioned assumptions. For instance, by juxtaposing contemporary philosophical views regarding morality within a pre-Christian era, Nietzsche's genealogical method makes explicit the presuppositions of the 'slave morality' which are embedded in society today (Nietzsche 1967). Second, self-referential knowledge acquisition entails a critical stance. It encourages individuals to examine and question their hitherto unquestioned presuppositions. It helps to scrutinize the validity, consistency and coherence of this set of presuppositions and it assists in assessing their suitability for the context in which people operate. For example, by showing that the origins of our current moral views tie in with power struggles (whereby the weak managed to domesticate the strong by reverting values), Nietzsche's genealogy shows that our moral system today is not as innocuous or noble as it might appear.

Third, this type of knowledge is edifying. We are referring here to the German idealist notion of *Bildung*, which indicates the process of self-formation that accompanies genuine knowledge acquisition. Contrary to Richard Rorty (1980), who argues that philosophy leads to edifying knowledge, we argue that social research, as long as it pursues self-understanding, is better placed to achieve *Bildung* given its strong empirical component. By being exposed to different forms of life, individuals are confronted with the ethnocentricity and locality of their views, expectations and perceptions. They then no longer take their beliefs and values as natural, fixed or universal, but see them as culturally specific and time- and space-bound. Nietzsche's genealogical method does precisely that, demonstrating that certain key concepts currently employed (for instance, 'bad' as charitable and caring) used to have a different meaning ('bad' as strong, powerful and aristocratic). Fourth, self-referential knowledge acquisition implies the broadening of our imaginative scope. Through this type of knowledge, people become aware of the existence of alternative socio-political scenarios, and they learn to think beyond the frameworks and practices that are currently in operation. This imaginative dimension is central to Foucault's history of the present and his notion of the new intellectual, who no longer preaches from above but who provides tools for a broadening of perspective. In contrast, the model of the old intellectual imposes orthodoxies and bars imaginative politics (Baert 1998).

The proposal outlined here is likely to be challenged on at least three dimensions. A first question refers to the nature of collective selfhood. Sceptics might argue that there is ambiguity as to which community we are referring to. Our answer is that we refer to a potentially infinite number of communities as long as they involve the audience or readership of the researchers. Each of us belongs to various communities at once: for instance, we belong to professional groups, socio-economic categories, ethnic or religious entities, and regional or national communities. The reflectivity which we are advocating can apply to each of those groups. Self-referential research confronts people with, and challenges, the presuppositions which they hold in virtue of their membership to a larger community, but the precise nature of this collective selfhood remains open. Amongst these different communities is also the academic community to which the social researcher belongs. Indeed, self-referential knowledge will affect the presuppositions of the academic discipline in which the researcher functions. For example, anthropologists, who work within the critical turn, use empirical research to explore how the intricate relationship between colonialism and anthropological knowledge has affected the latter, or to expose and challenge the assumptions regarding gender and identity that are widely shared within the discipline (Marcus and Fischer 1999; Clifford and Marcus 1986).

A second question goes deeper. Sceptics might ask why we should be interested in research in pursuit of self-understanding. After all, they would argue, research ought to provide knowledge about the external world – not about ourselves. To pursue self-referential knowledge seems the epitome of professional navel-gazing. Our answer to this critique is that the ultimate aim of the research which we are propagating is to become aware of, conceptualize, and possibly unsettle the presuppositions that make possible knowledge in the first place. There is no such thing as unmediated access to the external world. Any knowledge of the social world relies on a set of presuppositions, and self-referential knowledge brings these presuppositions to the foreground. For instance, since the arrival of post-processual archaeology, archaeologists have become sensitive to the ways in which empirical research can be used to become aware of how contemporary categories have hitherto been projected onto the past (Hodder 1991; Shanks and Hodder 1998; Tilley 1998). Post-processual archaeology is not solely preoccupied with the present or, worse, with the current state of the discipline of archaeology. This growing awareness of the practices and assumptions of the discipline should only be a phase in a broader intellectual process: it should be a stepping-stone towards a more self-conscious, more mature and richer account of the past.

A final question deals with truth. Some will ask: how do we know whether or not a discursive formulation of previously latent presuppositions is correct? How can we judge that our rearticulation of the set of presuppositions is truthful? For instance, which criteria do we use to assess whether Foucault's genealogy of madness is right? Our answer to this riposte is threefold. First, the question as to whether our accounts are correct is not specific to self-referential knowledge acquisition. This question can be asked about any narrative, whether or not its aim is self-understanding. So leaving aside the issue of whether this question might be a fruitful one to ask, it does not constitute a critique of the specific programme which we advocate. Second, researchers can assess questions regarding truth validity based on an open dialogue about the specific case involved. We prefer to talk about persuasiveness rather than truth in this matter, to emphasize the way in which decisions of this kind are both provisional and socially negotiated by the researchers involved. We do not believe that it is fruitful for philosophers, or for anyone, to search for a set of criteria prior to this conversation and supposedly applicable to any kind of setting. To do so would run the risk either of presenting criteria which are applicable to only a limited number of settings or of proposing such general guidelines that they are no longer informative to researchers. There is no neutral algorithm prior to the conversation between the researchers, or at least not one that would be enlightening or helpful to those very same researchers.

Third, the strength of self-referential knowledge acquisition lies to a large extent in its ability to make people see things in a different light – to adopt an innovative perspective. This is not to say that issues regarding cognitive validity are irrelevant. However, once the aim of study is self-understanding, people should not only be persuaded by the coherence and plausibility of the narrative presented. They also need to be convinced by the originality and depth of the narrative, the extent to which it stretches their self-understanding against the context of the received wisdom of the past. The ultimate aim of this type of research is to encourage a *Gestalt* switch so that people think very differently about things. Note that this means that the bar is put quite high. Many pieces of research appear sound and credible, but add little to our self-understanding in the way in which we have spelled out. Also, while some research might help us articulate a narrative about ourselves, this story might not be substantially different from the dominant one. According to our pragmatist agenda, none of those cases would do. We might have substituted persuasiveness for truth, but this has not made social research less demanding: self-referential knowledge acquisition is particularly difficult to achieve.

Social research, reflexivity and societal engagement

In contrast to their contemporaries in Vienna and Cambridge, classical pragmatists, like Dewey and Mead, wanted philosophy and the social sciences to engage with the social world, to make it a richer, more diverse and altogether more interesting place. Dewey's contributions to educational theory are a case in point, and so is the sociological research conducted by members of the Chicago School (see, e.g., Abbott 1999; Joas 1993). These examples show philosophy and the social sciences at their best, interacting with and learning from the external world, and attempting to give something back to the communities that are being studied. Since then, the further institutionalization of academics within university establishments and the intense professionalization of the social sciences has led to quite a different set-up (see, e.g., Jacoby 1986). This shift has certainly not been altogether negative, bringing legitimacy and outside recognition, securing improved work conditions and setting rigorous standards of intellectual quality. However, in relation to the initial pragmatist ambitions about the relationship between knowledge and practice, those institutional transformations have meant that intellectual legitimacy and academic recognition have become stronger priorities than practical engagement. Whereas earlier sociologists addressed significant political and social concerns, the upshot of the structural changes is that social scientists increasingly address other social scientists and that their language and intellectual interests reflect and reinforce this narrowing of horizons.

Against this backdrop, our argument for a new way of thinking about social research, centred around an integration of American neo-pragmatism and continental philosophy, acquires an element of urgency.

In contrast with the academic setting today, social research in pursuit of self-understanding encourages researchers to be sufficiently open to the unfamiliar, to take a broader perspective and reflect on the world we took for granted hitherto. This type of research is about expanding our imaginative canvas and practical reach, something to be achieved by learning from and reaching out to those beyond the safe contours of the academy.

Our argument in particular shows affinities with Michael Burawoy's recent plea for a 'public sociology', which uses expert knowledge to promote debate with and amongst various non-academic publics, thereby responding and adjusting to their demands and ultimately providing 'dialogue' and 'mutual education' (Burawoy 2004; 2005). Burawoy compares his notion of 'organic' public sociology with 'traditional' public sociology: whereas the latter addresses an amorphous, invisible and mainstream public, the former actively engages with a specific, visible and politically organized group of people. Both forms of public sociology can perfectly coexist and indeed feed into each other, but Burawoy argues particularly in favour of the organic version because its political mandate is better articulated, it has clearer direction and its practical pay-off is less ambiguous. Public sociology, so he argues, is not only different from mainstream 'professional sociology' but also from 'policy sociology'. While policy sociology attempts to provide technical answers to questions provided by an external client, public sociology develops a 'dialogic relationship' between sociology and the public whereby the issues of each partner are brought to the attention of the other, and each adjusts or responds accordingly. Whereas both professional and policy sociology construct 'instrumental knowledge', public sociology shares with 'critical sociology' a preoccupation with 'reflexive knowledge' or 'dialogue about ends'. Public sociology should not be conflated with critical sociology, however. Whereas both professional and critical sociology target an academic audience, public sociology, like policy sociology, embarks on a dialogue with non-academic publics about the 'normative foundations' of society.

While Burawoy's passionate argument for a more socially engaged sociology is appealing and, indeed, has obtained worldwide attention, he focuses mainly on the actual practical engagement of sociologists with their publics. Less attention is given to exploring the type of knowledge acquisition involved in the kind of reflexive sociology which he promotes. Following the distinction by the Frankfurt School between substantive and instrumental rationality, Burawoy differentiates between reflexive sociology and policy sociology on the basis that it establishes goals and values rather than means. But this definition remains notoriously vague, especially given that what counts as a value in one context can be a means for acquiring a value in a different context. Meta-theoretical discussions about the future of the discipline of sociology, as the debate around public sociology certainly is, need to be accompanied by philosophical explorations of the methodological issues involved. Otherwise the arguments presented have a hollow ring to them and can easily be dismissed as mere statements of intent, devoid of any substance.

The pragmatist-inspired proposal outlined here – with its rejection of foundationalism, naturalism and representationalism, its emphasis on self-understanding, and its exploration of the link between knowledge and action – provides the right philosophical backing to support and define the type of social scientific knowledge that engages with groups and communities outside the safe contours of the ivory tower. However, this is not to say that the Gadamerian dialogical model of knowledge, for which we have been arguing, is solely relevant for non-academic publics. Social research in the pursuit of self-understanding cuts right across Burawoy's distinction between critical and public sociology because the reflexivity that is built in affects presuppositions that are held within academic as well as non-academic communities.

This is particularly clear in the case of Bauman's *Modernity and the Holocaust* (1989), a book we analysed in the previous chapter and that constitutes a prime example of the type of research we have in mind. *Modernity and the Holocaust* not only invites a broader non-academic audience to rethink the nature of the atrocities during the Third Reich, but also challenges some of the presuppositions that sociologists and philosophers hold about the value, the possibilities and the dangers of the transition towards modernity. Challenging the *Sonderweg* thesis and opposing the orthodox view that modernity and the Holocaust are antithetical, Bauman persuasively argues that key features of modernity – the 'garden' notion of the nation-state, and a process of bureaucratization with its increasing instrumental rationality and decreasing sense of individual responsibility – were necessary conditions for the emergence of the Holocaust. By doing so, Bauman goes further than arguing against the popular conception that the atrocities committed during that period were somehow irrational outbursts or indicative of the fact that the project of modernity had not quite been accomplished. Crucially, his analysis also implies that sociologists ought to reassess their views about the project of modernity itself, a reassessment which ultimately affects how they conceive of their own discipline, entrenched as it is in the Enlightenment vision. In short, this example indicates that, in practice, the rigid distinction between Burawoy's critical and public sociology may be less relevant than he assumes it is. This is because any substantial dialogical knowledge, of the kind we have been arguing for and which Bauman epitomizes, will be relevant to both academic and non-academic communities.

Final remarks

This final chapter has sought to demonstrate the fruitfulness of an ongoing dialogue between American neo-pragmatism and continental philosophy, which, for far too long, have been regarded as addressing irreconcilable intellectual concerns. It has explored the affinities which exist between our neo-pragmatist agenda in the field of philosophy of the social sciences and the philosophical outlook developed by Gadamer. Rather than conceiving of social research as, primarily, an explanatory or predictive endeavour, we have tried to show that this neo-pragmatist view promotes social research in terms of an ongoing engagement with otherness, a process which ultimately contributes to the pursuit of richer forms of collective redescription. In this view, research takes a central role in the ability of communities to distance themselves from their hitherto unacknowledged presuppositions, to assume different points of view and, ultimately, to make a difference to the social world which those communities have helped to create and which they inhabit. This neo-pragmatist approach, we have argued, presents a philosophical basis for the reflexive knowledge entailed in both critical and public sociology.

One final issue needs to be addressed. As our neo-pragmatist perspective aims to contribute to the philosophy of the social sciences, the question inevitably arises which theories are well (or ill-) suited to bringing about the reflexivity which we have been advocating? From the above, it should be clear that our answer is that, unlike other philosophies of social science such as falsificationism or critical realism, this pragmatist-inspired proposal is neutral vis-à-vis theory choice insofar as it refuses to invoke external criteria – such as falsifiability, explanatory power or predictive success – to decide on the value of a given theory. Instead, it suggests that we should take into account the context of the dominant presuppositions of the discipline or indeed of a community at large before evaluating the theory under consideration because it is only against this background that such an evaluation can be achieved. Alfred Schutz's notion of 'stock of knowledge at hand' is particularly applicable here because it captures very well how, in their everyday life, people approach the social world in terms of 'familiarity and pre-acquaintanceship' (Schutz and Luckmann 1973). Just as everyday life is embedded in the *Lebenswelt* – a world of everyday life governed by the 'natural attitude' – so social researchers take for granted a number of theoretical and metaphysical beliefs and methodological strategies. It follows from the above that theories ought to be evaluated on the basis of how much of a *Gestalt*-switch they manage to bring about – to what extent they could bring researchers to rethink those hitherto deeply entrenched and often unacknowledged presuppositions. In opposition to the ritualistic hero worship, which is so endemic in the social sciences today and which is tied in with the representational model of social researcher, the pragmatist-inspired perspective calls for less deference and bolder claims – an intellectual iconoclasm of sorts. The question should no longer be how we can apply the works of our intellectual heroes or preferred models (whatever they are) to the empirical data, but how we can learn from the encounter with the unfamiliar to challenge them and think differently.

References

Abbott, A. 1999. *Department and Discipline: Chicago School at One Hundred.* Chicago, IL: University of Chicago Press.

Archer, M. 1995. *Realist Social Theory: The Morphogenetic Approach.* Cambridge: Cambridge University Press.

Archer, M. 1996. *Culture and Agency: The Place of Culture in Social Theory.* Cambridge: Cambridge University Press.

Baert, P. 1998. Foucault's history of the present as self-referential knowledge acquisition. *Philosophy and Social Criticism* 24(6): 111–26.

Baert, P. 2005. Social theory and the social sciences. In G. Delanty (ed.), *The Handbook of Contemporary European Social Theory.* London: Routledge, pp. 14–24.

Baert, P. 2007. Why study the social. In P. Baert and B. S. Turner (eds), *Pragmatism and European Social Theory.* Oxford: Bardwell, pp. 45–68.

Baert, P. 2009. A neopragmatist agenda for social research: integrating Levinas, Gadamer and Mead. In H. Bauer and E. Brighi (eds), *Pragmatism in International Relations.* London: Routledge, pp. 44–62.

Bernstein, R. 1991. *The New Constellation: The Ethical-Political Horizons of Modernity/Postmodernity.* Cambridge: Polity.

Bhaskar, R. 1998. *The Possibility of Naturalism: A Philosophical Critique of the Contemporary Human Sciences.* London: Routledge.

Burawoy, M. 2004. Public sociologies: a symposium from Boston College. *Social Problems* 51: 103–30.

Burawoy, M. 2005. 2004 Presidential Address: for public sociology. *American Sociological Review* 70: 4–28.

Clifford, J. and Marcus, G. (eds) 1986. *Writing Culture: The Poetics and the Politics of Ethnography.* Berkeley: University of California Press.

Dahlgren, P. 1995. *Television and the Public Sphere: Citizenship, Democracy and the Media.* London: Sage.

Dewey, J. 1929. *The Quest for Certainty.* New York: Henry Holt.

Dewey, J. 1938. *Logic: The Theory of Inquiry.* New York: Holt, Rinehart and Winston.

Gadamer, H.-G. 1989. *Truth and Method.* New York: Continuum (originally in German, 1960).

Gell, A. 1998. *Art and Agency: An Anthropological Theory.* Oxford: Oxford University Press.

Giddens, A. 1984. *The Constitution of Society: Outline of a Theory of Structuration.* Cambridge: Polity.

Habermas, J. 1989. *The Structural Transformation of the Public Sphere: An Inquiry into a Category of Bourgeois Society.* Cambridge: Polity (originally in German, 1962).

Hempel, C. G. 1965. *Aspects of Scientific Explanation, and Other Essays in the Philosophy of Science.* New York: Free Press.

Hodder, I. 1991. *Reading the Past.* Cambridge: Cambridge University Press.

Hooper, C. 2000. *Manly States: Masculinities, International Relations, and Gender Politics.* New York: Columbia University Press.

Jacoby, R. 1986. *The Last Intellectuals: American Culture in the Age of the Academe.* New York: Noonday Press.

James, W. 1907. *Pragmatism, a New Name for Some Old Ways of Thinking: Popular Lectures on Philosophy.* London: Longmans, Green & Co.

James, W. 1911. *The Meaning of Truth.* New York: Longman Green.

Joas, H. 1993. *Pragmatism and Social Theory.* Chicago, IL: University of Chicago Press.

Lakatos, I. 1970. Falsification and the methodology of scientific research. In I. Lakatos and A. Musgrave (eds), *Criticism and the Growth of Knowledge.* Cambridge: Cambridge University Press, pp. 91–196.

Landes, J. 1988. *Women and the Public Sphere in the Age of the French Revolution.* Ithaca, NY: Cornell University Press.

Latour, B. 1993. *We Have Never Been Modern.* London: Harvester Wheatsheaf.

Law, J. and Hassard, J. (eds) 1999. *Actor Network Theory, and After.* Oxford: Blackwell.

Lawson, T. 1997. *Economics and Reality.* London: Routledge.

Lawson, T. 2003. *Reorienting Economics.* London: Routledge.

Layder, D. 1993. *New Strategies in Social Research: An Introduction and Guide.* Cambridge: Polity.

Marcus, G. and Fischer, M. 1999. *Anthropology as a Cultural Critique.* Chicago, IL: University of Chicago Press.

Marsh, D. et al. 1999. *Postwar British Politics in Perspective.* Cambridge: Polity.

McDowell, L. 1999. *Gender, Identity and Place: Understanding Feminist Geographies.* Cambridge: Polity.

Nietzsche, F. 1967. *Beyond Good and Evil; Prelude to a Philosophy of the Future.* London: George Allen & Unwin (originally in German, 1886).

Peirce, C.S. 1877. The fixation of beliefs. *Popular Science Monthly* 12: 1–15.

Peirce, C.S. 1878. How to make our ideas clear. *Popular Science Monthly* 12: 286–302.

Popper, K. 1959 [1934]. *The Logic of Scientific Discovery.* London: Hutchinson & Co.

Popper, K. 1991 [1963]. *Conjectures and Refutations.* London: Routledge.

Putnam, H. 2004. *The Collapse of the Fact/Value Dichotomy and Other Essays.* Cambridge, MA: Harvard University Press.

Rockefeller, S. 1994. *John Dewey: Religious Faith and Democratic Humanism.* New York: Columbia University Press.

Rorty, R. 1980. *Philosophy and the Mirror of Nature.* Oxford: Blackwell.

Rorty, R. 1982. *Consequences of Pragmatism.* New York: University of Minnesota Press.

Rorty, R. 1999. *Philosophy and Social Hope.* Harmondsworth: Penguin.

Schiller, F. C. S. 1903. *Humanism: Philosophical Essays.* London: Macmillan.

Schiller, F. C. S. 1907. *Studies in Humanism.* London: Macmillan.

Schutz, A. and Luckmann, T. 1973. *The Structures of the Life-World.* Chicago, IL: Northwestern University Press.

Shanks, M. and Hodder, I. 1998. Processual, postprocessual and interpretative archaeologies. In D. Whitley (ed.), *Reader in Archaeological Theory.* London: Routledge, pp. 69–98.

Siltanen, J. and Stanworth, M. (eds) 1984. *Women and the Public Sphere: A Critique of Sociology and Politics.* London: Hutchinson.

Silva, F. C. da 2008. *Mead and Modernity. Science, Selfhood and Democratic Politics.* Lanham, MD: Lexington Books.

Tilley, C. 1998. Archaeology as socio-political action in the present. In D. Whitley (ed.), *Reader in Archaeological Theory.* London: Routledge, pp. 315–30.

Notes

Chapter 1: One Hundred Years of French Social Theory

1 We very much recommend Lukes (1973) as a semi-biographical introduction to Durkheim.
2 For an excellent discussion, see Lukes 1973: 435–49.
3 For an overview of the history of the *Annales* school, see, e.g., Burke 1990.
4 This is not to say that Durkheim's methodology is necessarily without criticism.
5 We are referring here to Foucault's genealogical writings. See, e.g., the interviews and articles in his *Language, Counter-memory, Practice* and *Power/Knowledge*.
6 With regard to the notion of *habitus*, see, e.g., Bourdieu 1969; 1977: 78–86; 1990: 52–65.
7 With regard to the relationship between field and *habitus*, see, e.g., Bourdieu 1971.
8 Obvious examples can be found in Bourdieu 1969; 1971; 1973; 1977: 171–82.
9 For a comparison with rational choice theory, see, e.g., Wacquant 1992: 24ff.
10 In its original sense, the phrase 'the hermeneutic of suspicion' refers to the work of Marx, Nietzsche and Freud. See Ricoeur 1970: 32ff.

Chapter 2: The Biological Metaphor

1 Radcliffe-Brown was far more sympathetic towards French sociology (1958: 85–6).
2 This increased solidarity is often orchestrated so that the mobilization of forces can take place more smoothly.
3 With regard to this third point, see Giddens 1977: 106ff.
4 The term 'strong programme' is taken from science studies. See, e.g., Latour and Woolgar 1986.

Chapter 3: The Enigma of Everyday Life

1 We thank one of the anonymous referees for this suggestion.

2 Take, for instance, Mead's article, 'A Behaviorist Account of the Significant Symbol', which can be found in his *Selected Writings* (1964: 240–7).

3 The term was first introduced by Blumer in an article in *Man and Society* in 1937.

4 Related notions are Maturana's notion of 'social- or self-consciousness' and Giddens's concept of 'institutional reflectivity'. See Maturana 1980; and Giddens 1989: especially 36–44; 1992.

5 This issue is taken up in chapter 5. See also Giddens 1984.

6 See Schutz's paper: 'Concept and Theory Formation in the Social Sciences' (1962: 48–66).

7 See Schutz's papers: 'Commonsense and Scientific Interpretations of Human Action' and 'On Multiple Rationalities' (1962: 3–47, 207–59).

8 The term was coined by Mannheim in his essay 'On the Interpretation of *Weltanschauung*' (1952: 33–83).

Chapter 4: The Invasion of Economic Man

1 See, for instance, Boudon 1982; Elster 1985. Serious objections have been raised to the reconstruction of Marx along these lines (e.g. Cohen 1982).

2 Obviously, in cases of uncertainty, where Pi is incalculable, expected utility is likewise indeterminable.

3 For a more elaborate account of the applications of game theory in this area, see, e.g., Jervis 1978. For an overview of the relevance of game theory to political science in general, see, e.g., Riker 1992.

4 The concept of 'bounded rationality' was originally coined by Simon in the 1950s. See Simon 1957.

Chapter 5: Sociology Meets History

1 An instance of this need for self-reflection is the criticism of 'methodological nationalism' first undertaken by Hermínio Martins and Niklas Luhmann in the 1970s and recently re-edited by Ulrich Beck (see chapter 8).

2 Unlike Tilly, Homans kept his sociological and historical research interests separated: see, on the latter, Homans 1941; and, on the former, Homans 1961.

3 On a par with Eisenstadt's *Revolution and the Transformation of Societies*, this is arguably the most influential text on the topic of 'revolution' of the second half of the twentieth century. See Eisenstadt 1978.

4 On Mann's analysis of the state, see also Mann 1988.

5 On 'entangled modernities', see Therborn 2003.

Chapter 6: The History of the Present

1 For a discussion of the stratified conception of reality in realist philosophy, see Baert 1996.

2 The article appeared initially as 'Nietzsche, la généalogie, l'histoire' in a volume in memory of Jean Hyppolite.
3 With respect to genealogy, see the excellent contribution by Geuss 1994.
4 For a genealogical account of the topic of governmentality in Foucault's work, see Dean 1999: 40–59.
5 For a similar argument, see Poster 1990: 161–2.

Chapter 7: The Spread of Reason

1 Adorno et al. 1976; Habermas 1987b; 1987c: 1–49; 1987d; Habermas and Luhmann 1971. For an overview of Habermas's participation in public debates, see Holub 1991.
2 Habermas 1989. Like the French *doctorat d'État*, the German *Habilitations-schrift* refers to an extensive doctoral dissertation.
3 For a critical overview of Habermas's theory of cognitive interests, see, e.g., Ottmann 1982.
4 For a preliminary study on the theory of communicative action, see Habermas 2001b. See also, e.g., Honneth and Joas 1991.
5 See also the debate between Habermas and Rawls (1997), and the comparative analysis by Baynes (1992).
6 On the influence of classic American pragmatism on Habermas, see Aboulafia et al. 2002.
7 For a similar argument, see also Giddens 1985b: 114–16; and Held 1980: 397–8.
8 A good example is his discussion of the politics of social welfare in Offe 1996: 105–223.

Chapter 8: A Brave New World?

1 Even though, in his most recent work, Wagner does make an effort to provincialize the European experience of modernity. See Wagner 2008: 215ff.
2 For a critique, see Chernilo 2006; 2007.
3 Sennett has actually written fictional works. See, e.g., Sennett 1986b.
4 Hegel's influence on American philosophical pragmatism is an established, well-documented fact. See, e.g., Joas 1993.

Chapter 9: Conclusion

1 This chapter includes material published elsewhere, namely Baert 2005; 2007; 2009.

Index